WOMEN IN THE DAMASCUS DOCUMENT

Society of Biblical Literature

Academia Biblica

Steven L. McKenzie,
Hebrew Bible/Old Testament Editor

Mark Allan Powell,
New Testament Editor

Number 21

WOMEN IN THE DAMASCUS DOCUMENT

WOMEN IN THE DAMASCUS DOCUMENT

Cecilia Wassen

Society of Biblical Literature
Atlanta

WOMEN IN THE DAMASCUS DOCUMENT

Copyright © 2005 by the Society of Biblical Literature

All rights reserved. No part of this work may be reproduced or transmitted in any form or by any means, electronic or mechanical, including photocopying and recording, or by means of any information storage or retrieval system, except as may be expressly permitted by the 1976 Copyright Act or in writing from the publisher. Requests for permission should be addressed in writing to the Rights and Permissions Office, Society of Biblical Literature, 825 Houston Mill Road, Atlanta, GA 30329, USA.

Library of Congress Cataloging-in-Publication Data

Wassen, Cecilia, 1962-
  Women in the Damascus document / by Cecilia Wassen.
    p. cm. — (Academia Biblica ; no. 21)
  Includes bibliographical references and index.
  ISBN-13: 978-1-58983-168-1 (paper binding : alk. paper)
  ISBN-10: 1-58983-168-3 (paper binding : alk. paper)
  1. Damascus document. 2. Women—Legal status, laws, etc. (Jewish law)—History—To 1500. 3. Qumran community. 4. Dead Sea scrolls. 5. Essenes. I. Title. II. Series: Academia Biblica (Series) (Society of Biblical Literature) ; no. 21.

BM175.Z3W37 2005
296.1'55—dc22

2005017607

Printed in the United States of America
on acid-free paper

TABLE OF CONTENTS

ACKNOWLEDGEMENTS ix

LIST OF TABLES xi

ABBREVIATIONS xiii

1. INTRODUCTION 1
   1.1 INTRODUCTION 1
   1.2 QUMRAN SCHOLARSHIP ON WOMEN 2
      1.2.1 The Essenes 2
      1.2.2 Celibacy and Marriage 5
      1.2.3 Studies on Women in the Dead Sea Scrolls 9
   1.3 CONTRIBUTION 11
   1.4 METHODOLOGY 13

2. THE DAMASCUS DOCUMENT 19
   2.1 MANUSCRIPTS 19
   2.2 CONTENT 22
   2.3 DATE OF COMPOSITION 23
   2.4 HISTORY IN D 24
   2.5 PURPOSE AND AUDIENCE 25
   2.6 THE PLACE OF D AMONG THE DEAD SEA SCROLLS 27
   2.7 LITERARY DEVELOPMENT 32
      2.7.1 The Admonition 32
      2.7.2 The Composition of the Laws 33
      2.7.3 References to Women in the Literary Strata 42

3. THE EARLY LAW CODE 45
   3.1 INTRODUCTION 45
   3.2. A TEXT ON THE *ZAVAH*, THE *NIDDAH*, AND CHILDBIRTH: 4Q266 6 I 14–16;
      4Q272 1 II 3–18; 4Q266 6 II 1–13 45
      3.2.1 Introduction 45
      3.2.2 4Q272 1 ii 3–18; parallel: 4Q266 6 i 14–16 underlined 47
      3.2.3 4Q266 6 ii 1–13 51
      3.2.4 Conclusion 58
   3.3 THE RITE OF THE *SOTAH* AND INTERCOURSE WITH A SLAVE WOMAN:
      4Q270 4 1–21; 4Q266 12 1–9 59
      3.3.1 The Text 59
      3.3.2 The Rite of the Sotah 61
         3.3.2.1 The Rite of the Sotah 61

3.3.2.2 Conclusion 67
3.3.4 Intercourse with a Slave Woman: 4Q270 4 12–21; 4Q266 12 4–9 68
  3.3.4.1 Intercourse with a Slave Woman 68
  3.3.4.2 Conclusion 71
3.4 A TEXT ON MARITAL ARRANGEMENTS: 4Q271 3 4B–15; 4Q270 5 14–21;
  4Q267 7 12–14; 4Q269 9 1–8 71
  3.4.1 Introduction 71
  3.4.2 The Text: 4Q271 3 4b–15; parallels: 4Q270 5 14–21 and 10 1–2
    underlined; 4Q267 7 12–14 italics; 4Q269 9 1–8 dotted underline 72
  3.4.3 Fraud in Connection to Marriage 74
  3.4.4 The Choice of a Suitable Groom 76
  3.4.5 Prohibition Against Marrying a Woman Who Has Had Sexual
    Experience Outside of Marriage 80
  3.4.6 Physical Examination 85
  3.4.7 The Female Experts 87
  3.4.8 4Q273 5 89
  3.4.9 Conclusion 89
3.5 BINDING OATHS AND WOMEN'S OATHS: CD XVI 6B–12; PARALLELS:
  4Q270 6 II 19–21; 4Q271 4 II 7–12 90
  3.5.1 The Text: CD XVI 6b–12; parallels: 4Q270 6 ii 19–21 dotted
    underline and 4Q271 4 ii 7–12 underlined 90
  3.5.2 Laws Concerning Oaths 90
  3.5.3 Conclusion 93
3.6 THE SABBATH CODE 93
  3.6.1 Introduction 93
  3.6.2 Intermingling on the Sabbath 94
  3.6.3 Carrying Perfume/Spices and an Infant on the Sabbath 95
  3.6.4 Treatment of Slaves 97
  3.6.5 Conclusion 97
3.7 A LAW AGAINST SEXUAL INTERCOURSE IN עיר המקדש : CD XII 1–2;
  4Q271 5 I 17–18 97
  3.7.1 Introduction 97
  3.7.2 The Temple Scroll 99
  3.7.3 The Damascus Document 101
  3.7.4 Conclusion 102
3.8 CONCLUSION: HALAKHAH 102

4. THE CATALOGUE OF TRANSGRESSORS 107

4.1 INTRODUCTION 107
4.2 SEXUAL TRANSGRESSORS: 4Q270 2 I 16–19 107
4.3 MORE SEXUAL TRANSGRESSORS: 4Q270 2 II 15–17 109
4.4 CONCLUSION 112

5. THE ADMONITION 113

5.1 INTRODUCTION 113
5.2 NETS OF BELIAL: CD IV 12B–V 15A 113
5.2.1 Introduction 113
5.2.2 Polygyny 114
5.2.3 Defiling the Sanctuary 118
5.2.4 Marriage to a Niece 120
5.3 CD VII 4B–10A: A BIFURCATION OF LIFESTYLES? 122
5.3.1 Introduction 122
5.3.2 Phraseology in D similar to CD VII 4–5 123
5.3.3 The Context of CD VII 4b–10a 125
5.4 CONCLUSION 128

6. COMMUNAL LAWS 131

6.1 INTRODUCTION 131
6.2 THE INITIATION PROCESS AND EXCLUDED CATEGORIES: CD XV 5–XVI 2; 4Q266 8 I 1–10; 4Q270 6 II 5–10; 4Q271 4 II 1–4A 131
6.2.1 Introduction 131
6.2.2 Key Aspects of the Initiation Rite in D 133
6.2.3 The Oath of the Covenant and its Biblical Background 136
6.2.4 Mustering Among the Essenes 139
6.2.5 1QSa 140
6.2.6 Lists of Excluded Persons 144
6.2.6.1 The List in D 144
6.2.6.2 Exclusion From What? 145
6.2.6.3 Principles for Exclusion: A Comparison 146
6.2.7 Conclusion 154
6.3 MARRIAGE, DIVORCE, AND THE EDUCATION OF CHILDREN: 4Q266 9 III 1–10; CD XIII 15–19 156
6.3.1 Introduction 156
6.3.2 The Text: 4Q266 9 iii 1–10; CD XIII 15b–19 underlined. 156
6.3.3 Comments on the Text and Reconstruction 157
6.3.4 Literary Strata 158
6.3.5 A Reference to Divorce 159
6.3.6 Business, Marriage, and Divorce: the Role of the Examiner ... 160
6.3.7 Education 164
6.3.8 Conclusion 167
6.4 THE VIRGIN WITH NO REDEEMER: CD XIV 15–16; 4Q266 10 I 9 167
6.4.1 Introduction 167
6.4.2 The Text: CD XIV 12b–17a; parallel: 4Q266 10 i 5–10 underlined 168
6.4.3 Communal Support 169

6.5 The Penal Code: CD XIV 20–23; 4Q266 10 i 14–15; ii 1–15;
   4Q269 11 i 4–8, ii 1–2; 4Q270 7 i 1–15 171
   6.5.1 Introduction 171
   6.5.2 The Penal Codes 171
   6.5.3 Fornication with a Wife: 4Q270 7 i 12–13; parallel: 4Q267 9 vi 4–5
         underlined 173
      6.5.3.1 Scholarly Points of Views 173
      6.5.3.2 Interpreting לזנות 174
      6.5.3.3 Sexual Intercourse and Procreation: Opinions by Jewish
              Authors 179
      6.5.3.4 Enforcing the Law about Fornication 181
      6.5.3.5 Conclusion 182
   6.5.4 The Fathers and Mothers in the Penal Code 184
      6.5.4.1 The Text: 4Q270 7 i 13b–15a 184
      6.5.4.2. The Fathers and the Mothers 185
         6.5.4.2.1 Introduction 185
         6.5.4.2.2. The Titles Fathers and Mothers 185
         6.5.4.2.3 The Offenses in 4Q270 7 i 13–14 188
      6.5.4.3 רוקמה 189
      6.5.4.4 *rwqmh* outside of the Dead Sea Scrolls 194
      6.5.4.5 Conclusion 196
6.6 CONCLUSION: COMMUNAL LAWS 197

7. CONCLUSION 207

BIBLIOGRAPHY 213

1. EDITIONS AND TRANSLATIONS CITED OR QUOTED 213
   Bibles 215
   The Dead Sea Scrolls and Related Documents 213
   Discoveries in the Judaean Desert 214
   Rabbinic Literature 215
   Other Jewish Texts 215
   Other Early Texts 216
2. REFERENCE WORKS 216
3. GENERAL BIBLIOGRAPHY 216

INDICES 239

1. BIBLICAL TEXTS 239
2. DEAD SEA SCROLLS 245
3. ANCIENT AUTHORS 257

Acknowledgements

I would like to thank my thesis supervisor, Dr. Eileen Schuller, for her advice throughout the course of writing this dissertation. I have greatly benefited from her expertise in the field of Qumran studies. I am grateful for her enthusiasm for my project, her commitment to her students, and her attention to detail.

I would also like to thank the two other members of my supervisory committee, Dr. Adele Reinhartz and Dr. Stephen Westerholm, for their generous assistance. Their many thoughtful comments and suggestions are greatly appreciated.

I am indebted to Jennifer Nettleton and Jennifer Parsons for proofreading my manuscripts and giving me encouraging comments along the way.

I want to thank my parents, Ingemar and Ulla Thorolfson, for giving me confidence in my own abilities and encouraging me to pursue an academic career. I also want to thank my two sons, Jacob and Max, for being the wonderful persons that they are and for always reminding me what is most important in life. Finally, I want to express deep gratitude to my husband Magnus, who has supported me in all possible ways throughout my graduate studies. With love, I dedicate this study to you.

LIST OF TABLES

Table 1: Passages assigned by Robert Davis to "CDS1" compared to
  delineation by Charlotte Hemple..38
Table 2: Passages concerning women placed according to their literary strata:
  A comparison between models by Charlotte Hempel and Robert Davis.......42
Table 3: Confinement of ritually impure people in 11QT.....................................100
Table 4: Excluded categories of people in D, 1QSa, and M.................................147

ABBREVIATIONS

ASTI	*Annual of the Swedish Theological Institute*
B.	Babylonian Talmud
BA	*Biblical Archaeologist*
BASOR	*Bulletin of the American Schools of Oriental Research*
BDB	The New Brown–Driver–Briggs–Geseniugs Hebrew and English Lexicon
BJS	Brown Judaic Studies
BTB	*Biblical Theological Bulletin*
CurBS	*Currents in Research: Biblical Studies*
DJD	Discoveries in the Judaean Desert
DJDJ	Discoveries in the Judaean Desert of Jordan
DSD	*Dead Sea Discoveries*
ErIsr	*Eretz–Israel*
EvT	*Evangelische Theologie*
HAR	*Hebrew Annual Review*
HR	*History of Religions*
HS	*Hebrew Studies*
HSS	Harvard Semitic Studies
HTR	*Harvard Theological Review*
HUCA	*Hebrew Union College Annual*
IEJ	*Israel Exploration Journal*
JAGNES	*Journal of the Association of Graduates in Near Eastern Studies*
JANES	*Journal of Ancient Near Eastern Studies*
JBL	*Journal of Biblical Literature*
JJS	*Journal of Jewish Studies*
JNSL	*Journal of Northwest Semitic Languages*
JQR	*Jewish Quarterly Review*
JQRMS	Jewish Quarterly Review Monograph Series
JSOT	*Journal for the Study of the Old Testament*
JSOTSup	Journal for the Study of the Old Testament: Supplement Series
JSP	*Journal for the Study of the Pseudepigrapha*
JSPSup	Journal for the Study of the Pseudepigrapha: Supplement Series
M.	Mishnah
NTOA	Novum Testamentum et Orbis Antiquus
NTS	*New Testament Studies*
PG	Patrologia Graeca
PL	Patrologia Latina
PVTG	Pseudepigrapha Veteris Testamenti Graece
RB	*Revue Biblique*
RevQ	*Revue de Qumran*

SAOC	Studies in Ancient Oriental Civilization
SBLMS	Society of Biblical Literature Monograph Series
SBLSymS	Society of Biblical Literature Symposium Series
SJLA	Studies in Judaism in Late Antiquity
SJSJ	Supplements to the Journal for the Study of Judaism
SNTSMS	Society for New Testament Studies Monograph Series
SR	*Studies in Religion*
STDJ	*Studies on the Texts of the Desert of Judah*
T.	Tosefta
TS	*Theological Studies*
VT	*Vetus Testamentum*
VTSup	Vetus Testamentum, Supplements
ZAW	*Zeitschrift für die Altentestamentlische Wissenschaft*

1. INTRODUCTION

1.1 INTRODUCTION

The Damascus Document (D) is widely accepted as a foundational document amongst the sectarian literature of the Dead Sea Scrolls.[1] The document pertains to members living in "camps," who married and had children. Many of its laws concern women specifically, such as laws regarding marriage, oaths, and purity. My study offers a detailed analysis of all the passages that relate to women. It addresses issues of the role, status, and participation of women in the community behind the text, as well as the attitudes towards women that the text reflects. Key issues that pertain to the status of women include purity, membership, and marriage.

In spite of the rich material related to women in D, no study until now has undertaken a detailed and *comprehensive* examination of its references to women. The present study aims to fill this void, so as to enrich our understanding of women in the Dead Sea Scrolls.

---

[1] By "sectarian literature," I refer to those documents that are generally viewed as being composed within the sect behind the Scrolls; see Carol Newsom, "'Sectually Explicit' Literature from Qumran," in *The Hebrew Bible and Its Interpreters* (eds. William Propp, Baruch Halpern, and David Noel Freedman; Winona Lake, Ind.: Eisenbrauns, 1990), 167–87; Devorah Dimant, "The Qumran Manuscripts: Contents and Significance," in *Time to Prepare the Way in the Wilderness: Papers on the Qumran Scrolls by Fellows of the Institute for Advanced Studies of the Hebrew University, Jerusalem, 1989–1990* (eds. Devorah Dimant and Lawrence Schiffman; STDJ 16; Leiden: Brill, 1995), 23–58. For a definition of "sect," see below, n.50.

1.2 QUMRAN SCHOLARSHIP ON WOMEN

1.2.1 THE ESSENES

Soon after the discovery of Cave 1 in 1947, the Dead Sea Scrolls became linked to the Essenes, as they are depicted by Josephus, Philo and Pliny the Elder.[2] The famous description by Pliny of the celibate life of the Essenes reads: "They are a people unique of its kind and admirable beyond all other in the whole world, without women and renouncing love entirely, without money, and having for company only the palm-trees"; and further, "thus, unbelievable though this may seem, for thousands of centuries a people has existed which is eternal yet into which no one is born."[3] In his second book of the *Jewish War* (II 119–61), Josephus gives a lengthy description of the communal life of the Essenes.[4] According to him, the Essenes are characterized by a simple lifestyle, mutual affection between members, and a strict adherence to the sacred laws, and they form communities in every town in Palestine. Instead of marrying, they adopt the children of others and teach them their way of life (120). He explains that "it is not that they abolish marriage, or the propagation of the species resulting from it, but they are on guard against the licentiousness of women and are convinced that none of them are faithful to one man" (121). Josephus adds a short note on "another order of Essenes," ἕτερον Ἐσσηνῶν τάγμα, who marry (160–61):[5]

---

[2] When only a few documents from Cave 1 were known, Eleazar Sukenik identified the authors as Essenes (*Otzar Ha-Megilloth Ha-Genuzoth* [Jerusalem: Bialik, 1954] [Hebrew]). For support of the Essene identification, see André Dupont-Sommer, *The Essene Writings from Qumran* (trans. G. Vermes; Gloucester, Mass.: Peter Smith, 1973), 42–61; Todd Beall, *Josephus' Description of the Essenes Illustrated by the Dead Sea Scrolls* (SNTSMS 58; Cambridge: Cambridge University Press, 1988); Hartmut Stegemann, "Qumran Essenes: Local Members of the Main Jewish Union in Late Second Temple Times," in *The Madrid Qumran Congress: Proceedings of the International Congress on the Dead Sea Scrolls, Madrid 18–21 March 1991* (eds. Julio Trebolle Barrera and Luis Vegas Montaner; STDJ 11; Leiden: Brill, 1992), 2:83–166; Joseph M. Baumgarten, "The Disqualifications of Priests in 4Q Fragments of the 'Damascus Document,' a Specimen of Recovery of Pre-Rabbinic Halakha," in *The Madrid Qumran Congress*, 2:503–13; Geza Vermes and Martin Goodman, *The Essenes According to the Classical Sources* (Sheffield: JSOT Press, 1989), 2–14; Geza Vermes, *The Complete Dead Sea Scrolls in English* (New York: Allen Lane The Penguin Press, 1997), 46–8; James VanderKam and Peter Flint, *The Meaning of the Dead Sea Scrolls: Their Significance for Understanding the Bible, Judaism, Jesus, and Christianity* (San Francisco: HarperSanFrancisco, 2002), 240–50.

[3] *Natural History* V 17.4. Translation by Dupont-Sommer, *The Essene Writings*, 37.

[4] He also describes the Essenes in *Ant.* XVIII 18–22.

[5] Translation by Dupont-Sommer, *The Essene Writings*, 35. Translations of Josephus' works are based on *Loeb Classical Library*, unless I state another source.

There exists another order of Essenes who, although in agreement with the others on the way of life, usages, and customs, are separated from them on the subject of marriage. Indeed, they believe that people who do not marry cut off a very important part of life, namely, the propagation of the species; and all the more so that if everyone adopted the same opinion the human race (τὸ γένος) would very quickly disappear.

Like Josephus, Philo ascribes a misogynist rationale for the celibacy of the Essenes: "For no one of the Essenes ever marries a wife, because woman is a selfish creature and one addicted to jealousy in an immoderate degree, and terribly calculated to agitate and overturn the natural inclinations of a man, and to mislead him by her continual tricks."[6] The condescending views of women ascribed to the Essenes are strikingly similar to views expressed by Josephus and Philo themselves about women, and may say more about the ancient authors than about the Essenes.[7]

Most scholars reconstruct the history of the group behind the Dead Sea Scrolls in light of the emergence of the Essenes in Second Temple Palestine. Proponents of this theory include, among others, Roland de Vaux, Frank Moore Cross, J. T. Milik, John Strugnell, Geza Vermes, James VanderKam, and John Collins.[8] It should be noted that the reconstructions made by the individual scholars have never been entirely uniform. Theories that modify the traditional Essene model include Jerome Murphy-O'Connor's thesis of a Babylonian origin.[9] According to him, at an unknown date after the Exile, a group of pious Jews in Babylonia founded an Essene community. In the wake of the Maccabean success, some of the Essenes returned to Palestine and, after having come in conflict with Jewish religious authorities, they settled in Qumran. His theory has been supported and further developed by Philip Davies.[10] Alternatively, the

---

[6]*Hypoth.* 11.14; all translations from Philo's works are based on C. D. Yonge, ed., *The Works of Philo: Completed and Unabridged: New Updated Edition* (Peabody, Mass.: Hendrickson, 1993).

[7]See e.g., Josephus, *Ant.* VI 8.15; Philo, *Hypoth.* 11.15–17. For a detailed analysis on Philo's views on women, see Dorothy Sly, *Philo's Perception of Women* (Atlanta: Scholars Press, 1990); Richard A. Baer Jr., *Philo's Use of the Categories Male and Female* (Leiden: Brill, 1970).

[8]For an outline of the majority view, see Emil Schürer, *The History of the Jewish People in the Age of Jesus Christ (175 B.C.–A.D. 135)*, (edited and revised by Geza Vermes and Fergus Millar; trans. T. A. Burkill; Edinburgh: Clark, 1979), 2:555–90.

[9]Murphy-O'Connor explains that the Maccabees' creation of a state attracted the immigration of Jews from the diaspora, as well as creating a wave of anti-semitism that forced some Jews to flee ("The Essenes and Their History," *RB* 81 [1974], 224). For a critique of Murphy-O'Connor's thesis, see Michael Knibb, "Exile in the Damascus Document," *JSOT* 25 (1983), 99–117.

[10]According to Davies, the ideological beginning of the *yahad* goes back to sixth century Babylonia with the emergence of two parallel calendric traditions. Davies notes that D preserves similar traditions regarding the calendar, halakhah, and historiography as do Jubilees, 1 Enoch

Groningen hypothesis postulates a Palestinian origin and a split between the Essenes and the Qumran community.[11] This hypothesis maintains that the Essenes began as a Palestinian movement in the end of third century within the context of the apocalyptic traditions of that time, reflected in documents like Jubilees and 1 Enoch. Halakhic differences led the Teacher of Righteousness to split from the Essenes and to bring with him a splinter group to Qumran. Thus, the Qumran community is significantly different from the Essenes, which becomes a "parent movement." Stegemann has offered a new twist to the Essene hypothesis by arguing that the Essenes were not a sect, but a major religious movement in Second Temple Jewish life.[12]

Other scholars argue for a different identification of the people behind the Scrolls. Lawrence Schiffman, for example, emphasizes a common heritage with the Sadducees.[13] He identifies the founders of the sect with Sadducean priests who opposed the Hasmonean high priesthood. Michael Wise, Martin Abegg and Edward Cook refrain from identifying the authors of the Scrolls with any given party, describing them as a diverse and religiously conservative movement, which originated

---

and the Temple Scroll. He argues that the halakhic conflict and the polemic over the calendar reflected in these documents stem from the third and second centuries B.C.E. The social segregation of the group behind D took place later, after the return to Palestine. Furthermore, the term "Essenes" may have been used in a much looser and broader sense than scholars usually assume, and he would therefore include D and S among Essene writings. See Philip Davies, "The Birthplace of the Essenes: Where is 'Damascus,'" *RevQ* 14 (1990), 503–19.

[11]See Florentino García Martínez and A. S. van der Woude, "A 'Groningen' Hypothesis of Qumran Origins and Early History," *RevQ* 14 (1990), 521–41; Martínez and Julio Trebolle Barrera, *The People of the Dead Sea Scrolls* (trans. Wilfred Watson; Leiden: Brill, 1995), 77–96. John J. Collins, among others, has criticised the hypothesis; "The Origin of the Qumran Community: A Review of the Evidence," in *To Touch the Text: Biblical and Related Studies in Honor of Joseph A. Fitzmyer, S.J.* (eds. M. Horgan and P. Kobelski; New York: Crossroad, 1989), 175.

[12]Hartmut Stegemann, *The Library of Qumran: On the Essenes, Qumran, John the Baptist, and Jesus* (Grand Rapids, Mich.: Eerdmans, 1998), 150. See also "The Qumran Essenes."

[13]Lawrence Schiffman has written extensively on this topic; see, e.g., *Reclaiming the Dead Sea Scrolls* (Philadelphia: The Jewish Publication Society, 1994), 73–6; "The Place of 4QMMT in the Corpus of Qumran Manuscripts," in *Reading 4QMMT: New Perspectives on Qumran Law and History* (eds. John Kampen and Moshe Bernestein; SBLSymS 2; Atlanta: Scholars Press, 1996), 81–98.

Introduction 5

in the beginning of the first century B.C.E.[14] Several other theories have similarly questioned some of the basic assumptions about Qumran and its library.[15]

There are many striking similarities between the Essene sect, as it is depicted by first century C.E. Latin and Greek writers, and the communities behind the Dead Sea Scrolls, but to list all the reasons in favour of an Essene identification of the community at Qumran is beyond the scope of this study. Given the many parallels, which range from the ascetic lifestyle to minor details, I accept the identification of the community behind the Scrolls as Essene, whose origins likely began in the early second century B.C.E. Furthermore, I do not envision the Qumran group as a splinter group from the rest of the Essene movement because I find it unlikely that the community at Qumran would have treasured and copied documents from a parent-movement that it—according to this hypothesis—would have considered the enemy.

1.2.2 CELIBACY AND MARRIAGE

The portrayals by the Greek and Latin writers of the Essenes as predominantly male and celibate contradict the picture that emerges from the sectarian literature of the Dead Sea Scrolls of communities that include women and children. One of the first major documents from Qumran to be published, the Rule of the Community (1QS), does not mention women (with the exception of the expression, "one born of a woman" in 1QS XI 21) and has therefore commonly been seen as reflecting a community of celibate men. Amongst other sectarian documents that were published early, the Rule of the Congregation (1QSa) and CD—contrary to 1QS—take the presence of women and children for granted. In order to harmonize the conflicting sources, the majority of scholars identified the *yahad* ("community") of 1QS as a male, celibate group who lived in solitude in the desert at Khirbet Qumran, which was presumed to be the central headquarters of the Essene sect. At the same time, scholars assigned those documents that assumed a married community, such as CD and 1QSa, to the order of married Essenes that Josephus mentions; families living in camps,

---

[14]M. Wise, M. Abegg, and E. Cook identify the Wicked Priest as John Hyrcanus II (63–40 B.C.E.) and suggest that the Teacher of Righteousness began his ministry in the late second or early first century B.C.E. (*The Dead Sea Scrolls: A New Translation* [San Francisco: Harper Collins, 1996], 26–35).

[15]Norman Golb argues that Khirbet Qumran was a fortress. The Scrolls stem from the library in the Jerusalem temple and were hidden at Qumran during the war against the Romans. See "The Problem of Origin and Identification of the Dead Sea Scrolls," *Proceedings of the American Philosophical Society* 124 (1980), 1–24; "The Dead Sea Scrolls: A New Perspective," *The American Scholar* 58 (1989), 177–207; *Who Wrote the Dead Sea Scrolls: The Search for the Secret of Qumran* (New York: Scribner, 1995). Robert Eisenman attempts to link the Qumran group with the early Christians. See *James, the Brother of Jesus: the Key to Unlocking the Secrets of Early Christianity and the Dead Sea Scrolls* (New York: Viking, 1996); *The Dead Sea Scrolls and the First Christians* (Rockport, Mass.: Element Books, 1996).

according to D (CD VII 6–9), were thereby understood as members living in various towns across Palestine, but not at Qumran.[16] The relatively few skeletons of women and children compared to those of males discovered at the cemetery at Khirbet Qumran were often used as evidence to prove that the community at Qumran was all male, although the very existence of the female skeletons still remained a difficulty for the hypothesis.

As all the Dead Sea Scrolls now are published, there are a large number of additional texts that mention women, such as 4QMMT (4Q394–399), the War Scroll (1QM),[17] 4QMiscellaneous Rules (4Q265), the Temple Scroll (11QT), 4QOrdinances[a,b,c] (4Q159, 4Q513, 4Q514), 4QTohorot A,C (4Q274, 4Q278), 4QInstruction[b] (4Q416), 4QRitual of Marriage (4Q502), and 4QHalakha A (4Q251). Although most scholars still hold on to the standard model described above, the strict division between a male, celibate order versus an order of married men and women is becoming increasingly difficult to retain.[18] Consequently, some scholars who highlight the large number of documents that include references to women and the lack of explicit evidence for celibacy have challenged the traditional perspective.[19]

The question of celibacy in the movement behind the Dead Sea Scrolls is obviously tied to the question of Essene identification. Scholars who oppose the identification, such as Schiffman, commonly hold that celibacy was not practised by the sect behind the Scrolls.[20] Schiffman argues that the Qumran complex was a centre

---

[16]For example, see Godfrey R. Driver, *The Judaean Scrolls: The Problem and a Solution* (Oxford: B. Blackwell, 1965), 51; Vermes, *The Complete Dead Sea Scrolls*, 34; Michael A. Knibb, *The Qumran Community* (Cambridge, N.Y.: Cambridge University Press, 1987), 14–15; James VanderKam, *The Dead Sea Scrolls Today* (Grand Rapids, Mich.: Eerdmans, 1994), 57, 91. Frank Moore Cross states, "The term *yahad*, community, seems to apply to the community par excellence; i.e., the principal settlement in the desert. The Qumran settlement is probably unique, not only in being the original 'exile in the desert,' the home of the founder of the sect, but also in following a celibate rule" (*The Ancient Library of Qumran,* [3d ed.; Minneapolis: Fortress Press, 1995], 70–1).

[17]See 1QM VII 1–7.

[18]Murphy-O'Connor questioned the standard model before most new texts were published; see "The Judean Desert," in *Early Judaism and its Modern Interpreters* (eds. Robert Kraft and George Nickelsburg; vol. 2 of *The Bible and Its Modern Interpreters*; Philadelphia: Fortress Press, 1986), 126.

[19]Stegemann, *The Library of Qumran*, 193–8; Schiffman, *Reclaiming*, 133–5. Already H. Hübner disputed that celibacy was the norm ("Zolibat in Qumran," *NTS* 16 [1970–71], 153–67).

[20]According to Schiffman, the sect behind the Scrolls may still fall into the category of those marrying Essenes that Josephus describes, since the Essenes may have been an inclusive term used for a number of groups (*Reclaiming*, 143, 129). Norman Golb observes, "no doctrine of celibacy can be located in any of the Scrolls" ("The Problem of Origin and Identification of the Dead Sea Scrolls," 1).

for the sect, where members would go in order to complete required studies to become full members, thus temporarily leaving their wives and children. A few permanent residents, however, would have kept their families with them.[21] Taking the lack of evidence for celibacy in the Scrolls into account, Hartmut Stegemann, a main proponent of the identification of the Qumran community as Essene, holds that marriage was the norm in the Essene movement.[22] According to him, the writers of antiquity mistakenly believed that the Essene men were unmarried, because the Essene women were marginalised and almost invisible in the movement. There was also a high mortality among women and a prohibition against remarriage.[23] Other scholars also hold that marriage was the norm among the Essenes. Joseph Baumgarten questions the view that celibacy among the Essenes was a life-long commitment, suggesting instead that elderly men and women renounced sexual relationship, thus taking on the lifestyle of celibacy at a later stage in their lives.[24] Another theory proposes that Essene men, after having married and had children, renounced sexual intercourse at the age of twenty-five when they entered the holy army.[25] Alternatively, scholars have proposed a development in the history of Essene communal life from celibacy to married life. Arguing that D is later than S, Cross holds that it is possible that the skeletons of women represent a later stage of the Qumran community, when the previously celibate community had changed into the married one.[26] As Davies puts it: "a century, after all, is a long time to wait for the eschaton."[27]

Despite the absence of explicit evidence of celibacy in the Scrolls and the lack of evidence of any rationale for abstention from marriage, scholars have nonetheless tried to infer an explanation for the celibate lifestyle of the Essenes. Thus, celibacy has commonly been explained in terms of purity and holiness; it is often described as an

---

[21] Schiffman, Reclaiming, 53, 135; cf. *Sectarian Law in the Dead Sea Scrolls: Courts, Testimony and the Penal Code* (BJS 38; Chico, Calif.: Scholars Press, 1983), 214–15.

[22] Stegemann argues that Qumran was not the centre of the movement, but a place for the production of scrolls (*The Library of Qumran,* 51–5).

[23] Ibid., 196–7; "The Qumran Essenes," 126–32.

[24] Baumgarten points to 4Q502, which he takes to be evidence of a ritual of such renunciation; "Qumran-Essene Restraints on Marriage, in *Archaeology and History in the Dead Sea Scrolls: The New York Conference in Memory of Yigael Yadin* (ed. Lawrence H. Schiffman; JSPSup 8; Sheffield: JSOT Press 1990), 13–24.

[25] Abel Isaksson, *Marriage and Ministry in the New Temple: A Study with Special Reference to Mt. 19.12–13 and 1 Cor. 11.3–6* (Uppsala Universitet Nytestamentliga Seminar Acta 24; Lund: C. W. K Gleerup, 1965), 45–65.

[26] Cross, *Ancient Library,* 82. R. De Vaux suggested that the original rule of celibacy may have been relaxed later; see *Archaeology and the Dead Sea Scrolls: The Schweich Lectures of the British Academy 1959* (London: Oxford University Press, 1973), 128–9.

[27] Philip Davies, *Behind the Essenes: History and Ideology in the Dead Sea Scrolls* (BJS 94; Atlanta: Scholars Press, 1987), 84–5.

attempt by the Essenes to imitate the priestly level of purity in the temple.[28] Celibacy has also been compared to the sexual abstention of warriors of the Holy War in the Pentateuchal narratives.[29] The ideal of celibacy has also been traced to the eschatological outlook of the sect. Accordingly, sexual intercourse may have been renounced in anticipation of the world-to-come, a world devoid of sexual pleasures. Also, procreation served no purpose if the present world were to end soon.[30] These rationales are often combined to explain the alleged phenomenon of celibacy among the Essenes.

Few scholars have considered the possibility that the celibate branch of the Essenes included women, although ascetic women are known from the Jewish group of men and women that made up the Therapeutae in Egypt, described by Philo.[31] Indeed, some scholars hold that the Therapeutae are related to the Essenes. If they are correct, this would support the hypothesis that Essenism may have included celibate women.[32]

---

[28] Elisha Qimron argues that the members of the *yahad* saw themselves as a substitute for the temple. Hence they did not take wives because sexual intercourse was prohibited in the Temple City (CD XII 1–12; 11QT XLV 7–12); see "Celibacy in the Dead Sea Scrolls and the Two Kinds of Sectarians," in *The Madrid Qumran Congress*, 1:290–4. Antoine Guillaumont points to Moses' renunciation of sexual relations as background to the celibate ideal ("A propos du célibat des Esseniens," in *Hommages à André Dupont-Sommer* [Paris: Librarie Adrien Maisonneuve, 1971], 395–404); see also A. Marx, "Les racines du célibat essénien," *RevQ* 7 (1970), 323–42; Joseph Coppens, "Le célibate esséniens," in *Qumrân: Sa piété, sa théologie et son milieu* (eds. Mathias Delcor et al.; Bibliotheca Ephemeridum Theologicarum Lovaniensium. 46; Paris: Duculot, 1978),

[29] On this topic, see Cross, *Ancient Library*, 83–4; Matthew Black, "The Tradition of Hasidean-Essene Asceticism: Its Origins and Influence," in *Aspects du Judéo-Christianisme: Collogue de Strasbourg 23–25 avril 1964* (ed. Universitée des sciences humaines de Strasbourg. Centre de recherches d'histoire des religions; Paris: Presses Universitaires de France, 1965), 19–33; Gary Anderson, "Celibacy or Consummation in the Garden? Reflections on Early Jewish and Christian Interpretations of the Garden of Eden," *HTR* 82 (1989), 121–48.

[30] See, for example, Davies, who compares the celibacy of the Essenes to that of the early Christians who were facing the coming eschaton (*Behind the Essenes*, 84–5).

[31] Baumgarten suggests that there were female ascetics among the Essenes; "Qumran-Essene Restraints on Marriage," 13–24. In contrast, Ross Kraemer claims, "...the entire cosmology, theology, and symbolic universe of Qumran was so pervasively male that no women would have found it acceptable, let alone compelling" ("Monastic Jewish Women in Greco-Roman Egypt: Philo Judaeus on the Therapeutrides," *Signs* 14 [1989], 365). Her comments are not convincing since Jewish and Christian women have found spiritual comfort in scriptures that are thoroughly patriarchal, such as the Hebrew Bible and the New Testament.

[32] Proponents of a connection between the Therapeutae and the Essenes include Marcel Simon, *Jewish Sects at the Time of Jesus* (trans. James Farley; Philadelphia: Fortress Press, 1967), 120–30; for a survey, see J. Riaud, "Les Thérapeutes d'Alexandria dans la Tradition et dans la recherche critique jusqu'aux découvertes de Qumran," in *Aufstieg und Niedergang der*

Introduction 9

If the sectarian literature of the Dead Sea Scrolls is written by the Essenes themselves, it remains the primary witness of the ancient sect, whereas the descriptions by the ancient observers, who, as outsiders to the sect could be mistaken about details, are secondary evidence. From this perspective, it becomes clear that the sect behind the Scrolls held marriage to be the common way of life. At the same time, since the ancient writers insist that celibacy was characteristic among the Essenes, it is likely that *some* Essenes— likely a minority—were celibate. The latter branch may or may not have included ascetic women. Josephus chose to describe the celibate Essenes at length rather than the married Essenes, so as to satisfy the Roman readers' interest in the curious and unique customs of the Jews. A description of the celibate, self-denying Essenes, rather than the more usual married ones, was likely of more interest to his readers. In addition, within Josephus' and Philo's encompassing apologetic strategy of defending the Jewish way of life, describing Jews who practised celibacy provided an opportunity to show the Roman world that some Jews had perfected control over bodily passions even more than the Romans. Philo therefore chose to ignore the married Essenes completely in favour of the celibate branch. Furthermore, Pliny's description of the Essenes borders on the fantastic, as several scholars have pointed out.[33] From this perspective, D provides information about one of the many Essene communities in Palestine in which marriage was the common way of life.

1.2.3 STUDIES ON WOMEN IN THE DEAD SEA SCROLLS

Issues relating to women in the Dead Sea Scrolls have been the subject of several studies and academic presentations. Eileen Schuller's article "Women in the Dead Sea Scrolls," an examination of some key texts concerning women, raises important questions about the status and membership of women in the sect behind the Scrolls.[34]

---

römischen Welt: Geschichte und Kultur Roms im Spiegel der neureren Forschung 2/20/2 (Berlin: De Gruyter, 1987), 1241–64. See also Philip Davies and Joan Taylor, who oppose a link between the Therapeutae and the Essenes ("The So-Called 'Therapeutae' of De Vita Contemplativa: Identity and Character," *HTR* 91 [1998], 3–24).

[33] I share the sentiment that Matthew Black expresses: "one cannot suppress the suspicion that Josephus' account may have been an exaggerated one"; and "He [Josephus] may well be guilty of selecting the exceptions and making them the rule; in Pliny (H.N. V, 15) Essene celibacy has been promoted to the marvellous"; see "The Tradition of Hasidean-Essene Asceticism," 28. Stegemann, similarly, likens Pliny's account to "tourist information," filled with errors (the Essenes did marry, did use coins, and had no palm-trees close by); see "The Qumran Essenes," 83–5.

[34] Eileen Schuller, "Women in the Dead Sea Scrolls," in *Methods of Investigation of the Dead Sea Scrolls and the Khirbet Qumran Site: Present Realities and Future Prospects* (eds. Michael Wise et al.; Annals of the New York Academy of Sciences 722; New York: New York Academy of Sciences, 1994), 115–32. Her article also appeared in modified forms in *The Dead Sea Scrolls after Fifty Years: A Comprehensive Assessment* (eds. Peter W. Flint and James VanderKam; Leiden: Brill, 1998), 2:117–44, and as "Evidence for Women in the Community

Schiffman offers an analysis of all the references to women in the Temple Scroll.[35] Furthermore, "Women and Qumran" was the topic of a session at the Society of Biblical Literature meeting in Nashville, Tennessee, in 2000. It included the papers "Women and Children in Legal and Liturgical Texts from Qumran" (by Moshe Bernstein) and "Wisdom and the Women at Qumran" (by Benjamin G. Wright III).[36] A study on the Damascus Document by Maxine Grossman contains the chapter "Gender in the Damascus Document."[37] In his book *Reclaiming the Dead Sea Scrolls*, Schiffman devotes one chapter to "Women in the Scrolls," which surveys several documents that take the presence of women for granted.[38] The *Encyclopedia of the Dead Sea Scrolls* dedicates two articles specifically to the topic of women in the scrolls: "Women" and "Family Life."[39] An article by Sidnie White Crawford examines female titles in the Scrolls.[40] Furthermore, there have been many studies on specific topics related to women, such as divorce laws, laws on marriage, purity issues, and restrictions on sexual intercourse.[41] In addition, texts pertaining to women in the Dead Sea Scrolls are in some cases included in general surveys of women in Second Temple

---

of the Dead Sea Scrolls," in *Voluntary Associations in the Graeco-Roman World* (eds. John S. Kloppenborg and Stephen G. Wilson; New York: Routledge, 1996), 252–65. See also Lena Cansdale, "Women Members of the *Yahad* according to the Qumran Scrolls," in *Proceedings of the Eleventh World Congress of Jewish Studies* (Jerusalem: World Union of Jewish Studies, 1994), 215–22.

[35] Schiffman, "Laws Pertaining to Women in the Temple Scroll," in *The Dead Sea Scrolls: Forty Years of Research* (eds. Devorah Dimant and Uriel Rappaport; Leiden: Brill, 1992), 210–28.

[36] This collection of papers has been published in *DSD 11* (2004). Unfortunately, they appeared in print after the completion of my study.

[37] Maxine Grossman, *Reading for History in the Damascus Document: A Methodological Study* (STDJ 45; Leiden: Brill, 2002).

[38] Schiffman, *Reclaiming*, 127-43.

[39] Eileen Schuller and Cecilia Wassen, "Women: Daily Life," in *Encyclopedia of the Dead Sea Scrolls* (eds. L. Schiffman and J. VanderKam; New York: Oxford University Press, 1999), 2: 981–4; John Collins, "Family Life," 1:287–90; see also Joseph Fitzmyer, "Marriage and Divorce," 1:511–14.

[40] Sidnie White Crawford, "Mothers, Sisters, and Elders: Titles for Women in Second Temple Jewish and Early Christian Communities," in *The Dead Sea Scrolls as Background to Postbiblical Judaism and Early Christianity* (ed. James Davila; STDJ 46; Leiden: Brill, 2003), 177–91.

[41] For example, Gershon Brin, "Divorce at Qumran" in *Legal Texts and Legal Issues: Proceedings of the Second Meeting of the International Organization for Qumran Studies, Cambridge, 1995: Published in Honour of Joseph M. Baumgarten* (eds. Moshe J. Bernstein, Florentino García Martínez, and John Kampen; STDJ 23; Leiden: Brill, 1997), 231–44; Sarah Japhet, "The Prohibition of the Habitation of Women: The Temple Scroll's Attitude Toward Sexual Impurity and Its Biblical Precedents," *JANES* 22 (1993), 69–87.

Introduction

Judaism, such as those by Leoni Archer and Tal Ilan.[42] Still, the number of gender-related studies on the Dead Sea Scrolls remains few.

1.3 CONTRIBUTION

My study differs from general surveys on women in Palestine in Hellenistic times, as well as surveys on women in the Dead Sea Scrolls such as the chapter by Schiffman, in that through a detailed analysis of references to women in one single document, D, it presents a glimpse of the presence and participation of women in one particular community.[43] In addition, whereas general surveys look for commonalities and social trends of a certain period, my study reveals a complex picture of women's position in the community, highlighting the sometimes conflicting traces of evidence that relate to the status of women. My study of the references to women in D is comparable in subject matter to the valuable article on women in the Temple Scroll by Schiffman, in which he offers a detailed examination of key passages on women in that document.[44] My analysis goes beyond the scope of his article, however, since in addition to interpreting the text, it also investigates women's role and status in the community behind the text and examines changes that appear over time.

The present exploration into the role and status of women in the community behind D will be an important contribution to the debate about the position of women in the sect behind the Scrolls. In spite of differing views concerning the history of the group behind the Scrolls and the question of marriage or celibacy, scholars are nearly unanimous in ascribing a very limited, marginalized role to women in the sect. It is revealing that both Stegemann and Schiffman, in spite of their opposing views on the nature of the group behind the Scrolls, agree as to the very subordinate role of women in the communities behind the Scrolls.[45] Frequently, the low status of women is explained in terms of purity: for example, Magen Broshi calls women "a source of impurity," and Steven Fraade writes, "They [the Dead Sea Scrolls] seem to *assume* the

---

[42]Tal Ilan, *Jewish Women in Greco-Roman Palestine* (Peabody, Mass.: Hendrickson Publishers, 1995); Leoni J. Archer, *Her Price is Beyond Rubies: The Jewish Woman in Greco-Roman Palestine* (Sheffield: Sheffield Academic Press, 1990). See also Evelyn and Frank Stagg, *Woman in the World of Jesus* (Philadelphia: Westminster Press, 1978), 36–40.

[43]See Schiffman, *Reclaiming*, 127-43.

[44]See Schiffman, "Laws Pertaining to Women in the Temple Scroll."

[45]Stegemann asserts that women did not become full members, and were left out of worship services and common meals ("The Qumran Essenes," 132-4; cf. *The Library of Qumran*, 193.) He provides no textual evidence for the assumptions that women did not participate in any of the communal activities. Schiffman holds that men would leave their wives for periods of time in order to study at the centre at Qumran and thereby gain full membership, a status not attainable for women (*Reclaiming*, 53, 101). Similarly, Philip Davies and Joan Taylor argue that a woman was a member by virtue of her attachment to a man ("On the Testimony of Women in 1QSa," *DSD* 3 [1996], 223-35).

existence of women and marriage within the order and do not speak of celibacy, being instead careful to exclude women from aspects of the community's life in which they might threaten its ritual purity."[46] In contrast to most scholars, Schuller has very tentatively explored the possible evidence in the Scrolls indicating that women were full members of the community.[47] Furthermore, Mayer Gruber paints a picture of a society with egalitarian traits behind the Scrolls, in which women had extensive rights.[48] I am following their lead by reexamining old assumptions about, and questioning general depictions of, women in the Scrolls.

My analysis of the representation of women in D presents a highly complex picture in which women in some cases are depicted as inferior to men and in other cases as their equals. Thus, by offering a balanced picture of the status and role of women, my study challenges the common assumption that the Essene women were extensively marginalised in communal life. My examination enhances our understanding of the particular laws in D that relate to women, such as purity laws and marital laws. By analysing the implications of the legislation in D concerning the communal life of women, this study offers new insights in the historical-cultural

---

[46]Broshi writes: "In the *Rule of the Community*, no women and children are mentioned, a most significant omission as women are quite problematic creatures, a source of impurity" ("Was Qumran, Indeed, a Monastery? The Consensus and Its Challengers: An Archaeologist's View," in *Caves of Enlightenment: Proceedings of the American Schools of Oriental Research Dead Sea Scrolls Jubilee Symposium [1947–1997]*, [ed. James H. Charlesworth; North Richland Hills, Tex.: Bibal Press, 1998], 23). Fraade refers to 1QSa I 26, which requires sexual abstinence during three days before a meeting of the council, and 1QM VII 1–7, which prohibits boys and women from entering the war camp ("Ascetical Aspects of Ancient Judaism," in vol.1 of *Jewish Spirituality* [ed. Arthur Green; World Spirituality 13; New York: Crossroad, 1986], 270); cf. Albert Baumgarten: "the relatively minor place occupied by women in most of these movements would accord well with their concern for purity" (*The Flourishing of Jewish Sects in the Maccabean Era: An Interpretation* [Kinderhook, N.Y.: Brill, 1997], 45); J. Baumgarten explains that women and boys were prohibited from eating the paschal lamb (4Q265 3) out of concern for purity; see *Qumran Cave 4. XXV: Halakhic Texts* (ed. J. Baumgarten et al.; DJD XXXV; Oxford: Clarendon Press, 1999), 63.

[47]Schuller, "Women in the Dead Sea Scrolls," in *Methods of Investigation of the Dead Sea Scrolls*, 121–3. She has since reformulated the question about female membership: "The question, rather is: Could women choose independently to join the sect or did they become part only by birth or by marriage to a member? Did they go through much the same initiation process as male initiates and take the solemn oath (CD 15:5–10)?" ("Women in the Dead Sea Scrolls," in *The Dead Sea Scrolls after Fifty Years*, 129). See also Cansdale, who argues that women were full members of the *Yahad*, which she takes as evidence that the authors of the scrolls were not Essene ("Women Members of the *Yahad* according to the Qumran Scrolls," 215–22).

[48]Mayer I. Gruber, "Women in the Religious System of Qumran," in *The Judaism of Qumran: A Systematic Reading of the Dead Sea Scrolls* (eds. Alan Avery-Peck and Jacob Neusner; vol. 5 of *Judaism in Late Antiquity*; Leiden: Brill, 2001), 1:173–96.

position of women within the group of Essenes. My study aims to contribute to the body of Qumran research that continues to grow and broaden in its scope.

1.4 METHODOLOGY

My study consists of a close reading of selected passages in D, which in turn are analysed from a socio-historical perspective. The approach used in this investigation is grounded in the historical-critical method developed in biblical studies. This method assumes that it is possible, to some extent, to reconstruct historical realities based on close textual studies. However, it also recognizes that this has to be done by very careful exegesis of the text, taking questions of authorial intent and redactional activities into account, in combination with an examination of the broader historical and social context. At the same time, one has to accept that the task of recovering the roles of men and women in societies from antiquity primarily concerns the spectrum of probabilities, ranging from high to low, but almost never certainties.

My study offers an in-depth analysis of all the relevant passages on women in D. I discuss those passages that explicitly mention women and deal with issues that are clearly pertinent to women, for example, legislation concerning women's oaths and purity laws in relation to childbirth and menstruation. The majority of the passages that I will study belong to this category. Moreover, I examine those passages that do not mention women, but are relevant to the subject matter of women. To this category belong a text on initiation ritual (CD XV 1–XV 2), in which it is unclear whether or not women undertook the ritual alongside men, and a passage from the Sabbath code (CD XI 9–11) that legislates the carrying of an infant and the wearing of spices, but does not mention women.

I examine the passages concerning women in D within the context of their literary layers and according to the approximate chronological order of the strata. For this, I use the source-critical and redactional studies on the laws in D by Charlotte Hempel and Robert Davis.[49] As I will explain in detail in Chapter 2, there are two main blocks of material of laws: an early law code whose exact origin is shrouded by uncertainties but was likely composed in a non-sectarian setting, and a second block of legislative material stemming from a specific Essene community at a time when the movement had developed sectarian traits.[50] The latter legislation is devoted to the organization of

---

[49]Hempel, *The Laws of the Damascus Document: Sources, Tradition, and Redaction* (STDJ 29; Leiden: Brill, 1998); Davis, "The History of the Composition of the 'Damascus Document'" (Ph.D. diss., Harvard University, 1992).

[50]I subscribe to the definition of a sect by Rodney Stark and William Bainbridge: "A *sect movement* is a deviant religious organization with traditional beliefs and practices" (p.124). "Deviance" is explained as tension with the socio-cultural environment. By their definition they see a "continuum running from high to low tension," whereby a sect is found at one pole where the tension is high and a church at the opposite pole where there is no tension; see "Sects: Emergence of Schismatic Religious Movements," in *A Theory of Religion* (ed. Donald Wiebe;

a specific community and includes laws, for example, concerning initiation, functions of different officials, and penalties. This block of material is distinct from the early law code that Hempel calls Halakhah, which is directed to the society as a whole and is comprised of biblically based laws, such as purity laws in connection with childbirth and menstruation.

The division of blocks of text according to their literary layers provides a useful methodological framework that allows for studying the components relating to women within their appropriate literary context, as well as in their underlying social environment. Laws pertaining to women from the early layer will be studied in relation to the block of laws from the same layer that all stem from the same non-sectarian context. I will examine the laws relating to women among the communal laws within the context of the communal legislation as a whole. For the purpose of understanding women's position within the social environment of a sect I will also highlight some sectarian traits in the communal legislation (Ch. 6).

My study will expose the complexity of the representations of women in each literary layer that is apparent in that women sometimes appear subordinate to men, as is consistent with a patriarchal society, but in other instances they appear to be on an equal footing with men. My methodological approach enables me to compare and contrast women's status and the attitudes towards women in the two main literary layers and to offer insights into aspects of women's position from a pre-Essene setting to a later sectarian setting in one specific Essene community. Possible outcomes are that the representations of women in the layers are similar, or that the position of women has deteriorated or improved over time. Another possibility is that no specific trend is noticeable. Since my study includes all passages that refer to women, I examine sections that do not reveal much about women in terms of status and role in the community; nevertheless, these passages provide a general sense of which issues are important in relation to women.

The method for my study is closely aligned with feminist biblical criticism in its focus on passages relevant to women, in asking specific questions related to the role and status of women, and in uncovering implicit attitudes to women and men. In the words of Bernadette Brooten, this study "will place women in the center of the

---

Toronto Studies in Religion 2; New York: Peter Lang in association with the Centre of Religious Studies at the University of Toronto, 1987), 124–8. The community behind D displayed a strong tension with the general Jewish society. As I explain in chapter two, the Essene community behind D to some extent kept apart from the surrounding society in terms of ideology and religious praxis, as well as by following its own regulations and having its own leadership and officials. I will highlight sectarian traits in my analysis of the communal laws (Ch. 6), and I will elaborate on the implications of a sectarian environment for the position of women in my conclusion to Communal Laws (section 6.6).

frame."⁵¹ It recognizes that gender, as it appears in the text, is a social construction that should be deconstructed and analysed in order to properly understand social values in relation to women and men. With the limited explicit information on women in D, every minute detail about them needs to be scrutinized and put in its historical-social context. Questions about why references to women are included or, in some cases, why women are not mentioned, need to be addressed as well.

Feminist biblical scholarship has often exposed the inherent bias in all investigations into texts and shown that value-free or objective scholarship is not possible. When deconstructed by feminist scholars, scholarship has often revealed an androcentric bias. Similarly, Qumran scholarship on women often exhibits an androcentric and pro-male bias by simply assuming that women were in a subordinate position vis-à-vis men and were barred from public functions, without pointing to any particular evidence. My own position is to reject an *a priori* assumption that women were in a subordinate and submissive position and instead analyse the texts to uncover all possible clues that could shed light on women's status. This position may lead to a very different view on women in the Dead Sea Scrolls.

In my study I will occasionally highlight passages from other Qumran documents that can shed light on the legislation in D. I will do so very carefully, recognising that there are difficulties involved in any comparison of Qumran texts, and that the relationships among the various documents from the Dead Sea Scrolls are far from certain. In that task it is crucial to take the literary development of D into account, since the stages reflect different social environments and time periods. Hempel argues that the laws in the Halakhah stratum are reminiscent in form, terminology, and outlook of 11QT, 4Q159 and 4QMMT.⁵² These documents, 11QT in particular, include laws that are relevant for my analysis and I will consequently include them in my discussion. The language, form, and content of the communal legislation in D are closest to 1QSa, and there are also important similarities with S. Although I do not presume a common provenance for any of these documents, the similar character of the community organization of 1QSa compared to D indicates that the communities behind the two documents influenced each other and exchanged ideas.⁵³ In relation to S, there is evidence of direct textual dependence in a few instances where the texts

---

⁵¹Bernadette Brooten, "Early Christian Women and Their Cultural Context: Issues of Method in Historical Reconstruction," in *Feminist Perspectives on Biblical Scholarship* (ed. Adela Yarbro Collins; Chico, Ca.: Scholars Press, 1985), 65; Marie-Therese Wacker explains that feminist exegesis is not a methodology on its own, but "it makes use of existing methods to uncover findings relevant to women or supplement them with specific ways of asking questions" ("Methods of Feminist Exegesis," in *Feminist Interpretation: The Bible in Women's Perspective* [eds. Luise Schottroff, Silva Schroerer, and Marie-Therese Wacker; Minneapolis: Fortress Press, 1998], 63).

⁵²Hempel, *Laws*, 172, 188. For further references, see below p. 29.

⁵³On this topic, see below, p. 28, especially n. 44.

correspond closely to each other. Nevertheless, their relationship is not easily reconstructed.[54] In Chapter 2 I will explain on the basis of chronological and other considerations why I argue that neither D nor S were composed at Khirbet Qumran (although they continued to be revised at Qumran), but that they both were written in different Essene communities elsewhere in Palestine.

Both the Admonition and the laws in D are thoroughly informed by the Hebrew Bible. In the cases where laws concerning women in D are interpretations of biblical laws, I will compare these to their biblical *Vorlage* and discuss whether these laws as found in D improve the legal position of women or not, compared to the biblical laws. Furthermore, Second Temple literature will be considered to the extent that it will aid the interpretation of the passages in D. In some cases, non-Qumranic Jewish literature, both from Palestine and from the Diaspora, can help in understanding the meaning of ambiguous expressions (for example, "not established for her" לוא הוכן לה in 4Q271 3 9); other times, I will explore the Second Temple literature in order to situate specific laws in D within the contemporary Jewish society. Furthermore I will, on occasion, cautiously refer to Mishnaic halakhah. Given that there are very old traditions incorporated into the Mishnah, there is the possibility that the Mishnah can, in some cases, illuminate issues addressed in D.

The study is divided into six segments. Chapter 2 gives the necessary background information to D, including a description of the document and the manuscripts, date of composition, genre, purpose, and the place of D among the Dead Sea Scrolls. A major section of chapter 2 is devoted to defining the underlying literary strata of the laws. The division of the laws into original literary units provides the framework for my interpretation of the selected passages, which will be examined according to the chronological order of the literary strata. The subsequent chapters entail close examinations of the selected passages from D, grouped together according to their literary strata, in the approximate chronological order of the literary strata. Hence, Chapter 3 comprises a close analysis of passages pertaining to women in the Early Law Code. Chapter 4 discusses the Catalogue of Transgressors; Chapter 5 concerns

---

[54]For a discussion of the methodological difficulties involved in studying the relationship between D and S, see Sarianna Metso, "The Relationship between the Damascus Document and the Community Rule," in *The Damascus Document: A Centennial of Discovery. Proceedings of the Third International Symposium of the Orion Center for the Study of the Dead Sea Scrolls and Associated Literature, 4–8 February, 1998* (eds. Joseph M. Baumgarten, Esther G. Chazon, and Avital Pinnick; STDJ 35; Leiden: Brill, 2000), 85–93.

the Admonition; Chapter 6 treats passages related to women in the communal laws; Chapter 7 forms the conclusion.

2. THE DAMASCUS DOCUMENT

2.1 MANUSCRIPTS

The Damascus Document (D) is unique among the Dead Sea Scrolls in that two medieval manuscripts of this document exist. MSS A and B were discovered in 1896, in the Genizah of an old Karaite synagogue in Cairo. First published by Solomon Schechter in 1910 as *Fragments of a Zadokite Work*, these manuscripts are dated to the tenth (MS A) and twelfth centuries (MS B) respectively and together are labelled as the Cairo Damascus Document (CD).[1] The discovery in the early 1950s of ten copies of D among the Dead Sea Scrolls identified D as part of the Qumran library, and as such, the document was widely held to be Essene.[2] Fragments of the document were discovered in Caves 4, 5 and 6.[3] Cave 4 contained fragments from eight copies of

---

[1] Solomon Schechter, *Fragments of a Zadokite Work: Documents of Jewish Sectaries*, vol. 1 (Cambridge: Cambridge University Press, 1910; repr. with "Prolegomenon" by J. A. Fitzmyer; New York: Ktav, 1970). Further editions are: S. Zeitlin, *The Zadokite Fragments: Facsimile of the Manuscripts in the Cairo Genizah Collection in the Possession of the University Library, Cambridge, England* (JQRMS 1; Philadelphia: Dropsie College, 1952); Chaim Rabin, *The Zadokite Documents* (2nd ed.; Oxford: Clarendon, 1958); Joseph Baumgarten and Daniel Schwartz, "Damascus Document (CD)," in *Damascus Document, War Scroll, and Related Documents* (vol. 2 of *The Dead Sea Scrolls: Hebrew, Aramaic, and Greek Texts with English Translations*; eds. James Charlesworth et al.; Tübingen: J. C. B. Mohr/Louisville, Ky.: Westminster John Knox Press, 1995), 4–79; Elisha Qimron "The Text of CDC," in *The Damascus Document Reconsidered* (ed. Magen Broshi; Jerusalem: The Israel Exploration Society, 1992), 9–49. This edition also includes quality photographs of the medieval MSS.

[2] For bibliographies of scholarly studies on D, see Fitzmyer, "Prolegomenon" in the reprint of Schechter, *Fragments of a Zadokite Work*, 9–37; García Martínez, "Damascus Document: A Bibliography of Studies 1970–89," in *The Damascus Document Reconsidered*, 63–83.

[3] 5Q12 contains CD IX: 7–9; see M. Baillet, J. T. Milik et R. de Vaux, *Les 'petites grottes' de Qumran* (DJDJ III; Oxford: Clarendon Press, 1962), 181. 6Q15 frgs 1–4 corresponds to CD

the document (4Q266–273), which were assigned to József T. Milik, who assembled and transcribed them. The fragments of 4Q266–273 have subsequently been published by Baumgarten in *DJD XVIII*, based on Milik's transcription.[4]

In the copies found in the Cairo Genizah, MS A contains sixteen pages (I–XVI), while MS B comprises only two pages that the editor has designated XIX and XX. MS B page XIX partly duplicates MS A VII–VIII, following MS A closely in parts, but also displaying significant variants. The relationship between the variant portions of the two manuscripts (CD VII 9b–VIII 2a/XIX 5b–14) is unclear and has been the subject of much debate.[5] In light of the finds in Cave 4, Milik rearranged Schechter's order by placing pages XV–XVI before page IX. The order is now accepted as I–VIII,

---

IV 19–21; V 13–15; V 18–VI 2, VI 20–VII 1 plus a legal section parallel to 4Q270 2 ii 15–19; see Baillet, *DJDJ III*, 128–31.

[4] J. M. Baumgarten, *The Damascus Document (4Q266–273): Qumran Cave 4, XIII* (DJD XVIII; Oxford: Clarendon Press, 1996). For a description of the foundational work done by Milik, see Baumgarten, *DJD XVIII*, 1.

[5] Several theories have been proposed to explain the major variants of the manuscripts which occur in the section CD VII 9b–VIII 2a (MS A)/CD XIX 5b–14 (MS B). Rabin argues that MSS A and B depend on a common archetype (*Zadokite Documents*, viii). Jerome Murphy-O'Connor suggests that the original source contained segments from both MSS A and B, namely CD VII 9b–13a (MS A; the Isaiah midrash) followed by CD XIX 7b–14 (MS B; the Zechariah-Ezekiel midrash) ("The Original Text of CD 7:9–8:2' 19:5–14," *HTR* 64 [1971], 379–86). His views have been accepted by many, including Michael Knibb, who also considers the Amos-Numbers midrash in VII 13b–VIII 2a (MS A) as secondary ("The Interpretation of Damascus Document VII, 9b–VIII, 2a and XIX 5b–14," *RevQ* 15 [1991], 243–51). Philip Davies maintains that MS A is more original than B at this point, although the section VII 10–VIII 2 belongs to a later supplement of the Admonition (*Damascus Covenant: An Interpretation of the "Damascus Document"* [JSOTSS 25; Sheffield: JSOT Press, 1983], 143–72). Arguing that both the Amos-Numbers midrash (MS A) and the Zechariah-Ezekiel midrash (MS B) are original, Sidnie White Crawford maintains that the differences between MSS A and B can be explained as scribal errors rather than deliberate redactions ("A Comparison of the 'A' and 'B' Manuscripts of the Damascus Document," *RevQ* 12 [1987], 537–53). It is significant that the contested segment, CD VII 14–VIII 2a (MS A; the Amos-Numbers midrash), is attested in 4Q266 3 iii (*DJD XVIII*, 43–5). Based on this, John J. Collins argues that the Amos-Numbers midrash is original (*The Sceptre and the Star: The Messiahs of the Dead Sea Scrolls and Other Ancient Literature* [New York: Doubleday, 1995], 80–2). In her review of scholarly hypotheses on the divergences between MS A and B, Charlotte Hempel notes that there is scant textual material in 4QD in support of the MS B recension. Although there is no trace of the Zechariah-Ezekiel midrash, she correctly points out that it is theoretically possible that the lost part in 4Q266 may have included this midrash as well (*The Damascus Texts* [Companion to the Qumran Scrolls 1; Sheffield: Sheffield Academic Press, 2000], 78).

XIX–XX (MS B), XV–XVI, IX–XIV.⁶ Overall, MS A follows the Cave 4 material closely where the two overlap, but the length of the Cairo Genizah manuscript is significantly shorter than the version preserved in the 4QD fragments.⁷ This discrepancy, however, is more likely to be the result of accidental loss of text than intentional omission of material.⁸

Based on style and content, the document naturally divides into two parts: an exhortation called Admonition (CD I–VIII, XIX–XX) and a legal portion (IX–XVI and 4QD text). The 4QD text preserves previously unknown material from the opening of the Admonition (4Q266 1 a–b, 1 c–f, 2 i 1–5 and parallels). Most of the new material, however, belongs to the legal section. The discovery of the 4QD copies made it apparent that the legal section comprises about two thirds of the original document.⁹ The 4QD text provides a number of new laws concerning the priesthood, tithing, and purity; also, it supplies the ending of the document (4Q266 11), which describes an expulsion ceremony.¹⁰ The latter fragment may provide the original title of the work, מדרש התורה האחרון ("the final interpretation of the Law") with which the document ends.¹¹

Of the eight copies of D in Cave 4, 4Q266 is the most extensive and best preserved text, as well as the only copy that preserves both the introduction and the end of the document. It is also the oldest copy, dated from the beginning to the middle of the first century B.C.E., while the rest of the copies range from the middle of the first century B.C.E. to the first century C.E.¹² Seven of the manuscripts are written on hide, while 4Q273 is written on papyrus. Unlike the Cave 4 copies of S, which contain

---

⁶J. T. Milik, *Ten Years of Discovery in the Judean Wilderness* (London: SCM Press, 1959), 151–2, n.3. The book was originally published in French: *Dix ans de découvertes dans le Désert de Juda* (Paris: Cerf, 1957).

⁷Baumgarten counts less than thirty significant variants between MS A and the 4Q text from the parallel text of about 326 lines (*DJD XVIII*, 6). One overlap with MS B appears in 4Q266 4 7–8, according to Milik's arrangement, in which two fragments contain words corresponding to CD XX 33–34 (*DJD XVIII, 46–7*). So also Hartmut Stegemann, who places fragment 4Q266 4 at the beginning of col. X ("Towards Physical Reconstructions of the Qumran Damascus Document Scrolls," in *The Damascus Document: A Centennial of Discovery*, 180).

⁸Hempel, *The Damascus Texts*, 24

⁹Joseph Baumgarten, "The Laws of the Damascus Document in Current Research," in *The Damascus Document Reconsidered*, 61.

¹⁰For an outline of the document, see the summary tables of contents provided by Baumgarten in *DJD XVIII*, 3–5. See also Joseph Baumgarten, "Damascus Document" in *Encyclopedia of the Dead Sea Scrolls*, 1:167; Hempel, *The Damascus Texts*, 26–42.

¹¹See Stegemann, "Physical Reconstructions," 193; contra Baumgarten (*DJD XVIII*, 78).

¹²Baumgarten, *DJD XVIII*, 26, 30.

different versions of the text, the 4QD manuscripts are copies of the same recension with minor variances between them.[13]

Baumgarten presents a tentative order for the fragments (where there is no overlap with CD), according to Milik's arrangement. Stegemann together with his assistants, Annette Steudel and Alexander Maurer, are in the process of reconstructing a composite text of D. According to Stegemann, the best preserved manuscript from Cave 4, 4Q266, originally had thirty-two columns.[14]

In the present study on D, I primarily follow the transcription and restoration of CD by Baumgarten and Schwartz. I have also benefited from the edition of CD by Qimron in *The Damascus Document Reconsidered*, and indicate in my study the points at which I have been particularly influenced by his transcription.[15] For the manuscripts of D from Cave 4, I follow Baumgarten's edition in *DJD XVIII*.

2.2 CONTENT

The two parts, the Admonition and the Laws, are of very different character. The Admonition (I–VIII, XIX–XX) explains the relationship between God and his people; it stresses that Israel by and large has gone astray (for example, CD I 2; II 5–III 16; IV 12–VI 2) and that a return to the covenant and renewed obedience to its laws represent the only hope for Israel. A polemical edge is conspicuous, particularly in the community's self-identification as a remnant (for example, CD I 7, II 11) and the establishment of "the New Covenant."[16] The boundaries between the faithful and the faithless are drawn within Israel between the insiders, who are obedient to the covenant, and the outsiders, who are ruled by Belial (CD IV 12–V 15).

The discourse reflects an eschatological perspective, familiar from other sectarian texts, according to which the sect sees itself living at the end of the present age, in "the period of wickedness" (CD VI 10, 14), awaiting the eschaton. In a sermon-like fashion, the speaker encourages the audience to remain committed to the covenant and to be obedient to its laws. Frequent allusions to scripture are used to illuminate the history of the community and of Israel, as well as to justify the sect's authority and

---

[13] For the recensional history of S, see Philip Alexander and Geza Vermes, *Qumran Cave 4 XIX: Serekh Ha-yahad and Two Related Text* (DJD XXVI; Oxford: Clarendon Press, 1998), 9–12; Sarianna Metso, *Textual Development of the Qumran Community Rule* (STDJ 21; Leiden: Brill, 1997).

[14] In his preliminary report, Stegemann points out that based on CD and the 4QD copies the order of the first ten columns of 4Q266 and the final ten columns can be reconstructed in a straightforward way. For preliminary results, see Stegemann, "Physical Reconstructions," 177–212. See also Stegemann, *The Library of Qumran*, 117.

[15] Qimron's edition includes restorations based on the 4QD MSS, as well as references in footnotes to variant readings in 4QD.

[16] For a description of the ideology of the members of the "New Covenant," see Stegemann, "The Qumran Essenes," 146–7.

ideology. In addition to explicit references to scripture, the influence from biblical texts is apparent throughout the discourse.[17]

The legal section in D contains lists of laws addressing a variety of topics. Organised according to topics, the laws are often, but not always, introduced by a heading, such as וזה סרך "this is the rule for..."[18] In this section, the Hebrew Bible is occasionally cited to prove a specific halakhic view point, and the biblical text is often introduced with the formula אשר אמר, "as he said" (for example, CD IX 2).

The Admonition and the Laws function well together as a unit. Dupont-Sommer, for example, stresses their close relationship by explaining that the first part functions as an introduction to the second and that "the whole purpose of the Exhortation [the Admonition] is to advise the members of the sect to obey its ordinances."[19] Davies describes the relationship well when he explains that the Laws provide the "what" and the Admonition the "why," that is, "the ideological context in which this halakhah operates."[20]

2.3 DATE OF COMPOSITION

The dating of 4Q266, the oldest copy of D, to the beginning to the middle of the first century B.C.E. provides the *terminus ante quem*. Allusions to the death of the Teacher of Righteousness (CD XIX 35b–XX 1a; XX 13b–15a)[21] may point to a date of composition later than 110 B.C.E., when the Teacher presumably died.[22] These

---

[17] See Jonathan Campbell, *The Use of Scripture in the Damascus Document 1–8, 19–20* (Berlin/New York: Walter de Gruyter, 1995).

[18] See, for example, CD X 4 וזה סרך לשפטי העדה, "And this is the rule for the judges of the congregation"; see also XII 19, 22; XIII 7. Another form of introduction is על; for example, על הטהר במים, "Concerning one who purifies himself in water" (CD X 10), and על השבת "Concerning the Sabbath" (CD X 14).

[19] Dupont-Sommer, *The Essene Writings*, 117; contra Rabin, who argued that the two parts are separate works (*Zadokite Documents*, x). Joseph Baumgarten comments: "It is now evident that the 'elaboration of the laws,' *perush ha-mishpatim*, was the central purpose of D, with the hortatory sections at the beginning and end serving to call for the renewal of the covenant to follow the true interpretation of the Torah" ("The Damascus Document Reconsidered," in *The Dead Sea Scrolls at Fifty: Proceedings of the 1997 Society of Biblical Literature Qumran Section Meetings*, vol. 2 [eds. Robert Kugler and Eileen Schuller; Early Judaism and Its Literature 15; Atlanta: Society of Biblical Literature, 1999], 150).

[20] Davies, "Reflections on DJD XVIII," in *The Dead Sea Scrolls at Fifty*, 154.

[21] For an interpretation of these passages, see Joseph Fitzmyer, "The Gathering in of the Teacher of Righteousness," in *The Dead Sea Scrolls and Christian Origins* (Studies in the Dead Sea Scrolls and Related Literature; Grand Rapids, Mich.: Eerdmans, 2000), 261–5.

[22] Most scholars date the arrival of the Teacher of Righteousness to mid-second century B.C.E., to the time of Jonathan Maccabee; see, e.g., Antii Laato, "The Chronology of the Damascus Document of Qumran," *RevQ* 15 (1992), 605–7; Collins, "The Origin of the

references belong to a section that is usually seen as the latest layer of the Admonition (CD XIX 33b–XX 22b). Scholars commonly date the composition of the document to the very end of the second century B.C.E.[23] It is important to note, however, that parts of the document stem from an earlier time. In light of the studies by Davies, Hempel and others (see below), it is evident that the main segments were composed over a long period prior to a final completion around 100 B.C.E.

2.4 HISTORY IN D

D provides some information about the early period of the sect and scholars have used this text in conjunction with passages of other Qumran documents to outline the beginning and early period of the sectarian movement.[24] CD I 3–11 contains a recollection of the origin of the movement before the arrival of the Teacher of Righteousness and is often seen as a key for understanding the origin of the sect. CD I 5–7 alludes to the formation of the movement: "And at the end of (his) wrath (ובקץ חרון) 390 years after giving them into the hand of Nebuchadnezzar, king of Babylon, he visited them and caused a root of planting (שורש מטעת) to grow." According to CD I 9–11, the Teacher of Righteousness appeared 20 years thereafter.[25] Most scholars connect the activities of the Teacher of Righteousness to the time of Jonathan

---

Qumran Community," 159–78. For the date of the death of the Teacher of Righteousness, see Baumgarten, "Damascus Document (CD)," 169.

[23]See, for example, John Collins, "Was the Dead Sea Sect an Apocalyptic Movement?" in *Archaeology and History in the Dead Sea Scrolls*, 40; Hempel, *The Damascus Texts,* 23. Those who date the document to about 100 B.C.E. include Martínez and Trebolle Barrera (*The People of the Dead Sea Scrolls*, 52), Michael A. Knibb ("The Place of the Damascus Document," in *Methods of Investigation of the Dead Sea Scroll*, 150), Stegemann (*The Library of Qumran*, 117), Devorah Dimant ("Qumran Sectarian Literature," in *Jewish Writings of the Second Temple Period* [ed. Michael E. Stone; Compendia Rerum Iudaicarum ad Novum Testamentum, Section 2; The Literature of the Jewish People in the Period of the Second Temple and the Talmud 2; Assen, The Netherlands: Van Gorcum/Philadelphia: Fortress Press, 1984], 490), and Vermes (*The Complete Dead Sea Scrolls*, 125).

[24]See, e.g., Philip Callaway, *The History of the Qumran Community: An Investigation* (JSPSup 3; Sheffield: Sheffield Academic Press, 1988); "Qumran Origins: From the *Doresh* to the *Moreh*," *RevQ* 14 (1990), 637–50; Collins, "The Origin of the Qumran Community," 167–72. For a survey of interpretations of passages in CD, see Campbell, *The Use of Scripture,* 4–8. In a series of articles Davies has attempted to reconstruct the history of the movement, in which he highlights the difficulties and uncertainties involved in such a task; see, e.g., "Was There Really a Qumran Community?" *CurBS* 3 (1995), 9–35; "The Teacher of Righteousness and the 'End of Days,'" *RevQ* 13 (1988), 313–17; "The Birthplace of the Essenes: Where is 'Damascus'?" 503–20; "Communities at Qumran and the Case of the Missing 'Teacher,'" *RevQ* 15 (1991), 275–86.

[25]The full title מורה צדק appears in CD I 11; XX 32. CD XX 1 refers to מורה היחיד "the unique teacher"; XX 14 reads יורה היחיד and XX 28 refers to "the teacher," מורה.

Maccabee (152–142 B.C.E.) or to that of Simon Maccabee (142–134 B.C.E.), the two primary candidates for הכוהן הרשע "the Wicked Priest," known from Pesher Habakkuk (1QpHab).[26]

In the Admonition "Damascus" is a key word that distinguishes the Damascus Document from other Qumran documents, as D recalls a journey to Damascus and back.[27] Many scholars understand the word symbolically for Qumran.[28] Alternatively, Murphy-O'Connor argues that it is a cipher for Babylon.[29] Other scholars, such as J. T. Milik, Stegemann, Samuel Iwry, and Philip Callaway argue in favour of a literal interpretation of Damascus.[30] In contrast to the many explicit interpretations of symbols that are provided to the readers throughout the document, nothing in the text alerts the reader that "Damascus" carries a symbolic meaning.[31] For this reason, the references to Damascus should be taken literally. From this perspective it becomes apparent that the journey to Damascus and back was perceived as an important event by the growing community.

2.5 Purpose and Audience

The mixture of legal and homiletic material in D makes it hard to uncover the purpose of the document. Scholars have called attention to the personal call in the second person plural to listen, שמעו, repeated several times in the beginning of the document; for example, ועתה שמעו כול יודעי צדק, "And now listen, all you who know righteousness" (CD I 1).[32] These exhortations give the Admonition a sermon-like character, suggesting that the Admonition was intended to be heard. The addressees are called "children" בנים (CD II 14) in a familial model by which the speaker takes a

---

[26]E.g., 1QpHab VIII 8; IX 9–10, XI 4–5. For more discussion see Stegemann, *The Library of Qumran*, 147–52; Collins, "The Origin of the Qumran Community," 170–72; Knibb, "Exile in the Damascus Document," 99–117.

[27]"Damascus" appears six times: CD VI 5, 19; VII 15, 19; VIII 21/XIX 33–34; XX 12.

[28]Those who espouse a symbolic interpretation include T. Gaster, *The Dead Sea Scriptures in English Translation* (Garden City: Doubleday, 1956), 4; Cross, *Ancient Library*, 73; Schiffman, *Reclaiming*, 92–4.

[29]Murphy-O'Connor, "The Essenes and Their History," 221.

[30]Milik, *Ten Years of Discovery in the Judean Wilderness* (London: SCM Press, 1959), 91; Stegemann, "The Qumran Essenes," 100–1; 146–8; Samuel Iwry, "Was There a Migration to Damascus? The Problem of שבי ישראל," *ErIsr* 9 (1969), 80–8. Callaway claims that the author of D had a literal exile to Damascus in mind in four of the references to the city, and that "Damascus" possibly also carried a symbolic meaning (*The History of the Qumran Community*, 121–7, 132).

[31]See Callaway, "Qumran Origins: From the *Doresh* to the *Moreh*," 644.

[32]Cf. ועתה שמעון] לי ואודיעה לכם "And now, [listen] to me, and I will make known to you" (4Q266 1 a–b 5); ועתה שמעו אלי כל באי ברית "And now listen to me, all who enter the covenant" (CD II 2); ועתה בנים שמעו לי "And now, children, listen to me" (CD II 14).

parental role.³³ Although the identity of the speaker is not revealed in the text that is preserved, it may have been the *maskil* as Baumgarten suggests in his reconstruction of the introductory line.³⁴

It has been suggested that the intended audience is primarily new converts. However, the designation "children of light" (4Q266 1 1) as well as the emphasis on the knowledge of righteousness that the audience already possesses (CD I 1; 4Q270 2 ii 19), certainly point to the whole community—senior members as well as newcomers—as addressees.³⁵ By assuring the listeners that they already have knowledge, the discourse serves to boost their loyalty and commitment to the covenant and the community.

Knibb, Vermes, and Daniel Falk associate the document with the annual Festival of the Renewal of the Covenant.³⁶ There are several hints of a connection to such a festival in D. First, the structure of D shows an influence from biblical covenant formulas in a general way, as several scholars have highlighted.³⁷ Second, there are several allusions in D to the liturgy of the Festival: the admission of new members (CD XV 5–XVI 6), the annual gathering of all members (CD XIV 3–6), a confession

---

³³The literary style of personal calls is also found in 4QWords of the Sage to the Sons of Dawn (4Q298 1–2 i; 3-4 ii); in this case the speaker is the *maskil*; see Menachem Kister and S. Pfann, "4Q298 4QCrypt A Words of the Maskil to all Sons of Dawn," in *Qumran Cave 4: XV, Sapiential Texts* (eds. T. Elgvin et al.; DJD XX; Oxford: Clarendon Press, 1997), 1:1–34.

³⁴Baumgarten reconstructs 4Q266 1 a-b 1: [פרוש המשפטים למשכיל לב]ני אור להנזר מדר[כי רשעה], "[The Elaboration of the laws by the Sage for the ch]ildren of light to keep apart from the way[s of wickedness]" (*DJD XVIII*, 31–2). The word משכיל, common in S, is attested D in 4Q266 9 iii 15. For different reconstructions of 4Q266 1 a-b 1 see Stegemann, "Physical Reconstruction," 193; Ben Zion Wacholder, "The Preamble to the Damascus Document: A Composition Edition of 4Q266–4Q268," *HUCA* 69 (1998), 31–47.

³⁵In agreement with Dupont-Sommer, *The Essene Writings*, 118.

³⁶Knibb, *The Qumran Community*, 14; Vermes, *The Complete Dead Sea Scrolls*, 43–5; Daniel Falk, *Daily, Sabbath and Festival Prayers in the Dead Sea Scroll* (STDJ 27; Leiden: Brill, 1998), 236ff.

³⁷Although differing in their delineations, Klaus Baltzer, Davies, and Falk all argue that D has the structure of a covenant formulary according to biblical models. Baltzer suggests the following structure: Dogmatic Section (Antecedent History) CD I–VI 11, Ethical Section (Statement of Substance) VI 11–VII 4, Blessings and Curses VII 5 ff (the conclusion of Admonition is considered to be later), Laws IX 1–XVI 20. Baltzar was not aware of the expulsion ceremony, which makes for a very fitting ending to a document patterned on a covenant formulary; see *The Covenant Formulary in Old Testament, Jewish, and Early Christian Writings* (Philadelphia: Fortress Press, 1971), 179. Davies excludes the laws, but Baltzer and Falk rightly consider the structure of the whole document to reflect the shape of a covenant formulary since a legal section is paramount in the biblical covenant formulas; see Davies, *Damascus Covenant*, 52; Falk, *Daily, Sabbath and Festival Prayers*, 220–21; 226.

(CD XX 28b–30), and an expulsion ceremony in 4Q266 11 8–21.[38] Third, the main theme of the Admonition—allegiance to the covenant and the importance of observing its laws—coincides with the theme of the covenantal renewal. The legal section subsequently provides the content of these laws, which is the foundation of the Covenant relationship to which members affirm their loyalty. The suggestion that D was read as a sermon at the annual Festival is highly plausible, especially in light of the sermon-like style at the beginning of the document and at the end of the Admonition (4Q270 2 ii 19–21).

2.6 THE PLACE OF D AMONG THE DEAD SEA SCROLLS

Since ten copies of D were discovered at Qumran, it is generally accepted that the document should be considered foundational to the sect.[39] D shares both ideology and terminology with other Qumran documents, for example, sobriquets for individuals important to the movement, such as "Teacher of Righteousness" and "the Liar" (or "Spouter of Lies") known from 1QpHab.[40]

The collection of laws in D represents one of the examples of "rules" (*serakim*) from the Qumran corpus, that is, a document that contains a set of rules for a community. The other main rule texts are S and 1QSa. In addition, the War Scroll, M, outlines the rules for a final war.[41] There are other documents that comprise legislation

---

[38]The confession in CD XX 28b–30 corresponds closely to the confession from the liturgy of the Festival of the Renewal of the Covenant in 1QS I 24b–25. The expulsion ceremony in D contains elements that are reminiscent of the liturgy for the festival in 1QS, namely, blessings, curses of apostates, and a reference to God's saving acts in the past. This text places the expulsion ceremony "in the third month," בחודש השלישי (4Q266 11 17), connecting the event to the theophany at Sinai (Exod 19:1) and the Festival of the Renewal of the Covenant (cf. Jubilees 6:17–21); see Milik, *Ten Years*, 117.

[39]For a discussion of the position of D within the Dead Sea Scrolls, see Michael Knibb, "The Place of the Damascus Document," in *Methods of Investigation*, 149–60.

[40]CD VIII 12c–13 (Spouter of Lies); for references to the Teacher, see above, p. 24, n. 25. Concerning sobriquets in the Dead Sea Scrolls, see the doctoral dissertation by Håkan Bengtsson, *What's in a Name? A Study of Sobriquets in the Pesharim* (Uppsala: Uppsala University, 2000).

[41]Dimant suggests that also 1QSb may be described as a kind of rule ("Qumran Sectarian Literature," 490). I am here using "rules" in a loose sense for describing documents that provide laws and regulations to a community. A more narrow definition only considers a document a "rule" that contains the word *serekh* ("rule"), that is, 1QSa, S, D and M; see Philip Alexander, "Rules," *Encyclopedia of the Dead Sea Scrolls*, 2:799–803. Vermes includes 4QMMT, 11QT, and 4QRebukes by the Overseer (4Q477), under the rubric "Rules" (*The Complete Dead Sea Scrolls*, vii–viii). Schiffman describes 5Q13 as a "rule for the conduct of the covenant renewal and the mustering ceremony of the Qumran sect" ("Sectarian Rule [5Q13]," in *Rule of the Community and Related Documents* [vol.1 of The Dead Sea Scrolls: Hebrew, Aramaic, and

that reflect a specific community organisation as opposed to laws of more general nature; these include 4QTohorot A–C (4Q274, 4Q276–278)[42] and 4QMiscellaneous Rules (4Q265).[43] These documents assume a married community, which makes S unique in its lack of stipulations relating to women.

Amongst the rules, there are considerable similarities between D and 1QSa which both prescribe ordinances for communal organisations that include women and children. These two documents share administrative concerns as well as language, which indicate a close relationship between the two communities that produced the documents. Striking parallels are the common use of עדה ("congregation") as self-designation, references to "camps," and to the otherwise unknown document ספר ההגו, "the Book of Hagu." Given the similarities, Hempel suggests that the communal laws of D and the larger part of 1QSa (I 6–II 11a) "emerged from a similar—if not identical—social situation."[44]

Its range of literary styles and a mixture of homiletic material and laws make D most similar in genre to S, a document which contains a combination of didactic material, communal legislation, and hymns.[45] D displays close similarities with S in its communal laws, and shares language, ideology, and legislation with that document.[46] Nonetheless, S lacks the elaboration of biblical laws that occupies a substantial portion of the legal section in D. These laws in D often coincide with the halakhah displayed in

---

Greek Texts with English Translations; eds James Charlesworth et al., Tübingen: J. C. B. Mohr/Louisville, Ky.: Westminster John Knox Press, 1994], 133).

[42] See Baumgarten, "274–278. 4QTohorot A–C," in *DJD XXXV*, 79–122.

[43] See Baumgarten, "265. 4QMiscellaneous Rules," in *DJD XXXV*, 57–79. See also Sarianna Metso, "Constitutional Rules at Qumran," in *The Dead Sea Scrolls after Fifty Years*, 1: 206.

[44] Charlotte Hempel, "The Earthly Nucleus of 1QSa," *DSD* 3 (1996), 256. Both documents refer to "camps" (1QSa II 15; CD XII 23, XIII 20; XIV 3 [CD XIII 5, 7, 16 in the singular]) and to the Book of Hagu (CD X 6; XIII 2; XIV 8 [restored]; 1QSa I 7). Other similarities include: a prominent position of priests (1QSa I 2,15–18; CD XIII 2–7), disqualification of physically disabled from entering into the "midst of the congregation" (1QSa II 8–9; 4Q266 8 i 9), positions within the community according to age (4Q266 8 iii 6–9; 1QSa I 7–17), ranking according to ability (CD XIII 11–12; 1QSa I 17–19), and groupings into thousands, hundreds, fifties, and tens (CD XIII 1–2; 1QSa I 14, 29–II 1). Davis points out commonalities between CD X 4–10; XII 22–XIII 7; XIII 20–21 (what he calls "CDS2") and 1QSa ("History," 48–9). A notable difference is the lack of any reference to the Examiner in 1QSa, who is a prominent official in D (e.g., CD XIII 7–19).

[45] 4QMiscellaneous Rules as well as 4QOrdinances[a] (4Q159) also comprise a mix of literary genres; see Baumgarten, "265. 4QMiscellaneous Rules," in *DJD XXXV*, 58.

[46] For instances of literary dependency between the Admonition and 1QS, see J. T. Milik, "Milki-sedeq and Milki-reša' dans les anciens ecrits juifs et chretiens," *JJS* 23 (1972), 136; Davies, "Communities at Qumran and the Case of the Missing 'Teacher,'" 275–86; Knibb, "The Place of the Damascus Document," 157–8.

other Qumran texts, though occasional differences appear. Specifically, the biblically based halakhah in D is similar in many instances to the legislation in the Temple Scroll; for example, the prohibition of uncle-niece marriages and sexual intercourse in עיר המקדש ("the city of the sanctuary").[47] D also shares halakhic concerns with 4QMMT, 4QHalakha A (4Q251), and 4QOrd^a.[48] The distinctive characteristic in D of dividing laws into topics introduced by headings is a feature that is also found in 4QOrdinances^a (4Q159) and 4QHalakha A. 4QOrd^a, like D, presents laws whose topical arrangement does not follow any biblical sequence. There are significant similarities also with 4QMiscellaneous Rules (4Q265), which like D preserves biblically based laws, such as Sabbath laws, side by side with communal legislation.[49] Parallel to S and 4Q265, D contains a penal code, which stipulates harsh punishments for members of a specific community.[50] 4QTohorot A (4Q274) like D, utilizes "camp" language, and prescribes strict purity rules for men and women.[51]

The relationship among the various Qumran documents is a complex issue; hence scholars have proposed differing scenarios. Metso, for example, argues that various

---

[47] See CD V 9–11; XII 12; 11QT XLV 11–12; LXVI 15–17. For a list of parallel laws in D and 11QT, see Lawrence Schiffman, "The Relationship of the Zadokite Fragments to the Temple Scroll," in *The Damascus Document: A Centennial of Discovery*, 133–44. See also Callaway, "Qumran Origins: From the *Doresh* to the *Moreh*," 648–50. Philip Davies suspects a common origin of 11QT and D, and suggests this is the community behind D ("The Temple Scroll and the Damascus Document," in *Temple Scrolls Studies: Papers Presented at the International Symposium on the Temple Scroll, Manchester, December 1987* [ed. George Brooke; JSPSup 7; Sheffield: JSOT Press, 1987], 201–10).

[48] See Schiffman, "The Relationship of the Zadokite Fragments to the Temple Scroll," 144. For a comparison of 4QMMT and D, see Schiffman, "The Place of 4QMMT in the Corpus of Qumran Manuscripts," 90–4; Charlotte Hempel, "The Laws of the Damascus Document and 4QMMT," in *The Damascus Document: A Centennial of Discovery*, 69–84. Baumgarten highlights similarities between the laws in D and 4QOrd^a ("The Laws of the Damascus Document in Current Research," 56). See also Hempel, "4QOrd^a (4Q159) and the Laws of the Damascus Document," in *The Dead Sea Scrolls: Fifty Years after Their Discovery: Proceedings of the Jerusalem Congress, July 20–25, 1997* (eds. Lawrence Schiffman, Emanuel Tov, and James VanderKam; Jerusalem: Israel Exploration Society in cooperation with the Shrine of the Book, Israel Museum, 2000), 372–6. Martínez and Trebolle Barrera discuss similarities between segments of the Temple Scroll, 4QMMT, D and S in relation to purity (*The People of the Dead Sea Scrolls*, 141–57).

[49] Pointed out by Hempel, "The Laws of the Damascus Document and 4QMMT," 71.

[50] For the parallels between sectarian regulations in S and D, see Moshe Weinfeld, *The Organizational Patterns and the Penal Code of the Qumran Sect: A Comparison with Guilds and Religious Associations* (NTAO 2; Göttingen: Vandenhoeck & Ruprecht, 1986), 7–80. Concerning the similarity between the penal codes in S and D, see Charlotte Hempel, "The Penal Code Reconsidered," in *Legal Texts and Legal Issues*, 337–48; Joseph Baumgarten, "The Cave 4 Versions of the Qumran Penal Code," *JJS* 43 (1991), 268–76.

[51] For references to "camp," see 4Q274 1 i 6; 2 i 6.

groups "used common sources and borrowed material from each other," to produce the various rule books.[52] Stegemann, on the other hand, proposes a chronological relationship between various rule texts, whereby the rules have succeeded each other.[53] This question is related to the issue of origin of the documents, and especially how they relate to the Qumran location. It is generally accepted that the library at Qumran represents a collection of texts of two kinds: works that were *composed* by the movement, usually labelled "sectarian" texts, and works that were *read and copied* at Qumran, but not produced by the movement.[54] Furthermore, not all sectarian texts among the Scrolls were written at the Qumran location; instead, many texts likely were composed by the wider sectarian movement. Since the majority of scholars view Qumran as the site of a celibate community, they associate S (which does not mention women) with Qumran, while assigning D (which presumes a married community) to an Essene community different from that of Qumran.[55] In addition, S appears to reflect a community that has withdrawn from the outside world, which fits well with a desert location. D, on the other hand, refers to members living in camps (CD VII 6; IX 11; X 23; XII 23) and towns in Israel (CD XII 19), who are involved in trade (CD XII 8–11; XIII 15–16), own property, including slaves (CD XII 10; XIV 12–13), and have extensive contact with Gentiles (CD XII 8–11).[56] Thus D and S are often seen as blueprints for two different social organisations: the wider Essene movement of married members in towns and villages and a celibate community at Qumran. However, such a scenario conflicts with chronological assessments. De Vaux dated the first occupational phase at Qumran, "Phase Ia," to ca.135–104 B.C.E., i.e., the reign of

---

[52] Metso, "Constitutional Rules at Qumran," 86–210; "The Relationship between the Damascus Document and the Community Rule," 85–93. Cf. Davies: "Quite obviously 1QS has *not* been composed as a rule for a community. It is incoherent, unsystematic and contradictory" ("Redaction and Sectarianism in the Qumran Scrolls," in *Scriptures and Scrolls: Studies in Honour of A. S. Van der Woude on the Occasion of His 65th Birthday* [eds. F. García Martínez, A. Hilhorst and C. J. Labuschagne; Leiden: Brill, 1992], 157).

[53] According to Stegemann, 1QSa constitutes the oldest rule book while D is the last. The two main works of S (1QS I 1–III 12; V–XI) developed apart from, or after 1QSa; see "Some Remarks to 1QSa, to 1QSb, and to Qumran Messianism," *RevQ* 17 (1996), 479–505; *The Library of Qumran*, 107–18.

[54] See e.g., Carol Newsom, "'Sectually Explicit' Literature from Qumran," 167–87.

[55] Baumgarten and Schwartz endorse this perspective; "The Damascus Document (CD)," 6–7. VanderKam's description is representative of this perspective: "the former [S] governs an isolated male society, while the latter [D] legislates for camps of Essenes who live among non–Essenes and also have families." And, "one may fairly call the Manual [S] a constitution for the Qumran community" (*The Dead Sea Scrolls Today*, 91, 57). For a critique of this perspective, see Metso, "The Relationship between the Damascus Document and the Community Rule," 85–93.

[56] See for example, Philip Davies, "Damascus Rule," in the *Anchor Bible Dictionary*, 2:8–10, who lists differences between the community of D and the one at Qumran.

John Hyrcanus.[57] His chronology has been challenged by Magness, among others, who claims that phase Ia never existed and redates the initial establishment of the Qumran community to 100–50 B.C.E.[58] One consequence of this new date is that both D and S, in developed forms, antedate the settlement (though S underwent further redactions in the first part of first century B.C.E.).[59] It is thus likely that both S and D were composed in Palestine prior to the establishment of the community at Qumran, and that they were studied and used in some manner at Qumran, as indicated by the respective ten (D) and eleven (S) copies discovered there. Still their exact status in the Qumran community and the extent to which the rules were employed by the Qumran community remains an elusive issue.[60]

---

[57] De Vaux, *Archaeology and the Dead Sea Scrolls*, 3-5.

[58] According to Jodi Magness, there is no evidence of a settlement before the first half of the first century B.C.E. ("The Chronology of the Settlement of Qumran in the Herodian Period," *DSD* 2 [1995], 58–65; *The Archaeology of Qumran and the Dead Sea Scrolls* [Grand Rapids, Mich.: Eerdmans, 2002], 63–9). Davies claims that phase Ia was invented to fit literary data in spite of archeological evidence pointing to the later date ("How Not to Do Archaeology: The Story of Qumran," [*BA*, Dec. 1988], 203–7); see also Ernest-Marie Laperrousaz, who proposes a beginning of the settlement around 100 B.C.E. ("Breves remarques archaeologiques concernant la chronologie des occupations esseniens de Qoumran," *RevQ* 12 [1986], 199–212).

[59] The MS of 1QS is dated to 100–75 B.C.E.; see Frank M. Cross, "Introduction" in *Scrolls from Cave I: The Great Isaiah Scroll, The Order of the Community, The Pesher to Habakkuk* (eds. Frank Moore Cross, David Noel Freedman, James Sanders and John Trevor; Jerusalem: Albright Institute of Archaeological Research and the Shrine of the Book, 1974), 4. S is commonly estimated to have been composed around mid-second century B.C.E., with subsequent redactions until mid-first century B.C.E. and possible scribal emendations even later; see Marcus Bockmuehl, "Redaction and Ideology in the *Rule of the Community*," *RevQ* 18 (1998), 541–57. Metso postulates that an even earlier version of S, an original document, "O," precedes the recensions of S known from Qumran. The original version, "O," was a shorter version of 1QS V–IX. Two literary traditions developed from "O," represented by, on the one hand, 4QS^e (originating 150–100 B.C.E.) and, on the other, 4QS^{b,d}. These two traditions were combined into 1QS, dated 100–75 B.C.E. She emphasizes that no standard text of S existed, since different versions of S continued to be copied; see *Textual Development of the Qumran Community Rule*, 107–49. See also G. Vermes and P. Alexander, *DJD XXVI*, 9–12.

[60] See for example, Philip Davies ("Halakhah at Qumran," in *A Tribute to Geza Vermes: Essays on Jewish and Christian Literature and History* [eds. Philip Davies and Richard White; JSOTSup 100; Sheffield: JSOT Press, 1990], 37–50) and Sarianna Metso ("In Search of the Sitz im Leben of the Community Rule," in *Provo International Conference on the Dead Sea Scrolls: Technological Innovations, New Texts, and Reformulated Issues* [eds. Donald Parry and Eugene Ulrich; STDJ 30; Leiden: Brill, 1999], 306–15) who raise important questions and point out difficulties with historical reconstructions.

2.7 LITERARY DEVELOPMENT

2.7.1 THE ADMONITION

For a modern reader, the Admonition appears inconsistent in parts and at times difficult to read as a unified whole.[61] Apparent seams indicate development within the text and the use of sources. Scholarly appreciation for the coherence of the document differs widely. For example, Abegg, Wise, and Cook introduce D in the following way:

> Although many broad themes are easy to notice—the greatness of God and his covenant with Israel, the perfidy of apostates, the necessity of obeying the rules of God and the group, and so on—the train of thought rambles from subject to subject, with many digressions, asides, and pauses to explain a difficult or important quotation from Scripture. Apparently the *Document* was expanded at different times, often without care for the lucidity of the discourse.[62]

Jonathan Campbell, on the other hand, views the Admonition as a well-constructed text. He states: "Contrary to the difficulties usually encountered upon an initial reading of the work, it appears that it is in the document's skilled employment of the bible that its integrity and unity can be found."[63]

In the past, there has been wide agreement that the Admonition is a composite work, and several scholars have attempted to outline its literary development.[64] Nevertheless, the source-critical approach has been criticized by Dimant and Campbell.[65] Still, since also these scholars admit that there are sources underlying the document, redaction- and source-critical works are in my estimate well worth considering.

Davies' source-critical literary analysis of the Admonition has been highly influential in Qumran scholarship. Davies assigns most of the first seven columns to

---

[61] Davies, for example, puts within brackets words or phrases that he considers secondary because they do not fit within the context (*Damascus Covenant*, 232–67).

[62] Wise, Abegg, and Cook, *The Dead Sea Scrolls*, 49.

[63] Campbell, *The Use of Scripture*, 205–6.

[64] For example, studies by R. H. Charles, K. G. Kuhn, J. Becker, A-M.Denis, Murphy-O'Connor; see Murphy-O'Connor, "The Judean Desert," 126–28; see also Davies' survey of the main compositional theories (*Damascus Covenant*, 3–48).

[65] Campbell, *The Use of Scripture*, especially 183, 205–8. Dimant claims that D is a literary work of an author who may have used sources, but these, in turn, have been worked into "one overall framework which expresses the intention of the author." It is therefore futile to attempt to trace any sources. She offers an outline of the document in an attempt to show that the work is a unity; see "Qumran Sectarian Literature," 496–7. For a critique of Dimant's proposed structure, see Davis, "History," 6–8.

the original work (CD I 1–VII 9), with the exception of the numerous interpolations.[66] CD VII 10–VIII 2a and later VIII 2b–18 were added to a brief original warning in CD VII 9.[67] While these warnings were originally uttered towards outsiders, they are now redirected towards members of the community as well as towards the parent community.[68] CD XIX 33–XX 34, which Davies labels "The New Covenant," is the product of a Qumranic redaction, but it also contains the original ending of the Admonition, CD XX 27b–34, in a revised form.[69] Davies' overall hypothesis, that the first seven columns of CD form an original composition that later has been expanded, is convincing.

Two passages in the Admonition relate to women in particular: one concerns marital and sexual laws and the other pertains to family life. The discourse on the nets of Belial in CD IV 16–V 11 puts unlawful marriages and illegal sexual practices at the forefront in its condemnation of Israel. Moreover, CD VII 6–9 describes the members who live in camps as observing "the rule of the land," marrying and having children. These passages that mention women appear in the original core document and they will be analysed in my study below (Ch. 5).

2.7.2 THE COMPOSITION OF THE LAWS

The beginning and the end of the legal part of D reveal parallels with the introduction to the Admonition in both terminology and content. This shows the care with which the two main parts have been put together in order to create a well-rounded composition.[70] Immediately following CD XX comes the so-called Catalogue of Transgressors (4Q270 2 i–ii), a list denouncing those who transgress certain laws.[71]

---

[66] Amongst those segments Davies views as additions, those reflecting an inter-polemical dispute are clearly secondary. This perspective is found in CD I 13–18a; IV 19c–20a; VII 10b–VIII 2a; VIII 2b–18/XIX 7–32a (note the Spouter of Lies in VIII 12c–13); XIX 33b–XX 22. This time frame can be tied to the period after the death of the Teacher of Righteousness, alluded to in CD XX 1 and 14. The supposedly secondary nature of the chronological references in CD I,1–II,1 and the references to the Teacher of Righteousness, however, are not convincing. Davies admits that there is no literary reason for excluding these segments (*Damascus Covenant*, 200).

[67] These two sections have been added in two stages, CD VIII 2b–18, being the latest addition; see Davies, *Damascus Covenant*, 156ff.

[68] Ibid., 143–71; 203.

[69] This sections reflects several layers; ibid., 173–97.

[70] 4Q266 4 contains the ending of the Admonition, corresponding to CD XX 33–34 plus subsequent lines from an original ending, longer than the one preserved in CD, if Milik's combination of four fragments is correct; see *DJD XVIII*, 46–47; plate V.

[71] Milik identified the first three lines of 4Q270 2 i with CD XX 32–33, which would secure the placement of the Catalogue of Transgressors as following immediately after the Admonition. However, the traces from the first three lines are tiny and, as Baumgarten points out, the identification is speculative; *DJD XVIII*, 143. Stegemann supports the placement of

This Catalogue serves as a solemn introduction to the laws, warning the listeners about the dire consequences of not observing the laws that follow.[72] The damaged lines 17–18 of column ii, by which the Catalogue ends, allude to God's wrath toward transgressors. The Catalogue is followed by an exhortatory section (lines 19–21) resembling the Admonition.[73] A personal call to listen (4Q270 2 ii 19) is strikingly similar to the repeated calls for attention in the introduction to the Admonition (CD I 1; II 2, 14; 4Q266 1 a–b 5).[74] Furthermore, this passage picks up main themes from the Admonition with a warning about the "paths of destruction" ונתיבות שחת (4Q270 2 ii 20) and an exhortation to consider "the deeds of each generation," ובהבינכם במעשי דור ודור (line 21), alluding to the sinful history of the people. These allusions to the Admonition subsequent to the Catalogue facilitate the transition from the Admonition to the Laws.

The Laws section ends, appropriately, with a description of an expulsion ceremony (4Q266 11 5–21), whose details recall the first part of the Admonition.[75] The members are here referred to as "children of his truth," בני אמתו (4Q266 11 7), similar to "children," בנים, in CD II 14 and the partially reconstructed expression "chil]dren of light," לב[ני אור, in 4Q266 1 a–b 1. Furthermore, the passage displays a historical framework similar to that in the Admonition.[76] The phrase מדרש ה[תורה האחרון, "the last interpretation of the Law," occurs both at the beginning (4Q266 5 i 17)[77] and the end of the Laws (4Q266 11 21), linking together the beginning and the conclusion of the Laws. Thus, formal cohesion in the outer framework of D and the introduction to the legal section provides evidence that the final product is a well structured composition.

There is evidence pointing to a composite nature of the collection of laws. The document itself distinguishes between early laws, ראשונים, and later ones אחרונים (CD XX 8–9, 31). Thus the redactor highlights that there are laws that stem from different periods and emphasizes that all the laws should be observed. Laws

---

4Q270 2 i–ii as following immediately subsequent to CD XX ("Physical Reconstructions," 190–1).

[72] In his commentary on the fragment 4Q270 2 i Baumgarten argues that the fragment "is introductory to the laws" (*DJD XVIII*, 143). Nevertheless, in the summary chart of the Admonition and the Laws (pp. 3–4), he places the Catalogue at the end of the Admonition. According to Hempel, the Catalogue forms part of the Laws (*Laws*, 170).

[73] I agree with Hempel who argues that lines 19–20 mark a new beginning (*Laws*, 170).

[74] 4Q270 2 ii 19 reads, ועתה שמעו לי כל יודעי צדק "And now listen to me, all who know righteousness."

[75] Hempel also highlights concepts in the prayer within the expulsion ceremony that are reminiscent of the Admonition (*Laws*, 180–5).

[76] 4Q266 11 9b–13 presents Israel as elected among the sinful peoples and states that correct interpretation of the laws was given to their descendants, i.e., the community.

[77] Stegemann places this fragment in column XII, subsequent to CD XX (the end of Admonition) ("Physical Reconstructions," 185, 199).

originating with the Teacher of Righteousness are viewed as later than the "the first precepts" (CD XX 31).[78] There are other hints of literary layers, such as conflicting rules; for example, while the authority of the Examiner, המבקר, is in most cases supreme, in a few passages it is undermined by that of the priests.[79]

Over the years, many scholars have observed in a general way that the legal section seems to be a composite containing laws dating from different times. Stegemann, for example, argues that "The Damascus Document is so extensive because it includes many earlier congregational and disciplinary rules, especially a number from pre-Essene times."[80] Emphasizing the composite nature of the ordinances, Dupont-Sommer argues that a number of laws are archaic and that they are preserved "out of respect for their very antiquity."[81] Similarly, Strugnell points out that "the nucleus of the legal code in the Damascus Document might conceivably go back to a prior period [than Qumran]."[82] While suggesting that the collection of laws may be older than the Admonition and antedate the settlement at Qumran, Knibb claims that contradictions in the laws "reflect different stages in the evolution of the beliefs and attitudes of the movement."[83] Davies distinguishes between original laws in CD, which are based on scriptural exegesis or derived from scripture, and later laws

---

[78] In addition, differences in the 4QD MSS attest to some minor redactional activity: 4Q270 6 v does not include the rule concerning spending the Sabbath near the Gentiles (CD XI 14–15), which is included in 4Q271 5 i 9. The penal code in 4Q270 7 i includes rules that are not part of the penal code in 4Q266 10 ii; see Baumgarten, *DJD XVIII*, 74–5.

[79] For example, the authority of the Examiner is emphasized in CD XIV 11–12: "and any matter about which a person may wish to speak, let him address the Examiner, whether concerning a dispute or judgement." The authority of the priests is, on the contrary, implied in CD XIII 2–4: "And where there are ten, let there not be absent a priest versed in the Book of Hagu; by his word they shall all be ruled. But if he is not experienced in these (matters) while one of the Levites is experienced in these (matters), then the lot shall be for all those who belong to the camp to conduct themselves by his word." The responsibility of the priest to judge in such case is contradicted by the gloss in CD XIII 5b–6a: "and the Examiner shall explain to him the interpretation of the Torah," (see Davis; "History," 89). According to CD XIV 6–8, the "priest appointed to preside over the Many" is responsible for interpreting the Torah, and offering judgement. However, the authority over judgement is taken over by the Examiner in CD XIV 11–12.

[80] Stegemann, *The Library of Qumran*, 117.

[81] Dupont-Sommer, *The Essene Writings*, 142–3.

[82] Strugnell, "The Qumran Scrolls: A Report on Work in Progress," in *Jewish Civilization in the Hellenistic Roman Period* (ed. S. Talmon; Philadelphia: Sheffield Academy Press, 1991), 103.

[83] Knibb, *The Qumran Community*, 15, 53; "The Place of the Damascus Document," 152.

stemming from a *yahad* redaction, which base their authority on the Teacher of Righteousness.[84]

Though many scholars have asserted the composite character of the laws, few have undertaken a literary critical study of the laws. Many years ago, a preliminary source-critical study of the laws was offered by Arie Rubinstein, who distinguished between "camp rules" and "halakhah proper."[85] Davis and Hempel have each more recently written a dissertation on the composition and development of the laws in D.[86] Written only a few years apart and independent of each other, the two studies reach both similar and different conclusions. Whereas Davis only had access to a few fragments of the copies of D from Qumran, Hempel's book has the added advantage of covering the Cave 4 material.

The two scholars presume a long history of composition of the laws in D. Hempel identifies two main blocks of material, an early law code that she calls "Halakhah" and a later stratum she labels "Community Organization." Influenced by the Groningen Hypothesis, Hempel distinguishes between an Essene movement that developed prior to the establishment of the Qumran community, and the development of the Qumran community as an "off-shoot" of the Essene parent movement.[87] Subsequently, she assigns the laws in the stratum "Community Organization" to the Essene parent community.[88] The Community layer reflects an organized community, which is the basic feature that distinguishes it from the Halakhah. According to Hempel, the latter stratum, on the other hand, originates in pre-Essene circles. Since the Halakhah stratum reflects a "national self-perception as comprising the whole spectrum of Israelite society" rather than a specific community setting, the laws have a wide application in Second Temple Judaism.[89] Hempel points to affinities between the early law code and legislation in 4Q159, 4QMMT, 11QT, which, like the Halakhah stratum, do not reflect a sectarian background.[90] At the same time, she notes a thorough priestly concern in the Halakhah, conspicuous especially in the 4QD material, and suggests

---

[84]Davies suggests that the laws in CD IX–XVI may be a collection of laws from various communities ("Halakhah at Qumran," 44–5). Abegg, Cook, Wise, instead claim that the main section of laws apply to Israel as a whole, while another section at the end concern regulations for internal life of the sect (*Dead Sea Scrolls*, 61).

[85]Arie Rubenstein, "Urban Halakhah and Camp Rules in the Cairo Fragments of the Damescene Covenant," *Sefared* 12 (1952), 283–96.

[86]Davis, "History"; Hempel, *The Laws of the Damascus Document*, which is a revised version of her doctoral dissertation. For my study, I am relying on the book by Hempel.

[87]Contrary to Martínez, she doubts that a distinction can be made between a pre-Qumranic Essene phase and a "formative period" in the Dead Sea Scrolls. In addition, she downplays the supposed split between the Qumran community and its parent movement (*Laws*, 4–7).

[88]The parent movement of the *yahad*, reflected in Community Organization, stems from a time prior to the leadership of the Teacher (*Laws*, 150).

[89]Ibid., 4–5, 42, 70.

[90]Ibid., 70–2, 169, 188.

that priestly circles may be behind much of the early law code.[91] In addition to the two main literary strata, Hempel detects "miscellaneous halakhah," "miscellaneous traditions," and redactional material. The latter comprises seven categories, and includes the works of two redactors.[92]

Davis distinguishes between four stages in the development of the laws (CDS 1–4), which he lists chronologically: the earliest layer, CDS1, stems from rural, possibly "mildly-sectarian" Essene camps (as opposed to the more "fully developed Essenes" at Qumran); CDS2 and 3 represent later legislation among non-Qumranic communities of Essenes from mid-second century B.C.E. to the first century C.E.; and CDS4 contains material from a Qumranic redaction.[93] He also detects several glosses.[94]

Both Davis and Hempel accept Philip Davies' hypothesis that D was redacted by the *yahad*. Unfortunately, neither of them goes into much detail regarding the literary relationship between the Laws and the Admonition.[95] They both note formal characteristics which set the earliest layer apart from the rest of the laws in D: (a) the laws are often grouped according to topics and introduced by the formula על plus topic; (b) scriptural citations, paraphrases, or explicit references are common, often introduced by an introductory formula; (c) the halakhic exposition usually employs the basic form of apodictic law, אל plus jussive plus איש.[96] Not all the elements are present in all sections of the layer Hempel labels Halakhah.[97]

A large part of the earliest law code that Davis calls CDS1 corresponds to the Halakhah stratum in Hempel's delineation. To this section belong the Sabbath code, laws regarding oaths, a variety of purity laws, and more. Still, some portions of the material that Davis assigns to CDS1, Hempel labels "miscellaneous halakhah" rather

---

[91] Hempel traces this legislation to "priestly groups long before the emergence of the *yahad* and probably also prior to the emergence of the parent movement of the *yahad*;" (p.70); and "the material in this [Halakhah] stratum comprises traditional halakhic exegesis that was cherished and handed on in priestly circles" (*Laws*, 189).

[92] Miscellaneous pieces of Halakhah are laws of disparate nature that do not belong to any of the major strata (*Laws*, 153–63).

[93] According to Davis, CDS2 concerns laws for several camps while CDS3 relate to the same camps at a time when they have become federally organized and assemble annually (CD XIV 3–10); see "History," 66–76.

[94] Ibid., 77, 89.

[95] In a summary chart of the literary development of the Laws, Davis assigns the Admonition to mid-second century B.C.E., shortly after the emergence of the Teacher of Righteousness. According to this chart, the Admonition is written after CDS1, and slightly before CDS2, CDS3 ("History", 112–13). Hempel notes that her conclusions that D was subject to a revision aimed at harmonizing the laws with those of S (the "Serekh redaction") fits well with Davies' hypothesis of a revision by the *yahad* (*Laws*, 151).

[96] While Davis highlights the first two of the formal features that Hempel lists, he does not include the third point (point [c] above); see Davis, "History," 37–9; Hempel, *Laws*, 26–8.

[97] Hempel, *Laws*, 26–7.

than Halakhah, and they reach different conclusions concerning the law on lost property (CD IX 10b–14).[98] The chart below compares the portion Davis assigns to CDS1 to Hempel's stratification:

Table 1: Passages assigned by Robert Davis to "CDS1" compared to delineation by Charlotte Hemple

Davis CDS1	Hempel
XV 1–5a: swearing	not assigned to any strata[99]
XVI 6–15: oaths, a wife's oath, free-will offerings	Halakhah
IX 1–10a: reproof, oaths	Halakhah
IX 10b–14a: lost property	Community Organization
X 10b–13: purification by washing	Halakhah
X 14–XI 18b: the Sabbath code	Halakhah
XI 18c–21a: sacrifices and worship	Halakhah
XI 21b–XII 2a entering the Temple, sexual intercourse in עיר המקדש	Miscellaneous halakhah
XII 2b–6a: apostasy, profanation of the Sabbath and holidays	Miscellaneous halakhah
XII 6b–11a: relations with gentiles	Halakhah
XII 11b–18: impure animals, dietary restrictions, impurity of oil, corpse impurity	Miscellaneous halakhah
4Q266 6 i: skin disease	Halakhah

In addition to the text in CD, Hempel assigns the following passages from the 4QD texts—material to which Davis did not have access—to Halakhah:

---

[98] It is difficult to know exactly why the two scholars differ when they do, partly because Davis presents his findings as a *fait a compli*. Rather than outlining his methodology in any depth, he encourages the readers to evaluate his conclusion and see if it resolves the problems in the text: "the proof, as they say, is in the pudding" ("History," 9 n.10). At the same time, his findings of formal elements that are characteristic of the CDS1 stratum are very similar to those listed as criteria for isolating the early law code in the methodology that Hempel outlines; see Davis, "History," 14, 38–9.

[99] This segment, together with a few others, falls outside of the general categorization because of lack of context; see Hempel, *Laws*, 162, 190.

4Q266 5 ii 1–16 (and parallels): disqualification of priests.
4Q266 6 i–iii; 4Q272 i–ii; 4Q269 7 (and parallels): skin disease, fluxes and childbirth.
4Q266 6 iii–iv; 4Q267 6; 4Q271 2 1–6 (and parallels): agricultural halakhah.
4Q269 8 i 3–ii (and parallels): ritual defilement and purification.
4Q270 4 (and parallels): the *Sotah* and the betrothed slave woman.
4Q271 3 1–14a, 15 (and parallels): Jubilee Year, transvestism, business and marital arrangements.

Apart from formal features, both Davis and Hempel emphasize the general, non-sectarian nature of the early laws and the strong scriptural basis.[100] Davis observes that the presence of women and children is taken for granted (CD XII 1; XVI 6–12), and that members owned property, servants and businesses (CD XI 7–9, XII 9–10). Furthermore, he notes that they seem to have at least working relations with the Jerusalem priesthood (CD XVI 13f.; IX 14; XI 17–21). There is also significant contact with non-Jews (CD XII 6–11).[101]

The lack of association with any particular organized community speaks in favour of Hempel's assignment of the law code to a time prior to the organization of Essenes into communities. Furthermore, given the emphasis on priestly concerns in the 4QD material (to which Davis did not have access), Hempel's assignment of the Halakhah to priestly circles is also compelling.[102] However, one may question Hempel's conclusion that the legislation in the Halakhah stratum applied widely across the Second Temple Jewish society. Although intended as legislation for all Israel, the early laws represent a highly stringent exegesis, which suggests that the formulators of the law code belonged to particular priestly circles that were marked by a strict halakhic position. Examples of stringent halakhah include the Sabbath prohibitions against using tools to save human lives (CD XI 17) and moving soil (CD XI 10–11), the injunction against spending the Sabbath near the Gentiles (CD XI 14–15), and the prohibition against sexual intercourse on the Sabbath (CD XI 4).[103] Moreover, the legislation concerning priestly issues includes the requirement to pay tithes from gleanings (4Q270 3 ii 18), and the disqualification of priests for temple service who have been captive or lived abroad (4Q266 5 ii 5–8), which are also examples of a stringent halakhah.[104]

---

[100]Davis points out that the group behind CDS1 is not an "isolationist sectarian" community ("History," 29).

[101]Ibid., 28–37.

[102]*Laws*, 42, 49.

[103]For an interpretation of this law, see below section 4.2

[104]Baumgarten argues that the laws concerning disqualification represent "a more stringent position" compared to common traditional law without going beyond the parameters of "customary law" ("The Disqualification of Priests," 513).

Additionally, there are laws among the material that Hempel assigns to "miscellaneous pieces of halakhah" (CD XI 21b–XII 2a; XII 11b–20a) that appear highly stringent, such as a prohibition against sexual intercourse in Jerusalem (CD XII 1–2), the requirement for the ritual slaughter of fish (CD XII 13–14), and the transmission of impurity through oil on wood, stones, and dust (CD XII 15–16). By their stringent halakhah, these priestly circles likely distinguished themselves as a specific group amongst other priests. Quite possibly, this group should be identified with the "root planting" (CD I 7–9) that was formed about twenty years prior to the emergence of the Teacher of Righteousness.

Since Davis includes this collection of laws without hesitation in the early law code, CDS1, it is worth briefly examining whether the whole block of "miscellaneous pieces of halakhah" should indeed be separate from the early law code. Hempel excludes the collection of "miscellaneous pieces of halakhah" from the Halakhah stratum because they lack the formal cohesion of the rest of the material.[105] But many of the laws among the "miscellaneous halakhah," like the other laws in the Halakhah section, do not reflect a specific community organization and do display a scriptural orientation, both of which are characteristic of the Halakhah stratum.[106] In fact, many of the segments of the Halakhah, parallel to the "miscellaneous halakhah," do not show formal consistency, such as the long section on skin disease, fluxes and childbirth, in which the criteria of non-communal character and scriptural orientation are sufficient to assign it to the Halakhah section.[107] Furthermore, the lack of association with a particular community alone suffices to assign the laws on priestly matters (4Q266 5 ii 1–16 parallels) to the Halakhah stratum.[108] Judging by the same criteria, I would argue the purity laws from the "miscellaneous halakhah," (CD XII 11b–18) should belong to the Halakhah layer.[109]

Based on the similarity in content and form, the section CD XI 18c–XII 2a, which Hempel divides between Halakhah and "miscellanous laws," should be seen as one

---

[105] *Laws*, 161.

[106] The purity regulations in CD XII 11b–15a are based on Leviticus 11. A few passages display similar Halakhic concerns as found in 11QT, which speaks in favour of an early origin for these laws: CD XII 1–2 prohibits sexual intercourse in עיר המקדש (cf.11QT XLV 11–12); CD XII 15–17 concerns defilement through oil (cf. 11QT XLIX 12); for the latter law, see Joseph Baumgarten, "The Essene Avoidance of Oil and the Laws of Purity," *RevQ* 6 (1967), 183–92.

[107] The texts on skin disease, fluxes and childbirth (4Q266 6 i–iii; 4Q269 7; 4Q272 1 i–ii; 4Q273 4 ii) have little formal similarity with the bulk of the Halakhah section, but share the firm dependence on scripture; see Hempel, *Laws*, 49.

[108] Hempel, *Laws*, 42.

[109] The pattern of 'אל plus jussive plus איש' also appears in the introduction to the collection of purity laws in CD XII 11b. It should be noticed that the introduction of topics by the repetition of כול in CD XII 14–18 is reminiscent of 4Q266 6 iii 2–5 from a section of agricultural laws that Hempel assigns to Halakhah (*Laws*, 58).

unit. CD XI 18b uses the common format 'אל plus jussive plus איש', "Let no man send to the altar a burnt offering... by a man who is defiled," which links the law to XII 1–2a (a prohibition against sexual intercourse within עיר המקדש) that uses the same form, אל ישכב איש. Because of the lack of association to a particular community and the use of the form 'אל plus jussive plus איש', CD XII 1–2a also belongs to the Halakhah.[110] If my assessment is correct, then the formulators of the early law code distinguished themselves from other groups within Second Temple Judaism by their stringent interpretation of purity laws. These priestly circles may well be seen as the specific forerunners who formulated a stringent halakhah and, in time, evolved into a movement that would eventually be known as the Essenes.

While there are strong similarities in the delineations by Davis and Hempel concerning the early law code, their analyses of the later literary strata differ significantly. Whereas Davis detects three layers—CDS2, 3 and 4—Hempel discovers one main literary tradition, the Community Organization, plus some additional material that she attributes to two redactors: the Serekh redactor who copied and updated the legislation of D, and a Damascus redactor who attempted to bring the Laws in line with the Admonition.[111] Hempel points to characteristic features of the community that emerge in the stratum Community Organization: the community includes communal functionaries such as the Examiner; there is a formal admission process; family, property, and participation in the temple cult are taken for granted.[112] Davis, on the other hand, underscores the eschatological orientation of the sectarian community behind CDS 2–3, its family lifestyle, and the organizational similarities of CDS2 with the community where 1QSa originated.[113]

Since Hempel and Davis assume very different development in the later layers, a detailed comparison between these two different sets of stratifications is simply not possible.[114] Their difference of opinion regarding later redactional activity in the

---

[110] Hempel describes the material in CD XI 21b–XII 6a and XII 11b–20a as patchy and as "the most disparate and haphazard collection of rulings in the Laws of D" (*Laws*, 153). She divides the material into four parts (XI 21b–XII 1a; XII 1b–2a, 2b–6a, 11b–20a) and assigns the concluding statement in XII 19–20a to a Damascus redactor and lines 2b–6a to a Jubilees redactor (*Laws*, 153–9). Scholars differ in their delineation of the material. Since CD XI 18b does not concern the Sabbath like the previous laws, it marks the beginning of a new section; see Dupont-Sommer, *The Essene Writings*, 153.

[111] Hempel, *Laws*, 80.

[112] Ibid., 149–50.

[113] Davis, "History," 42, 64

[114] Both scholars postulate a Qumran or *serekh* redaction at the last stage of the development of the text of the Laws in D. In spite of the fact that both are looking for similarities with S in their evaluation, there is hardly any agreement as to which segments they associate with a Qumranic redaction. The disagreement stems from differing views of which key words signal a *yahad* redaction. While Hempel focuses on references to "the many" הרבים, Davis looks

communal legislation attests to the great difficulty of delineating the precise stratification. Hempel's number of literary strata, as well as the sheer number of redactors and miscellaneous traditions involved, makes her delineation difficult to assess.[115] For my study, I will follow the distinction between two main literary strata— an early law code and later communal laws— recognizing that the latter has undergone development. In addition, I agree with Hempel that the Catalogue of Transgressors falls outside the parameters of the two main literary layers of the laws and I will consequently treat laws concerning women in this section separately.[116]

2.7.3 REFERENCES TO WOMEN IN THE LITERARY STRATA

The references to women in the legal section of D are found within all the literary strata, from the early law code to the later communal laws. Thus women have been present among those groups who framed the legislation throughout the entire time of their development. The references to women and passages relevant to my study of women fall into the following categories, according to the delineation of the material by Hempel and Davis:

Table 2: Passages concerning women placed according to their literary strata: A comparison between models by Charlotte Hempel and Robert Davis

Early Laws	Davis	Hempel
4Q266 6 i 14–16, ii 1–13; 4Q272 1 ii 3–18: menstruation, flux and childbirth	not included	Halakhah
4Q270 4 1–21: Sotah, sex with slave woman	not included	Halakhah
4Q271 3 7b–14a, 15b: marriage arrangements	not included	Halakhah
CD XVI 10–12: a woman's oath	CDS1	Halakhah

---

for references to "the camp" in the singular and "the *maskil*" as indicators of Qumranic redactional activity; see Davis, "History," 77–97; Hempel, *Laws*, 191.

[115] *Laws*, 189–90. The discovery of a "Damascus Redactor," who harmonizes the Laws with the Admonition, is problematic. Such a claim needs to be substantiated by a detailed examination of the relationship between the Laws and the Admonition, an issue that Hempel never addresses.

[116] Hempel notes that many of the transgressions are dealt with in the laws that follow, particularly in the Halakhah stratum. She is uncertain whether the list should be viewed as an originally independent unit that was incorporated as an introduction to the laws or whether it was created as a summary of the laws (*Laws*, 168–70).

Early Laws (continued)	Davis	Hempel
CD XI 9–12 (the Sabbath code): wearing perfume bottles, carrying an infant, provoking a female slave	CDS1	Halakhah
CD XII 1–2a: sexual intercourse in עיר המקדש	CDS1	Miscellaneous halakhah
CD XII 10–11: sale of female slave to Gentiles	CDS1	Halakhah
Catalogue of Transgressors	**Davis**	**Hempel**
4Q270 2 i 16–19: reproach of sexual transgressors (male and female)	not included	Catalogue of Transgressors
4Q270 2 ii 15–17: sexual intercourse with pregnant woman, intercourse with a niece	not included	Catalogue of Transgressors
Communal Laws		
CD XV 5–XVI 2: process of admission	CDS4	Community Organization
CD XIV 15–16: support for the virgin with no relatives	CDS3	Community Organization
4Q270 7 i 12–15 (the penal code): fornication with wife, murmur against the Mothers	not included	Community Organization
4Q266 9 iii 1–10: the Examiner's role in marriage, divorce, and education	not included	Community Organization
4Q271 3 14b–15a: the Examiner's power to select women to perform physical exams	not included	Community Organization

In addition to the above passages from the legal part of D that are relevant to women, I will examine those segments that refer to women in the Admonition. The Admonition clearly reflects an origin in a specific organized community, parallel to the communal layer of laws. By emphasising a monopoly of exegetical truth and of correct observance of the laws of the covenant, the discourse aims at communicating a strong "us-versus-them" mentality as well as a conviction as to the exclusive status of the "in-group." Given the particularistic outlook of the Admonition, I will assume that the Admonition originated and developed approximately in tandem with the communal laws.

In conclusion, the subsequent analysis of those segments in D that are relevant for the study of various aspects of women's lives is based on the premise that the communal laws, together with the Admonition, reflect a specific Essene community that was established long before the settlement at Qumran was built. By highlighting some sectarian traits in the communal organization—as far as these concern the position of women— this study will examine the general character of this particular community. Moreover, this study will assume that laws from the early law code originated, not within an Essene community, but among pre-Essene circles. Although these early laws primarily cast light on the views of their formulaters, they also reflect the concerns of the Essene community behind D. Their inclusion in D shows that these laws were approved by the community.

3. THE EARLY LAW CODE

3.1 INTRODUCTION

This chapter examines the segments concerning women that belong to the earliest layer, in accordance with the literary stratification based on the works by Hempel and Davis. The following passages are included in the analysis: purity rules for a *zavah*, a *niddah* and a parturient, the *Sotah*, laws concerning intercourse with a slave woman, laws on sexual relations and marital arrangements, Sabbaths laws, and a prohibition of sexual intercourse in Jerusalem (CD XII 1–2a), a segment that Hempel has assigned to "miscellaneous pieces of halakhah," but which I have argued is part of Halakhah.[1]

In line with the biblical orientation of the Halakhah section in general, these segments are firmly based on biblical laws. At the same time, the biblical texts are used in an innovative way to support the halakhic position of the document. An important task in the analysis below will be to compare the legislation on women in D with that in the Hebrew Bible and examine the implications concerning the legal position of women in D. Such a comparison will determine whether the legal status of women has improved or deteriorated in D compared with that in the Hebrew Bible, or whether there is evidence of both tendencies.

3.2. A TEXT ON THE *ZAVAH*, THE *NIDDAH*, AND CHILDBIRTH: 4Q266 6 I 14–16; 4Q272 1 II 3–18; 4Q266 6 II 1–13

3.2.1 INTRODUCTION

There is a section in D, preserved in fragments from 4Q266 and 4Q272, that deals with "source" impurity, that is, impurity related to genital discharges of both men

---

[1] See above pp. 40–1.

and women, as well as childbirth.² The section on source impurity follows immediately after a section on scale disease (4Q266 6 i 1–13 and parallels).³ The beginning of this section is found in 4Q266 6 i 14 (and in the parallel text of 4Q272 1 ii 3), which preserves a *vacat*, followed by the introduction, "[And the r]ule concerning one who has a discharge," [ומ]שפט הזב את זובו. After 6 i 15, the 4Q266 text lacks about 10 lines. Fragments from this section are, however, preserved in 4Q272 1 ii 3–18, which focuses on the *zav* and *zavah*. Finally, 4Q266 6 ii 1–13 provides the last extant segment of the passage on source impurity in D and details laws concerning impurity caused by flux, menstruation, and childbirth.⁴ Taken together, these fragments indicate that the section on genital discharges and childbirth is at least one column long (4Q266 6 i 14–6 ii 13), which is about the same length as the Sabbath code (CD X 14–XI 18). However, since the end of column 6 ii is not preserved, it may have been considerably longer.⁵

The topics covered in D's section on purity laws, including the passage on scale disease, loosely follow Leviticus 12–15, which provides laws for scale disease

---

²I use "genital discharge" and "source impurity" as overarching terms that include male and female flux (associated with gonorrhea), seminal emission, and menstruation. מקור "source" is used as a euphemism for genitals in Lev 12:7; 20:18, the Temple Scroll, and Rabbinic literature.

³To the section of source impurity may belong some of five small fragments (4Q266 6 i a–e) that appear to pertain to purity issues. Although Baumgarten suggests "scale disease and its purification" as a context, references to "touch," נגע (6 i e; though this is crossed out), הבשר, "the flesh" (6 i b), and "he should wash [his] clothes," ויכבס בגד[יו] (6 i c), may equally well relate to transmission of impurity from persons impure from genital discharges and subsequent purification; see DJD *XVIII*, 54–5.

⁴A simple line count based on the similar number of letter spaces in 4Q272 and 4Q266 (about 50) suggests that 4Q272 1 ii 15–18 should overlap with the first lines of 4Q266 6 ii. According to Stegemann, 4Q266 6 ii (which he places in col XV) should be placed very close to the top of the column (Stegemann, "Physical Reconstruction" 185–89, 198). Baumgarten does not include any words from 4Q272 1 ii in his reconstruction of the first lines of 4Q266 6 ii. Since most of the text in 4Q272 1 ii is unknown and could be a different version, I will not suggest a new reconstruction based on this possibility. Hempel puts 4Q266 6 ii immediately after 4Q272 1 ii in her composite text (*Laws*, 44–8).

⁵The top of the next column, 4Q266 6 iii 1–3, contains the words מי הנדה, "sprinkling water" (line 2), which might suggest that source impurity still is the subject because sprinkling water is required at the purification of genital discharges (see Joseph Baumgarten, "The Use of מי הנדה for General Purification," in *The Dead Sea Scroll: Fifty Years After their Discovery*, 481–5). 4Q266 6 iii 3 introduces the new topic of gleanings, which is indicated by the *vacat* in line 3. Both Baumgarten and Stegemann consider it likely that the section prior to 4Q266 iii 3 also relates to agriculture. Both scholars understand 4Q270 3 i as the introduction to agricultural laws, indicated by the red ink in line 19. At the same time, the specific placement of fragment 4Q270 3 i is not certain; see Stegemann, "Physical Reconstruction," 189–90; Baumgarten, *DJD XVIII*, 57–8, 147.

The Early Law Code

(Leviticus 13–14), flux of males and females (Lev 15:1–15, 25–30), emission of semen (Lev 15:16–18), and menstruation (Lev 15:19–24). The one difference in order is that Leviticus 12 treats the purity laws on childbirth before the section on scale disease, whereas 4Q266 6 ii discusses impurity resulting from childbirth together with genital discharges. These two types of impurities may be treated together in D because of the obvious parallels: childbirth involves genital discharge of the woman and the means of purification after childbirth is similar to that of a *zavah*.

Although my focus is primarily on laws concerning female impurity in 4Q266 and 4Q272, male impurity will also be considered because the impurity prescriptions constitute an elaborate, coherent system with parallel laws for men and women affected by similar kinds of impurity. In the following discussion, the segments will be analysed in sequence, starting with 4Q272 1 ii 3–18, and followed by 4Q266 6 ii 3–13.

3.2.2 4Q272 1 II 3–18 (PARALLEL: 4Q266 6 I 14–16 UNDERLINED)

```
3   va]cat                                    [ ומ]שֹׁ[פט הזב את זוֹ[בוֹ כֹ]ול איש]
4                           [אשר יזוב מבשרו או אשר יעלה עלוֹ מ]חשבת זמה או אשרֹ
5                                                [ מגעו כמגע הֹooo
6                           וכבס בג]ד]וֹ[ן] ורחץ במים                            [
7            ו]משפט [הזבה כול אשה]    בו הנוגע בו וֹרֹ]חץ
8            ת[שֹׁב אֹ[ת]    הזבה דם שבֹ[עת ימים תהיה בנד]תה ב]
9            הֹנדה וכ]ול]    שבעת הימיםֹ]
10                        [הנו]גֹע בהֹ]                                          [
11                        ובעֹ]וֹ                                                [
12                        תקוץ [דם זובה                                          [
13                        המים]                                                  [
14                        נוֹ]6                                                  [
15   המים[                 ובמי הנדהֹ]
16   [                    החיי]ם [שנֹיֹ]
17                        ידהֹ]
18   [                    ]וֹ
```

3   va[cat] And the la[w concerning one who has a dis]charge: A[ny man]
4   [with a discharge from his flesh or one who brings upon himself] lustful [th]oughts or who
5   [   ] his touch is like the touch of *hooo*[
6   and he shall wash his clo[th]es [and bathe in water]
7   him, who touches him shall ba[the   And] the law [of a woman who has a discharge: Any woman]

---

[6] See PAM 43.302; *DJD XVIII*, Plate XL. Baumgarten marks four illegible letters: oooo (*DJD XVIII*, 190).

8   who has a discharge of blood [shall be in her men]strual impurity se[ven days] b[she] shall remain fo[r]
9   the seven days [   ]the menstruant and a[ll]
10 [tou]ch her[ ]
11 wb'o[ ]
12 stir up [the blood of her discharge]
13 the water[ ]
14 nwo[ ]
15 and with the waters of sprinkling[ ]
16 the livin[g water] šny[ ]
17 her hand[ ]
18 wo[ ]

The first five lines pertain to male impurity, and thereafter the topic switches to female impurity. I will first discuss male impurity and second female impurity, according to the order of the text. The fragmentary text in lines 3–7 outlines laws concerning the impurity transmitted through the touch of an impure male person (line 5), and by touching such a person (line 7), and the required purification from that contact.[7] These issues are at the core of Lev 15:2–12.

The text lists three kinds of genital discharges together: first a *zav* [8], "a[ny man with a discharge from his flesh]," [כ]ול איש אשר יזוב מבשרו; secondly, a man who ejaculates due to "lustful thoughts," that is, masturbates, "[or one who brings himself] lustful [th]oughts **or** who....," [או אשר יעלה עלו מ]חשבת זמה או אשר. The text breaks off after "or who," leaving the third case unknown. On the basis of Lev 15:13–15 the third case may be the emission of semen resulting from sexual intercourse, as Martha Himmelfarb suggests.[9]

---

[7] Leviticus 15 distinguishes between touching the body of an impure person (Lev 15:7) and being touched by an impure person (Lev 15:11); the prescribed purification in both instances is identical. 4Q272 1 ii 6 reads וכבס בג[ד]יו, "and he shall wash his clothes," which likely refers to a person touched by a *zav*, parallel to Lev 15:11 ("all those whom the one with the discharge touches without his having rinsed his hands in water shall wash their clothes, וכבס בגדיו, and bathe in water and be unclean until evening"). The statement in line 7, "who touches him shall ba[the]," is similar to Lev 15:7 and likely refers to the purification necessary for a person touching a *zav*; Lev 15:7 reads: "All who touch the body of the one with the discharge shall wash their clothes and bathe in water (יכבס בגדיו ורחץ במים) and be unclean until the evening."

[8] *Zav* impurity is introduced in words reminiscent of Lev 15:2. Compare ומש[פט הזב את זו[בו כ]ול איש אשר יזוב מבשרו (lines 3–4a) and Lev 15:2: איש איש כי יהיה זב מבשרו זובו, "when any man has a discharge from his member."

[9] Martha Himmelfarb, "Impurity and Sin in 4QD, 1QS, and 4Q512," *DSD* 8 (2001), 17–20. She argues that the text places discharge due to lustful thoughts and sexual intercourse within the category of *zav*. This interpretation seems highly unlikely. *Zav* impurity is clearly distinguished from ejaculation of semen in biblical legislation (Lev 15:13–15) as well as in

The main issue in the text appears to be the transmission of impurity through touch, and most likely, in this respect, the three kinds of impurities are considered equal.[10] Accordingly, the ways by which a person impure from seminal emission transmits impurity are the same as those of a *zav*. If this interpretation is correct, it would make impurity from seminal emission more severe than the biblical stipulation in Leviticus 15. Whereas Leviticus dwells on the impurity transmitted by touching a *zav* or anything the *zav* has defiled (Lev 15:4–12) and specifies that semen transmits impurity (Lev 15:16–18), it fails to mention whether touching a *person* impure from ejaculation or sexual intercourse is defiling. 4Q272 1 ii likely clarifies the law in Leviticus, stating that two additional categories of unclean persons (those who have contracted impurity through either ejaculation or sexual relations) are able to transmit impurity by touch (and by being touched), parallel to the *zav*. Since both the woman and the man become impure from sexual intercourse (Lev 15:18), physical contact with either a man or a woman would thus be defiling.

From 4Q272 1 ii 7b the subject switches to the impurity of a woman. Baumgarten's reconstruction, [ומשפט] הזבה ["and the law [of a woman who has a flow" is probable, since it provides a parallel for the introduction to the law of discharge of a man (line 3). *Zavah* should be taken as an inclusive term for any kind of female discharge, regular (*niddah*) or irregular (*zavah*), parallel to its use in biblical Hebrew (Lev 15:19).[11] Both categories are likely dealt with in the text that follows.

The wording in lines 7–10 displays some similarities to the law regarding the menstruating woman in Lev 15:19, and Baumgarten has reconstructed the lines accordingly.[12] The partially reconstructed phrase "and all who touch her," וכ[ול הנו]גע בה (line 9–10) is taken from Lev 15:19, "whoever touches her [the menstruant] shall be unclean until the evening" and makes clear that the transmission of impurity through touch is still the focus. The similarity to Lev 15:19 indicates the general

---

11QT (XLV 7–8, 11–12, 15–16). Furthermore, since sacrifices were required after the purification from *zav* impurity, it is unfeasible that D would require offering sacrifices after each occasion of sexual intercourse. Furthermore, 11QT XLV 11–12 extends the purification period after sexual intercourse to three days, not seven days, which is required for the *zav*. In addition, early rabbinic halakhah clearly distinguished between discharge from an infection, *zav*, and emission that resulted from sexual arousal; see Baumgarten, *DJD XVIII*, 54; *m. Zabim* 2.2.

[10] 4QTohA 1 i 8b–9a supports this interpretation since the text states that a person impure from emission of semen transmits impurity through his touch: ואם תצ[א מאיש] שכבת הזרע מגעו יטמא, "and when [a man has] an emiss[ion] of semen his touch is defiling"; see DJD *XXXV*, 100–1.

[11] Jacob Milgrom, *Leviticus 1–16: A New Translation with Introduction and Commentary* (The Anchor Bible 3; New York: Doubleday, 1991), 934, 948.

[12] Compare 4Q272 1 ii 7b–9a to Lev 15:19 with the parallel words underlined:

4Q272 1 ii: [וכול אשה] הזבה דם שב[עת ימים תהיה בנד]תה ב]   ת[שב א]ת] שבעת הימים].
Lev 15:19: ואשה כי־תהיה הזבה דם זבה יהיה בבשרה שבעת ימים תהיה בנדתה

content of the lines.[13] Lines 8–10 refer to the impurity of a menstruant, and like Lev 15:20–23, lay down the rules for purification after contact with her. According to Lev 15:19, a menstruating woman transmits impurity to anyone who touches her body as well as to anything upon which she sits or lies. Lev 15:25 also explains that a *zavah* shall be unclean "as in her impurity," כימי נדתה, that is, as in her menstruation. Hence, during the primary impurity of a *zavah* (during the flux), the potential to impart impurity to others through touch is the same as during menstruation.[14] Leviticus clarifies that the touch by a *zav* is defiling (Lev 15:11), but fails to mention whether the touch by a *niddah* or a *zavah* is defiling. One may thus hypothesize that the fragmentary text of 4Q272 1 ii 7–10 clarifies the biblical laws, by stating that the touch of a menstruant and the *zavah* is defiling. This would make this section parallel to the preceding passage, which applies the biblical purification rules for physical contact with a *zav* to a man impure from seminal emission, as discussed above. The effort to harmonize biblical laws by applying the same principle to several laws is a tendency that appears also in other Qumran documents. Jacob Milgrom calls this exegetical principle "homogenization."[15]

The fragmentary text in lines 11–17 contains three likely references to water for ablution, showing that the text is concerned with purification rituals.[16] The reference to ידה, "her hand" (4Q272 1 ii 17), is the last legible word of the fragment, and indicates that the issue still concerns a female impurity bearer.[17]

In sum, the fragmentary text of 4Q272 1 ii 3–18 concerns transmission of impurity by men and women defiled by source impurity. The first part lists the three types of male source impurity that are considered identical with regard to transmission of impurity through touch (by the impurity carrier himself, or by another touching the impurity carrier) as that of a *zav*. Thereby the text harmonizes the biblical stipulations

---

[13]Touching the body of a menstruant brings a less severe state of impurity than touching anything that she has sat or lain upon in Lev 15:19–22, which shows that the main fear is contact with the actual blood; cf. Milgrom, *Leviticus 1–16*, 934.

[14]"Touches her" refers to her body, not her clothes (cf. Lev 15:7); see Milgrom, *Leviticus 1–16*, 935. In addition, the *zav* transmits impurity to the person who touches him, and by analogy the same holds true for the *zavah*. For the parallel of status between *zav* and *zavah* according to biblical law, see Judith Hauptman, *Rereading the Rabbis: A Woman's Voice* (Boulder, Colo.: Westview Press, 1998), 148–9.

[15]Milgrom, "The Scriptural Foundations and Deviations in the Laws of Purity of the Temple Scroll," in *Archaeology and History in the Dead Sea Scrolls*, 91, 95.

[16]See 4Q272 1 ii 13,15. Lines 15b–16 is restored [ם]החיי [המים]. Line 15a reads במי הנדה "waters of sprinkling." In biblical law sprinkling water is required for the purification of corpse impurity (Numbers 19), but Qumran law requires immersion and sprinkling water for any of kind of genital uncleanliness, i.e., flux, emission of semen, and menstruation. See Baumgarten, "The Use of מי נדה for General Purification," 481–85; *DJD XXXV*, 83–7.

[17] The issue here may be impurity transmitted through touching by hands, although one would expect "hands" to be in the plural (cf. Lev 15:11).

The Early Law Code

as well as increases the stringency in regard to transmission of impurity for persons impure from the emission of semen. The second part concerns purity rules for *zavah* and *niddah* and likely reiterates biblical laws concerning the transmission of impurity. It is also likely that parallel to the laws for the male impurity carriers, the text harmonizes these laws concerning female impurity carriers with regard to the transmission of impurity; thus, physical contact with a *zavah* or a *niddah* is equal with regard to transmission of impurity.

3.2.3 4Q266 6 II 1–13

This column consists of three fragments. The first part, 4Q266 6 ii 1–4, may pertain to sexual relations during the impurity period of a woman; the second part, 4Q266 6 ii 5–13, deals with rules for childbirth.

1 [אותה] ק̇ר̇ב̇ [אשר י] o o [ה̇א̇ש̇ה̇] [ ] o [ ]
2 [תהיה ע̇ו̇ן]¹⁸ נדה עלו ואם ראתה [עו]ד̇ והיאה לו[א עת נדתה]
3 [טמא]שבעת ימים והיאה אל תוכל קודש ואל ת̇[ב]ו
4 אל המקד̇ש עד בו השמש ביום ה̇שמיני   *vacat*
5 ואשה אשר̇ [תזרי]ע̇ וילדה זכר [וטמאה א]ת̇ שבעת [הימים]
6 [כ]י̇[מי] נ̇ד̇ת̇ [דאותה וביום השמיני ימול בשר] ע̇ר̇ל̇ת̇[ו]
7 [ושלושת ושלושים יום תשב בדם טוהרה ואם נקבה תלד]
8 [וטמאה שבועים כנדת ד]אותה ו̇[ששה וששים יום תשב בדם]
9 [טוהרה והיאה] לא תוכ̇ל̇ [קודש ולא תבו אל המקדש]
10 [ ]כי מ[שפט מות הו]א̇ה
11 [הי]ל̇ד למנקת בטוה[רתה תביא כבש לעלה ובן־יונה או־תור לחטאת]¹⁹
12 [ו]אם לו̇א ה̇שיגה יד[ה די שה ולקחה בן יונה או תר לעולה]
13 [ו]המירה א̇[ת ה]שה [

1. [ ]o[ ]*h* ' o the wom[an] o   o [one who app]roaches [her]
2. [the s]in of menstrual impurity [will be] upon him. And if she sees (blood) ag[ain], and it is not [time of her menstrual period]
3. [(and he has sexual relations with her) he shall be impure] for seven days. She shall not eat anything hallowed, nor en[ter]
4. the sanctuary until sunset on the eighth day. *vacat*
5. And a woman who [conceiv]es and gives birth to a male child [shall be impure] for seven [days,]
6. [as] in [the day]s of her menstrual [impurity. And on the eighth day the flesh of his] foreskin [shall be circumcised. For]
7. [thirty-three days shall she remain in her blood purification. If she bears a female child]

---

[18] For the reconstruction of lines 1–3, which differs from the text in *DJD XVIII*, see discussion below.

[19] My own reconstruction; see discussion below.

8. [she shall be impure two weeks as in her menstrual i]mpurity. [For sixty-six days she shall remain in her blood]
9. [purification. And she] shall not eat [any sacred thing, nor enter the sanctuary,]
10. [for] it is a capital cr[ime   ]
11. [the i]nfant to a wet-nurse. At [her] purification, [she shall bring a lamb for a burnt offering and a pigeon or a turtledove for a sin offering].
12. [And] if she cannot afford [a lamb, she shall take a turtledove or a pigeon for burnt-offering]
13. [and she] shall substitute [it for the lamb   ]

The fragmentary text in lines 1–2 is problematic. Of the several reconstructions that have been proposed I have adopted the reconstruction (with minor adjustments) by Ben Zion Wacholder and Martin Abegg.[20] It is generally agreed that the phrase [תהיה ע]ן נדה עלו], "[the s]in of menstrual impurity [will be] upon him" (line 2), recalls the law about sexual intercourse with a menstruant recorded in Lev 15:24: "if any man lies with her, and her *impurity falls on him* (ותהי נדתה עליו), he shall be unclean for seven days." The reconstruction of the subsequent words in line 2 is disputed. Baumgarten suggests the following reconstruction of lines 2b–3a: ואם ראתה [עו]ד והיאה לו [בעת נדתה] שבעת ימים והיאה אל תוכל קודש "If she ag[ain] sees (blood), and it is not [at the time of her menstruation] of seven days, she shall not eat anything hallowed." According to this reconstruction, lines 2b–3 refer to food restrictions of a *zavah* and are not related to sexual intercourse.[21] The reconstruction by Wacholder and Abegg allows for the subject matter to follow in a logical way. Accordingly, the text presents two laws as parallels: just as a man who has sexual intercourse with a *niddah* is impure for seven days (Lev 15:24), so is a man who has intercourse with a *zavah*. The latter is a non-biblical law and there may have been a need to provide a law for such a case. This reconstruction is particularly likely in light of the partially parallel laws of the menstruant and the *zavah* in Leviticus 15, which invite the

---

[20] See Ben Zion Wacholder and Martin G. Abegg, A *Preliminary Edition of the Unpublished Dead Sea Scrolls: The Hebrew and Aramaic Texts from Cave 4* (Fascicle 1; Washington DC: Biblical Archaeology Society, 1991), 13. Lawrence Schiffman accepts Wacholder-Abegg's reconstruction of line 2 in "Pharisaic and Sadducean Halakhah in Light of the Dead Sea Scrolls," *DSD* 3 (1994), 285–99, which was published prior the publication of *DJD XVIII*.

[21] Qimron proposes yet another reconstruction. He maintains that the text continues to speak of a *niddah* (not a *zavah*). He suggests the following reconstruction: ואם ראתה [ד]ם והיאה לו [תקרב אל אישה] שבעת ימים "and if she sees blood then she should not approach her husband for seven days." See Qimron, "לשיפור המהדורות של מגילות מדבר יהודה" ("Improvements to the Editions of the Dead Sea Scrolls") *ErIsr* 26 (1999), 144. In light of the context it is more likely that lines 3–4 concern a *zavah* than a *niddah*, since only the former is required to enter the temple (lines 3–4) in order to offer sacrifices (cf. Lev 15:29). On Lev 15:24, see Milgrom, *Leviticus 1–16*, 940–1.

application of laws of transmission of impurity from the one category to the other (Lev 15:25).[22] Consequently, the impurity of a man who has intercourse with a *niddah* or a *zavah* would be the same: seven days' impurity with all the laws for transmission of impurity of the menstruant applied to him. Nevertheless, although D may prescribe identical laws for transmission of impurity by a *zavah* and a *niddah*, the means of purification after the periods of primary impurity for the two categories still remain different according to the purification procedures outlined in Leviticus 15.

The law concerning the *zavah* in 4Q266 ii 2–3 implies that any blood discovered between the periods of menstruation is indicative of the state of a *zavah*. This injunction is more stringent than both biblical (Lev 15:25: "if a woman has a discharge of blood for *many days*") and early rabbinic views on this matter.[23]

4Q266 6 ii 3b continues by prohibiting a woman suffering from a flux from entering the temple or eating sacred food until the end of the purification period. The prohibition is reminiscent of the restrictions in Lev 12:4 concerning a parturient.[24] There are clear similarities between the impurity of a *zavah* and that of a parturient in Leviticus; in both cases, the woman has a primary impurity period (seven or fourteen days for a parturient and as many days as her discharge lasts for a *zavah*). Both periods of primary impurity are compared to that of a *niddah* (Lev 12:2; 15:25). A period of purification follows subsequent to the primary impurity period (thirty-three or sixty-six days for a parturient,[25] seven days for a *zavah*), ending with offerings (burnt and sin

---

[22]In comparison, 4QTohA presents the impurity transmitted by the blood of a *zavah* during her primary impurity and that of a *niddah* as parallel cases. 4QTohA 1 i 7–8 reads: "And the one who is counting (seven days), whether male of female, shall not tou[ch one who has an unclea]n [flux] or a menstruating woman in her uncleanliness, unless she was purified of her [unclean]liness; for the blood of menstruation is like the flux and the one touching it," (כי הנה דם הנדה כזוב ואשר נוגע בו); see *DJD XXXV* 101.

Hannah Harrington notices the similarity in severity of impurity between the two categories and explains that although the *zavah* is a more severe impurity in the Hebrew Bible, there is no indication in the Scrolls of any difference in status between the two. For a more extreme level of impurity of the *zavah* compared to the *niddah* in the Hebrew Bible, she refers to the ban of the *zavah* from the camp (Num 5:2) and the requirement of bathing and of laundering of clothes after physical contact with a *zavah* (Lev 15:7 concerning a *zav*) compared to merely bathing after contact with a *niddah* (15:19); see *The Impurity Systems of Qumran and the Rabbis: Biblical Foundation* (SBL Dissertation Series 143; Atlanta: Scholars Press, 1993), 87.

[23]According to the Rabbis, a woman must be bleeding for three days before being considered a *zavah*; see Baumgarten, *DJD XVIII*, 56; Milgrom, *Leviticus 1–16*, 942; *Sifra*, Mezora Zabim 5:9.

[24]Compare. 4Q266 6 ii 3–4 והיאה אל תוכל קודש ואל ת[בו] אל המקדש עד בו השמש ביום השמיני and Lev 12:4 בכל־קדש לא־תגע ואל־המקדש לא תבא עד־מלאת ימי טהרה ("She shall not touch any holy thing, nor come into the sanctuary, until the days of her purification are completed").

[25]Depending on the sex of the baby; see Lev 12:1–5.

offerings). In light of the similarities, it is logical to apply the rules of a parturient to a *zavah,* as does D.[26]

There are two significant differences between 4Q266 ii 3–4 and Leviticus 12: 4Q266 6 ii 3 uses תוכל, "eat," rather than תגע, "touch," in Lev 12: 4; and there is a non-biblical reference to "sunset." In his examination of Lev 12:4, Milgrom concludes that the primary sacred object a lay person would be able to "touch" would be sacred food at his or her table and points to rabbinic literature which understands "touch" as "eat" in this instance.[27] Thus 4Q266 6 ii 3 similarly clarifies the biblical injunction. The reference to "sunset of the eighth day" emphasizes that the impure person is unclean until the sunset of the last day of the purification period, a view that is also expressed in 11QT, 4QMMT, and 4QTohorot.[28] While the law in 4Q266 6 ii 3–4 prohibits any contact between an impure person and the sacred realm—the temple and sacred food— until the sunset of the eighth day, it also assumes that a *zavah* who is cleansed will enter the temple in order to offer sacrifices in accordance with Lev 15:29. Thus, this law reflects a time when participation in the temple service was assumed. That a woman *is* able to eat of the sacred food when she is ritually pure is also taken for granted in the text.[29]

---

[26] This can be compared to the sectarian laws on emission of semen in 4QToh A (4Q274) 2 i, which expands the impurity transmitted by a person impure from seminal emission in analogy with the biblical rules of a *zav*; see *DJD XXXV,* 104; Joseph Baumgarten, "Zab impurity in Qumran and Rabbinic Law," *JJS* 14 (1994), 273–7.

[27] "Sacred food" includes any offering a lay person would eat, including the "well-being sacrifice" (Num 7:11–18), Passover offering (Num 9:9–14), as well as sacrifices and tithes consumed by the priests and their families; see Himmelfarb, "Impurity and Sin," 22; Milgrom *Leviticus 1–16,* (referring to *b. Yebam.* 75a; *b. Mak.* 14b), 751–2.

[28] 11QT XLV 9–10; XLIX 20–21; L 12, 15–16; LI 3, 5; 4Q394 (4QMMT) 3–7 i 16–19; 4Q277 (4QToh B^b) 1 ii 13 (*DJD XXXV* 116–17); see Harrington, *The Impurity Systems,* 64. The importance of waiting until sunset is part of the polemic surrounding the purity level of a *tevul yom* (a person who has finished ablutions and laundering on the final day of purification, but has not waited until sunset) in relation to the ritual of the burning of the Red Heifer. Baumgarten detects a polemic against the Pharisaic view of *tevul yom* behind the reference to sunset in 4Q266 6 ii 4; see *DJD XVIII,* 56; "The Red Cow Purification Rites in Qumran Texts," *JJS* 46 (1995), 112–19; "The Pharisaic-Sadducean Controversies about Purity," *JJS* 31 (1980), 161.

[29] According to the reconstruction by Baumgarten of 4Q265 3 3, a woman is prohibited from eating the paschal sacrifice: [אל] יואכל נער זעטוט ואשה [בזב]ח הפסח, "[Let no] young lad nor a woman partake [of] the paschal [sacri]fice." But the אל is reconstructed and not certain. See *DJD XXXV,* 63; Joseph Baumgarten, "Scripture and Law in 4Q265," in *Biblical Perspectives: Early Use and Interpretation of the Bible in Light of the Dead Sea Scrolls. Proceedings of the First International Symposium of the Orion Center for the Study of the Dead Sea Scrolls and Associated Literature, 12–14 May 1996* (eds. Michael Stone and Esther Chazon; STDJ 28; Leiden: Brill, 1998), 30–3.

Line 5 introduces the topic of purification after childbirth. This is also the subject of 4Q265 7 (4QMiscellaneous Rules), which outlines the regulations for a parturient based on Lev 12:2–5. 4Q265 provides an aetiology for the discrepancy in the length of time of impurity and purification for a woman after childbirth depending on the sex of the child, tracing it to the period of time Adam and Eve waited before entering the sacred garden.[30] A similar explanation for the biblical law of the parturient appears in Jub. 3:8–14.[31] In contrast to 4Q265 7 and Jubilees, D is not concerned with the reason behind the difference in time in the two cases, but simply presents the biblical legislation with the addition of non-biblical details.

There are clear parallels between 4Q266 6 ii 5–13 and the rules for the parturient in Lev 12:2–8, and it is reasonable to conclude that this section closely follows the biblical text as Baumgarten proposes.[32] However, a close look at the words of the bottom fragment of 4Q266 6 ii (lines 8–13) reveals that none of the extant words duplicates those of Lev 12: 2–8. Still, the reference to a wet nurse in line 11 and the plausible reference to substituting the sacrifice do suggest that the subject matter continues to be purification after childbirth, which is clearly the topic in lines 5–7.

4Q266 6 ii 10–11 refers to a capital offense (line 10) and to a wet nurse (line 11), both of which are without parallels in the biblical text. The reference to a capital crime likely refers to the punishment for transgressing any of the prohibitions imposed upon the parturient; that is, eating anything sacred or entering the temple (Lev 12:4). Given that the same prohibition is imposed on a *zavah* in lines 3–4, the punishment for transgressions applies to a *zavah* as well.[33] There are several instances in biblical legislation where capital punishment is imposed for polluting of the sacred realm.[34] It may be that the reference in 4Q266 6 ii 10 is particularly inspired by Lev 15:31, which outlines the fatal consequence for polluting the sanctuary in relation to the preceding purity laws concerning discharge, emission of semen, and menstruation: "Thus you shall keep the people of Israel separate from their uncleanness, so that they do not die (ולא ימתו) in their uncleanness by defiling my tabernacle that is in their midst." The

---

[30] While the primary impurity period is 7 days followed by 33 days of purification after the birth of a boy, the length of primary impurity after having a girl is 14 days, followed by a purification period of 66 days (Lev 12:1–5).

[31] For a discussion on Jewish and Christian views on the garden of Eden as a prototype for the temple, see Anderson "Celibacy or Consummation in the Garden?" 121–48.

[32] Baumgarten reconstructs 4Q266 6 ii 5–13 in light of 4Q265 7 14–17. By following the order of 4Q265 7, Baumgarten is able to connect the fragments of 4Q266 6 ii 5–13 to the same underlying biblical passage, Lev 12:2–8.

[33] The expression משפט מות is not known from any other document in the Scrolls, except for a possible reconstruction of a text from Jubilees, 4Q221 7 6. Elsewhere D uses דבר מות: 4Q266 5 ii 3; 10 ii 1; CD IX 6. In the Hebrew Bible, משפט מות appear only once (Deut 21:22) and then with reference to hanging.

[34] See Milgrom's discussion on death through divine agency, *karet* (*Leviticus* 1–16, 945–46).

root מות is used in both cases, and in both Lev 15:31 and 4Q266 6 ii 10 the punishment of death is considered to take place through divine agency.³⁵

With the reference to a wet nurse (line 11), D deviates intriguingly from the biblical passage concerning the parturient (Lev 12:2–8). According to Baumgarten's reconstruction, the infant [הי]לד should be given to a wet nurse who should nurse it in purity, [למנקת בטוה[רה. He explains that the mother is not allowed to nurse the baby during her days of purification—an interpretation that has been accepted by scholars as yet another example of the general Qumran tendency to make biblical laws more stringent.³⁶ This interpretation seems unlikely since such a law has no parallel in any other Jewish source. The ramifications of prohibiting new mothers from nursing for 40 to 80 days after childbirth would be serious and dangerous for the health of the babies, since breast-milk is obviously their main source of nourishment.³⁷ If a woman were prohibited from breast-feeding for up to two months after giving birth, it would be virtually impossible for her to start nursing after that. She would consequently have to rely on a wet-nurse for the whole time the baby was being nursed, generally about three years.³⁸ An obvious obstacle to a prohibition of that kind would be the availability of surrogate nurses. Since women who observed these laws would not be able to become wet-nurses, a nurse would have to be found among other women. The hiring of wet-nurses also involved a considerable cost to the parents, one that not everyone could afford.³⁹ Furthermore, infant mortality was high in ancient times, as

---

³⁵Similarly, priests (Num 7: 20–1; 22:23; Lev 22:3) as well as lay-people (Lev 7 :20) are subject to being "cut off" if they eat sacred food in a polluted state.

³⁶See e.g., Himmelfarb, "Impurity and Sin," 25; Hempel, *Laws*, 46. *DJD XVIII*, 56. See also Joseph Baumgarten, "Purification after Childbirth and the Sacred Garden in 4Q265 and Jubilees" in *New Qumran Texts and Studies: Proceedings of the First Meeting of the International Organization for Qumran Studies, Paris 1992* (eds. George Brooke, Florentino García Martínez; STDJ 15; Leiden: Brill, 1994), 3–10.

³⁷Although cow or goat milk is a possible source of nutrition for a baby, it cannot provide the same nutritional value as breast milk. Use of animal milk as substitute for breast-milk results in a poor immune system for the baby resulting in increased risk of sickness and death. (From conversation with Patricia Seymour, MD, Hamilton, Ontario).

³⁸Milgrom, *Leviticus 1–16*, 953; Mayer I. Gruber, "Women in the Cult according to the Priestly Code," in *Judaic Perspectives on Ancient Israel* (eds. J. Neusner et al.; Philadelphia: Fortress Press, 1987), n.40. The early Rabbis propose that women should nurse their babies for between 18 and 24 months at a minimum; see Ilan, *Jewish Women*, 121.

³⁹The practice of wet-nursing is well recorded in the Roman world, where it was not only practised extensively among the upper classes, but also among the lower classes, including slaves. Though most information comes from Rome, the practice was known in many other parts of the Roman world. By the end of first century C.E., "most upper-class women had given up breast-feeding their babies" (Beryl Rawson, "The Roman Family," in *The Family in Ancient Roman: New Perspective* [ed. B. Rawson; Ithaca, N.Y.: Cornell University Press, 1986], 30). For studies on wet-nursing in the Roman world, see Keith Bradley, "Wet-Nursing at Rome: A

was the rate of child deaths. It is very hard to envision that Jewish laws would be created that effectively would increase infant and early childhood mortality. Finally, a prohibition of nursing goes against the general appreciation of breast-feeding as a life-giving activity, found in the literature of late antiquity, including early rabbinic literature.[40] According to *m. Ketub.* 5, breast-feeding is part of the duties of a wife. In early rabbinic literature, a nursing woman is allowed several privileges, all designed to protect the infant.[41]

A wet-nurse may be mentioned in the text for reasons other than those suggested by Baumgarten. The word טוה[רתה may, in fact, begin a new sentence, in which case the mention of a wet-nurse does not necessarily relate to purity. Since line 12 pertains to the case of a parturient who cannot afford a lamb, line 11b may provide a condensed form of the command in Lev 12:6–7 to bring offerings (a lamb, a pigeon and a turtle dove). The law in Lev 12:6 begins with the phrase ובמלאת ימי טהרה "when the days of her purification are completed." The remainder of the word בטוה[in 4Q266 6 ii 11 may similarly refer to the completion of the woman's purification, as I have proposed in my reconstruction of line 11: [בטוה[רתה תביא כבש לעלה ובן־יונה או־תור לחטאת], "At [her] purification, [she shall bring a lamb for a burnt offering and a pigeon or a turtledove for a sin offering]."[42]

There could be a number of reasons for mentioning a wet-nurse. First, the reference may relate to cases where a mother is prevented from nursing her baby. It may be that she cannot produce milk, which is a problem for some women who try to

---

Study in Social Relations," in *The Family in Ancient Rome: New Perspectives* (Ithaca, N.Y.: Cornell University Press, 1986), 201–29; Bradley, "The Social Role of the Nurse in the Roman World," in *Discovering the Roman Family: Studies in Roman Social History* (New York: Oxford University Press, 1991), 13–36. Ilan points out that there is no information on wet-nursing in Palestine and assumes that most mothers nursed their own infants. There is, however, first century B.C.E. evidence of Jewish wet-nurses in Egypt; see *Jewish Women*, 121.

[40] Cf. Lk 11:27; Gail Paterson Corrington discusses the common images of Isis as a nursing goddess and Mary nursing infant Jesus; see "The Milk of Salvation: Redemption by the Mother in Later Antiquity and Early Christianity," *HRT* 82:4 (1989), 393–420. See also the second century Christian composition *Odes of Solomon* (35:5–6), where God is depicted as nursing a child. On evidence of breast-feeding in the Ancient Near East, see Mayer Gruber, "Breast-Feeding Practices in Biblical Israel and in Old Babylonian Mesopotamia," in *The Motherhood of God and Other Studies* (eds. Jacob Neusner et al.; South Florida Studies in the History of Judaism 57; Atlanta: Scholars Press, 1992), 69–107.

[41] E.g., *m. Ketub.* 5.9; *t. Shabb.* 9:22; see Ilan, *Jewish Women*, 120–1.

[42] Since the text already has specified in detail how many days of primary impurity and subsequent purification periods a woman must undergo after childbirth (4Q266 6 ii 5–9), it is feasible that no further specification was necessary. A simple reference to "her purification" was likely sufficient to indicate the completion of her purification period, in contrast to phrases that specify the length of purification; e.g., [ובמילא[ת לו שבעת ימי טה[רתה], [when he] has [completed] the seven days of [his] puri[fication]"; 4QRitual of Purification (4Q512) 10–11 5.

nurse. Or it may relate to a woman dying in child birth, not an uncommon incident in ancient times, and in which case her husband would be required to find a wet-nurse.[43] In short, it is more reasonable to assume that a wet-nurse is mentioned in relation to a problem that prevents a mother from nursing rather than as part of a law that prohibits a woman from breast-feeding. The law in 4Q266 6 ii 10b–11 likely gives a short statement about the obligation of saving the life of the baby by using a wet-nurse. A second possibility is that the law *prohibits* the use of wet nurses, perhaps in response to the increasing tendency to use wet-nurses in place of mothers breast-feeding their babies in the Roman world. We really do not know why there is a reference to a wet-nurse in the text; as illustrated above, there are other possible explanations than presuming that the impurity of the mother was a concern and that breast-feeding was prohibited for the parturient. Most likely, the text gives a general command about saving the life of an infant by hiring a wet-nurse in the case of a mother's death.

3.2.4 CONCLUSION

The long section on purity laws concerning genital discharges and childbirth in 4Q266 6 i 14–16/4Q272 1 ii 3–18/4Q266 6 ii 1–13 gives an indication of the importance attached to this subject in the circles that produced the early law code. These purity laws represent a stringent interpretation of biblical legislation. Waiting until sunset for a *zavah* at the end of her purification is a detail which is not specified in Lev 12:4. Furthermore, compared with Leviticus, legislation that imposes the death penalty for a parturient for entering the temple in a ritually impure state is an innovation. Whereas Leviticus describes the condition of the *zavah* as bleeding for "many days" (Lev 15: 25), the sense in 4Q266 6 ii 2–3 appears to be that *any* blood outside of the time of menstruation makes a woman a *zavah*. Considering the long process of purification for a *zavah*, which was only terminated with offerings, this is a stringent interpretation of the biblical law. In addition, if my interpretation of the fragmentary text of 4Q272 1 ii is correct, the ways by which impurity is transmitted by a person impure from any kind of genital discharge is the same as that of a *zav*. Since Leviticus does not state that a couple after intercourse (or a man after ejaculation) transmits impurity by touch, a halakhic position that posits that they do transmit impurity by touch, parallal to a *zav,* represents a stringent interpretation of Leviticus 15.

---

[43]See, for example, Gen 35:16–19 (Rachel dies in child birth). Rabbinic law, in comparison, demands that a husband provides a wet-nurse for the baby if he divorces his wife shortly after childbirth. If the baby knows the mother, she is obliged to continue nursing and is eligible to receive a salary as wet-nurse; see Ilan, *Jewish Women,* 120–1.

3.3 The Rite of the *Sotah* and Intercourse with a Slave Woman: 4Q270 4 1–21; 4Q266 12 1–9

3.3.1 The Text

4Q270 4 consists of five fragments that are extensively cracked (PAM 43.296 and 43.298), but which together make up the left side of a column. With the upper margin visible, fragment 'a' is clearly the top of the column; the placement of the bottom fragments (lines 11–21) is uncertain.[44] A few key phrases in the top fragment (lines 1–10) show with certainty that the first part of the column relates to the ordeal of the *Sotah*, the suspected adulteress (Num 5:11–31). Baumgarten places the second, narrow fragment at lines 11–17. Lines 13–16 appear to deal with illicit intercourse with a slave woman and to be based on Lev 19:20–22.

Lines 9–16 may overlap with 4Q266 12 1–9, but the identification as parallels is not certain. 4Q266 12 was put together by Milik from four fragments (a–d) as a parallel text to 4Q270 4.[45] Baumgarten tentatively adds a fifth fragment (e).[46] Baumgarten does not use the top fragment of 4Q266 12, fragment a (lines 1–5a), for his reconstruction of 4Q270 4 10–12. Still, he underlines the *aleph* in 4Q266 12 1 and מלכים in line 4 as parallels to the text of 4Q270 4 9, 12 and reconstructs [אל יתן איש] in line 1 from 4Q270 4 9. At the same time, he uses the fragments 4Q266 12 b and c (corresponding to 4Q266 12 6, 8–9) for reconstructing 4Q270 4 13–15.[47] The appearance of the unusual word מלכים in both 4Q266 12 4 (fragment a) and 4Q270 4 12, (although with a possible definite article in the latter) makes the parallel highly likely. The problem is in the next two lines where the two copies do not seem to be exactly the same, but the identification is somewhat easier when fragment e is not included in 4Q266 12. For the reconstruction of 4Q270 4 10–12 I will follow a preliminary transcription of these lines by Hartmut Stegemann whose transcription is based on Milik's notes.[48]

Milik had also proposed that the fragment 4Q266 13 is linked to the passage on the *Sotah*; there is a reference to someone testifying (4Q266 13 4) and to blood (line 5), which is suggestive of a connection to the text on the *Sotah*. Nevertheless, since the

---

[44] Baumgarten, *DJD XVIII*, 154.

[45] Baumgarten lists 4Q266 12 under "Unidentified Fragments," but does note overlaps between 4Q266 12 1, 4, 6, 7, 9 and 4Q270 4 (*DJD XVIII*, 78–9).

[46] Baumgarten writes, "Frg. e, אל [י]קרב[may perhaps belong to the same group" (*DJD XVIII*, 79).

[47] Hempel, inserts line 2 from 4Q266 12 (לפני עדים ש[נים]) in the composite text of 4Q270 4 and 4Q266 12; *Laws*, 62–3.

[48] I have received permission from Hartmut Stegemann (through Annette Steudel) to refer to the placement of 4Q266 12 1–5 (fragment a) in the column according to an unpublished transcription of the column by Stegemann for my analysis of the text on the *Sotah*.

fragment does not include any parallels to 4Q270 4, a connection to 4Q270 4 is hard to verify and I will not use 4Q266 13 for reconstructing 4Q270 4.

According to Baumgarten's arrangements of the D fragments, the passage on the *Sotah* and the ensuing laws on sexual relations come before further marital laws and laws on business deals (4Q270 5/4Q271 3) in the middle section of the document. The content and order of this part of the document, however, remains unclear.⁴⁹

4Q270 4 (parallel 4Q266 12 underlined)

top margin

[יֹבא איש אשה להאלותה]	1
[הרואה אם יראה אשת]	2
[רעהו אם] אָמרה אנוֹסהֹ הֹיתי	3
[לא יב]יֹאָהֹ כי אם דמהֹ יצוֹאֵ	4
[לא יצא יביאה לפני אי]שׁ [מן] הֹכֹהנים ופרע	5
[הכהן את ראשה והשביע את]הֹאָשה והשקה את	6
[האשה את מי המרים המאררים] לֹאֵ תקח מידֹ[ו כֹ]לֹ	7
[המים] הקדושים	8
[א]לֹ יתן איש אֶ[ת]	9
[ל]פֹני [ ]	10
[עדים שנים א]ם יֵשׁ[ ]	11
[רעה לה כאשר ל]הֹמלכים	12
[אל ישכב איש] עם אשה	13
[ה]שׁופחה החרופהooאֵ	14
[שבע שנים כאשר] אמר לא תֹ[ ]	15
[יֹ[קתנה אוֹ לב]נו ייעדנה]	16
[ ]ה אֶתֹ אשֶׁרֹ ל[ ]	17
[ ]ooooo	18
[מן הקד]שׁ] לחמוֹ	19
[הש[מיני] יֹ]שכב עם	20
[עֹ]ולה oo[ ]	21

Translation
1. [ ] a man shall bring a woman to place a curse upon her
2. [ ] who sees, if he sees the wife of
3. [his neighbour if] she said I was raped
4. [he shall not br]ing her unless her blood does [not] come forth⁵⁰

---

⁴⁹Several columns are missing, and the order of the extant fragments is not certain; see *DJD XVIII*, 79–80.

⁵⁰The phrase דמה יצוא is an unusual expression for menstruation. Nevertheless, יצא is likely used with reference to semen "going out" from a man in 4QTohA 1 i 8 as Baumgarten restores the phrase: ואם תצ]א מאיש[שכבת הזרע, "And when [a man has] an emis[sion] of semen" (*DJD XXXV*, 100–1).

The Early Law Code

5. [he shall bring her before o]ne [of] the priests and [the priest] shall unbind
6. [her hair, and he shall make] the woman [take an oath] and make [the woman] drink
7. [the bitter water of the curse.] She shall not take from [his] hand [a]ny
8. [ ] the holy [water]
9. [ ]let [n]o man give
10. [ ]b[efore]
11. [two witnesses i]f there is
12. [a neighbour of her according to /] the kings
13. [let no man lie] with a woman
14. [the] female slave who was designated oo' [ ]
15. [seven years as] he said y[ou shall] not[ ]
16. [ ] take her or [assign her] for [his so]n[51]
17. [ ]h that which /[ ]
18. [ ]ooooo
19. [ ]from the sac[red] his bread
20. [the] eig[hth] he lies with
21. [ ] burnt offering oo[ ]

The text that emerges from the combination of these fragments concerns two different subjects, the *Sotah* (lines 1–10) and a slave woman (lines 13–16). It is not clear where in lines 11–12 the first section ends, or where the subsequent section begins. I will first discuss the text that relates to the Sotah, and then I will examine the text that pertains to the slave woman.

3.3.2 THE RITE OF THE *SOTAH*

3.3.2.1 The Rite of the Sotah

A modern reader may be rightfully upset when reading the prescribed ordeal for a suspected adulteress in Num 5:11–31. The text depicts a cruel, public humiliation of a woman whose guilt is not yet "proven."[52] The text relates how a husband, suspecting his wife of adultery, will bring her to the temple where she will be put through an ordeal of drinking "water of bitterness" to establish her guilt or innocence. The text emphasizes that the woman's guilt is not established: "she is undetected," "there is no witness against her," "she was not caught in the act" (Num 5:13). Had she been caught

---

[51] Baumgarten suggests this translation in light of Exod 21:10, but does not include the word ייעדנה (Exod 21:9) in his reconstruction of the text.

[52] In order to address possible critique of my description I should share my assumption. I assume that women in an ancient society would feel humiliated by being publically shamed in the same way as women today would react to such treatment. My assumption is based on a general belief that humans are fundamentally the same with regard to their basic emotions, desires, and reponses to crises today as in the past.

in the act, or had there been evidence against her, she and her lover would have suffered the death penalty (Lev 20:10; Deut 22:20–24). The case of the *Sotah* is unique in biblical law since it allows a person to be tried for a crime without evidence (cf. Deut 19:15; Num 35:30). According to Tikva Frymer-Kensky the reason for this unusual procedure is that the suspected crime—adultery—poses a real danger to the society as a whole and must therefore be "solved" through a quasi-legal procedure, although there are no witnesses. She compares the procedure to the case of an unsolved murder (Deut 21:1–9), for which the rite of killing a heifer is prescribed.[53]

Repetitions and obscure Hebrew expressions (Num 5: 21, 22, 24 and 27) make the biblical description of the rite and the nature of the punishment hard to comprehend fully. Some commentators postulate two sources, while others attempt to understand the text as a unit.[54] Ancient readers would certainly have read the text as a whole, which makes the debate over possible sources irrelevant for my discussion. The main elements of the rite are as follows: after an offering by the husband, a priest will "set her [the suspected adulteress] before the Lord" and unbind her hair. The priest will then pronounce the oath, whereupon she will respond by saying "Amen, Amen," thereby accepting the consequences of the oath. Throughout the ordeal the woman is silent, except when she is forced to accept the words pronounced by the priest. The priest will make her drink "the water of bitterness," a mix of water, dust from the temple floor, and ink from the curse on a parchment dissolved in the water. The two possible outcomes of the curse are linked to her reproductive organs: infertility versus successful pregnancy (Num 5:27–28). The text focuses on the repercussions in the case of guilt, which consists of physical afflictions.[55]

Although the focus is on pregnancy, it is uncertain whether or not the woman is assumed to be pregnant already.[56] The curse promises to cause pain and ailments in her womb and uterus: וצבתה בטנה ונפלה ירכה, "your belly shall swell up and your

---

[53] Tikva Frymer-Kensky, "The Strange Case of the Suspected Sotah (Numbers V 11–31)," *VT* 34 (1984), 11–26.

[54] See Frymer-Kensky, "The Strange Case of the Suspected Sotah"; Jacob Milgrom, "The Case of the Suspected Adultress, Numbers 5:11–31: Redaction and Meaning," in *Women in the Hebrew Bible: A Reader* (ed. Alice Bach; New York: Routledge, 1999), 475–82 (first published in *Creation of Sacred Literature: Composition and Redaction of the Biblical Text* [ed. Richard Elliot Freedman; Berkeley: University of California Press, 1981], 69–75).

[55] The text does not state whether the curse will take effect immediately or later. For a description of the rite, see Katherine Doob Sakenfeld, "Numbers," in *The Women's Bible Commentary* (eds. Carol A. Newsom and Sharon H. Ringe; London: SPCK, Louisville, Ky.: Westminster John Knox Press, 1992), 49.

[56] W. McKane argues that the woman is pregnant; "Poison, Trial by Ordeal and the Cup of Wrath," *VT* 30 (1980), 475–92; so also Judith R. Wegner, *Chattel or Person? The Status of Women in the Mishnah* (New York: Oxford University Press, 1992), 52; see also Anthony Phillips, *Ancient Israel's Criminal Law: A New Approach to the Decalogue* (New York: Schocken Books, 1970), 147, 118 ff.

uterus [literally "thigh"] shall discharge" (Num 5:27). The precise nature of the affliction is uncertain.⁵⁷ Possibly, ונפלה ירכה (the falling of the thigh) describes a prolapsed uterus, when the uterus falls down, causing sexual dysfunction and sterility.⁵⁸ Another possibility is that the phrase refers to miscarriage. The punishment does not consist of the death penalty, which one might expect for adultery, but it does result in her being shamed, becoming an "execration among her people." If innocent, however, the woman will ונזרעה זרע, which can mean either to be able to "to retain seed" or to "be able to conceive" (Num 5:28).

The rite testifies to the ancient male anxiety over women's sexuality, as well as male domination and female powerlessness. The biblical double standard on sexuality that considers female adultery a crime but men's infidelity acceptable (as long as any female sexual partner is not under another man's authority) comes to the fore in the ordeal. To understand the rite as a mechanism for protecting a woman from an irate husband, or from a lynch mob, as Milgrom proposes, is an optimistic reading of the text.⁵⁹

There are several words and expressions in 4Q270 4/4Q266 12 that are similar to the wording in Numbers 5 and clearly show that the text concerns the case of the Sotah. The first line (4Q270 4 1) refers explicitly to the ordeal of the Sotah with the reference to a man (the husband) *bringing* a woman to undergo the ordeal, יבא איש[

---

⁵⁷*NRSV* reads: "when the Lord makes your uterus drop and your womb discharge."*JPS Hebrew-English Tanakh* reads "so that her belly shall distend and her thigh shall sag." "Thigh," ירך, is elsewhere an euphemism for the male sexual organ (Gen 46:26; Exod 1:5; Judg 7:30) and in Num 5:21 likely refers to a woman's reproductive organs. צבה constitutes a lexicographical difficulty. If the verb is related to the Akkadian *sabu,* "flood," it may allude to the uterus being flooded; see Jacob Milgrom, *JPS Torah Commentary: Numbers* (Philadelphia: Jewish Publication Society, 1990), 41. G.R. Driver argues that the phrase can refer to both sterility and miscarriage; see "Two Problems in the Old Testament Examined in the Light of Archaeology," *Syria* 33 (1956), 73–7. See also Rachel Biale, *Women and Jewish Law: An Exploration of Women's Issues in Halakhic Sources* (New York: Schocken Books, 1984), 186.

⁵⁸Frymer-Kensky, "The Strange Case of the Suspected Sotah," 11–26.

⁵⁹Milgrom, *JSP Torah Commentary: Numbers*, 354. See also "The Case of the Suspected Adulteress, Number 5:11–31," 69–75. Hauptman agrees with Milgrom; *Rereading the Rabbis, 28–9.* Similarly, Biale suggests that the ordeal is not a real ordeal compared to other ancient tests by which the accused was usually killed (the ordeal by water in ancient Babylonia and Medieval Europe). Instead, the ordeal would "practically guarantee that a woman could prove her innocence" (*Women and Jewish Law*, 187). But oaths were taken very seriously in the ancient world. The ordeal described in the Code of Hammurabi presents two alternatives: to take an oath or to leap into the river (depending on who makes the allegation). Thus the first alternative is very similar to the one prescribed in Numbers 5 and gives evidence of the serious nature of an oath; see McKane, "Poison, Trial by Ordeal and the Cup of Wrath," 492–3; Michael Fishbane, "Accusations of Adultery: A Study of Law and Scribal Practice in Numbers 5:11–31," *HUCA* 45 (1974), 25–45.

האלותה. והביא האיש את־אשתו אל־הכהן ‎:5:15 this is similar to Num ;אשה להאלותה "to put a curse upon her" is reminiscent of references to the adjuration of curses in Num 5:21–3 by the priest. Lines 5–8 describe the ordeal itself. ופרע, line 5, "to unbind," is the same verb used in Num 5:18 for loosening the hair of the suspected adulteress: ופרע את־ראש האשה. והשקה, line 6, "cause her to drink," is parallel to Num 5:24, where the priest makes the woman drink "the water of bitterness": והשקה את־האשה את־מי המרים המאררים. The reference to "holy [water]" [המים] הקדושים in line 8 likely refers to "the holy water" in Num 5:17, that is, the water used by the priest to which he will add dust of the temple and the dissolved ink from the curse. On the basis of the text extant in lines 5–8, the description of the ordeal follows the biblical account and gives a brief summary of the successive stages (the bringing of the woman to the priest, the priest's unbinding of her hair, the pronouncement of the curse, her drinking of the water).

Whereas lines 5–8 describe the actual rite, lines 2–4 do not correspond to the biblical account. Instead, lines 2–4 appear to discuss cases when a man should or should not impose the ordeal on his wife. Line 2 refers to someone observing something ("one who sees" and "if he sees the wife" of somebody), evidently a witness. The reference to עדים in line 11, reconstructed from 4Q266 12 2, supports the suggestion that line 2 also alludes to a witness. Baumgarten suggests that a plausible reference to a witness in line 2 can be understood in comparison with early rabbinic laws.[60] Rabbinic legislation required certain events to take place before a husband could force a woman to undergo the ordeal. First, a man must warn his wife in front of two witnesses not to seclude herself with a certain man (*m. Sotah* 1:1–2).[61] Second, a subsequent seclusion with the man (the suspected lover) must be witnessed by two witnesses, one witness, or only the husband, depending on the tradition.[62] The Mishnah clarifies that mere social contact between the woman and the suspected paramour would not suffice as evidence against her (*m. Sotah* 1:2). As a final judicial step, the case was heard by the Sanhedrin (*m. Sotah* 1:4–5) with the intent of forcing a confession from a guilty woman. If the woman confessed, she would be divorced without receiving her *ketubah*, but if she still claimed innocence she was brought to the temple to undergo the ordeal. As Hauptman comments, "This series of events is a

---

[60] *DJD XVIII*, 153.

[61] קנא is used in Num 5:14 with respect to "be jealous, zealous" (*BDB*, 888), but was interpreted by the rabbis as "to warn" (Marcus Jastrow, ספר מלים: *Dictionary of the Targumim, Talmud Babli, Yerushalmi and Midrashic Literature* [New York: The Judaica Press, 1989], 1390). See Hauptman, *Rereading the Rabbis*, 17.

[62] Following an initial warning before two witnesses, R. Eliezer claims that one witness—who can be the husband—of the rendezvous is enough to force the woman to go through the ordeal. According to R. Joshuah two witnesses are required to have seen the seclusion, which would provide more protection for the woman (*m. Sotah* 1:1–2; 6:3; *t. Sotah* 1:1–2).

far cry from the Torah's mere 'fit of jealousy.'"⁶³ These requirements brought the ordeal closer to the regular justice system that required witnesses to unlawful acts for a trial and a verdict (based on Deut 19:15).

The wording in 4Q270 4 2 suggests that a witness would see a suspicious act done by someone's wife, such as secluding herself with a possible lover. Hence it is likely that, as in rabbinic tradition, the text requires a witness observing a rendezvous (the opportunity to commit adultery) before a husband could bring his wife to the temple. It should be noted that D refers to the witness in the singular, which corresponds to the opinion of R. Eliezer. Thus two witnesses would not be required, as R. Joshuah holds. The requirement of a single witness differs from biblical law (Deut 19:15), which prescribes two witnesses for any offence.⁶⁴ In the case of the *Sotah*, however, one witness may have sufficed to have a woman tested by the ordeal, since the ritual itself—however oppressive to women—was not perceived as a punishment, but as a substitute for a trial.

These changes to the biblical law in 4Q270 4 and 4Q266 12 correspond to the general trend in rabbinic tradition to introduce witnesses—though rabbinic opinions differ as to how many witnesses are necessary—and hold hearings before judges. Judith Hauptman suggests that such rabbinic legislation reflects "a growing dissatisfaction with the ordeal" and was a reaction against an earlier, more positive view.⁶⁵ Since 4Q270 4 legislates changes to the ordeal that increase the rights of the woman, a critical or more "reasonable" view of the ordeal may date much earlier than Hauptman suspects. It is likely that opposing views about the ordeal existed simultaneously for a long time, since the law code in D, with its legislation for a reform of the ordeal, likely goes back to the early second century B.C.E.

The barely legible third line of 4Q270 4 may refer to the case of a woman who claims to have been raped: "[if] she said, I was raped," אנוסה היתי.⁶⁶ Unfortunately, the rest of the ruling is not preserved. According to rabbinic references, a rape victim was exempt from the ordeal, since it was not disputed that sexual intercourse occurred. Baumgarten suggests that the ruling in 4Q270 4 is the same; the phrase והוא לא נתפשה

---

⁶³Hauptman, *Rereading the Rabbis*, 18.

⁶⁴Communal laws in D on testimonies in CD IX 16b–X 3 are based on Deut 17:6 and 19:15. The meaning of the passage in D has been subject to much scholarly debate; see Schiffman, *Sectarian Law*, 73–81; Hempel, *Laws*, 93–8; Joseph Baumgarten, "Judicial Procedures," in *Encyclopedia of the Dead Sea Scrolls*, 1: 456; Jacob Neusner, "'By the Testimony of Two Witnesses' in the Damascus Document IX, 17–22 and in Pharisaic-Rabbinic Law," *RevQ* 8 (1972–5), 197–217; Bernard Jackson, "Damascus Document IX, 16–23 and Parallels," *RevQ* 9 (1977–8), 445–50; N.L. Rabinovitch, "Damascus Document IX, 17–22 and Rabbinic Parallels," *RevQ* 9 (1977–8), 113–16.

⁶⁵Hauptman, *Rereading the Rabbis*, 21.

⁶⁶Rape may also be the subject of legal discussion in the fragmentary text in 4Q266 5 i 1–2.

(Num 5:13), "she was not caught in the act," was understood by the rabbis as "she was not seized violently."⁶⁷

The words in line 3 are remarkable in that they record the words of the accused woman. This is in sharp contrast to the biblical account in which the voice of the woman is never heard, with the exception of her accepting the curse spoken by a priest by saying "Amen, Amen" (Num 5:22). The words by the accused woman in 4Q270 4 3 constitute her testimony of defence. Thus the text presumes that a woman suspected of adultery was questioned and given the opportunity to defend herself in order to establish whether or not the ordeal should be imposed. This procedure is in line not only with rabbinic law, but also with Philo's account of judicial hearings. In his detailed account of the ritual, he describes how the case is first brought before the judges in Jerusalem, who will evaluate the evidence in the form of the spouses' testimonies.⁶⁸ The woman may thus defend herself. Only if the case remains unsolved, with the woman continuing to state her innocence, is she forced to undergo the ordeal.

Line 4 concerns blood "coming forth" (דמה יצוא) from a woman. The text may read "[he shall not br]ing her, unless her blood does [not] come forth," as the phrase is restored by Milik, in which case the phrase indicates pregnancy. Alternatively, one may read, "unless her blood comes forth," which may allude to blood as evidence of rape.⁶⁹ The latter possibility hardly makes sense within this context of the *Sotah*, because if a woman claimed she was raped, no further inquiry into the question of adultery would be necessary. The reconstruction [לא יצא] is, in my view, preferable. Possibly the formulators of the early law code interpreted the ambiguous wording of Num 5:27–8 as an allusion to pregnancy. The law would then limit the ordeal to women who were suspected of being pregnant, when the question of possible adultery would be especially important. Similarly, the early rabbis limited the ordeal to women who could have conceived from an adulterous union.⁷⁰ *M. Sotah* 4:3 exempts the following categories of women from the rite of the *Sotah*: a woman who is already pregnant by a previous husband, a nursing woman (being unable to become pregnant), a sterile woman, an aged woman (post menopausal), and "one that is incapable of bearing children."⁷¹ However, while the rabbis exempted those women from the ordeal who could not have conceived from an adulterous relationship, 4Q270 4 would require that a woman was pregnant before she could undergo the ordeal. Both

---

⁶⁷Baumgarten (*DJD XVIII*, 153) refers to *Sifre Numbers* 7; *b. Yebam.* 56b and the use of the verb תפש for rape in Deut. 22:28; see also *b. Sotah* 2b.

⁶⁸Philo, *Special Laws* 3: 52–63; see also references in *Cherubim* 14; *Planting* 108.

⁶⁹Baumgarten mentions this reading as a possibility; *DJD XVIII*, 153–4.

⁷⁰Women who could not conceive could still be divorced without receiving the *ketubah* on the suspicion of adultery (*m. Sotah* 4:3).

⁷¹According to Philip Blackman, this phrase refers to a woman who is using some contraceptive device; *Nashim* (vol. 3 of *Mishnayoth*; 3rd ed.; Gateshead, Eng.: Judaica Press, 1973), 353.

approaches focus on pregnancy, but D takes the emphasis on pregnancy further, effectively limiting the number of women who would risk being forced to undergo the ordeal.

Line 7 differs from the details in Num 5:11–21 by prohibiting the woman from taking something from "his hand," presumably that of the priest. Baumgarten suggests that the woman is prohibited from touching the vessel containing the water because of fear of contamination from an impure woman.[72] Though sectarian Qumran rhetoric occasionally fuses moral and ritual defilement, it would be a unique case if an immoral person—an adulterous wife—actually transmitted impurity. Instead, the phrase may simply reiterate what the biblical text is already saying, that the priest should hold the water while she drinks (Num 5:18b).[73]

The expression "let [n]o man give" [ת]א שיא ןתי ל[א in line 9 is reminiscent of Num 5:20, where ותבכש־תא ךב שיא ןתיו refers to sexual intercourse. The partially restored negative particle, however, lacking in the biblical text, makes the subject matter hard to conjecture. The parallel text in 4Q266 12 adds in the next line "tw]o witnesses" and the line below includes the word הל "to her." If rabbinic law has any bearing, the context may relate to cases where the husband was allowed to withhold the *ketubah* in divorce. If a woman was found guilty according to the ordeal of *Sotah*, or if she refused to drink (which was understood as indicative of guilt), then the husband could divorce her without giving her the *ketubah*.[74] This would also be the case when there were witnesses to the affair, to which line 11 may refer.[75] However, this possibility remains speculative.

3.3.2.2 Conclusion

The fragmentary text of 4Q270 4 and 4Q266 12 prescribes laws for the ordeal of the *Sotah*. The language of the husband *bringing* the wife to undergo the ordeal is similar to the biblical account (Num 5:15), which evokes the same imagery of a woman who is brought as a passive object to the temple. Though the passage endorses the ritual *per se*, it appears to introduce changes to the ordeal compared to its biblical *Vorlage*. Most significantly, the text likely demands some kind of evidence of the amorous affair before a man could bring his wife to the temple. The reference to seeing (in the singular) a neighbour's wife (4Q270 4 2) reveals that a witness—probably to the seclusion of the wife with a suspected lover—was necessary before a trial by ordeal could take place. In addition, the case of a woman who claims that she was

---

[72] *DJD XVIII*, 154.

[73] The biblical text explicitly says, "In his own hands the priest shall have the water of bitterness that brings the curse" (Num 5:18b). *M. Sotah* 3:4 states that the woman should be taken away immediately after she has drunk the water in order that the temple court not be made unclean. Thus the woman is assumed to be clean but there is a danger that the curse will affect her womb and she might hemorrhage and defile the temple.

[74] For the expression "to give her her *ketubbah*," הבותכ ןתיו, see *m. Sotah* 6:2.

[75] *M. Sotah* 4:2.

raped shows that the woman had a chance to defend herself. Thus, some kind of preliminary hearings are presumed to take place before she could be forced to undergo the ordeal. Philo, writing in the first half of the first century C.E. in Alexandria, describes a similar legal procedure preceding the ordeal. Information given on the *Sotah* in Philo's writings and rabbinic laws shows that the legal procedures surrounding the ordeal had changed in late Second Temple times from the biblical legislation. The fragmentary text concerning the *Sotah* in D may suggest that changes to the ordeal took place much earlier. Still, it is not known whether the legislation in D concerning the *Sotah* reflects actual praxis or if it represents a proposal for change. At the very least, the text gives evidence of a discontent with certain aspects of the biblical law on the *Sotah*.

3.3.4 INTERCOURSE WITH A SLAVE WOMAN: 4Q270 4 12–21; 4Q266 12 4–9

3.3.4.1 Intercourse with a Slave Woman

The topic in lines 13–16 is sexual or marital relations. It is not clear if the previous line, which has the word "the kings" המלכים in 4Q270 12, parallel to 4Q266 12 4, relates to the same topic.[76] The fragmentary nature of lines 12–21 in 4Q270 4 makes interpretations of the content highly uncertain. Baumgarten proposes links to Lev 19:20–2 and very tentatively with Exod 21:10, both of which legislate about sexual relations with a slave woman. Line 13 pertains to sexual relations, evident from the restored phrase based on 4Q266 12 6 אשה עם [איש ישכב אל] "[let no man lie] with a woman." The reference in line 14 to a slave woman ה]שופחה, who is "designated" החרופה, points to Lev 19:20–2, in which a similar expression is used in the law concerning intercourse with a slave woman.[77] The biblical law prescribes a minor penalty to a man who has intercourse with a slave woman designated for another man.[78] Since the woman is a slave, the issue is not adultery (Deut 22:23–7) but

---

[76] It is not evident why Milik suggests a connection to Ps 68:30 (*DJD XVIII*, 79).

[77] Lev 19:20 reads: "If a man has sexual relations with a woman who is a slave, designated for another man (והוא שפחה נחרפת לאיש)." חרופה in rabbinic literature denotes "betrothed" or "designated" (Jastrow, *Dictionary*, 500).

[78] Louis Epstein, *Marriage Laws in the Bible and the Talmud* (Cambridge, Mass.: Harvard University Press, 1942), 59. Because the maidservant is designated for someone else, the present master is only partially owner and therefore has no right to compensation; Jacob Milgrom, "The Bethrothed Slave-Girl, Lev 19:20–22," *ZAW* 89 (1977), 43–50. It is debated who the seducer is. Whereas one view holds that the man is the owner and the woman has been assigned to someone else, the majority hold that the seducer is someone other than the owner; see Philip Budd, *Leviticus* (The New Century Bible Commentary; Grand Rapids, Mich.: Eerdmans, 1996), 281.

property rights.⁷⁹ י[קחנה או לב]נו in line 16 may relate to acquiring a slave woman for a son, similar to Exod 21:9.⁸⁰

In line 15, between these apparent allusions to a slave woman, are the words [שבע שנים], seven years (as restored from 4Q266 12), followed by the introduction to a scriptural quotation, אמר [כאשר], "[as] he said." The reference to seven years is reminiscent of a law in 11QT LXIII 10–15, which paraphrases the law in Deut 21:10–14 on marrying a woman taken captive during war. In contrast to the biblical account, the Temple Scroll (TS) imposes seven years of probation on a captive woman before she may "touch your purity," תגע לכה בטהרה, and a full seven years before she may eat a "sacrifice of peace offering," וזבח שלמים לוא תואכל עד יעבורו שבע שנים.⁸¹ טהרה in this context in TS may pertain to the husband's pure food and also to other pure objects.⁸² Highlighting the reference to seven years in the two laws of D and TS, Baumgarten cannot see any connection between a slave woman and a captive, unless they both are presumed to be gentiles and therefore in need of an extended period of purification.⁸³ Nevertheless, the law in 4Q270 4 may refer specifically to gentile slaves, in light of another law about slaves in the early law code that alludes to the gentile origin of slaves. In prohibiting the sale of slaves to foreigners CD XII 10–11

---

⁷⁹Epstein, *Marriage Laws*, 50–1. Budd, on Lev 19:20 in *Leviticus*, 281.

⁸⁰Baumgarten points to a possible connection to Exod 21:9 (*DJD XVIII*, 154).

⁸¹For an analysis of this passage, see Yigael Yadin, *The Temple Scroll I–III* (Jerusalem: Israel Exploration Society, Archaeological Institute of the Hebrew University, Shrine of the Book, 1983) 2:285–6, 364–7; Schiffman, "Laws Pertaining to Women in the Temple Scroll," 218–19.

⁸²In sectarian writings, טהרה (often in the expression טהרת הרבים, "the purity of the many") pertains to pure food eaten in common by members (e.g., 1QS V 13; VI 16–21; VIII 24–25). Members were excluded from "the purity" if they violated the community rules (e.g., 1QS VI 25; VII 3; CD IX 21, 23). The term טהרה, however, carries a wide range of meanings and each specific occurrence has to be carefully analysed in its context. In 11QT, which does not reflect a sectarian perspective, טהרה denotes pure objects, sometimes pure food, but also purification and purity as a quality. On the usage of טהרה in 11QT, see Friedrich Avemarie, "'Tohorat Ha-Rabbim' and 'Maqsheh Ha-Rabbim': Jacob Licht Reconsidered," in *Legal Texts and Legal Issues*, 222–3. According to Jacob Milgrom, טהרה in 11QT LXIII 14 denotes the pure food of the husband ("Further Studies in the Temple Scroll," *JQR* 71 [1980/2], 104–5). Alternatively, Hempel links טהרה in 11QT LXIII 14 to table fellowship (*Laws*, 99). Brin considers the reference to טהרה in 11QT LXIII 14 a sectarian interpolation ("Divorce at Qumran," 236). For general studies on the term, see Saul Lieberman, "The Discipline in the So-Called Dead Sea Manual of Discipline," *JBL* 71 (1951) 199–206; Jacob Licht, *The Rule Scroll: A Scroll from the Wilderness of Judaea: 1QS, 1QSa, 1QSb, Text, Introduction, and Commentary* (Jerusalem: Bialik Institute, 1965 [Hebrew]), 294–303; "Some Terms and Concepts of Ritual Purity in The Qumran Writings," in *Studies in the Bible Presented to Professor M.H. Segal* (eds. J.M. Grintz and J. Liver; Publications of the Israel Society for Biblical Research 17; Jerusalem: Kiryat Sepher, 1964), 300–9.

⁸³Baumgarten, *DJD XVIII*, 154.

states, "because they entered with him into the covenant of Abraham." The expression "with him"— the master— suggests that the slaves were of non-Jewish origin.[84] If the law in 4Q270 4 pertains to a man taking a gentile slave woman as a wife/concubine, the text may impose a seven year probation period for a slave woman before she is fully included in all aspects of Jewish society and fully trusted in terms of purity.[85] Nevertheless, any connection between the laws remains speculative.

The relation of the last three lines (19–21) from three small fragments to the previous segment remains uncertain. ישכב עם (line 20) indicates that the topic still is sexual relations. If the topic still revolves around sexual relations with a slave woman, references to "his bread" and "sacred" [מן הקד[ש] לחמו (line 19) may be part of further restrictions to the woman's access to pure items. The reference to הש[מיני], "ei]ghth," if this is the correct reconstruction,[86] may refer to the first year the woman may partake of the sacrificial food. The last line (line 21) may read עולה "burnt offering," and could relate to the guilt offering prescribed for the man who has had sexual intercourse with a slave woman designated for someone else in Lev 19:22.[87] These suggestions, however, are only a few of several possibilities.

The law about the slave woman is but one law among several in the early law code that relates to slaves. A law from the Sabbath Code warns against provoking "his slave, his maidservant or his hired man," on the Sabbath (CD XI 12).[88] In this case, the concern is not for the well-being of the slaves, but for keeping the Sabbath peaceful. Finally, CD XII 10–11 regulates the trade of male and female slaves as part of the restrictions on trade of other property (clean animals and food products) to the gentiles. While clearly considered as property, the slaves' humanity is also

---

[84]See Lawrence Schiffman, *The Halakah at Qumran* (ed. Jacob Neusner; SJLA16; Leiden: Brill, 1975), 121; "Legislation Concerning Relations with Non-Jews in the Zadokite Fragments and in Tannaitic Literature," *RevQ* 11 (1983), 388–9; so also Hempel (*Laws*, 135).

[85]In addition, the period of seven years recalls the time of probation for anyone who transgressed the Sabbath rules (CD XII 5–6), which is part of an interpolation according to Hempel. She does not discuss its chronological relationship with the main literary layers (*Laws*, 190).

[86]On the photo few traces of the word are visible (Plate XXX).

[87]Leviticus 5 elaborates on guilt offerings. According to Lev 5: 7, 10, a burnt offering in the form of a pigeon is part of the sacrifices required for a poor person who cannot afford a costly animal.

[88]4Q270 6 v 16–17 omits שוכרו "his hired man"; see *DJD XVIII*, 161. Baumgarten explains that מרה, "to resist" or "to provoke," indicates that the rule aims at preventing "secular confrontations" on the Sabbath ("The Damascus Document [CD])," 49. According to Schiffman, the law prohibits urging slaves to work on the Sabbath (Exod 20:10) (*The Halakhah at Qumran*, 120–1). If Schiffman is correct, then also this law presumes that slaves are non-Jewish. He points out that Philo provides the same view (referring to *Spec. Laws* II, 66–8).

acknowledged by the inclusion in the "covenant with Abraham."[89] Notably, both the male and female slave are explicitly included in the covenant: "because *they* have entered," באו (XII 11). The several references to slaves in the early law make the law code unusual within the Scrolls, which rarely mention slaves.[90]

3.3.4.2 Conclusion

The use of female slaves for reproductive purposes and sexual pleasure was common in biblical times, according to texts such as Exod 21:7–11 and Lev 19:20–22.[91] These biblical passages may underlie the rules in the second half of 4Q270 4. Possibly, the law in 4Q270 4 elaborates upon Lev 19:20–22, concerning a man taking a slave woman designated for someone else, and imposes some kind of purity restrictions on the slave woman for seven years. Apart from these prescriptions, the halakhic opinion on the matter of sexual relations with slave women is not preserved.

3.4 A Text on Marital Arrangements: 4Q271 3 4b–15; 4Q270 5 14–21; 4Q267 7 12–14; 4Q269 9 1–8

3.4.1 Introduction

4Q271 3 4b–15 contains detailed rules for the arrangement of marriages, with a particular concern for the choice of bride and groom. The section is introduced by the formula ואשר אמר and is marked off from the previous segment by a *vacat*; the end of the passage is missing. Almost all of the text can be restored from parallel copies, and thus the content is fairly clear. There are similarities with 4QOrdinances[a] (4Q159), which are discussed below.

Four specific topics are dealt with in this section: (a) fraud in business transactions and marriage arrangements (lines 4b–9a); (b) criteria for the choice of a

---

[89]Hempel includes CD XII 6b–11a in the Halakhah stratum (*Laws*, 35,186). Davis includes the segment in CDS1 ("History," 14).

[90]4QHalakha A (4Q251) 8 1–2, paraphrasing Exod 21:26–7, legislates improvements for slaves injured by the owner; see *DJD XXXV*, 33–4. 4Q416 2 i–iii (4QInstruction[b]) sides with the poor as opposed to the wealthy, urging the poor man not to sell himself "for money," which may allude to slavery (ii 17). It is uncertain whether an ostracon found at Qumran refers to the gift of a slave. The original editors, Frank Moore Cross and Esther Eshel, suggested that a personal name, Hisdai, is the name of a slave given as gift to the community ("Ostraca from Khirbet Qumran," *IEJ* 47 [1997], 17–28). On slavery in the Scrolls, see Douglas Gropp, "Slavery," in *Encyclopedia of the Dead Sea Scrolls*, 2: 884–6.

[91]On the plight of female slaves, see Raymond Westbrook, "The Female Slave," in *Gender and Law in the Hebrew Bible and the Ancient Near East* (eds. Victor Matthews, Bernard Levinson and Tikva Frymer-Kensky; JSOTSup 262; Sheffield: Sheffield Academic Press, 1998), 214–38; Carolyn Pressler, "Wives and Daughters, Bond and Free: Views of Women in the Slave Laws of Exodus 21:2–11," in *Gender and Law in the Hebrew Bible and the Ancient Near East*, 147–72.

groom (lines 9b–10a); (c) prohibition against marrying a woman who has had non-marital sexual experience (lines 10b–12a); and (d) the case when the virginity of a prospective bride is disputed (lines 12b–15). The section on marital arrangements is preceded by a rule on the redemption of property for the Jubilee and a rule on transvestism (4Q271 3 1–4a). In addition to 4Q271 3 4b–15, I will briefly examine the fragment 4Q273 5, which likely relates to marital laws. This discussion appears at the end of this section (3.4.8).

3.4.2 THE TEXT: 4Q271 3 4B–15; PARALLELS: 4Q270 5 14–21 AND 10 1–2 UNDERLINED; 4Q267 7 12–14 ITALICS; 4Q269 9 1–8 DOTTED UNDERLINE[92]

4 vac וֹאשר אמר כי[תמכור]
5 [ממכר או קנה מיד]עֲמִיתך לוא תונו איש את עמיתו vac וזה פרוֹ[ש]
6 [ ]oooo[בכול אשר הוא יודע אשר ימצא]יודיענו[93 נתן]
7 [ ] וגם אל[94 ימכו]ר והוא יודע אשר הוא מועל בו באדם וּבֲבֲהֵמָה ואם
8 [את בתו יתן איש לאי]שׁ את כול מומיה יספר לו למה יביא עליו את משפט
9 הארור אשר אמ[ר משג]ה עור בדרך וגם אל יתנהה לאשר לוא הוכן לה כי
10 הוא כלאים ש[ו]ר וחמור ולבוש צמר ו(1)ופשתים יחדיו vac אל יבא איש
11 אשה בברית הקו[דש אש]ר ידעה לעשות מעשה במדבר ואשר ידעה
12 [מעשה בבית]אביה או אלמנה אשר נשכבה מאשר התארמלה וכול
13 [אשר עליה ש]ם רע בבתוליה בבית אביה אל יקחה איש כי אם
14 [בראות נשים]נאמנות וידעות ברורות ממאמר המבקר אשר על
15 [הרבים ואחר]יקחנה ובלוקחו אותה יעשה כמש[פ]ט [ולוא]יגיד עלי[ה]

4 vac And concerning what he said ['When you sell]
5 [anything to or buy anything from] your neighbour, you shall not defraud one another.' vac This is the expla[nation]
6 [let him inform him] of everything he knows that is found oooo [
   ]ogive
7 [and also he should not sel]l while he knows that he is wronging him, whether it concerns man or beast. And if
8 [a man gives his daughter to a ma]n (in marriage), let him disclose all her blemishes to him, lest he bring upon himself the judgement

---

[92] Double underline marks the overlap between 4Q270 5 10 and 4Q269 9.
[93] Following Qimron's reconstruction as reported by Baumgarten (*DJD XVIII*, 176).
[94] I am following Eibert Tigchelaar's suggestion that the small fragment 4Q270 10 should be placed to the right of 4Q270 5 because of partial overlapping with 4Q271 3 7–8. Fragment 10 contains letters from two lines. Line 1 reads]גם אל[(אל instead of אש as Baumgarten reads the word). Tigchelaar proposes the reconstruction [ימכור וגם אל], which corresponds to the lacuna at the beginning of 4Q271 3 7. See Tigchelaar, "More Identifications of Scraps and Overlaps," *RevQ* 19 (1999), 61–8

The Early Law Code

9 [of the curse which is sai]d (of the one) 'that makes the blind to wander out of the way.' And also, he should not give her to someone not established for her, for

10 [that is (like) *kila'yim*, (plowing with) o]x and ass and wearing wool and linen together. *vac* Let no man bring

11 [a woman into the ho]ly [covenant][95] who has had sexual experience so as to do an unseemly deed,[96] (whether) she had such

12 [experience in the home] of her father or (as) a widow who had sexual experience after she was widowed. And any

13 [woman upon whom there is a] bad [na]me in her maidenhood in her father's home, let no man take her, except

14 [upon examination] by reliable and knowledgeable [women] selected by command of the Examiner over

15 [the many. After]ward he may take her, and when he takes her he shall act in accordance with the l[a]w [and he shall not t]ell about [her]

This text provides an anthology of laws, drawing on Leviticus 25, and Deuteronomy 22 and 27. The link between marriage arrangements (line 4 ff) and the law on transvestism in the preceding section (lines 3b–4a) is found in Deuteronomy 22. This chapter of Deuteronomy includes a prohibition against cross dressing (Deut 22:5), a law on defamation of a virgin (Deut 22:13–19), and a prohibition against ploughing with two different animals and wearing clothes of a wool and linen mix (Deut 22:10–11).[97] 4Q271 3 also paraphrases laws from Lev 25:14 (concerning fraud) and Deut 27:18 (the curse for misleading the blind), as well as making other allusions to Leviticus.[98] 4Q159 2–4 6–10 also presents a law on transvestism (Deut 22:5) followed by a law on defamation of a virgin (based on Deut 22:13–19). The similarity between 4Q159 2–4 and 4Q271 3 suggests that collections of halahkic material based on biblical texts were circulating at the time of the composition of D.[99] Although the section on marital arrangements in 4Q271 3 forms a part of the Halakhah stratum, Hempel assigns the reference to the Examiner (4Q271 3 14b–15a) to the communal stratum.[100] The discussion below is divided into five topics related to

---

[95] For ברית as a possible reference to marriage, see 4QInstruction[a] (4Q415) 2 ii 7. Baumgarten points to Ezek 16:8 and Mal 2:14 (*DJD XVIII*, 177).

[96] ידעה literally, "she has known" (sexually); for woman as a subject see Gen 19:8; Num 31:17, 18, 35 (and possibly Ruth 3:3). John Kampen translates מעשה בדבר "unseemly deed," pointing to ערות דבר in Deut 24:1 (cf. *m. Git.* 9:10; *m. Ketub.* 3.5). See "The Matthean Divorce Texts Reexamined," in *New Qumran Texts and Studies*, 155–6.

[97] For Deuteronomy 22 as the exegetical basis, see Hempel, *Laws*, 68.

[98] On blemishes, see Lev 21:17; on virginity of a bride, see Lev 21:7, 13.

[99] Hempel, "4QOrd[a] (4Q159) and the Laws of the Damascus Document," 376.

[100] Hempel points to 4Q159 2–4, which preserves a similar interpretation of the law on the defamation of a bride in Deut 22:13–21 without ascribing any role to the Examiner. While the

marriage, following the subject matter in the text: (a) fraud, (b) choice of groom, (c) marital prohibitions, (d) physical examination, and (e) female experts.

3.4.3 FRAUD IN CONNECTION TO MARRIAGE

4Q271 3 4–5 paraphrases the biblical law regarding fraud in business transactions (Lev 25:14), followed by the formulaic expression [ש]וזה פרו, "this is the explanation."[101] Unfortunately, the exegesis of the Levitical law is not clear, due to the missing text. Nevertheless, the subsequent phrases in lines 6–7, as well as the parallel case of fraud in marital arrangements, provide good clues for determining the underlying meaning.[102] The point seems to be that in a business transaction the vendor is responsible for disclosing any defects in the object or the animal of which he is aware.

The end of line 7 begins a new clause, ואם "and if." The words in line 8, את כול מומיה יספר לו, "all her blemishes he should tell him," suggests that the context still concerns fraud, but the object is not clear. Baumgarten's reconstruction for the beginning of line 8: [את בתו יתן איש לאי]ש fits well in this context.[103] Just as a person must disclose all defects of an object in a business transaction, so too in marriage arrangements a person—likely the father—must disclose all the blemishes[104] of a woman prior to her betrothal or marriage.

The same requirement to reveal the blemishes of a bride is found in 4QInstruction[a] (4Q415) 11 6–7.[105] In this Wisdom text, the father is admonished to recount to the groom-to-be any blemishes his daughter might have. Otherwise, it is

---

rest of the passage on the arrangement of marriages is general in nature in 4Q271 3, the reference to the Examiner breaks this pattern (*Laws*, 65–70).

[101] The law on fraud in Lev 25:14 is connected to the Jubilee year. Although a law on the redemption of slaves in the Jubilee year precedes the segment on fraud (4Q271 3 1–2), there is no apparent association between the laws that pertain to the Jubilee year and those concerning fraud, since the reference to transvestism (lines 3–4) separates the two segments.

[102] Particularly noteworthy is the repetition of the verb ידע, which in line 6 refers to something that is found (probably a defect) and in line 7 to knowingly doing another person wrong.

[103] The next topic (line 9) concerns marriage arrangements and is connected with the previous case by וגם "and also he should not give her to someone not established for her." מומיה "her blemishes" in line 8 therefore refers to blemishes of a woman given away in marriage.

[104] מום refers to a variety of physical defects. In biblical Hebrew מום (or מואם) is a collective term that includes a wide range of physical defects for both humans and animals (e.g., Lev 21:17–23). Similarly, in the lists of physical defects in 1QSa II 5b–9a and 1QM VII 4–5 מום refers to bodily imperfections.

[105] See John Strugnell and Daniel Harrington, in consultation with Joseph Fitzmyer, *Qumran Cave 4 XXIV: Sapiential Texts, Part 2: 4QInstruction (Musar leMevin): 4Q415ff.* (DJD XXXIV; Oxford: Clarendon Press, 1999), 41–72.

like "stumbling in the darkness," an image strikingly similar to misleading the blind in 4Q271 3 9. The composite text reads (4QInstruction^a 11 6–7; parallel text from 4Q418a [4QInstruction^e]167 6 is underlined):

6 [כ]ול מומיה ספר לו ובגויתיה הבינה[ו   כי נגף]
7 באו[פ]ל[ ]תהיה לו <u>כמכשול לפניו</u> [ ]   [

6 [A]ll her blemishes recount to him and make [him] understand her bodily
   defects [   ] And it shall be stumbling
7 in the da[r]kness. [Then] she will be for him like a stumbling block in front of
   him.

The principle that demands revealing defects of a prospective bride is also found in *m. Qidd.* 2:5:[106]

> If he [betrothed a woman] on condition that she had no defects and defects were found in her, she has not become betrothed. If he wedded her without conditions and defects (מומין) were found in her, she is to be divorced without marriage settlement (כתובה). All blemishes that disqualify priests also disqualify women.[107]

In the first case, a betrothal is not valid if it was made on the condition that a woman has no defects. In the second case there are no conditions. Nevertheless, if any unseen blemishes are discovered, her punishment is divorce without receiving the *ketubah* (the marriage settlement promised to a woman in the marriage contract in the case of a divorce, which includes her dowry). To forfeit the *ketubah* would be a monetary loss for her whole family.[108] In D, in contrast, there is no mention of divorce. Instead the guilty person, in this case the father, would have a curse inflicted upon him, leaving the punishment in God's hands. Similarly, in 4Q415 no penalty is mentioned either, only the unfortunate consequences for the groom. In addition, both texts explicitly lay the responsibility for disclosing blemishes on the father, not the daughter herself.

It is possible that the law aims to protect the daughter from a quick divorce, since the husband would find out about hidden blemishes after the wedding. Nevertheless, neither D nor 4Q415 displays any concern about the daughter, and instead seeks to protect the groom from any unpleasant discoveries after the wedding. Furthermore, the

---

[106] Gershon Brin draws attention to the similarity between the law in 4Q271 3 and the Mishnah (he points to *m. Ketub.* 7:7–10; *t. Ketub.* 7:8–10; *t. B.Bat.* 4:5–7); "שתי הוראות בעניני נישואין מקומראן" ("Two Instructions on Marital Matters from Qumran"), *Bet Miqra* 142 (year 40) Nisan 5755 (1995) [Hebrew], 224–31.

[107] Cf. *m. Ketub.* 7:7

[108] See "Appendix," note 8, in Philip Blackman, *Mishnayot Nashim*, 490.

texts overtly favour the groom by requiring that any defects of a prospective bride alone be revealed but not those of the groom.[109]

A woman is seen as property in the marital transfer from the father to the husband. By presenting the marital arrangements as a business transaction, D treats the woman as a commodity, and a woman with hidden blemishes is viewed as damaged goods.[110] It is not the woman who is responsible for disclosing any blemishes, but her father, and he is subject to the punishment of a curse. The non-liability on the woman's part makes clear that she is not treated as a legal person, but as someone fully dependent on her father.[111] This does not necessarily mean that she is a minor. Instead, it seems that a woman simply passed from living in "her father's house" (lines 12 and 13) to living with her husband, moving from being under the authority of the father to being under the authority of the husband.[112]

3.4.4 THE CHOICE OF A SUITABLE GROOM

The father is responsible for not giving his daughter to someone not established for her: אל יתנהה לאשר לוא הוכן לה (line 9). An improper marital match is strongly condemned as *kila'yim*, the improper mixing of two different kinds (Deut 22:9–11; Lev 19:19). Since כון is not usually used in the passive with reference to persons, but rather to objects that are established or prepared, it is not clear what the term specifically denotes in this case.[113] There are several proposals in recent scholarship. Drawing on various rabbinic sources, Gershon Brin interprets the phrase as a demand to find a compatible groom who suits the woman's qualities; that is, there is to be no incompatibility between the two for physical or social reasons, discrepancies in age or education. Also, by implication this means that the match is already established in

---

[109] According to the Mishnah there are cases when the defects of the husband are grounds for a divorce: e.g., skin-disease, polypus, and a foul body odour. Nevertheless, in these cases the rhetoric is very different; he is forced to divorce her, it is not "an acquisition of error" (*m. Ketub.* 7:10).

[110] A similar perspective surfaces in *m. Ketub.* 7: 8.

[111] Though the reference to her "father" in the text is based on a reconstruction, it is clear that a male person, and not the woman, is subject to the punishment.

[112] For a similar perspective in rabbinic literature, see *m. Qidd.* 1:1–5; 2:3; Ilan points out that the acquisition of a wife, a Hebrew slave, a Canaanite slave, large cattle, secured and unsecured property, are described with identical formulas (*Jewish Women*, 88). Wegner claims that "the procedure for acquiring a wife...treats marriage as the formal sale and purchase of a woman's sexual function—a commercial transaction in which a man pays for the bride's virginity just as for any other object of value" (*Chattel or Person?* 42–5).

[113] See e.g., CD V 12 ("against the statutes of God's covenant, saying *they are not established,*" נבונו) ; CD X 22 ("let no man eat on the Sabbath except for that which *has been prepared,*" המוכן); 1QS VIII 5 ("council of community *established,* נבונה, in truth"); 1QS XI 11 ("All which is occurring he [God] *establishes,* יכינו, by his design"). In 1QH there are many references to what is established by God: his glory, his plans, his congregation, etc.

heaven.¹¹⁴ Baumgarten makes two suggestions; arguing that the expression most likely refers to "some overt incompatibility," such as a big age difference (*b. Yebam*. 44a), he also points to the notion that a spouse is prepared by destiny in Tob 6:18. By interpreting *kila'yim* as an allusion to a woman having sexual relationship with two different men, Aaron Shemesh argues that the wording הוכן denotes someone established for the woman through betrothal.¹¹⁵ The law then prohibits the father from giving the woman in marriage to someone other than the man to whom she is already betrothed. However, it is hard to imagine that such a command would be necessary since marriage with a woman betrothed to another man would be illegal.¹¹⁶

Any explanation of the pericope should take 4QMMT B 75–82 into consideration. This text likens some kind of improper marital union among priests and laymen alike with כלאים. The segment gives three examples of כלאים from Deuteronomy 22 (mating with different species, clothes of mixed stuff, sowing the field and vineyard with mixed seeds).¹¹⁷ Qimron and Strugnell argue that the illicit union in this text concerns intermarriage between priests and Israelites and point to evidence that priests in the Second Temple period often married women from the same family.¹¹⁸ The metaphoric use of *kila'yim* in 4QMMT suggests that improper marital

---

¹¹⁴Brin, "שתי הוראות בעניני נישואין מקומראן," 224–31.

¹¹⁵Shemesh suggests that sexual relations prior to marriage were common between a betrothed couple. He interprets the imagery of plowing a field with two different animals as the woman/the field, being plowed/having sexual relationship, with two animals/two men—the one to whom she was promised and with whom she has had sexual relations and the other to whom her father gives her; see Shemesh, "4Q271.3: A Key to Sectarian Matrimonial Law," *JJS* (1998), 244–63. But the imagery of plowing with two kinds of animals does not support Shemesh' interpretation: plowing does not allude to fertilization, and the animals are yoked together, thus only plowing once. If two different sexual partners had been the underlying issue, surely a better image would have been the prohibition of sowing the vineyard with two different seeds (Deut 22:9), which is another example of *kila'yim*. Moreover, the reference to wearing wool and linen together (line 10) does not evoke any allusion to two partners but to an improper mixing.

¹¹⁶The similarity between Deut 22:22 and Deut 22:23–24 suggests that sexual relations with a woman betrothed to another was considered adultery.

¹¹⁷Shemesh interprets the slight difference in examples given of *kila'yim* in 4QMMT (especially, mating of different animals) compared to 4QD (plowing of two animals) as evidence for two different underlying situations: inter-marriage (4QMMT) versus two sexual partners (D); "4Q271.3: A Key to Sectarian Matrimonial Law," 261–3. Nevertheless, the reference to wearing clothes of mixed stuff occurs in both documents.

¹¹⁸The editors point to 1 Chr 23:13 as a plausible biblical basis for the halakhah. In addition, they suggest that the commandment to the High Priest to marry someone מעמיו may have been interpreted as "from his own tribe (or family)" rather than "his people." The sectarians may have extended the statute to all priests. Another possibility is that זונה in Lev 21:7, 14 was interpreted as an outsider rather than "harlot"; see E. Qimron and J. Strugnell. *Qumran Cave 4.V. Miqsat Ma'ase ha-Torah* (DJD X; Oxford: Clarendon Press, 1994), 172–3.

matching based on descent may also be the key concern in D. It may also be relevant that 4QTestament of Qahat ar (4Q542) uses the term כילאין with reference to priests of doubtful lineage (1 i 5–6).[119]

Second Temple Judaism was highly concerned with genealogical purity.[120] Priests, more than others, had to be careful with regard to the lineage of their spouses.[121] Often, therefore, children of priests married into other priestly families, or married within the same family.[122] Endogamous marriages were common among the general population as well, not only because of genealogical concerns, but also in order to keep property within the family.[123]

Baumgarten proposes that the text instead condemns inter-marriage between Israelites and non-Israelites; see *DJD X*, 54–7 especially n.75; 171–75. The editors allow for other plausible reconstructions: "it is possible that more that one type of illegal marriage was included under the heading" (*DJD X*, 171 n.178a).

[119] Émile Puech, *Qumran Grotte 4.XXII. Textes Araméens Première Partie 4Q529–549* (DJD XXXI; Oxford: Clarendon Press, 2001), 257–82; André Caqout, "Grandeur et pureté du sacerdoce: Remarques sur le Testament de Qahat (4Q542)," in *Solving Riddles and Untying Knot: Biblical, Epigraphic, and Semetic Studies in Honor of Jonas C. Greenfield* (eds. Z. Zevit, Seymout Gitin, and Michaeld Sokoloff; Winona Lake, Ind.: Eisenbrauns, 1995), 39–44.

[120] See Adolph Büchler, "Purity and Family Impurity in Jerusalem before 70 C.E.," in *Studies in Jewish History* (London: Oxford University Press, 1956), 64–98. M. Broshi and A. Yardeni claim that 4QList of Netinim (4Q340)—a document consisting of the right side of six lines of a column—is a "list of blemished people unfit for marriage, a negative genealogical list"; see Qumran *Cave 4. XIV Parabiblical Texts, Part 2* (eds. M. Broshi et al.; DJD XIX; Oxford: Clarendon Press, 1995), 81–4. For a critique of this interpretation, see Shaye Cohen, "Hellenism in Unexpected Places," in *Hellenism in the Land of Israel,* (eds. John Collins and Gregory Sterling; Notre Dame, Ind.: University of Notre Dame Press, 2001), 217–23.

[121] The Tannaim demanded strict investigation into the genealogy of a prospective bride of a priest (*m. Qidd*. 4:4–6). The Damascus Document shows a particular concern for the genealogical purity of priests (4Q266 5 ii 4–14); see Baumgarten, "The Disqualification of Priests," 502–13.

[122] See Ilan, *Jewish Women*, 72–4.

[123] Ibid., 75–9. According to Philo, it was important that the bride and groom were relatives, or at least from the same tribe, so that the goods in the form of dowry would not be lost from that tribe (*Spec*. 2.125–6). For the custom of endogamous marriages, see K. C. Hanson, "The Herodians and Mediterranean Kinship, Part I: Genealogy and Descent," *BTB* 19 (1989), 75–84; "The Herodians and Mediterranean Kinship, Part II: Marriages and Divorce," *BTB* 19 (1989), 142–51. For the prevalence of endogamous marriages in the eastern Mediterranean society in the Second Temple Period, see K. C. Hanson and Douglas Oakman, *Palestine in the Time of Jesus: Social Structure and Social Conflicts* (Minneapolis: Fortress Press, 1998), 32–4. Ilan points out that marriage between cousins was common in Palestine (*Jewish Women*, 72–3). For categorisation of family types in general, see Emmanuel Todd, *The Explanation of Ideology: Family Structures and Social Systems* (Oxford: Blackwell, 1985).

The Apocryphal books Tobit and Judith, as well as Jubilees, testify to the practice of marriage between members of the close kinship group.[124] In light of the authoritative status of Jubilees both in D and at Qumran, where fragments of the document have been discovered, it is particularly noteworthy that Jubilees often speaks of close family relationships between spouses when Genesis does not state their relationship or does not mention the names of the wives.[125] By making the family relations explicit, Jubilees both legitimizes and promotes endogamous marriages. The book of Judith states that the deceased husband of Judith belonged "to her [Judith's] tribe and family" (Jdt 8:2). In the book of Tobit, the main couples (Tobit and Anna, Tobias and Sarah) are relatives (Tob 1:9; 6:12, 16–18).[126] Using an expression similar to הוכן, Tob 6:18 states that the marriage between Tobias and Sarah has been arranged in heaven; in the words of the angel Raphael, "she was set apart (חליקא) for you before the world was made."[127] At the same time, it is their close family relationship that makes them predestined for each other (Tob 6:16, 18).[128] The view that marriages are divinely prearranged also appears in Gen 24:14, where Isaac's servant prays to God that he will find the woman "You [God] have appointed" (הכחת) for Isaac. In this case as well, the marital predestination is manifested in the spouses' close family relations (Gen 24:15, 48).

Since the phraseology for predestined marriages in Tobit, Genesis and 4Q271 is similar, it is logical to surmise that the close family relation that Tobit and Genesis express by the notion of predestination is implied in D as well. I therefore propose that 4Q271 3 9–10 commands a father to find a man for his daughter who is from her close kin-group. Accordingly, *kil'ayim* in this context denotes marital unions between members of unrelated families. This symbolic meaning of *kil'ayim* in D comes close to its use in 4QMMT, where the term likely denotes intermingling between priestly and non-priestly families.

The legislation in D that sternly rejects marriage between a niece and her uncle, as reflected in the communal stratum of D as well as in the Admonition (CD V 7b–11a), does not conflict with a command to find a spouse within the close kinship group,

---

[124] Cf. biblical books, e.g., Ruth.

[125] Betsy Halpern-Amaru argues that Jubilees' concern with genealogical purity is associated with a view of Israel as a "priest-like" community; see *The Empowerment of Women in the Book of Jubilees* (SJSJ 60; Leiden: Brill, 1999), 147–59. See also Hanson, "The Herodians and Mediterranean Kinship, Part II: Marriages and Divorce," 143.

[126] Raphael's speech to Tobias begins with a reference to Tobit's command "to take a wife from your father's house" (Tob 6:16) and ends: "When Tobias heard the words of Raphael and learned that she was his kinswoman, related through his father's lineage, he loved her very much and his heart was drawn to her" (Tob 6:18).

[127] The Aramaic Tobit from Qumran (4QTobit[b ar] 4Q197) preserves the verse that speaks of Sarah being assigned for Tobias and uses the verb חלק: לך היא חליקא, 4Q197 4 ii 17; see Fitzmyer, "Tobit," in *DJD XIX*, 48–50.

[128] Cf. Tob 3:16–17.

since other marriages between relatives, such as that between cousins, are not prohibited in D.[129] The practice of endogamous marriages is one aspect of the social structure of the Eastern Mediterranean world in antiquity in which the kinship group was the essential social domain. The preference for endogamous marriages in the circles behind the early law code of D fits with an origin of the law code among priests.

3.4.5 Prohibition Against Marrying a Woman Who Has Had Sexual Experience Outside of Marriage

A *vacat* in 4Q271 3 10 delineates the passage on sexual experience as a subsection. Unlike 4Q271 3, 4Q270 5 19 has an additional *vacat* before או אלמנה (or [as] a widow), thereby marking a difference between the case of a widow and that of an unmarried woman. The topic in lines 4Q271 3 10–15 can be divided into two subcategories: (a) prohibition against marrying any woman with extra-marital sexual experience and (b) the requirement of examination prior to marriage in the case of a woman whose virginity is disputed. The relative length and detail of the prohibition against marrying women with non-marital sexual experiences testifies to its importance.

The halakhah of 4Q271 3 10b–12 prohibits a man from marrying a woman who has engaged in sexual relations outside of marriage, whether while living in her parents' house or as a widow. This list of women that a man is prohibited from marrying is reminiscent of similar lists found in the Holiness Code for priests; Lev 21:7–8a states, "They shall not marry a prostitute or a woman who has been defiled (אשה זנה וחללה לא לקחו); neither shall they marry a woman divorced from her husband. For they are holy to their God." The marital law for the High Priest is even more limiting: "He shall marry only a woman who is a virgin. A widow or a divorced woman, or a woman who has been defiled, a prostitute (וחללה זנה), these he shall not marry" (Lev 21:13–14a).[130] In contrast to Leviticus 21, 4Q271 3 does not prohibit marriage with a divorcee. Still, the laws in 4Q271 3 are likely influenced by the prohibitions in Leviticus 21 against marrying a woman who could be seen as a defiled woman or a *zonah*.[131] The mention of a widow in 4Q271 3 is similar to the

---

[129] Marriage between paternal cousins and a man and his niece are the most common forms of endogamous marriages in the Herodian family; see Hanson and Oakman, *Palestine in the Time of Jesus*, 34. Marriage between cousins is common in Jubilees; Halpern-Amaru, *The Empowerment of Women*, 148–9.

[130] Ezekiel extended the prohibition for the High Priest against marrying a widow to all priests, but allowed for the marriage to a widow of another priest (Ezek 44:22). The Mishnah follows the laws of Leviticus 21 and not Ezekiel 44 with regard to a widow (e.g., *m. Yebam.* 6:2–5).

[131] Shemesh points out the parallel halakhic view of Rabbi Eleazar (*Sifra*, Emor, pereq 1). Whereas the rabbis in general understood זונה as a promiscuous woman who engaged in casual

proscription for the High Priest, but, unlike the Levitical laws, D prohibits a man from marrying a widow *only* if she has had sexual relations after she became a widow, in other words, someone who could be described as a *zonah*.[132] The preoccupation with the sexual history of a widow demonstrates a desire to go beyond what is required in biblical law in order to strive for moral perfection.

Although the requirement of virginity for a young bride and chastity for a widow corresponds to general societal views, this conversion of general practice into codified law for all men—priests and laity alike—is unique.[133] The societal views that greatly value the virginity of an unmarried woman are part of an honour and shame system typical of the Mediterranean world in antiquity.[134]

This passage on marital arrangements typifies the traditional double standard imposed on male and female sexuality. The imbalance is particularly blatant in the subsequent law, which addresses the situation of doubtful virginity in a prospective bride. A man is prohibited from marrying a woman with a "bad name in her maidenhood in her father's house" (line 13), except, כי אם, if she is examined by reliable and knowledgeable women (lines 14–15); then (if she is exonerated) he may take her (line 15). The expression ש[ם] רע בבתולה בבית אביה (a bad [na]me in her maidenhood in her father's home) is similar to Deut 22:19, which is part of the law about slandering a virgin of Israel: כי הוציא שם רע על בתולת ישראל, "because he has brought a bad name onto a virgin of Israel."

Deut 22:13–21 concerns a husband who, after the consummation of the marriage, claims that his wife had not been a virgin. The text stipulates that the case should be tried before the Elders to whom the woman's parents must provide evidence of virginity, that is, showing blood stains on the sheets. If it turns out that the husband wrongfully slandered a "virgin of Israel" he shall pay a fine to her father—since it is *his* honour that he has damaged— and then be punished by whipping. As a final consequence, the husband is prohibited from ever divorcing the woman. If, however, the man is right, the woman should be stoned to death "because she committed a

---

sexual relations with several men, R. Eleazar defined the זונה as any woman who had engaged in sexual intercourse outside of marriage; see Shemesh, "4Q271.3: A Key to Sectarian Matrimonial Law," 246–7

[132] Talmudic rabbis deemed a widow who had sexual experience after widowhood a "prostitute" and as such she belonged to the category of prohibited women for regular priests to marry; *b. Yebam.* 59a–61a.

[133] Shemesh notes that this halakhah applies a priestly law to the "nation as a whole" ("4Q271.3 A Key to Sectarian Matrimonial Law," 248).

[134] A clear expression of this sentiment appears in Tob 3:14 with Sarah exclaiming "You know, O Master, that I am innocent of any defilement with a man, and that I have not disgraced my name or the name of my father in the land of my exile." For general studies on this value system, see Victor Matthews and Don Benjamin, "Social Sciences and Biblical Studies," *Semeia* 68 (1994), 7–21; John Chance, "The Anthropology of Honor and Shame: Culture, Values, and Practice," *Semeia* 68 (1994), 139–49.

disgraceful act in Israel by prostituting herself in her father's house" (Deut 22:21).[135] The execution of a non-virginal, "deceitful," bride should be seen as a community's response to the perceived threat from female sexuality that conflicts with the established norms and is outside of society's control. Just as apostates who threaten the community order and boundaries deserve death (Deut 13:2–19), so do women who have sexual relations outside of societal norms.

The law regarding slandering a virgin in Deut 22:13–21 is paraphrased in 11QT LXV 7–15 with no major deviations from the biblical text.[136] The law is also summarized with a minimum of details and some alterations in 4Q159 2–4 8–10. As in 4Q271 3 14, this passage uses the word נאמנות in the context of examining the bride. Though the original editor translated the word "trustworthiness," Jeffrey Tigay proposes the reconstruction, "trustworthy [women]," which is likely in light of 4Q271 3.[137] 4Q159 2–4 8–10 reads:

---

[135] The case belongs to a unit of six laws related to sexual relations (Deut 22:13–29), which imposes the death penalty for both parties in the case of adultery and consensual sex with a betrothed virgin, as well as for the one who violates a betrothed virgin. The basic principle is that female sexuality never belongs to the woman but to the man who possesses it (the father, the man to whom she is betrothed, the husband). The biblical laws provide some security for the woman in that it distinguishes between the woman's consent or lack thereof; see Carolyn Pressler, "Sexual Violence and Deuteronomic Law," *A Feminist Companion to Exodus to Deuteronomy* (ed. Athalya Brenner; Sheffield: Sheffield Academic Press, 1994), 102–12. Tikva Frymer-Kensky argues that although Deuteronomy transfers control from the father to the public sphere (the Elders), the ultimate control is in the hands of the father who could easily falsify the evidence to save his and his daughter's honour ("Deuteronomy," in *The Women's Bible Commentary*, 56–7). Noticing the tendency to transfer authority from the family to the public sphere, Louis Stulman argues that Deuteronomy in this way places "safeguards or controls on the authority of the paterfamilias." A similar case is that of the rebellious son whose fate is determined by local judges, not the father (Deut 21:18–21); see Stulman, "Enchroachment in Deuteronomy: An Analysis of the Social World of the D Code," *JBL* 109 (1990), 613–32. This unequivocal demand for execution—"purging" the evil from the community—of the guilty parties who engage in sexual relations that go contrary to social norms, represents a change in the criminal code compared to earlier practice. Anthony Phillips contends that at an earlier stage, adultery on the part of the woman did not necessarily result in her being killed. Instead, divorce was an option (Jer 3:8; however, cf. Gen 38). Similarly, Phillips suggests that the husband, who suspected his bride of not being a virgin, prior to Deuteronomy, would simply have sued the father for the bride price (*Ancients Israel's Criminal Law*, 121).

[136] Although the reference to the death penalty of the woman in Deut 22:20–1 is not preserved in the paraphrase in 11QT LXV, it was likely originally part of the damaged beginning of the next column. For a detailed account, see Schiffman, "Laws Pertaining to Woman in the Temple Scroll," 220–2.

[137] The text is published by John M. Allegro in *Qumran Cave 4* (DJD V; Oxford: Clarendon Press, 1968), 8. I follow the corrected readings by John Strugnell ("Notes en Marge du Volume V des 'Discoveries in the Judean Desert of Jordan'," *RevQ* 26 [1970], 178) and

8 כי יוצי איש שם רע על בתולת ישראל אם ב[ ] קחתו אותה יואמר ובקרוה] נשים[
9 נאמנות ואם לוא כחש עליה והומתה ואם ב[שקר]ענה בה ונענש שני מנים[ולוא]
10 ישלח כול ימיו כול] [אשר]

> If a man slanders (lit. brings up a bad name upon) a virgin of Israel, if b[ ] when he married her, let him say so. And trustworthy [women] shall examine her/it, [9] and if he has not lied about her, she shall be executed. But if he has testified against her false[ly] , he shall be fined two minas, [10] and he shall [not] divorce (her) all of his days. All [ ] who [

This passage affirms the Deuteronomic law, including the death penalty for the guilty woman, but alters the process radically by prescribing different means of investigation which leave the father out of the scenario altogether.[138] 4Q159 insists that the woman should be subjected to an examination by "trustworthy women." Tigay concludes that this refers to a physical exam and supports his claim by providing examples from different cultures and time periods of a similar practice of vaginal examinations to establish virginity.[139] While recognizing the problems and uncertainties involved in such a test, he still concludes that such an exam is a "far more reliable test than examining a cloth."[140] However, since it is not possible to prove with any certainty that a woman is a virgin *before* her first sexual intercourse (as will be discussed below), the assumption that an examination *after* sexual intercourse can provide some indication of a woman's prior virginal status, depending on the "sophistication of the examiners," as Tigay claims, is simply wrong.[141] The means of investigation has changed in 4Q159, but the underlying principles of injustice, and the

---

Jeffrey Tigay's reconstruction of ובקרוה] נשים[נאמנות (and trustworthy [women] shall examine her/it); see "Examination of the Accused Bride in 4Q159: Forensic Medicine at Qumran," *JANES* 22 (1993), 129–34.

[138] Unlike the biblical law, the husband is not flogged, only fined and prohibited from divorcing the wife.

[139] See discussion by Tigay, "Examination of the Accused Bride," 131. Witnesses are used in cases related to women's chastity according to the Mishnah, which takes for granted that both the parties involved are questioned: *m. Ketub.* 1:5–7; 2:6, 9; see also Wegner, *Chattel or Person?* 22–3.

[140] Tigay, "Examination of The Accused Bride," 133; in this opinion he is followed by Shemesh who states concerning the law in 4Q159 2–4: "it seems that these women's expertise actually enabled them to determine whether the present sexual act was truly the girl's first, or whether she had previously had intercourse" ("4Q271 3: A Key to Sectarian Matrimonial Law," 254).

[141] Still, he acknowledges that "there is no absolutely certain way to prove that a recent act of coitus was not a girl's first" ("Examination of The Accused Bride," 133).

promotion of a humiliating investigation for women based on ineffective "science," remains.[142]

The appearance of the word נאמנות (trustworthy) in 4Q271 3 and 4Q159 2–4 within a similar context is a striking parallel that presupposes literary or oral dependency, but it is hard to determine which tradition precedes the other. At any rate, 4Q271 3 describes a different case altogether compared to 4Q159 2–4 and its biblical *Vorlage*. Whereas Deut 22:13–22 and 4Q159 2–4 prescribe legal procedures in a virginity suit *after* the wedding, the case in 4Q271 3 concerns a situation *before* the wedding. It appears that the main purpose of the halakhah in 4Q271 3 is to ensure that the situation depicted in Deut 22:13–22 is avoided. If there is a suspicion that the prospective bride is not a virgin, the halakhah demands that the woman be examined prior to the wedding to settle the matter. Since the virginity, or lack thereof, of a woman is established prior to marriage, execution is not a possible outcome. Instead of facing an accusation that could lead to her death, the woman's reputation is at stake in the scenario depicted in 4Q271 3, which is still a very serious issue. A good name was crucial for the woman, since a bad reputation would spoil her chances of getting married and would bring shame to her family, the father in particular.[143]

The last preserved sentence in 4Q271 3 commands the husband to act in accordance with the law "when he takes her," and also possibly to refrain from slandering the bride: [ולוא] יגיד עלי[ה] "and he shall [not] tell about [her]," after which the text breaks off. A provision that prohibits a husband from accusing a bride of not being a virgin after she has already been exonerated appears redundant, and there may be another meaning that is now lost.

In spite of its provision to subject women to a humiliating examination, the law regarding the bride with a "bad name" represents an improvement in the legal situation for women in the case where she is suspected of not being a virgin. Of

---

[142] In comparison, Mishnah gives evidence of the continuous practice of virginity suits by husbands in courts; *m. Ketub.* 1:1 reads, "A virgin should be married on a Wednesday and a widow on a Thursday, for in towns the court sits twice in the week, on Mondays and on Thursdays; so if the husband would lodge a virginity suit he may forthwith go in the morning to the court." *M. Sanh.* 1:1 recognises the non-virginity suit as a capital case. The gravity of an accusation of non-virginity is evident in *m. 'Arak.* 3:5, which imposes double the fine (to the father) for slander compared to rape of an unbetrothed virgin, as Archer points out (*Her Price*, 59).

[143] See, for example, the Aramaic Levi[b] 4Q213a 3–4 (*Qumran Cave 4. XVII: Parabiblical Texts*, Part 3 [eds. G. J. Brooke, J. J. Collins, et al.; DJD XXII; Oxford: Clarendon Press, 1996], 33–5) which describes how a woman has "desecrated her name and the name of her father" and "shamed all her brothers." Unfortunately it is not known what sin this woman has committed, but some kind of sexual transgression is likely. The editors suggest that the woman is Dinah. But Dinah is not blamed (thankfully) for being raped in Genesis (34:1–31), Test Levi, or Jubilees 30, and it is unlikely that she would be accused here either. For the general anxiety over the unchastity of daughters, see Ben Sira 7:24; 26:10–12; 42:9–12.

course, a husband could still raise an accusation against the woman after the wedding if she had not been examined beforehand. However, the purpose of the law was likely to discourage husbands from accusing their new brides after the wedding, thus saving women from facing the death penalty.[144] An additional motive behind the law was surely to "save" men from defiling themselves with a *zonah*.

3.4.6 PHYSICAL EXAMINATION

4Q271 3 12b–14 prescribes an investigative physical examination on a woman by "reliable women," just as in 4Q159 2–4.[145] 4Q271 3 14 is distinctive in its insistence that the women be "knowledgeable," referring to them as נשים] נאמנות וידעות (reliable and knowledgeable). It is likely that these women investigated whether or not the hymen was intact. Roman medical writers from the second century C.E. confirm that the existence of a hymen in the vulvae of virgins was common knowledge in antiquity. Soranus disputes the popular belief that intercourse or menstruation ruptured the vaginal membrane.[146] The uterus was envisioned as an upside down jar, with the mouth at the bottom. Amulets, worn by women from all societal classes, reflect the belief that the womb was closed by a hymen which was subsequently opened with sexual intercourse.[147]

The Mishnah records several virginity suits. While the non-virginity of the woman is stated as a fact in these cases, the discussion centers on how the hymen of a woman

---

[144] It is highly unlikely that a woman would face the death penalty if she were discovered to be a non-virgin prior to the wedding. In order for a premarital sexual relation to be a capital crime, the woman has to be betrothed (Deut 22: 23–4). 4Q271 3 10–12 provides stipulations concerning choosing a bride prior to both betrothal and marriage.

[145] בראות in line 14 (reconstructed from 4Q270 5 21) denotes observation by the women. Similarly, ראה refers to the examination by priests of the discolouring of a person's skin and hair in 4Q266 6 i 4, 10 in the context of skin disease.

[146] Soranus, *Gynaikeia* 1.16–17. Parallel to the Hippocratics, Soranus considers the existence of a hymen in a woman's vagina an abnormality that should be removed in order for conception to take place (*Gyn*. 2.33); see Guilia Sissa, "Maidenhood Without Maidenhead: The Female Body in Ancient Greece," in *Before Sexuality: The Construction of the Erotic Experience in the Ancient Greek* (eds. David Halperin et al.; Princeton N.J.: Princeton University Press, 1990), 356. For a description of the general knowledge of virginity reflected in Roman medical literature as well as in Patristic sources, see Gillian Clark, *Women in Late Antiquity: Pagan and Christian Life-Styles* (Oxford: Clarendon Press: 1993), 73–6.

[147] Female amulets depicting a sealed jar have been discovered from all societal classes. These reflect a fear of an open womb, with the seal representing a replacement of an earlier seal, lost with sexual activity, which was crucial to close the uterus sufficiently to ensure successful pregnancies; see Ann Ellis Hansson, "The Medical Writer's Woman," in *Before Sexuality: The Construction of the Erotic Experience in the Ancient Greek*, 324–6.

was ruptured.[148] The Rabbis knew of cases where the hymen of a girl had been accidentally ruptured without sexual intercourse, which they called מוכת עץ "injured by a piece of wood."[149] Thus, the existence of a thin vaginal membrane in young girls was common knowledge. In both the Mishnah and the Talmud the rabbis distinguished between the full virginity of pre-pubescent girls and a partial virginity when the woman reached puberty, assuming that with the onset of menstruation some of the hymen would disintegrate.[150] In addition, the Babylonian Talmud reveals a familiarity with cases not only of virgins who have ruptured hymens, but also of the reverse, women with intact hymens in spite of sexual experience.[151]

Patristic writers knew of the practice of vaginal inspection by which a midwife looked for the hymen to authenticate virginity. Augustine, Ambrose and Cyprian show contempt for this practice.[152] The Protoevangelium of James (second century C.E.) records how Salome, the midwife, performs a physical examination on Mary after the birth of Jesus, only to discover that she is still a virgin with the membrane intact (19–20). These second century C.E. sources and later patristic writings testify to the practice of midwives performing physical examinations on women in order to determine their virginity (or lack thereof).

---

[148] *M. Ketub.* 1:1–7; subsequent traditions in the Talmuds show an increased awareness of the possibility that women do not necessarily bleed at their first sexual intercourse (*b. Ketub.* 10 a–b; *y. Ketub.* 1:1, 25a). Some sages also question the husbands' expertise in knowing when they experience an "open door," a euphemism for ruptured hymen (*b. Ketub.* 10a–b). One innovative way of testing the virginity of women demanded that women sit on wine-casks to see whether the odour of the wine would penetrate—likely through the mouth—in which case they would not be virgins (*b. Ketub.* 10a–b; cf. *b. Yebam.* 60b). This is based on the assumption that with sexual intercourse any barrier (i.e, the hymen) between the vagina and the mouth would be destroyed. For a discussion of these passages, see Tal Ilan, *Mine and Yours are Hers: Retrieving Women's History from Rabbinic Literature* (Leiden: Brill, 1997), 190–9.

[149] E.g., *m. Yebam.* 6:4.

[150] See *m. Ketub.* 1:3; according to *m. Yebam.* 6:4 any damage to the vaginal membrane would render the woman ineligible to be the wife of the High Priest (she was technically not considered a virgin any more). The High Priest should not marry a woman who had reached maturity, i.e., 12.5 years; presumably the onset of menstruation would render her less of a virgin. This line of reasoning becomes very clear in *b. Yebam.* 59a.

[151] Ilan traces a tradition in the Babylonian Talmud of rabbis who dismiss husbands' accusations in virginity suits (*Mine and Yours are Hers*, 191–9).

[152] Augustine recounts how a clumsy midwife can injure the virginal membrane; see *The City of God* I 18 (vol. 8 of *Fathers of the Church* [Washington: Catholic University of America Press, 1947-]). Ambrose vehemently disputes the benefit of such examinations; see *Letters to Bishops* 32, *Letter to Syagrius* (vol. 26 of *Fathers of the Church*). Cyprian believes a midwife can be mistaken in her assessment; see *Epistula ad Pomponium de virginibus* PL 4.375-83 (*To Pomponius, Concerning some Virgins*, Letter 4 in vol. 51 of *Fathers of the Church*). John Chrysostom claims that tests by midwives were common (*That Women under Rule should not Cohabit with Men*; PG 47.516.2).

From a medical point of view, although an intact hymen may be taken as indicative of virginity, it is not solid proof, since the hymen does not necessarily rupture during intercourse. Conversely, the loss of the hymen is not proof of non-virginity since the hymen may rupture due to physical activity (running around, jumping, etc.) or by insertion of something into the vagina. Knowing this, a physical examination whose purpose is to establish virginity or the lack thereof is a futile exercise. Although men cross-culturally and through the ages have wanted to certify the virginity of their brides, there is simply no foolproof means of doing so.

The ancient medical view that presupposes that a woman's vaginal hymen will rupture at the first intercourse provides a likely conceptual framework for the prescribed examination by female experts in 4Q271 3. This examination should be understood as a reference to vaginal examination.

3.4.7 THE FEMALE EXPERTS

The women responsible for the examination in D are called knowledgeable, ידעות. In this context the term likely refers to having the technical skills necessary to perform a vaginal examination. Thus, they were likely mid-wives. They are also said to be reliable, נשים נאמנות. Elsewhere in D, אמן is used with reference to reliable witnesses: in CD IX 21–23, נאמנים is used twice for "reliable witnesses" in cases concerning property. CD X 1–2 uses the verb in the context of establishing who would be considered a reliable witness. Although these latter texts are part of the community stratum, they testify to use of the verb as a technical term designating a reliable witness.

The Mishnah uses the verb אמן (*niph.* be reliable) in the same way and refers to reliable female witnesses by the female plural participle form of אמן in the *niphal*.[153] In rabbinic Judaism, from the Mishnah and onwards, women were normally not allowed as witnesses, since they were not considered as reliable as male witnesses.[154] There are, however, many exceptions to this principle, whereby a woman was allowed to testify and her testimony was believed. Accordingly, a woman's testimony was believed concerning the death of a husband (*m. Yebam.* 16:7) and sometimes deemed reliable with regard to sexual relations (*m. Ketub.* 1:1–7).[155] Josephus gives evidence

---

[153] See *m. Sanh.* 3:2; 4:5; *m. Yebam.* 15:4; for the feminine form, see *m. Yebam* 16:7 (end).

[154] On women and other categories of people not qualified to testify, see Ze'ev Falk, *Introduction to Jewish Law of the Second Commonwealth* (Leiden: Brill, 1972), 1:119–35.

[155] In virginity suits, a woman's account is sometimes accepted over that of the new husband (*m. Ketub.* 1:1–7); in cases of the captivity of a woman, a testimony by *another* woman that the woman has not been raped is accepted (*m. Ketub.* 2:6). Other cases where a woman's testimony is valid concern identifying a man as a priest (*m. Ketub.* 2:3); a claim to be divorced (*m. Ketub.* 1:5); defilement (*m. Sotah* 6:2). For discussion on cases of women's testimony, see Hauptman, *Rereading the Rabbis*, 196–220; Ilan, *Jewish Women*, 163–66. On

of a similar tension: on the one hand, he claims that women were disqualified from being witnesses;[156] on the other hand, he alleges that women's testimony, often procured under torture, was accepted in Herodian courts. Furthermore, Josephus also asserts that a woman—Herod's sister—served as a court judge.[157]

In 4Q271 3 14, the women who perform the examination are accepted as reliable witnesses. At first, the plural form for the women responsible for the examination seems surprising, since one midwife would be sufficient. But this plurality may reflect conformity with the biblical requirement of two witnesses (Deut 19:15). In light of Josephus' claim that women were disqualified from testifying, and the legal tradition in the Mishnah that severely limits women's capacity to testify, one may perhaps draw the conclusion that a similar principle underlies the law in 4Q271 3 and that women were allowed to testify only in this unique case. On the other hand, the disqualification of witnesses based on gender represents an innovation compared to biblical laws, which instead focus solely on the number of witnesses and their integrity, not their sex (Deut 19:15–20; Exod 20:16; 23:1–2). There is no evidence in the Hebrew Bible that a woman's testimony is considered unreliable. Similarly, nowhere does the sectarian literature of the Scrolls allude to women as unreliable witnesses. Communal law in D (CD IX 23–X 3) dictates that in a capital case a witness must be an adult and be "God-fearing," which disqualifies outsiders from testifying. In a non-capital case, no witness will be accepted who intentionally has transgressed any commandment until that person has repented.[158] These laws may have applied to men and women alike. Moreover, 1QSa explicitly requires a wife to testify about her husband (1QSa I 11).[159] The women who perform the physical examination in 4Q271 3 are credited with integrity and the moral capacity to testify. Consequently, it is certainly possible that the character of a person, and not the sex, was the main factor for determining whether or not a witness was reliable in the circles that produced the early law code. Lines 14–15a, ברורות ממאמר המבקר אשר על [הרבים] ("selected by command of the Examiner over [the many]"), which give the Examiner the right to select the "trustworthy women," is a communal interpolation; I will return to this reference in Chapter 6 "Communal Laws."[160]

---

women's testimony in Luke and in the Jewish society, see Turid Karlsen Seim, *The Double Message: Patterns of Gender in Luke and Acts* (Nashville: Abingdon Press, 1994), 155–7.

[156] *Ant.* XVII 64–5, 93; *War* I 584–90; Ilan, *Jewish Women*, 163–6.

[157] Herod's sister Salome served as one of several judges in the trial against Mariamne and her sons; *War* I 538.

[158] For a detailed analysis of the law, see Schiffman, *Sectarian Law*, 55–62.

[159] On this text, see below pp. 141–2.

[160] See pp. 201–2.

3.4.8 4Q273 5

It is possible that a fragment from the papyrus manuscript 4Q273 belongs to the same section as the marriage laws from 4Q271 3. This fragment may include a prohibition against marrying during the time of the woman's menstruation. This interpretation is tentative since only parts of the lines are preserved. The fragment includes the same expression אל יקח איש, as 4Q271 3 13, which makes the link particularly plausible.

Line 4–5 reads:

```
[ה]וֹת עולם המה אל יקח איש את האשׁ[ות     4
[              ]ךֹ אשר עד ooooo דֹם את ספרה מִיֹמִי     5
```

4]wt They are perpetual. Let no man take a wom[an]
5] from the days in which she counted the blood of ooooo until [ ]

3.4.9 CONCLUSION

The carefully outlined stipulations concerning marital arrangements in 4Q271 3, with their emphasis on women's chastity, reveal a traditional patriarchal view of the relation between spouses in marriage. The subordinate position of women is particularly evident in the requirement to disclose the blemishes of women prior to marriage. The father is instructed to find a groom who is "established" for the daughter, perhaps from among his near kinship group. Furthermore, according to a traditional double-standard, a woman may be ostracized for engaging in sexual relations prior to marriage, while the sexual past of a man is not an issue. The law in 4Q271 3 extends some of the biblical restrictions for priests to all men; thus in a unique feature of the text, all men are prohibited from marrying a *zonah*.

The legislation imposes extraordinary measures to decide whether or not a woman is a virgin by requiring mid-wives to perform physical exams. Thus, women midwives were agents in maintaining a legislative system that was oppressive to women. There are striking similarities between the laws in 4Q159 2–4 and 4Q271 3, which both are influenced by Deut 22:13–21, in their prescriptions to examine a woman suspected of not being a virgin. But whereas 4Q159 2–4 prescribes rules for examining the bride suspected of unchastity *after* the wedding, the rule in 4Q271 3 attempts to prevent such a situation. Instead of being examined after the wedding, a suspected non-virgin should be examined prior to the wedding. In this respect the law in D improves the legal situation for women, since a woman's reputation is at risk, but not her life.

3.5 BINDING OATHS AND WOMEN'S OATHS: CD XVI 6B–12; PARALLELS 4Q270 6 II 19–21; 4Q271 4 II 7–12

3.5.1 THE TEXT: CD XVI 6B–12; PARALLELS: 4Q270 6 II 19–21 DOTTED UNDERLINE AND 4Q271 4 II 7–12 UNDERLINED[161]

6 vac ואשר אמר מוצא שפתיך
7 תשמור להקים[162] vac כל שבועת אסר אשר יקום איש על נפשו
8 לעשות דבר מן התורה עד מחיר מות אל יפדהו vac כל אשר
9 [יק]ים איש על נפשו ל[ס]ו[ר][163] א[ת התו]רה עד מחיר מות אל יקימהו
10 [ע]ל שבועת האשה אשר אמ[ר לאיש]ה להניא את שבועתה אל
11 יניא איש שבועה אשר לא [י]דענה ה[ם][164] להקים היא vac ואם להניא
12 אם לעבור ברית היא יניאה ואל יקימנה vac וכן המשפט לאביה

6 vac   And concerning what he said, "whatever your lips utter,
7 you must diligently fulfill." vac Any binding oath by which a person takes upon himself
8 to keep a commandment of the Torah, even at the price of death, let him not redeem it. vac Anything by which
9 a person [tak]es upon himself to [de]part from the Torah, even at the price of death, let him not fulfill it.
10 [Conce]rning the oath of a woman of which he sai[d, "it is for] her[husband] to annul her oath." Let
11 no man annul an oath of which he does not [k]now if it should be fulfilled vac or annulled.
12 If it (the oath) is to transgress the covenant, let him annul it and not allow it to stand. vac And likewise is the rule for her father.

3.5.2 LAWS CONCERNING OATHS

CD XVI 6b–12 belongs to the stratum Halakhah together with the subsequent passage on freewill offerings (CD XVI 13–17a), which also concerns vows.[165] In the document's final form, CD XVI 6b–12 is part of a long section on laws related to

---

[161] Double underline marks the overlap between 4Q270 6 and 4Q271 4.

[162] 4Q271 4 ii does not have the *vacats* that appear in CD XVI 6b-12. 4Q271 4 ii has one *vacat* before לאביה in line 12 (corresponding to CD XVI 12).

[163] א[ת accords with Qimron's reading ("The text of CDC," 41).

[164] הם does not make sense in this context. Rabin reads אם and Baumgarten restores the word to א[ם in 4Q271 4 ii 11 (*DJD XVIII*, 178)

[165] Hempel, *Laws*, 30.

The Early Law Code 91

oaths and vows (CD XV 1–XVI 18), which includes the ordinances for the oath of entrance in column XV.[166]

The "binding oath," שבועת אסר, is the subject of our segment. The rules for oath-taking are understood according to the principle for a vow in Deut 23:23, which is quoted in lines 6–7: "whatever your lips utter, you must diligently fulfill."[167] Schiffman observes that for the author of D this law applied to both vows and binding oaths.[168] The obligation to fulfill an oath (or vow) is in accordance with the plain meaning of the biblical legislation (Deut 23:23; Num 30:2), but with the important addition that the oath had to be in accordance with the Torah, otherwise it should not be fulfilled "even at the price of death" (CD XVI 9). Scholars have noted the striking similarity to Josephus' claim that the Essenes would rather starve themselves to death than break the oath of abstaining from the food of outsiders (*War* II 143).[169] This legislation differs from the rabbinic law that makes provision for the annulment of a vow or an oath of a man.[170]

The subsequent law about the oath of a woman is based on biblical laws concerning a woman's vow (נדר) and pledge (אסר) by oath in Num 30:1–16.[171] As in biblical law, this text deals only with one aspect of a woman's pledge by oath, namely the annulment by her father or husband: "[Conce]rning the oath of a woman of which he sai[d 'it is for] her husband to annul her oath'" ע[ל שבועת האשה אשר אמ]ר ל[אישה להניא את שבועתה. In spite of the citation formula, no exact biblical parallel is known. Possibly the formula refers not to a specific passage, but to the substance of the law in Num 30: 6–15.[172]

---

[166] For a discussion of this passage, see below section 6.2 ("The Initiation Process and Excluded Categories").

[167] One minor difference is קום ("to fulfil") instead of עשה in Deut 23:23.

[168] Lawrence Schiffman, "The Law of Vows and Oaths (Num. 30, 3–16) in the Zadokite Fragments and the Temple Scroll," *RevQ* 15 (1991), 201.

[169] Rabin, *Zadokite Documents*, 76 n. 2; Dupont-Sommer, *The Essene Writings*, 162 n.3; Baumgarten and Schwartz, "The Damascus Document (CD)," 41 n.135; *DJD XVIII*, 180.

[170] According to the Tannaim, vows were possible to annul. But whereas the School of Hillel additionally accepted the annulment of oaths, the School of Shammai did not (*b. Ned.* 28b; *p. Ned.* 11:1); see Schiffman, "The Law of Vows and Oaths," 203. Baumgarten points out that Mishnah recognizes that the annulment of men's vows is without scriptural basis (*m. Hag.* 1:9); see "The Damascus Document (CD)," 41 n.135. There are several examples of rabbis releasing men from vows in the Mishnah (e.g., *m. Ned* 9:5–10).

[171] The biblical text refers frequently to "vow" נדר and "pledge" אסר; Num 30:3, 11, 13 refer to שבוה.

[172] Baumgarten, "Damascus Document (CD)," 41 n.136; É. Cothenet, "Le Document de Damas," in *Les Textes de Qumrân. Traduits et Annotés* (Paris: Letouzey et Ané, 1963), 2:186–7 n.8. Elisha Qimron suggests that the reader is expected to identify the passage through association ("Further Observations on the Laws of Oaths in the Damascus Document 15," *JQR*

According to Num 30: 3–16, a husband or father may annul any vow or obligation taken under oath by a woman, as long as he acts immediately upon hearing it.[173] At the same time, any vow of a widow or divorcee is binding according to Num 30:9, since such a woman is under no man's authority. The content of the obligation or vow is not a primary concern in the text and does not affect the right of the father or husband to cancel the woman's promise. However, the text mentions twice that the vow has been thoughtless, מבטא (Num 30: 6, 8), and it also refers to the case of a vow of abstinence (Num 30:13).

CD XVI 10–12 imposes the guiding principle for a vow from Deut 23:23 onto the law concerning a woman's obligation by oath in Numbers 30, and prohibits a husband from annulling a pledge by oath "of which he does not know if it should be fulfilled or annulled." Accordingly, it is no longer up to a man's own discretion to annul a pledge, and the decision should instead be based on external criteria. Pointing to Tannaitic laws that limit a husband's right to annul his wife's vows to certain types of vows (such as those of abstinence or self-affliction), Schiffman suggests that similar restrictions may have been in place within the sect.[174] However, there are no hints in the D text that additional principles are presumed. Instead, the guideline for whether a pledge by oath should be kept or not has already been specified in CD XVI 6–9, and this same principle is articulated again in line 12 in the instruction for a husband: "if it (the oath) is to transgress the covenant, let him annul it and not allow it to stand." Consequently, there is only one guiding principle for obligations taken by oaths, namely that a pledge must be fulfilled unless it leads to a transgression of the Torah. Thus, a father or a husband may annul a woman's oath only if it leads to a transgression, but not otherwise.[175] From this perspective, the law in CD XVI 6–9 applies to obligations by oaths of both men and women. The strict law in D allows for no recourse in the form of annulment for either men or women, if their pledges by oath

---

85 [1994], 255). Another possibility is that the reference is to an unknown passage. Rabin suggests it may be a reference to the Book of Hagu (*Zadokite Documents*, 76 n.10).

[173] Num 30:14 adds that a husband may annul a vow at a later date, but then "he shall bear her guilt."

[174] Schiffman explains that a husband only had the right to annul vows of abstinence, self-affliction, or vows that would affect a wife's responsibilities vis-à-vis her husband (referring to *m. Ned.* 11:1); "The Law of Vows and Oaths," 204. Although *m. Ned.* 11:1ff discusses the *content* of a vow as the criterion for whether a husband can annul it or not, elsewhere the man in authority over a woman is presumed to have the right to revoke any vow; *m. Ned.* 10:4 recounts that it was common that a husband revoked *all* vows that a woman had made before she married.

[175] Dupont-Sommer expresses the thrust of the law in CD XVI 10–12 well: "In Num. xxx. 7–16, the Law authorizes the husband, under certain conditions, to annul the oaths and vows of his wife; the present ordinance restricts this right to undertakings that might violate the Covenant" (*The Essene Writings,* 162).

are in agreement with the Torah. Thereby D considers women, just like men, accountable and responsible for the pledges they take.

The Temple Scroll paraphrases the law on women's vows in Numbers 30 and combines the texts of Deut 23:22–24 and Num 30:3–17 in a similar fashion to D.[176] In contrast to D, however, TS repeats the biblical texts at greater length and preserves the law on a woman's oath according to its original meaning.[177] A passage in the wisdom text 4QInstruction[b] (4Q416) takes the opposite stance on women's oaths compared to D and advises a husband to annul all the vows and oaths a wife makes.[178]

3.5.3 CONCLUSION

A husband's or a father's right to annul his wife's pledge by oath as outlined in Numbers 30 has been radically altered in CD XVI. This text restricts a man's authority over women's oaths to those cases in which the fulfillment of a pledge taken by oath violates the covenantal law. One significant consequence of this reinterpretation of Numbers 30 is that women are empowered to be responsible for their own pledges by oath and are allowed to express their religiosity by taking pledges as they themselves see fit. This halakhic position stands in sharp contrast to the legislation concerning women's oaths as found in 11QT and 4QInstruction[b].

3.6 THE SABBATH CODE

3.6.1 INTRODUCTION

Laws concerning the Sabbath are gathered in a list of prescriptions in the early law code under the heading על הש[ב]ת לשמרה כמשפטה ("concerning the Sa[bb]ath to guard it according to its precept" [CD X 14]).[179] Over all, the Sabbath Code provides a rigorous interpretation of the commandment to abstain from work on the seventh day (Exod 20:8; 31:12–17).[180] The Code uses the formulaic expression אל plus a third person masculine jussive to list the prohibitions. Four of the laws in the

---

[176] 11QT LIII 11–14a is a reworking of Deut 23:22–4, and LIII 14b–LIV 7 adapts Num 30:3–16. Much of the section outlining the husband's authority is damaged.

[177] For a comparison of these passages in D and 11QT, see Schiffman, "The Law of Vows and Oaths," 206–12.

[178] 4Q416 2 iv 7b–10 refers to both binding oaths and vows, כל שבועת אסרה לנדר נד[ר] ("and every obligatory oath of her, vowing a vo[w]").

[179] For a commentary on the Sabbath Code, see Schiffman, *Halakhah at Qumran*, 77–133. For a similar list of Sabbath laws, see Jubilees 50. Fragments of additional Sabbath codes are preserved in 4Q265 6, 7 1–5 (*DJD XXXV*, 68–72); 4QHalakha A (4Q251) 1–2 3–7 (*DJD XXXV*, 28–31); and 4QHalakha B I–II (4Q264a) (*DJD XXXV*, 54–6).

[180] For example, CD XI 13–14 prohibits aiding the delivery of animals on the Sabbath or rescuing an animal who falls in a pit (cf. Matt 12:11 and Lk 14:5) and CD X 19 restricts work-related talk on the Sabbath.

Sabbath Code in CD X 14–XI 18 pertain to women in particular. These include a prohibition against intermingling in CD XI 4–5, אל יתערב איש מרצונו בשבת, which most likely refers to sexual intercourse on the Sabbath. There are prohibitions against carrying spices (CD XI 9–10) and an infant (CD XI 11) on the Sabbath. In addition, the Sabbath Code includes a law that forbids contending with "a male or female slave" (CD XI 12). Each of these laws will be examined in turn.

3.6.2 INTERMINGLING ON THE SABBATH

CD XI 4–5 states אל יתערב איש מרצונו בשבת "let no one intentionally intermingle on the Sabbath."[181] The absence of an indirect object for the *hitpael* verb יתערב makes this law difficult to interpret. ערב carries the connotation "to intermingle" and "to mix" and is sometimes used within the context of impurity in the Qumran documents.[182] Scholars are divided in their interpretations of this law. Schiffman argues that CD XI 4–5 prohibits entering into a partnership.[183] Baumgarten proposes the interpretation, "Let no man intermingle (purities with others) voluntarily."[184] Highlighting instances where ערב is used with reference to defilement in the Scrolls, Qimron and Strugnell offer strong arguments that the law legislates against "defiling oneself on the Sabbath, especially by intentional sexual contact."[185] In support of their interpretation, Lutz Doering points out that a ban on sexual intercourse on the Sabbath fits well with the general requirement for Sabbath purity in the Qumran writings.[186] He suggests that the

---

[181] See parallel text in 4Q271 5 i 1–2 (אל יתערב [איש מרצ]ונו [בשבת]).

[182] For the use of ערב (in the context of purity of the temple, see 11QT XLV 4–7; 4Q274 1 i 5 admonishes a menstruating woman to refrain from intermingling, אל תתערב (*DJD XXXV*, 100).

[183] Schiffman, *Halakhah at Qumran*, 109–10. In addition, Rabin translates יתערב "to starve oneself" (*Zadokite Documents*, 54–5) and Dupont-Sommer translates "to fast" (*The Essene Writings*, 152).

[184] Baumgarten and Schwartz, "The Damascus Document (CD)," 47.

[185] Qimron and Strugnell point to 4QMMT B 48 where ערב refers to illicit sexual relations, and 11QT L 2, where ערב is used in the context of corpse-defilement; see *DJD X*, 140; see also Elisha Qimron, "The Halacha of Damascus Covenant. An Interpretation of 'Al Yitarev,'" *Proceedings of the Ninth World Congress of Jewish Studies Division* (Jerusalem: Magness, 1986), 1:13–14 [Hebrew]; Magen Broshi, "Anti-Qumranic Polemic in the Talmud," in *The Madrid Qumran Congress*, 596–7; E. Nodet, "La loi à Qumran et Schiffman," *RB* 102 (1995), 56.

[186] Doering points to the prohibition against wearing soiled clothes (CD XI 3–4) and the prohibition against spending the Sabbath near gentiles (CD XI 14–15). He also highlights evidence of legislation that requires ritual purification on the eve of the Sabbath (4QRitual of Purification [4Q512] iv [frg. 33+35] 1–5; 4QHalakha A [4Q251] 1 7); "Purity Regulations Concerning the Sabbath in the Dead Sea Scrolls and Related Literature," in *The Dead Sea Scrolls Fifty Years after their Discovery*, 600–9. For ritual purification before the Sabbath, see

prohibition refers to "intentional defilement relating to persons on the Sabbath," a prohibition that includes defilement resulting from sexual intercourse.[187] According to Broshi, the rabbinic encouragement of sexual intercourse on the Sabbath represents a polemical position against a ban on such a practice, represented by the Qumran legislation.[188] Jubilees also bans sexual intercourse on the Sabbath, a crime for which it imposes the death penalty (50:8).[189] Finally, there may be a reference to a prohibition of sexual intercourse on the Sabbath in the Catalogue of Transgressors (4Q270 2 i 18–19).[190] In light of the above, it is reasonable to conclude that the ban on "mingling" on the Sabbath concerns sexual intercourse. Such a prohibition is an expression of a general desire for purity during the Sabbath in the early legislation of D.

3.6.3 CARRYING PERFUME/SPICES AND AN INFANT ON THE SABBATH

The two laws concerning spices and infants appear in CD XI 9b–11 (parallels 4Q270 6 v 15–16 underlined; 4Q271 5 i 5–7 dotted underline)[191]:

9		אל ישא איש vac
10	עליו סמנים לצאת ולביא בשבת vac	אל יטול בבית מושבת
11	סלע ועפר vac האומן את היונק לצאת ולבוא בשבת [192] אל ישא vac	

9   vac Let no one carry
10 spices on him to go out or come in on the Sabbath vac Let no one lift within the house
11 a rock or soil.[193] vac Let no care-giver carry an infant to go out or come in on the Sabbath

---

Joseph Baumgarten, "The Purification Rituals in DJD 7," in *The Dead Sea Scrolls: Forty Years of Research*, 208.

[187] Doering, "Purity Regulations Concerning the Sabbath in the Dead Sea Scrolls and Related Literature," 607.

[188] Broshi points to a ban on sexual intercourse on the Sabbath among the Samaritans, Karaites, and Falasha; see "Anti-Qumranic Polemic," 96. See also S. Safrai, "Teaching of Pietists in Mishnaic Literature," *JJS* 16 (1965), 23–4.

[189] Jubilees shares many of its Sabbath laws with D, including the prohibition of the following activities: business talk, drawing up water, carrying things, and eating anything apart from what has been prepared in advance (Jub. 50:8–9; cf. CD X 17–19, 22; XI 1, 7–8).

[190] See below, pp. 108–9.

[191] Double underline marks the overlap between 4Q270 6 and 4Q271 5.

[192] There is a short space between ישא and האומן in 4Q270 v 16, which may indicate that 4Q270 originally had an additional word in the space

[193] The law about moving rock and soil inside the house deals with the problem of handling things on the Sabbath, corresponding to the rabbinic מקצה (*muqseh*); see Schiffman, *Halakhah at Qumran*, 117–19.

Two laws concerning carrying spices and infants are part of a general prohibition against transporting things from one domain to another on the Sabbath. Although written in the masculine, one may assume that they apply to women in particular. Drawing on the biblical injunction against going out on the Sabbath (Exod 16:29), CD XI 7–8 provides the general halakhic principle: "Let no one carry (things) from the house to outside and from outside into the house."[194] Other collections of Sabbath laws in Qumran documents similarly restrict carrying in and out on the Sabbath.[195]

According to Schiffman, the restrictions against carrying סמנים, "spices," likely "refers to the practice by women of wearing small ornamental perfume bottles around their necks."[196] This suggestion is supported by the Mishnah, which assumes that women wore these types of ornamental bottles with perfumes or spices. As part of a general prohibition against women wearing ornaments on the Sabbath (unless these are attached to the clothing) both the Mishnah and Tosefta emphasise that women are forbidden to carrying perfume or spice bottles.[197]

The restriction against carrying an infant concerns האומן. This word carries the meaning of someone caring for a child, or children, and can denote "foster-father," "pedagogue," "guardian," or "nurse."[198] Schiffman translates the word "parent."[199] In the context of the laws concerning carrying in and out, "care-giver" best captures the general nature of the law: anybody who is looking after the child, including a parent, may not carry the infant in or out on the Sabbath.

There are hints in the rabbinic tradition that the prohibition against carrying an infant from one domain to another on the Sabbath was controversial. While Tannaitic law prohibits carrying an infant (from one domain to another) on the Sabbath, the

---

[194] Schiffman points out that there is no indication of the rabbinic construction of an *'eruv* to permit carrying within a public domain; "Sabbath," *Encyclopedia of the Dead Sea Scrolls*, 2:805.

[195] 4Q265 6 4 prohibits carrying out any vessel or food on the Sabbath (*DJD XXXV*, 68) and 4Q251 1 4–5 legislates against carrying out anything on the Sabbath (*DJD XXXV*, 28).

[196] Schiffman, *Halakhah at Qumran*, 116–17.

[197] *M. Shabb.* 6:3; *t. Shabb.* 4:11.

[198] *BDB*, 52–3; Ludwig Koehler and Walter Baumgartner, *Lexicon in Veteris Testamenti Libros* (Leiden: Brill, 1953), 60–1. Compare different translations of אומן in CD XI 11: "a nurse" (Baumgarten, "The Damascus Document [CD]," 49); "a foster-father," (Dupont-Sommer, *The Essene Writings*, 153); "the pedagogue" (Rabin, *Zadokite Documents*, 56); "Ein(e) Pfleger(in)" (Johan Maier and Kurt Schubert, *Die Qumran-Essener: Texte der Schriftrollen und Lebensbild der Gemeinde*, [München: E. Reinhardt, 1973], 182). Num 11:12 likens Moses to a אומן, and 1QH[a] XV 21–2 (Sukenik: VII 21–2) compares the psalmist to a אומן in relation to his followers. For an analysis of the latter passage, see M. Delcor, *Les Hymnes de Qumrân* (Paris: Letouzy et Ané, 1962), 192–3; Svend Holm-Nielsen, *Hodayot: Psalms from Qumran* (Acta Theologica Danica 2; Aarhus: Universitetsforlaget i Aarhus, 1960), 134–5.

[199] Schiffman, *Halakhah at Qumran*, 119.

3.6.4 TREATMENT OF SLAVES

CD XI 12 prohibits disputing with slaves on the Sabbath: אל ימרא איש את עבדו ואת אמתו ואת שוכרו בשבת, "Let no one contend with his slave, his maidservant, or hired man on the Sabbath." The exact meaning of the verb מרא is disputed.[201] Nevertheless, taking מרא (or מרה) according to its literal sense of "be contentious, rebellious" makes sense in the context. Baumgarten explains that "the rule aims to prevent secular confrontations on the Sabbath."[202]

3.6.5 CONCLUSION

A prohibition in D against sexual intercourse during the Sabbath is an example of a legislation in the Scrolls that promotes ritual purity on that day. A desire to preserve Sabbath "purity" contradicts rabbinic legislation which encourages sexual intercourse during the Sabbath.

The prohibitions against carrying an infant and the law on perfume bottles are both expressed in the masculine form. But because of their specific subject matter—necklaces and infants—they can be assumed to pertain to women in particular.

The Sabbath law proscribing arguing with male and female slaves is one of several references to slaves in the early law code (CD XII 10–11; 4Q270 4 13–17). These laws presume that ownership of slaves was common-place.

3.7 A LAW AGAINST SEXUAL INTERCOURSE IN עיר המקדש: CD XII 1–2; 4Q271 5 I 17–18

3.7.1 INTRODUCTION

A law prohibiting sexual intercourse in עיר המקדש ("the city of the sanctuary") is part of a series of mixed injunctions in CD XI 18b–XII 20 that concern purity and holiness, criminal laws, and relations with gentiles. Hempel assigns most of this section to "miscellaneous pieces of halakhah," but considers the laws restricting

---

[200] At the same time, when the child can walk, it can be helped; *m. Shabb.* 18.2 reads, "A woman may pull her child along. R. Juda said: When? When the child can lift up one leg and put down the other; but if it is only dragged along this is forbidden." In addition *m. Shabb.* 10:5 allows the carrying of a sick man; see Rabin, *Zadokite Documents*, 56; Baumgarten and Schwartz, "The Damascus Document (CD)," 49.

[201] *BDB*, 598.

[202] Baumgarten and Schwartz, "The Damascus Document (CD)," 49. Schiffman argues that the law prohibits the use of slaves to do work for the masters on the Sabbath (cf. Philo *Spec. Laws* II 66–8). The verb in Arabic may denote "to urge on" (Schiffman, *Halakhah at Qumran*, 120–1); so also Rabin, *Zadokite Documents*, 56.

relations with gentiles (CD XII 6b–11a) as Halakhah material.²⁰³ In contrast to Hempel, I allocate the laws concerning the temple (CD XI 18b–XII 1a), the law prohibiting sexual intercourse in עיר המקדש (CD XII 1a–2a), and purity laws (CD XII 11b–18) to the earliest layer, in accordance with Davis' stratification.²⁰⁴ The immediate context of the law prohibiting sexual intercourse in עיר המקדש ("the city of the sanctuary") is purity laws relating to sacrifices and the temple (CD XI 18b–XII 2). This segment in turn ties in well with the preceding Sabbath Code from the same early literary layer, which ends with a law concerning sacrifices on the Sabbath (CD XI 18a).

CD XII 1–2 reads (parallel 4Q271 5 i 17–18 underlined):

אל ישכב איש עם אשה בעיר המקדש לטמא את עיר המקדש בנדתם

Let no man lie with a woman in the city of the sanctuary to defile the city of the sanctuary with their pollution.

The Temple Scroll includes a somewhat similar law, which also refers to עיר המקדש ("the city of the sanctuary"). Whereas D does not mention the time of impurity subsequent to sexual intercourse, 11QT extends the impurity period for a couple after sexual intercourse from one (Lev 15:18) to three days.²⁰⁵ 11QT XLV 11–12 reads:

ואיש כיא ישכב עם אשתו שכבת זרע לוא יבוא אל כול עיר המקדש אשר אשכין שמי בה שלושת ימים

And a man who lies with his wife and has an ejaculation shall not for three days enter the entire city of the sanctuary in which I shall cause my name to dwell.

The main exegetical difficulty with both texts lies in the phrase עיר המקדש, which scholars understand in two different ways: a designation of the temple complex, the *temenos*,²⁰⁶ or the entire city of Jerusalem.²⁰⁷ Considering the practical implications of

---

²⁰³Hempel attributes CD XII 19–20a as well as CD XII 23b–XIII 1a to a Damascus redaction (*Laws*, 154–62, 190).
²⁰⁴See my discussion above, pp. 40–1.
²⁰⁵Similarly, a nocturnal emission brings three days impurity according to 11QT XLV 7–12. The extension of the impurity period is derived from the command to the Israelites to stay pure and "be ready on the third day: do not go near a woman" (Exod 19:15); see Yadin, *Temple Scroll*, 1:287–8.
²⁰⁶Proponents for this view include Baruch A. Levine, "The Temple Scroll: Aspects of its Historical Provenance and Literary Character," *BASOR* 232 (1978), 14; Lawrence Schiffman, "*Ir Ha-Miqdash* and Its Meaning in the Temple Scroll and other Qumran Texts," in *Sanctity of Time and Space in Tradition and Modernity* (eds. A. Houtman, A. Poorthuis and J. Schwartz;

these interpretations, both proposals are somewhat problematic. On the one hand, it is very hard to imagine that CD XII 1–2 is a prohibition against sexual intercourse within the temple precincts, since such a law appears entirely redundant. On the other hand, a law that prohibits sexual intercourse in the *city* of Jerusalem appears to be quite extreme and virtually impossible to observe. These options have implications for the habitation of women and men that is envisioned in the two documents, as I will discuss below.

The interpretation of עיר המקדש is difficult because the expression does not occur in the Hebrew Bible and is rare in the Scrolls.[208] Elsewhere, D refers to the city Jerusalem by "the holy city" עיר הקדש (CD XX 22) and "Jerusalem" ירושלים (4Q266 5 i 12/4Q267 5 ii 5). In TS, the expression עיר המקדש is used only in the context of purity, and its specific connotation is elusive.[209] Since TS and the Halakhah section of D share common grounds, as I have discussed above, a brief examination of some of the purity laws in TS concerning Jerusalem and its temple may provide some background to the prohibition in CD XII 1–2.

3.7.2 THE TEMPLE SCROLL

The prohibition against a man entering עיר המקדש after sexual intercourse in 11QT LXV 12 is but one provision in an elaborate system of purity laws in TS that imposes confinement of impurity carriers to designated areas outside the cities (11QT XLVIII 14–17).[210] The stipulations differ concerning categories of impurity carriers in

---

Leiden: Brill, 1998), 95–109; "The Theology of the Temple Scroll," *JQR* 85 (1994), 118–21; "Exclusion from the Sanctuary and the City of the Sanctuary in the Temple Scroll," *HAR* 9 (1985), 307–9; Sarah Japhet, "The Prohibition of the Habitation of Women: The Temple Scroll's Attitude Toward Sexual Impurity and Its Biblical Precedents," *JANES* 22 (1993), 86.

[207] So Yadin, *The Temple Scroll*, 1:280; Jacob Milgrom, "The City of the Temple: A Response to Lawrence H. Schiffman," *JQR* 85 (1994), 125–8; "The Scriptural Foundations and Deviations in the Laws of Purity of the Temple Scroll," 85; "Studies in the Temple Scroll," *JBL* 97 (1978), 512–18; Harrington, *The Impurity Systems*, 57–8. Rabbin argues that CD XII 1–2 mainly refers to pilgrims (*Zadokite Documents*, 59). According to Sidnie White Crawford, TS never envisions the city of the sanctuary to be inhabited; instead it remains purely a pilgrimage city ("The Meaning of the Phrase עיר המקדש in the Temple Scroll," *DSD* 8 [2001], 242–53).

[208] The expression appears twice in D (in CD XII 1–2), four times in TS (11QT XLV 11–12; 15–17; XLVII 9; 12–13), and once in 4QHistorical Text A (4Q248) 7. 4Q248 consists of a single fragment. In this document, a Greek king is predicted to conquer עיר המקדש, which refers to the city of Jerusalem; see Magen Broshi and Hanan Eshel, "The Greek King is Antiochus IV (4QHistorical Text=4Q248)," *JJS* 48 (1997), 120–9.

[209] See White Crawford, "The Meaning of the Phrase עיר המקדש in the Temple Scroll," 242–3.

[210] These purity laws represent an adaptation of biblical legislation concerning the wilderness camp and the desert tabernacle. For the biblical background to the purity laws, see Lawrence Schiffman, "The Temple Scroll and the Nature of Its Law: The Status of the

relation to the holy city as opposed to a regular city. Since the places of confinement concerning the holy city are specifically located outside of the "city of the sanctuary" (11QT XLV 16–17), these laws are crucial for understanding the meaning of the expression the "city of the sanctuary." The categories of impure people who require confinement are shown in the following chart:

Table 3: Confinement of ritually impure people in 11QT

עיר המקדש (XLVI 17–18)	Every city (XLVIII 14–17)
scale disease, *zavim*, men after nocturnal emission	scale disease, *zavim*, menstruating women, women after childbirth

Without going into too much detail, I will state some of the reasons why I side with those scholars who identify עיר המקדש in TS with the city of Jerusalem, rather than with the *temenos*. In my view, 11QT XLVI 15–16 clearly locates the "places" of confinement *outside* of the city Jerusalem.[211] Furthermore, Milgrom (who argues that עיר המקדש refers to the entire city) offers, in my opinion, a credible explanation as to why the categories of impurity bearers differ for the city of Jerusalem compared to the other cities: since Jerusalem was to be completely holy, menstruating women and parturients were not expected to stay in Jerusalem at the time of their impurity, as they would know of their impurity in advance.[212] Furthermore, only those who experience

---

Question," in *The Community of the Renewed Covenant* (eds. E. Ulrich and J. VanderKam; Notre Dame, Ind.: University of Notre Dame, 1994), 44–5; "Architecture and Law: The Temple and its Courtyards in the Temple Scroll," in *From Ancient Israel to Modern Judaism: Intellect in Quest of Understanding, Essays in Honor of Marvin Fox* (eds. J. Neusner, Ernest Frerichs and Nahum Sarna; BJS 159; Atlanta: Scholars Press, 1989), 1:280–4. Yadin, *The Temple Scroll*, 1:288–9; Harrington, *The Impurity Systems*, 57–8. Japhet highlights the relevance of 2 Chr 8:11 for these laws, "The Prohibition of the Habitation of Women," 79–87; cf. Louis Ginzberg, *An Unknown Jewish Sect*, (New York: Jewish Theological Seminary of America, 1976), 73–4. The analogy between the wilderness camp and Jerusalem appears in 4QMMT B 59–62, "for Jerusalem is the holy camp... it is the chief camps of Israel" (see also B 29–33).

[211] 11QT XLVI 16b–18 reads: ועשיתם שלושה מקומות למזרח העיר מובדלים זה מזה אשר יהיו באים המצורים והזבים והאנשים אשר יהיה להמה מקרה "You shall make three places, to the East of the city, separate from each other, to which shall come lepers and those afflicted with a discharge and the men who have an emission of semen." The passage follows after a prescriptions for latrines (lines 13–16a), which should also be located outside of the city, to the North-West. That עיר refers to the whole city and not the temple is also clear from the previous prescription to make a trench around the temple that will "separate the holy temple from the city" יהיה מבדיל בין מקדש הקודש לעיר (11QT XLVI 9–10).

[212] Milgrom, "The Scriptural Foundations and Deviations in the Laws of Purity of the Temple Scroll," 85 ff.; "Studies in the Temple Scroll," 512–18; "The City of the Temple: A Response to Lawrence H. Schiffman," 125–8.

unintentional impurity are subject to the laws about confinement. Sexual intercourse was not expected to take place in the city, and thus a man engaged in intercourse should not *enter* the city for three days. Nocturnal emission, on the other hand, is unpredictable and can occur within the city; thus such a man is prohibited from entering the temple (11QT XLV 7b–8a) and should depart to the area set apart outside the city (11QT XLVI 18).[213] While caution and restrictions for impurity bearers are in place for "every city" as well, they are less strict than those imposed in the city of the sanctuary.[214] Although TS prescribes rules for an ideal Jerusalem that would be impossible for ordinary people to follow, this does not preclude the possibility that the author still held such views.

3.7.3 THE DAMASCUS DOCUMENT

Since the phrase עיר המקדש, "the city of the sanctuary," refers to the city of Jerusalem in TS, it is reasonable to assume that the expression carries the same connotation in CD XII 1–2. As noted above, there are considerable similarities between the laws in 11QT XLV 11–12 and CD XII 1–2, which both prohibit sexual intercourse in "the city of the sanctuary." In spite of the similarity between the two passages, the perspectives behind the two laws differ. While the rule in D prohibits sexual encounters to take place in the city, TS simply presumes that sexual intercourse takes place outside the city and demands that a man should wait three days before entering. Nothing in D indicates that impurity after sexual intercourse was extended for three days (from the one day of impurity prescribed in Lev 15:18) as TS holds. The law prohibiting entrance to the city of the sanctuary for three days after intercourse in TS is part of an elaborate system of purity rules regulating a variety of aspects of life in the city. The aim of the system is to preserve the temple and the holiness that radiates out from it and that affects the rest of Jerusalem.[215] In contrast, D has no elaborate system in place for impurity carriers in Jerusalem. Nothing in D suggests that impurity bearers were being confined to specific places outside the cities.[216] On the contrary, the laws in 4Q266 6 ii that deal with the impurity of a *niddah*, a *zavah*, and a parturient, require, as in Leviticus, that these impurity bearers do not eat anything

---

[213] Milgrom's views are reiterated by Martha Himmelfarb ("Sexual Relations and Purity in the Temple Scroll," *DSD* 6 [1999], 18–21), who points out that one would expect a place of confinement for menstruants, since menstrual impurity may come on unexpectedly. She speculates that the TS perhaps did not "imagine women spending a great deal of time in the city of the sanctuary" (p. 21). Harrington follows Milgrom's thesis (*Impurity Systems*, 47–67).

[214] Milgrom, "Studies in the Temple Scroll," 512–17.

[215] 11QT XLVII 3b–5a: "And the city which I will sanctify to make dwell my name and [my] templ[e within it] shall be holy and be clean from any case of whatever impurity with which they could be defiled."

[216] One possible exception concerns those afflicted with scale disease. See 4Q266 6 i 13; *DJD XVIII*, 52–3.

sacred or enter the temple (המקדש) until the end of their purification periods. There is no hint that they would be excluded from the entire city. D simply prohibits sexual intercourse in Jerusalem. Since other types of impurities, such as *niddah*, in the city are of no concern in this document, unmarried men and women would still be able to live in Jerusalem; married couples had to refrain from sexual intercourse within the city. In addition, the segment that precedes CD XII 1–2 prohibits a *tevul yom*—a person who has completed all purifications but has not waited until sunset—to enter the temple. One can therefore assume that a person who is a *tevul yom* could still enter the city. In consequence, persons who after sexual intercourse immersed themselves would be able to enter Jerusalem the same day.[217]

3.7.4 CONCLUSION

Both 11QT XLV 11–12 and CD XII 1–2 prohibit sexual intercourse in Jerusalem. TS presents a more stringent law than does CD XII 1–2, in that a man (and, by extension, a couple) has to wait three days after intercourse before entering the city. Nevertheless, both laws represent a very strict halakhah. According to legislation in D, it appears that a person who has washed himself or herself after intercourse, a *tevul yom*, can enter Jerusalem on the same day as he has or she had sexual intercourse without waiting for sunset. Although a law that prohibits sexual intercourse in Jerusalem makes it virtually impossible for ordinary married couples to live permanently in Jerusalem, D betrays no concern for their situation and offers no practical solutions to the dilemma. Instead, D presents the stringent law simply as a matter of fact.

3.8 CONCLUSION: HALAKHAH

A large portion of the early laws concern women. This is not surprising, since the early law code displays a strong biblical orientation and biblical laws pay much attention to sexual relations and purity issues related to women. These laws in D display an androcentric perspective, whereby women are viewed as other than male

---

[217] CD XI 21b–22a reads: "And whoever comes to the house of prostration, let him not come unclean after washing." According to Baumgarten, "the house of prostration," בית השתחות, refers to a specific area of the temple ("The Damascus Document [CD]," 51 n.178). For the view that the expression has no relation to the temple, see Annette Steudel, "The Houses of Prostration: CD XI, 21–XII, 1–Duplicates of the Temple (1)," *RevQ* 16 (1993), 49–67. The expression "unclean after washing," טמא כבוס, pertains to a *tevul yom*; see Avi Solomon, "The Prohibition Against Tevul Yom and Defilement of the Daily Whole Offering in the Jerusalem Temple in CD 11:21–12:1: A New Understanding," *DSD* 4 (1997), 1–10. Cf. the *zavah* who has to wait until *sunset* at her purification before entering the temple; 4Q266 6 ii 4 (see above, p. 54).

and "never subjects of their own lives."[218] This perspective parallels the general tendency in biblical literature. The main legal topics that pertain to women include marital laws and purity laws, which coincide with the spheres of life where a woman's behaviour most affects men. In other words, the choice of legal topics related to women reflects an androcentric viewpoint.

If the law code has a priestly origin, as has been suggested, then one can expect a special interest in laws about women that relate to purity in general as well as purity and the temple in particular, which are topics within the early legislation. 4Q266 6 ii 2–13 stipulates purification rules for a parturient and a *zavah* before they are allowed to enter the temple, as well as detailing laws concerning the sacrifices by a parturient. Other laws concerning women that may point to a priestly provenance for the early law code include regulations for the *Sotah* (4Q270 4 1–10 and parallels). In this case, the early law code adds several restrictions to the biblical law, which makes the ordeal more difficult for husbands to impose. The reluctance to allow husbands to use this means of trial may stem not only from a desire to protect the woman, but also from a profound respect for the temple institution and the use of a curse, which should not be used frivolously. A prohibition against sexual intercourse in the City of the Sanctuary (CD XII 1–2) aims to protect the holiness and purity of the entire city surrounding the temple. Concern for geneaology at marriage, which I detect behind the expression לוא הוכן לה (4Q271 3 9 and parallels), is typical of priestly families. And finally, the prohibition against marrying a non-virgin, or widow who has had a post-widowhood sexual relationship (4Q271 3 10b–12 and parallels), is an extension of the biblical restrictions against a priest marrying a *zonah*. These laws concerning women fit well within a priestly context.

Purity laws for women are a major concern in the early law code. The long section on purity laws concerning genital discharges and childbirth in 4Q266 6 i 14/4Q272 1 ii 3–4Q266 6 ii 13 gives an indication of the importance attached to this subject among the circles that produced the early law code. The close connection between male and female impurity in this section demonstrates that impurity is a basic halakhic concern for all and not a subject matter that particularly concerns women. The text, extant from 4Q272 1 ii, indicates that the column contained precise details about how impurity was transmitted and how it was removed, but these details are now lost. I suggest that the text harmonizes the ways by which impurity is transmitted by men and women with various types of source impurity so that the same laws apply to the transmission of comparable type of impurity for each sex. In addition, it appears that the text imposes the same laws for the transmission of impurity through sexual intercourse with a *niddah* as through intercourse with a *zavah* (4Q266 6 ii 1–2). The transmission of impurity and subsequent purification are important subjects in other

---

[218] This quote from Judith Baskin on rabbinic literature ("Rabbinic Judaism and the Creation of Woman," in *Judaism Since Gender* [eds. Miriam Peskowitz and Laura Levitt; London: Routledge, 1997], 126) holds true for D as well.

Qumran documents, and it is unfortunate that the exact legal position in the early law code on these matters is not known. Over all, as I demonstrate above, the purity laws on women express a stringent interpretation of biblical legislation, as in the case of a woman bleeding between menstrual periods immediately being giving the status of a *zavah* (4Q266 6 ii 2–3). A tendency to stringency in purity matters is also visible in the law that bans sexual intercourse in the city of the sanctuary (CD XII 1–2), making it impossible for married couples to live there.

The early law code does not address the subject of the seclusion of ritually impure men and women during their primary impurity period, a topic that is elaborated upon in the purity regulations in 11QT. Although the prohibition against sexual intercourse in the City of the Sanctuary in CD XII 1–2 is in line with the requirement in 11QT to keep the city pure by keeping impure people out, there is no hint anywhere that D has adopted a purity system that demands quarantine areas for ritually impure persons. Since the section on female and male source impurity and childbirth (4Q266 6 i 14/4Q272 1 ii 3–4Q266 6 ii 13) follows the outline of topics in Leviticus 12–15 and is similar to the biblical text that assumes contact between impure and pure persons did occur, this likely indicates that people impure from genital discharges as well as childbirth were not kept in seclusion. The mention of a wet-nurse is something of an enigma within the context of the purification laws for a parturient. I conclude that there is no reason to assume a prohibition against nursing behind the reference.

The Sabbath Code includes a prohibition of "intermingling" on the Sabbath, which I understand to be a reference to sexual intercourse. As in the law prohibiting sexual intercourse in the City of the Sanctuary, this law is an expression of heightened purity concerns and not a negative view of sexual intercourse *per se*. A desire to be ritually pure on the Sabbath, a perspective which surfaces sparsely in Qumran texts, is not part of biblical legislation, nor is it a common perspective in writings from the Second Temple Period. Hence this law represents another example of a distinct stringency in the early legislation of D. Two restrictions of the activities on the Sabbath pertain to women in particular in spite of being written in the masculine: a law prohibiting transporting an infant and one prohibiting carrying ornamental spice and perfume bottles. The former law is yet another example of a stringent halakhic interpretation of biblical law. These two laws do not reveal anything significant about the status of women, but it is noteworthy that men are assumed to be carrying infants and to be taking part in child care.

A law in 4Q270 4 13–17 (and parallels) addresses sexual relations with a slave woman. The fragmentary text appears to forbid a slave woman, whom a free man takes as his wife, from eating sacrificial food or touching pure items for seven years. The few preserved words of the fragments attest to the practice of using female slaves for sexual and reproductive purposes. This is but one of several laws relating to slaves in the early law code. Since few other Qumran documents touch on the topic of slavery, this feature makes D unusual within the Scrolls. Nevertheless, the acceptance of slavery in the circles that produced the early law code of D is in accordance with the rest of the Mediterranean world in antiquity. Presumably, the reason Josephus and Philo mention the absence of slaves among the Essenes is because this custom differed from the norm.[219] Since the laws that presume slavery in D are part of the oldest legislation in D, and do not reflect the practice of a sect that later developed, they are not necessarily at variance with the much later claims by Josephus and Philo that the Essenes did not own slaves.[220]

Marital laws in the early law code emphasize the importance of virginity for a woman, which corresponds to the general attitude towards marriage and women's sexuality found throughout the Hebrew Bible, in Jewish literature from the Second Temple Period, as well as in the later rabbinic tradition. The high societal value placed on female virginity, as well as the chastity of widows, may be understood within the context of the honour and shame system that was prevalent in the Mediterranean world in antiquity. A patriarchal perspective comes to the fore in the law that commands a father to disclose the possible blemishes of his daughter prior to marriage (4Q271 3 4b–9a), while the text does not raise the subject of a prospective groom's possible blemishes. Moreover, the discourse compares the marital transfer of a woman to a business transaction, and throughout the marital transaction a woman is treated like a chattel.

Several of the laws from the early law code reflect a stern patriarchal stance and a demeaning attitude toward women. The marital laws in 4Q271 3 1–15 testify to a traditional double-standard when it comes to marital arrangements: a woman may be ostracized for engaging in sexual relations prior to marriage, while the sexual experience of a man is not an issue. Nevertheless, whereas general societal values would discourage men from marrying women who had sexual experience outside of marriage, 4Q271 3 is unique in banning marriage with a woman who has had any pre-marital sexual relationship, or with a widow who has had a sexual relationship after the death of her husband. The law that requires a physical examination of a woman suspected of not being a virgin at the time of the marital arrangements epitomizes the objectification of women (4Q271 3 12b–15). The females who perform the gynecological examination are credited with knowledge and reliability. It is rather ironic that in one of the few cases where the high status and authority of women—in this case mid-wives—surface in the Scrolls it is with regard to their power to exercise control over other women and take part in a practice that is overtly demeaning for women. Moreover, the early law code includes the biblical law about the *Sotah*, which, more forcefully than anywhere else in the Hebrew Bible, expresses a woman's subordinate position in marriage and her lack of power.

In spite of the patriarchal outlook of much of the early law code, there are three laws that in their interpretations of biblical laws constitute a clear improvement of

---

[219]Dale Martin, "Slavery and the Ancient Jewish Family," in *The Jewish Family in Antiquity* (ed. Shaye Cohen; BJS 289; Atlanta: Scholars Press, 1993), 127.

[220]Philo, *Prob.* 79; Josephus, *Ant.* XVIII 21.

women's legal position compared to biblical law. The law about women's oaths in CD XVI 6–12 denies men the right given to them in Num 30:3–16 to annul women's oaths at will, and only allows those oaths that lead to transgressions to be annulled. Thereby D increases the responsibility of women taking oaths. A second case that improves the women's position is found in the fragmentary text concerning the *Sotah* in 4Q270 4 in that this law radically restricts a husband's right to subject his wife to the ordeal of the *Sotah* compared to Num 5:11–31. As a consequence of the changes to the ordeal introduced in D, it would be more difficult for a husband to force a woman to undergo this humiliating ordeal. A third case concerns the laws in connection to marriage with a woman suspected of not being a virgin. In comparison to the Deuteronomic law concerning a virginity suit (Deut 22:13–21), the law in 4Q271 3 12b–15 increases the security for the woman—however flawed the legislation may be—by forcing her virginal status to be examined *before* the wedding, if there are doubts about her virginity. Thus, the life of the woman is not at stake, but rather her honour.

In sum, in spite of the patriarchal perspective that permeates the early law code and the generally strict legal view of the document, several of the laws on women reflect an attempt to improve women's legal position. These laws show the complexity of women's status within the laws: women are treated as subordinate to men, but at the same time their position in several instances has been improved over that in biblical legislation. Thus, there are laws in the early law code that reveal a sympathetic view of women and express concern for the vulnerability of women to being treated unfairly.

4. THE CATALOGUE OF TRANSGRESSORS

4.1 INTRODUCTION

The Catalogue of Transgressors will be examined on its own because of the uncertainties associated with placing it within a particular literary stratum. 4Q270 2 i–ii contains fragments from a list of transgressors, which has parallel text in 6Q15 5.[1] Sexual transgressions are denounced in two short passages in each of the two columns, which will be discussed below.

The Catalogue serves as an introduction to the laws in D that reminds the audience about the importance of observing the laws and warns it about the destructive qualities of sinning. The exhortation that follows immediately after the Catalogue (4Q270 2 i 19–21) alludes to literary themes in the Admonition. Taken together, the Catalogue and the hortatory segment make for a smooth transition from the Admonition to the subsequent legal part.[2] Patterned on Deut 27:15–26, the Catalogue lists transgressors who will be subject to God's wrath.[3] The transgressors are introduced by the word או ("or") or אשר או ("or one who"). There is an interesting mix of biblical and non-biblical laws in the list; for example, prohibitions against both profaning the Name (Exod 20:7) and sexual intercourse during pregnancy (non-biblical) are included.

4.2 SEXUAL TRANSGRESSORS: 4Q270 2 I 16–19

או אשר עליה שם רע ב[בְּתוּלִיה בבית	]	16
או בתולה מארשה לאיש[4] אשר]ישכב אחר עמה	[אביה	17

---

[1] PAM 43.296; *DJD XVIII*, Plate XXVII.
[2] See above, pp. 33–4.
[3] See Baumgarten, *DJD XVIII*, 143.
[4] My reconstruction is based on Deut 22:23.

18 [	או יק]רֹב אל אשתו ביום
19 [השבת	ה֯ או אשר י[ ]

16 [or one who has a bad reputation in] her maidenhood in the house
17 [of her father   or a young woman who is engaged to a man] with whom another lies
18 [or one who ap]proaches his wife on the
19 [Sabbath] day[   ]or one who y[   ]

The nature of the sexual transgressions of lines 16–17 is not clear. Deut 27:16–26 offers no interpretive help, since the curses in Deuteronomy are directed against offenders of incestuous crimes, which do not seem to be the concern here.[5] Baumgarten reconstructs the lines with reference to (a) a woman with a bad reputation, and (b) a "[widow] with whom another lies." His reconstruction is based on 4Q271 3 12–13, which prohibits a man from marrying both kinds of female offenders: a woman who has a bad reputation "in her maidenhood in her father's house" ש[ם רע בבתוליה בבית אביה (unless she is examined and exonerated by reputable women) and a widow who has engaged in sexual relations after she was widowed, אלמנה אשר נשכבה מאשר התארמלה.[6] Whereas the words בבתוליה בבית in line 16 are parallel to the phrase in 4Q271 3 13, and the reconstruction by Baumgarten is plausible, there is no parallel between the words in line 17 and the reference to a widow in 4Q271 3 12. The word אחר, with reference to another man, does not easily fit in a context discussing a promiscuous widow, since her husband is dead (and hence "another" would be an odd expression). Instead, a more likely target is a woman belonging to a man, that is, a wife or a betrothed woman, with whom "another" man lies.[7]

Based on the content of line 16 and the reference to [אביה] בבית "the house of her father]"—reminiscent of Deut 22:21—Deut 22:13–29 is the likely backdrop to 4Q270 2 i 16–17. Deut 22:13–29 concerns sexual sins. The deuteronomic laws address the cases of a slandered virgin and three categories of women who engage in non-marital sexual relations: a wife, an engaged woman, and a non-engaged woman. This chapter devotes the most space to the law of a slandered virgin and laws concerning a woman who is betrothed. Since the offense in 4Q270 2 i 16 likely concerns a woman of bad reputation corresponding to Deut 22:13–21, it is probable that the object of condemnation in line 17 is an engaged woman, parallel to Deut 22:23–7 (but the Catalogue does not refer to the same circumstances as Deut 22: 23–7). Thus, line 17 may condemn a young, betrothed woman "with whom another lies."

---

[5] Deut 27:20–22.

[6] See my discussion on this passage above, pp. 80-1.

[7] Cf. the wording of Deut 28:30, which reads: אשה תארש ואיש אחר ישגלנה "You shall become engaged to a woman, but *another* man shall lie with her" (my italics). Some early traditions (e.g., the Samaritan Pentateuch) instead of ישגלנה (lit. ravish) read ישכב עמה.

Baumgarten reconstructs lines 18–19 as a reference to a man who has sexual relations "on the Sabbath day," ביום [השבת]. He mentions that, alternatively, the curse may concern sexual relations on the day of Yom Kippur. Nevertheless, in light of the general desire in the sectarian literature of the Scrolls to preserve ritual purity on the Sabbath, his reconstruction remains the most likely one.[8]

4.3 MORE SEXUAL TRANSGRESSORS: 4Q270 2 II 15–17

The second column of the Catalogue lists three sexual transgressions together: (1) sexual intercourse with a pregnant woman; (2) sleeping with a niece; (3) homosexual intercourse. The curses against sexual transgressors follow condemnations of anyone who reveals secrets to gentiles, curses (his own people?), rebels against true teachers[9] or against the word of God, or anyone who slaughters a pregnant animal or beast (lines 13–15). Homosexual relations between males are considered a capital offense in biblical legislation (Lev 18:22; 20:13). The prohibition against marriage to a niece is a sectarian law that is widely attested in the Qumran literature.[10] Since the rationale for the condemnation of the first sexual transgression—intercourse during pregnancy— is unclear, the discussion below will focus on that topic.

4Q270 2 ii 15b–17a (6Q15 5 underlined) reads:

15   [או אשר ישכב עם]
16   אשה הרה מקיץ דם] או יקרב א[ל בת] אחיו או ישכב עם זכר]
17   משכבי אשה vac

15   [or one who lies with a]
16 pregnant woman, stirring blood, [or approaches] the daughter [of his brother, or
     one who lies with a male]
17 as one lies with a woman vac

The meaning of the words מקיץ דם, "stirring blood," in the context of sex during pregnancy is not clear. Hempel takes מקיץ as מן ("from") and the noun קץ ("end") and interprets the phrase as a reference to cessation of menstrual blood.[11] In contrast, Baumgarten takes the form as the *hiphil* participle of קוץ and translates "causing blood

---

[8] See discussion above, section 3.6.2.

[9] 4Q270 2 ii 13b–14 reads: "[or preaches] sedition against those anointed with the holy spirit and error against [the seers of his truth]."

[10] CD V 7–11; 11QT LXVI 16–17; and 4QHalakha A (4Q251) 12 2-3.

[11] Hempel translates line 16: "a pregnant woman, a woman who no longer menstruates" (*Laws*, 165–6). According to Baumgarten, Qimron understands the phrase in a similar way (*DJD XVIII*, 146).

to stir."[12] Orthographically, it is less likely that קיץ is a noun since the word is not spelled with a *yod* anywhere else in D.[13]

In an article on 4Q270 2 ii, Baumgarten gives two options for interpreting the phrase: (a) a medical concern for harm to the fetus in connection with sexual intercourse, and (b) a concern that the women may be more susceptible to bleeding during pregnancy and therefore more likely to transmit impurity.[14] He opts for the second suggestion, concluding that a law which demands sexual abstention during pregnancy is founded on a fear of impurity. His suggestion that "מקיץ דם ('stirring blood') pertains to the fear that coital pressure during pregnancy might lead to bleeding" has no empirical basis, because pregnancy *per se* does not make women more susceptible to bleeding.

There are several reasons why the first interpretation (a) is the correct one. The curse against anyone who sleeps with a pregnant woman follows immediately after a reference to anyone who slaughters a pregnant animal and should likely be understood within this context.[15] Apart from the shared state of pregnancy, the issues appear to be quite different: killing (the animal) versus restrictions on sexual intercourse (with the woman). However, if a medical concern were the underlying issue behind a ban against sexual intercourse during pregnancy (the position which Baumgarten mentions but rejects), then the two curses may be linked together conceptually by concern for the life of the fetus. A brief discussion of Greco-Roman medicine will bring additional evidence to support this understanding of the phrase.

Greek and Roman medical sources provide a plausible background for a prohibition of intercourse because of the danger of "stirring blood." Pregnancy was considered to be beneficial for a woman and was a prescribed "cure" for many medical problems.[16] Regular menstruation was a sign of good health and Greek and Roman

---

[12] See *DJD XVIII*, 145–6.

[13] See, for example, CD IV 9; XV 10; 4Q266 11 18; 4Q269 8 ii 5; 4Q271 2 12. The verb קוץ also occurs in 4Q272 1 ii 12 as the only preserved word on that line, within the context of laws dealing with menstruation.

[14] Joseph Baumgarten, "A Fragment on Fetal Life, and Pregnancy in 4Q270," in *Pomegranates and Golden Bells: Studies in Biblical, Jewish, and Near Eastern Ritual, Law, and Literature in Honor of Jacob Milgrom* (eds. David P. Wright, et al.; Winona Lake, Ind.: Eisenbrauns, 1995), 445–8.

[15] Similarly, 11QT LII 5–7 prohibits sacrificing a pregnant animal (cf. 4QMMT B 36–8). A biblical background to the law in 4Q270 2 ii 15 is found in Deut 22:6–7 and Lev 22:28. See Baumgarten, "A Fragment on Fetal Life," 445; Robert Kugler, "Rewriting Rubrics: Sacrifice and the Religion of Qumran," in *Religion in the Dead Sea Scrolls* (eds. John J. Collins and Robert Kugler; Grand Rapids, Mich.: Eerdmans, 2000), 104–6.

[16] Both pregnancy and intercourse (providing wetness) was a prescribed cure in Hippocratic medicine for the common disease of the "wandering womb"; see Nancy Demand, *Birth, Death and Motherhood in Classical Greece* (Baltimore: The John Hopkins University Press, 1994), 32, 55–7; Aline Rouselle, *Porneia: On Desire and the Body in Antiquity* (trans. Felicia

doctors saw a connection between regular menstruation and fertility.[17] A persistent view in Greco-Roman medicine held that blood was crucial for the development of the fetus. Since the flow of blood ceased during pregnancy, medical doctors speculated that the blood now went to nourish the fetus. Therefore, blood-loss during pregnancy was considered harmful for the fetus as well as for the woman.[18]

The Hippocratic doctors believed that it was the first intercourse (rather than the onset of puberty) that brought on menstrual periods, and bleeding during pregnancy was therefore often attributed to intercourse.[19] In spite of that, according to the Hippocratic Collection a woman could have intercourse during pregnancy. Nevertheless, in light of the importance of retaining the blood in the uterus during pregnancy, a few Roman doctors argued for sexual restraint during pregnancy. Galen advised women not to have sex too often, while Soranus explicitly forbade sexual intercourse during pregnancy.[20]

This Greco-Roman view of the interrelationships between blood, sexual intercourse, and pregnancy supports the interpretation that 4Q270 2 ii 16 reflects a concern about retaining blood in the uterus for the developing fetus. Hence the phrase "stirring blood" may refer to a fear that intercourse would somehow shake the uterine blood and endanger the fetus.[21] This meaning of מקיץ דם ("stirring blood") would explain why the transgression of the ban on sexual intercourse was considered a particularly serious offense.

Pheasant; Oxford: Basil Blackwell, 1988), 28; Helen King, *Hippocrates' Woman: Reading the Female Body in Ancient Greece* (New York: Routledge, 1998), 25, 78–9.

[17] See Rousell, *Porneia*, 21.

[18] Hippocrates, *On the Diseases of Women* 1.25, 32; *Aphorisms* 5.31, 50, 60; Soranus, *Gynaecology* 1.19; see Helen King, "Producing Woman: Hippocratic Gynaecology," in *Women in Ancient Societies* (eds. Leonie Archer, S. Fischler, and M. Wyhe; New York: Routledge, 1994), 107–8; Lesley Dean-Jones, *Women's Bodies in Classical Greek Science* (Oxford: Clarendon Press, 1994), 60–5, 200–15.

[19] Dean-Jones refers to several passages in the Hippocratic Collection that presume that intercourse removed some impediment to menstruation. Since blood was accumulated in the young woman's body at the time of her puberty, it was paramount that she was "opened up" through intercourse; otherwise, the blood would move to the area around the heart, which was dangerous; Dean-Jones, *Women's Bodies in Classical Greek Science*, 50–3. See also Rouselle, *Porneia*, 42.

[20] Soranus, *Gynaecology* 1. 46, 56; see Rouselle, *Porneia*, 42.

[21] Some Rabbis believed that sexual intercourse during pregnancy might cause harm to the fetus. A baraita in *b. Nid.* 31a claims that sexual intercourse is harmful for the fetus during the first trimester, while it is beneficial for the fetus in the last two. Rabbinic law prohibits a pregnant woman from remarrying until delivery. According to Talmud, one reason for this is that careless intercourse with a new husband would endanger the fetus (*b. Yeb.* 42a; cf. *b. Nid* 45a); see Epstein, *Marriage Laws,* 305–6; Baumgarten, "A Fragment on Fetal Life," 448.

4.4 Conclusion

Parallel to the early law code and the Hebrew Bible, the Catalogue of Transgressors expresses a traditional view on women's sexuality that condemns any non-marital sexual relation a woman might have. It is worth noting that both men and women are condemned in this list. The fragmentary text from the Catalogue of Transgressors likely condemns any woman suspected of having pre-marital sexual relations, and, as I have reconstructed 4Q270 2 ii 17, anyone who during engagement has sexual relations with someone other than her fiancée. The list ends with a reference to the wrath of God (4Q270 2 ii 18), which indicates the rhetorical function of the Catalogue, namely, to warn the audience about the seriousness of the kind of transgressions that appear in the list. These rebukes show that the main נתיבות שחת, "paths of destruction" (line 20), that a woman can enter are sexual in nature.

The prohibition against sexual intercourse during pregnancy in D is one of the key parallels between sectarian documents and Josephus' description of the Essenes: "they [the Essenes] have no intercourse with them [their wives] during pregnancy, thus showing that their motive in marrying is not self-indulgence (ἡδονῇ), but the procreation of children."[22] In light of 4Q270 2 ii 16, a prohibition against intercourse during pregnancy may have originated not solely as an expression of asceticism, but also out of fear that intercourse during pregnancy may be harmful to the fetus.

---

[22] *War* II 161. For a detailed discussion on this passage, see below section 6.5.3, "Fornication with a Wife."

5. THE ADMONITION

5.1 INTRODUCTION

As I have discussed above, I consider the Admonition to be a composition written within the community behind D at about the same time as the communal laws because of the common perspective of the two parts.[1] Hence it is written after the Halakhah, and likely after the Catalogue of Transgressors, and has a provenance differing from that of the early laws. The Admonition contains a few references to women, which are mainly embedded within teachings on marriage and purity. CD IV 12b–V 15a criticises the general population for transgressing marital laws by taking two wives and allowing marriages between uncles and nieces. The people are also accused of transgressing purity laws with regard to sexual intercourse and entering the temple in a ritually defiled state. CD VII 6b–9a addresses those living in camps who "take wives and beget children," who are admonished to observe the laws of the Torah. These two passages will be discussed below.

5.2 NETS OF BELIAL: CD IV 12B–V 15A

5.2.1 INTRODUCTION

CD IV 12b–V 15a exposes the dominion of Belial over Israel.[2] This present state of affairs is explained as the fulfilment of Isa 24:17—"Fear and a pit and a snare are upon you, O inhabitant(s) of the land" (CD IV 14)—which is interpreted in the ensuing midrash as referring to the three nets with which Belial catches Israel. The

---

[1] See above, p. 43.
[2] There is a natural break between CD V 15a and b; in line 15 b, the focus changes from a contemporary perspective to an exposition of ancient times. See, e.g., Rabin, *Zadokite Documents*, 18; Campbell, *The Use of Scripture*, 116. Davies makes the division after CD V 16 (*Damascus Covenant*, 108, 119).

nets appear as three kinds of righteousness, ויתנם פניהם לשלושת מיני הצדק (IV 16–17), "making them seem as if they were three types of righteousness," which explains why Belial has been able to trap Israel by their sinful behaviour. The exposition of the traps of Belial forms a harsh critique of contemporary Jewish practice.[3] The three nets are identified as זנות, "fornication," ההון (emended from ההין),[4] "wealth," and טמא מקדש, "defilement of the temple" (CD IV 17–18).

There are noticeable discrepancies in the passage: the nets do not closely match the subsequent description of sins committed by "the builders of the wall" (CD IV 19–V 15), and the order of the specific sins does not follow the order of the nets. This discrepancy between the alignment of the nets and the list of sins likely reflects underlying layers of material in the text.[5] The author himself refers explicitly to one source used for this passage: "Levi son of Jacob" (IV 16).[6] Since the list of accusations focuses on transgressions of a marital and sexual nature, Davies convincingly argues that the author used a pre-existing list of sexual offences linked to his second source, a midrash on Isa 24:17, in the form of three nets of Belial.[7]

5.2.2 POLYGYNY

CD IV 20–21 specifies one example of the sin of fornication, but the exact meaning is debated; the lines read, בזנות לקחת שתי נשים בחייהם, (they are caught) "in

---

[3] A similar listing of three major sins appears in Jub. 7:20: "...preserve themselves from fornication and pollution and from all injustice. For on account of these three the flood came upon the earth." In Jub. 23:20–1 the critique against future generations (=contemporary society) includes wealth, corruption, and defilement of the temple; for accusations about defiling the temple, cf. Pss. Sol. 8:11–13. In the Aramaic Testament of Levi from the Cairo Geniza, Isaac instructs Levi to avoid fornication (זנות), defilement, (פחז), and uncleanliness (טמאה) (Bodleian B 11 14–16); טמאה refers to defiling the Temple. See Jonas Greenfield, "The Words of Levi Son of Jacob in Damascus Document IV 15–19," RevQ 13, (1988), 319–22.

[4] I am following the majority of scholars (e.g., Wise, Abegg, Cook, *The Dead Sea Scrolls*, 55; Vermes, *The Complete Dead Sea Scrolls*, 130). Schwarz argues that the form ההין (CD IV 17) should not be emended as it pertains to "arrogance" rather than "wealth," based on the use of ההון in Deut 1:41 ("Damascus Document [CD]," 21 n.45); so also Catherine Murphy, who points out that economic acts and arrogance are associated in D (*Wealth in the Dead Sea Scrolls and in the Qumran Community*, STDJ 40 [Leiden: Brill, 2002], 38–40).

[5] Davies argues that the redactor used two separate sources (*Damascus Covenant*, 110, 116). Others detect a secondary layer in CD V 6b–7; see Knibb, *The Qumran Community*, 42; Adiel Schremer, "Qumran Polemic on Marital Law: CD 4:20–5:11 and Its Social Background," in *The Damascus Document: A Centennial of Discovery*, 149–51; Jerome Murphy O'Connor, "An Essene Missionary Document? CD II, 14–VI,1," RB 77 (1970), 220–1; Rabin, *Zadokite Documents*, 17–19.

[6] Greenfield argues that the text refers to the Aramaic Testament of Levi ("The Words of Levi Son of Jacob in Damascus Document IV, 15–19," 319–22).

[7] Davies, *Damascus Covenant*, 110–16.

The Admonition

fornication by marrying two women in their (masc.) lives."[8] The masculine suffix in בחייהם, "their," (CD IV 21) poses a special problem.[9]

One interpretation, held by Murphy O'Connor, Davies and others, argues that the phrase prohibits any second marriage ever, even remarriage after the death of a spouse.[10] From 4Q271 3 10–12, we now know that a widow was allowed to remarry if she had remained chaste after the death of her husband.[11] Of course, the latter passage refers to a woman and not a widower. But in light of the permission for widows to remarry, one may safely assume the same rule concerning men. Hence, this interpretation is highly improbable.

According to another interpretation, the phrase is a prohibition against any second marriage as long as the *wife* is alive. Both polygyny and any remarriage after divorce (when the first wife is alive) are thereby prohibited. Fitzmyer, for example, argues that הם- ("their") refers to both the man and the wife and that the passage prohibits either of them from remarrying as long as both are alive.[12] Commonly these scholars point to the passage prohibiting the king from taking a second wife in 11QT LVII 17b–19a as support.[13]

ולוא יקח עליה אשה אחרת כי היאה לבדה תהיה עמו כול ימי חייה ואם מתה ונשא
לו אחרת מבית אביהו ממשפחתו

---

[8] For a detailed survey of the scholarly debate from 1910 to 1956, see Paul Winter, "Sadokite Fragments IV 20, 21 and the Exegesis of Genesis 1:27 in Late Judaism," *ZAW* 68 (1956), 71–84. For a description of the debate up to the early 1970s, see Geza Vermes, "Sectarian Matrimonial Halakhah in the Damascus Rule," *JJS* 25 (1974). For an extensive bibliography of scholarly works on this passage, see Schremer, "Qumran Polemic on Marital Law," 147–51.

[9] See John Kampen, "A Fresh Look at Masculine Plural Suffix in CD IV, 21," *RevQ* 16 (1993), 91–7.

[10] Murphy-O'Connor, "An Essene Missionary Document?" 220; Davies, *Behind the Essenes*, 73–85; *Damascus Covenant*, 116.

[11] In addition, remarriage after the death of the spouse is assumed in 11QT LVII 17–19.

[12] Joseph Fitzmyer, "Divorce Among First-Century Palestinian Jews," *ErIsr* 14 (1978), 106–10; "The Matthean Divorce Texts and Some New Palestinian Evidence," *TS* 37 (1976), 220. In his article "Marriage and Divorce" (*Encyclopedia of the Dead Sea Scrolls*, 1:511–14), Fitzmyer does not mention the possible reference to divorce in CD XIII 17/4Q266 9 iii 5. Other scholars who hold this position include Baumgarten ("The Qumran-Essene Restraints on Marriage," 14–15; *DJD XVIII*, 71), Schiffman (*Reclaiming*, 130; "Laws Pertaining to Women in the Temple Scroll," 217–18), Dupont-Sommer (*The Essene Writings*, 129 n.1), Brin ("Divorce at Qumran," 231–44), and Kampen ("A Fresh Look at Masculine Plural Suffix in CD IV, 21," 91–7).

[13] For example, according to Yadin, the passage in 11QT confirms that CD IV 20–21 prohibits polygamy and divorce ("L'attitude essénienne envers la poygamy et le divorce," *RB* 79 [1972], 98–9; cf. *The Temple Scroll*, 2:258).

He shall not take another wife in addition to her, for she alone shall be with him all the time of her life. But if she dies he may marry another from his father's house, from his family.

A third position is that polygyny alone is prohibited.[14] Vermes emphasizes that the three scriptural proof texts that follow CD IV 20–21 (Gen 1:27; 7:9; Deut 17:17) support monogamy as opposed to polygyny as the only legitimate marriage union; they do not touch upon the issue of remarriage after divorce. From this, it appears that only a prohibition of polygyny is at stake.[15] It is also important that the biblical basis for the prohibition, Lev 18:18, concerns bigamy—marrying two sisters—and not divorce and subsequent remarriage. Since the biblical text emphasizes that a husband is prohibited from simultaneously being married to two sisters, it is unlikely that divorce was even considered by the author in CD IV 20–21.[16] The crux for this interpretation is the use of the masculine suffix instead of the feminine one. However, this may be a simple scribal mistake, as Vermes argues.[17] In light of the 4QD fragments, it appears that D in fact recognises the legitimacy of divorce. Before the publication of 4QD, the reference to וכן למגרש (CD XIII 17) in the damaged section at the end of the column had been understood by some scholars as a reference to divorce. Nevertheless, this understanding remained uncertain because the context was unclear.[18] With the publication of the parallel text in 4Q266 9 iii 1–19 (=CD XIII 15–XIV 2), however, it is now apparent that the text concerns marriage: the Examiner is responsible for

---

[14]Vermes, "Sectarian Matrimonial Halakhah in the Damascus Rule," 197–202. For the same interpretation, see Ginzberg, *An Unknown Jewish Sect*, 20; Schremer, "Qumran Polemic on Marital Law," 147–60; David Instone Brewer, "Nomological Exegesis in Qumran 'Divorce' Texts," *RevQ* 18 (1998), 561–79. Cf. Tom Holmén, ("Divorce in CD 4:20–5:2 and 11QT 57:17–18: Some remarks on the Pertinence of the Question," *RevQ* 18 [1998], 397–408) who focuses on methodological issues in interpreting the passages CD IV 20–V 2 and 11QT LVII 17–18.

[15]Vermes, "Sectarian Matrimonial Halakah in the Damascus Rule," 197–202. According to the gospel traditions, Jesus refers to Gen 1:27 in support of a prohibition of divorce and remarriage (Mk 10:10–12; Mt 19:4). But the emphasis in the gospels is on the couple being joined together ("what God has joined together, let no one separate") compared to the stress on one man and one female (opposed to two wives) in CD IV 21.

[16]David Brewer stresses this point ("Nomological Exegesis in Qumran 'Divorce' Texts," *RevQ* 18 [1998], 576).

[17]Vermes asserts that "בחייהם ['their lives'] is either a mistake or else it is a linguistic peculiarity, attested in biblical and post-biblical Hebrew, whereby a masculine third person plural suffix stands for a corresponding feminine one" ("Sectarian Matrimonial Halakhah in the Damascus Rule," 202). According to Elisha Qimron, the form הם- as one form of 3rd person plural feminine suffix is attested in Qumran Hebrew (unfortunately he does not give a reference); see *The Hebrew of the Dead Sea Scrolls* (HSS 29; Atlanta: Scholars Press, 1986), 58, 322.

[18]Rabin, *Zadokite Documents*, 66.

The Admonition

supervising marriage (line 4), divorce (line 5), and the education of children (lines 6–8).[19]

Given that 4Q266 9 iii 5/CD XIII 17 assumes that divorce did occur in the community, two possible interpretations of CD IV 20–21 remain, if one assumes legal consistency within D: a) that the community recognised divorce, but not remarriage after divorce—the opinion of Baumgarten and Schiffman[20]—or b) that divorce and subsequent remarriage was accepted. The former view is highly unlikely, since divorce has always meant the freedom to remarry in Jewish legislation. Deut 24:1–4 and subsequent Jewish legislation testifies to this basic right of a woman.[21] Aramaic divorce certificates from Elephantine from the fifth century B.C.E. include the phrase "she may go wherever she wishes" (ותהך לה אן זי צבית).[22] A Jewish certificate from 72 C.E., discovered in Wadi Murabba'at, specifies that the woman is free to remarry, although her choice of a new husband is limited to "any Jewish man." This portion reads: די את רשיא בנפשכי למהך ולמהי אנת לכל גבר יהודי די תצבין, "that you are free on your part to go and become the wife of any Jewish man that you wish."[23] Given the long Jewish tradition of granting a woman the right to remarry upon divorce, it is hard to envision that the community behind D would accept divorce but not subsequent remarriage.

11QT, furthermore, accepts divorce among the general population as is evident in a paraphrase on Numbers 30 concerning the law on oaths of women (11QT LIV 4–5).[24] Additionally, Mal 2:16 in the Scroll of Minor Prophets from Cave 4 appears to

---

[19]See discussion below, sections 6.3.6 and 6.3.7.
[20]Schiffman, *Reclaiming*, 130; Baumgarten, *DJD XVIII*, 71.
[21]Cf. the Mishnaic claim: גופו של גט הרי את מותרת לכל אדם, "The essential formula of a letter of divorce is, Behold, you are permitted to any man" (*m. Git.* 9:3); see also *m. Qidd.* 1:1: "a woman is acquired by three means and she regains her freedom by two methods... and she recovers her freedom by a letter of divorce or on the death of the husband."
[22]Bezalel Porten and Ada Yardeni, *Contracts* (Vol. 2 of *Textbook of Aramaic Documents from Ancient Egypt: Newly Copied, Edited and Translated into Hebrew and English* [Jerusalem: Hebrew University/Winona Lake, In.: Eisenbrauns, 1986–96]). For a discussion on these papyri, see David Instone Brewer, "Deuteronomy 24:1–4," 239–41.
[23]Papyrus Murabba'at 20, lines 6b–7; see *Les grottes de Murabba'at* (eds. Benoit, P., J. T. Milik et R. de Vaux; DJD II; Oxford: Clarendon Press, 1961), 104–9; Brewer, "Deuteronomy 24:1–4," 238. According to the Rabbis no exception clause is accepted in a writ of divorce, contrary to the opinion of R. Eliezer (*m. Git.* 1:1, 3).
[24]See also 11QT LXVI 8–11, which prescribes that a seducer must marry the seduced woman with no chance of divorcing her (Deut 22:28–9). This case assumes that divorce under normal circumstances is allowed. The paraphrase of Deut 22:13–21 (the law about a slandered bride) in 11QT LXV 7–LXVI 4 may prohibit the false accuser to divorce his wife, but the end of the section is missing. Whereas the law in 11QT LVII 17–19 may prohibit divorce and remarriage for the king, the law is imposed on the king alone. Schiffman explains that the king is

advocate divorce, כי אם שנתה שלח "for if you hate her, send her away," which has a different connotation to that of the phrase in MT: כי שנא שלח אמר יהיה "for I hate divorce, says the Lord."[25]

To conclude, my analysis has shown that there is reason to believe that CD IV 20–1 prohibits polygyny only and not remarriage after divorce. If taken literally, the accusation against "taking two wives in their lives" proscribes any second marriage within a man's lifetime. Nevertheless, from the cumulative force of all the arguments I conclude that the accusation in CD IV 20–1 refers to polygyny.

A ban on polygyny did go against societal norms as well as biblical acceptance of the practice.[26] Although it is impossible to know how common the practice of polygyny was, there is evidence that some men still took more than one wife in late Second Temple period. Jospehus writes: "for it is an ancestral custom of ours to have several wives at the same time" (*Ant.* XVII 14).[27] While the practice of polygyny is well attested in royal circles, the Babatha archives show that such a marriage arrangement could also take place among the common people in the early second century C.E.[28] The accusation of fornication in the form of bigamy was addressed to all Israel, a society that allowed such a practice, and the prohibition of polygyny consequently set the community behind D apart from the rest of the society.

5.2.3 DEFILING THE SANCTUARY

The prohibition against marrying two wives is followed by a reference to defiling the sanctuary (CD V 6–7), corresponding to net number three. This sin is explained as lying with a woman who sees her bloody flux (CD V 6b–7a): וגם מטמאים הם את המקדש אשר אין הם מבדיל כתורה ושוכבים עם הרואה את דם זובה, "and they also continuously polluted the sanctuary by not separating according to the Torah, and they habitually lay with a woman who sees blood of flowing."[29] Scholars have variously

---

expected to follow the same standard of holiness as the High Priest ("Laws Pertaining to Women in the Temple Scroll," 215).

[25] See Brin, "Divorce at Qumran," 231–44; Russell Fuller, "Text-Critical Problems in Malachi 2:10–16," *JBL* 110 (1991), 54–6.

[26] The Rabbis allowed a man to have up to five wives (*m. Ketub.* 10:5; *m. Ker.* 3:7); Justin Martyr criticizes Jews for practicing polygyny (*Dialogue with Trypho*, 141; vol.6 of *Fathers of the Church*).

[27] See also *J.W.* I 477. For a discussion on these passages and polygamy in general in Second Temple Judaism, see John J. Collins, "Marriage, Divorce, and Family in Second Temple Judaism," in *Families in Ancient Israel* (eds. Leo Perdue, Joseph Blenkinsopp, and Carol Meyers; Lousville, Ky.: Westminster John Knox Press, 1997), 121–2.

[28] Naphtali Lewis, *Documents from the Bar Kokhba Period in the Cave of Letters* (Jerusalem: Israel Exploration Society, 1989), 26.

[29] Pss. Sol. 8:12 includes an accusation similar to that in CD V 6–7: "They walked on the place of sacrifice of the Lord, (coming) from all kinds of uncleanness; and (coming) with menstrual blood (on them), they defiled the sacrifices as if they were common meat."

assumed that the accusation in CD V 6–7 concerns sexual intercourse with menstruants[30] or women with irregular flux.[31] In biblical Hebrew דם זובה ("blood of flowing") can refer to either regular menstruation or irregular flux; the same is true in Qumranic literature.[32] In 4QTohorot A, the root זבה is used with reference to both types of impurities, while נדה refers to menstruation alone.[33] In D, נדה is consistently used with reference to menstruation.[34] If the author had meant either sort of impurity in CD V 7, he could have specified the accusation accordingly and clarified exactly what kind of impurity was under consideration. I will therefore take CD V 7 literally, as a reference to men sleeping with women who experience any kind of vaginal blood. Such practice is, of course, contrary to biblical law (Lev 15:24). Many scholars have suggested that the accusation is directed to a specific group and that it relates to a controversy about the interpretation of purity laws for women after menstruation or irregular flux.[35] Biblical proof texts are supplied to support the community's legislation concerning bigamy and marriage with a niece but not in this case, which suggests that the accusation relates to the transgression of a biblical law that was widely accepted.

The accusation regarding sleeping with a woman who sees her blood seems far-fetched: the taboo connected to a woman's menstrual blood was ancient and deeply ingrained in the Jewish consciousness in the Second Temple Period. It is hard to believe that transgressions of these purity laws were widespread among the people. Perhaps marriage or illicit sexual intercourse between Jews and non-Jews is the underlying issue here. If some laymen and priests married foreign women, perhaps some people would see a great danger with regard to purity issues. Foreign women would be suspect of not paying attention to Jewish purity laws and consequently—

---

[30] So Philip Davies, "The Ideology of the Temple in the Damascus Document," *JJS* 33 (1982), 289.

[31] Hans Kosmala believes it refers to both kinds of impurity; see "The Three Nets of Belial," *ASTI* 4 (1965), 99.

[32] Both menstruation and irregular flux can be described by a combination of the terms זבה and דם; דם זובה refers to regular "discharge of blood" (menstruation) in Lev 15:19, and ואשה כי־יזוב זוב דמה ימים רבים בלא עת־נדתה, "if a woman has a discharge of blood for many days, not at the time of her impurity" (Lev 15:25) concerns flux. The specific term for menstruation impurity is נדה (Lev 15:19, 24, 25).

[33] For the use of the root זבה with reference to a menstruant, see 4QTohorot A 1 i 4: והזבה דם ("who has a flow of blood"). For זבה in connection to irregular flux, see 4QTohorot A 1 i 6b אשה [זב]ה סדם לימים רב[ים] ("a woman with a blood [fl]ow lasting man[y] days"); and 1 i 7b–8, דם הנדה כזוב ("menstrual blood is like the flux"). See Baumgarten, *DJD XXXV*, 100–3; "The Laws about Fluxes in 4QTohora^a (4Q274)," in *Time to Prepare the Way in the Wilderness*, 1–8; Jacob Milgrom, "4QTohora^a: An Unpublished Qumran Text on Purities," in *Time to Prepare the Way in the Wilderness*, 59–68.

[34] See 4Q266 6 ii 2, 6; 4Q272 1 ii 8.

[35] E.g., Rabin, *Zadokite Documents*, 19 n.7²; Knibb, *The Qumran Community*, 43.

which was the greatest danger— transmitting impurity to their men. These in turn would go to the temple, and thus bring defilement to it. 4QMMT B 48–49 likely reflects a similar concern, linking forbidden marriage unions to a danger to the purity of the temple. The composite text reads (4QMMT C underlined; 4QMMT D dotted underline):

48 [כי לכול בני ישראל ראוי להזהר מִכֲּוֹלַ תַ̇]עֲרוֹבֶת [ה]גֶּבֶר
49 [ולהיות יראים מהמקדש

48 [For all the sons of Israel should beware] of any forbidden unions[36]
49 [and be full of reverence for the sanctuary].

The poorly preserved text in 4Q513 2 ii expresses a similar worry about the practical dangers of impurity in marriages to foreigners. Through their illicit unions, the priests are accused of polluting the holy offerings that they eat.[37] 4Q513 10 ii 3 reads "one may not mix with them" אין לערב בם[ו], which likely refers to sexual relations with non-Jews; such mixing brings defilement onto "the pure food," בטהרה, (line 6) and to the temple המקדש, (line 7). In light of these instances where the purity of the temple is threatened by sexual unions with foreigners, it is reasonable to conclude that CD V 6–7 pertains to the same issue.

5.2.4 MARRIAGE TO A NIECE

Instead of moving on to the second net—wealth—which logically follows the sequence outlined in the introduction (CD IV 17–18), the text returns to the topic of unlawful marriages (CD V 7b–11a). This time marriage between a man and his niece is condemned as incest. Since "the builders of the wall" in IV 20 were said to be caught in זנות ("fornication") twice, there is reason to understand this as the second instance of זנות.[38] Any transgression of the incest laws of Lev 18:6–18 is thus considered זנות ("fornication"). CD V 7b–11a reads:

---

[36] Lines 39–49 of 4QMMT B are poorly preserved. The discussion begins with a list of those who are forbidden to enter the congregation; references are made to the Ammonite (reconstructed), Moabite, the *mamzer*, the one with crushed testicles, and the eunuch. The text continues to discuss marriages within the prohibited categories (lines 40–45). Line 42 mentions טמאות, "impurities." "Forbidden unions" in line 48 likely refers to marriages between Jews and people from prohibited categories; see Qimron, *DJD X*, 50–1, 139–40.

[37] See 4Q513 2 ii, Schiffman, "Rules (4Q513=4QOrd^b)," in *Rule of the Community and Related Documents*, 161 n.19.

[38] See Fitzmyer, "The Matthean Divorce Texts and Some New Palestinian Evidence," 219; Murphy-O'Connor, "An Essene Missionary Document?," 220. For an analysis of the expression נתפשים בשתים בזנות ("caught in fornication twice"), see Schremer, "Qumran Polemic on Marital Law," 150–1.

7	ולוקחים
8	איש את בת אחיהו ואת בת אחותו ומשה אמר אל
9	אחות אמך לא תקרב שאר אמך היא ומשפט העריות לזכרים
10	הוא כתוב וכהם הנשים ואם תגלה בת האח את ערות אחי
11	אביה והיא שאר

[7] And they marry [8] each one his brother's daughter or sister's daughter. But Moses said [9] "You shall not approach your mother's sister; she is your mother's near kin." And the law against incest [10] is written with reference to males but the same (law) applies to women; so, if a brother's daughter uncovers the nakedness of [11] her father's brother, then she is his near kin.

It is striking that a biblical law, Lev 18:13, "written for males," in this case applies equally to women.

While the prohibition of polygyny is not found in other Qumran documents, the prohibition of marriage between an uncle and a niece is recorded also in 11QT LXVI 15–17 and 4QHalakha A (4Q251) 17 2. In comparison to D, the prohibition in TS lacks the polemical edge evident in D.

The prohibition against a man marrying his niece sets the community apart from the rest of Jewish society in which marriage between a man and his sister's daughter appears to have been common.[39] One may ask why marriage between an uncle and his niece would be prohibited. Schremer suggests that marrying a niece and bigamy are part of the same phenomenon. She points to tractate *Yevamot*, which depicts a society where men often married a niece in addition to another wife.[40] This may certainly be part of the reason for condemning the practice. However, it is more likely that biblical exegesis led the community to the ban. CD V 9–11 states that the prohibition against a man marrying his mother's sister in Lev 18:13 is "written for males" but applies equally to women. This gender-inclusive reading of biblical laws appears elsewhere in D, for example, in the laws concerning women's oaths in CD XVI 6–12. In its exegesis of the biblical law on women's oaths, D applies the principle to fulfill the promises one utters from Deut 23:24 to both men and women (see discussion above). Therefore, it is quite possible that reading biblical laws gender-inclusively was not an uncommon perspective in the community behind D. It is likely that a close reading of biblical law led the community to condemn marriages between uncles and nieces.

In sum, women are mentioned several times in the discourse on the Nets of Belial as part of the accusations about marital practices among the general population. The emphasis on marital laws in this section shows that the correct observance of these laws was at the centre of the conflicts that led the community behind D to separate to some extent from the general society. In contrast to societal norms, the community

---

[39] See Ilan, *Jewish Women*, 75–9.
[40] Schremer, "Qumran Polemic on Marital Law," 149–51.

banned polygyny and the marriage between an uncle and his niece. In addition, the author accuses men in general of having sexual relations with women who disregard basic purity rules. The women in the latter case are not accused directly, only by implication, perhaps because these women are assumed to be non-Jewish.

5.3 CD VII 4B–10A: A BIFURCATION OF LIFESTYLES?

5.3.1 INTRODUCTION

MS B overlaps with MS A from VII 5b to the end of MS A (MS A VII 5b–VIII 21 = MS B XIX 1–34a) and the two MSS display great variances, in particular in the use of the biblical references and their interpretations. There are differences between MSS A and B in the text under consideration (noted in the footnotes below). Unique to MS B (XIX 1–2) is a quote from Deut 7:9 that is usually viewed as original; it is therefore included in the text below.[41]

CD VII 4b–10a (MS A) with XIX 1–2 (MS B) inserted within brackets:

כל המתהלכים	4
באלה בתמים קדש על פי כל יסורו ברית אל נאמנות להם	5
לחיותם אלף דור (כב שומר הברית והחסד לאהב ולשמרי מצותי לאלף דור)	6
ואם מחנות ישבו כסרך הארץ[42] ולקחו	
נשים[43] והולידו בנים והתהלכו[44] על פי התורה וכמשפט	7
היסורים[45] כסרך התורה כאשר אמר בין איש לאשתו ובן אב	8
לבנו וכל המואסים[46] בפקד אל את הארץ להשיב גמול רשעים	9
עליהם	10

---

[41]CD VII 6–15 is not preserved in 4QD and it is not known which version 4QD follows at this point. The omission in MS A is likely due to haplography; White Crawford offers solid arguments for why the A text of CD VII 4b–10a should be considered the original apart from this instance; "A Comparison of the 'A' and 'B' Manuscripts of the Damascus Document," 537–54.

[42]CD XIX 3 (MS B) adds: אשר היה מקדם, "as it was from old."

[43]CD XIX 3 (MS B) adds: כמנהג התורה, "according to the custom of the Torah."

[44]While MS A's והתהלכו ("and they shall walk") continues the chain of waw-consecutive perfects, MS B modifies the verb form to ויתהלכו, which clarifies that the subject is the wives and children, "that *they* may walk" (CD XIX 4); see John Elwolde, "Distinguishing the Linguistic and the Exegetical: The Biblical Book of Numbers in the Damascus Document," *DSD* 7 (2000), 13.

[45]Rabin emends the word to האסרים, "binding vows," pointing to CD XVI 7; he is followed by Schiffman, "Laws of Vows and Oaths," 205. Still, the text makes sense as it reads and no emendation is necessary.

[46]CD XIX 5-6 (MS B) adds: במצות ובחקים, "the ordinances and statutes."

4 All those who walk
5 in these in holy perfection according to all his teaching, God's covenant is an assurance for them
6 to bring them life for a thousand generation(s) (MS B: as it is written, "He preserves the covenant and mercy to those who love him and for the observers of his ordinances to the thousandth generation"). And if they live in camps according to the rule of the land, and take
7 wives and beget children, then they shall walk according to the Torah and according to the precept
8 established according to the rule of the Torah, as he said, "Between a man and his wife, and between a father and his child."[47]
9 But all those who despise will be paid the reward of the wicked when God visits the earth.

Several scholars understand this text as key evidence in the Scrolls for a bifurcation in lifestyles, parallel to the passage by Josephus (*J.W.* II 160–1) in which he distinguishes between those who are celibate and those who marry.[48] Those who walk in "holy perfection," בתמים קדש, is taken as a reference to a celibate group of men and as antithetical to those who live in camps and marry and have children who, in turn, represent a married order.[49] The claim that the text contrasts a celibate "elite" group with a married "camp" group will be assessed below. By first examining sentences in D that use similar expressions to those of CD VII 4–5, and then by analysing the context of CD VII 4b–10a, I will show that a bifurcation between celibate and married is not evident in the text.

5.3.2 PHRASEOLOGY IN D SIMILAR TO CD VII 4–5

The closest parallel to the phrase "all those who walk in these in holy perfection according to all his teaching, God's covenant is an assurance to them to bring them life

---

[47] Some commentaries emend the text to correspond to Num 30:17, which reads "his daughter"; e.g., Cothenet, *Les textes de Qumran*, 171; Schiffman, "Laws of Vows and Oaths," 205.

[48] See, e.g., Collins, "Family Life," *Encyclopedia of the Dead Sea Scrolls*, 1:287.

[49] Qimron argues that the CD VII 4b–6a refers to a celibate group, the *yahad*, residing at Qumran ("Celibacy in the Dead Sea Scrolls," 290–1); cf. Qimron, "Davies' the Damascus Covenant," *JQR* 77 (1986), 84–7. Schwartz states, "lines 4–9 apparently contrast celibates, who 'walk in holy perfection' to whom God promises eternal life, with others who marry and have children." He adds that celibacy must have been the ideal lifestyle or even the norm, since there was a need to prove that marriage was acceptable and a proof-text (Num 30:17) is given in the text ("The Damascus Document [CD]," 25 n.64). Baumgarten argues that the men who walk in "holy perfection" refers to a specific, celibate, elite group within the wider movement ("Qumran-Essene Restraints on Marriage," 17–19, 23 n.23). According to Davies, CD VII 4–8 indicates that celibacy was "the more usual lifestyle" in the Damascus covenant community ("Reflections on DJD XVIII," 159).

for a thousand generation(s)" in CD VII 4–5 is found in CD XIV 1–2. The parallel words and parts of words are marked by underline in the comparison below.

CD XIV 1b–2a reads:

וכל המתהלכים באלה ברית אל נאמנות להם להנצילם מכל מוקשי שחת

And for all those who walk in these (precepts) God's covenant is an assurance to save them from all the snares of the pit.

CD VII 4b–6a reads:

כל המתהלכים באלה בתמים קדש על פי כל יסורו ברית אל נאמנות להם לחיותם אלף דור

All those who walk in these in holy perfection according to all his teaching, God's covenant is an assurance for them to bring them life for a thousand generations(s).

CD XIV 1–2 stresses that those who observe the commandments will be saved through God's covenant. Parallel to CD VII 4–5, the context of XIV 1–2 also speaks about the salvation of the just and punishment of the wicked at the time of visitation.[50] Nothing indicates that "those who walk in these (precepts)" in XIV 1–2 are a subgroup of a larger group.

Two phrases in the document's introductory sermon are also reminiscent of CD VII 4–5: an exhortation in CD II 15–16, להתהלך תמים בכל דרכיו, "to walk perfectly in all his ways," and the reference ולהולכים בתמים דרך, "and for those who walk the way in perfection" (4Q266 2 i 4). According to the fragmented text in lines 4Q266 2 i 1–6, the latter group is contrasted with לעם לא ידעהו (line 3), "for a people that does not know him." The initial sermon is addressed to the whole community and, as with CD XIV 1–2, no subgroup of elite members is assumed behind the wording.

The expression אנשי תמים הקדש ("men of perfect holiness"), which is close to the reference to those who "walk in these in holy perfection" in CD VII 4–5, appears three times in CD XX 1a–8a (XX 2, 5, 7). The section concerns secret apostates, "all those who have entered the congregation of *the men of perfect holiness*" (XX 2) but who in fact do not belong.[51] The expression אנשי תמים הקדש, "men of perfect holiness," is

---

[50]Parallel to CD VII 11, XIV 1 refers to the split between Judah and Ephraim. 4Q267 9 V1–2 provides more text corresponding to the fragmentary last lines of CD XIII; *DJD XVIII*, 109–10.

[51]CD XIX 33–XX 34 is generally taken as a later addition to the document. Because of its unique language, XX 1b–8a is often understood as an independent interpolation (Davies, *Damascus Covenant*, 181–2). If the passage is later than CD VII 4–5, the writer of XX 1b–8a

used all-inclusively to differentiate between the true members who live perfectly according to the rules and those who transgress the laws.⁵² "The congregation (עדת) of the men of perfect holiness" (XX 2) is used interchangeably with the "congregation" עדה (XX 3), the common label for the whole community throughout D.⁵³ In sum, expressions in D that are reminiscent of קדש בתמים באלה המתהלכים וכל, "all those who walk in these in holy perfection" (CD VII 4–5), do not allude to a separate group within the community, but to the entire congregation.

5.3.3 THE CONTEXT OF CD VII 4B–10A

CD VII 4b–10a is part of the section IV 12b–VII 10a, which criticises Israel (IV 12b–V16) and emphasizes the legal responsibilities of the members within the covenant. Davies calls this section "Laws" according to the prevailing theme of the section.⁵⁴ The comparison in CD VII is between two opposite groups, namely "those who walk in these in perfect holiness," בתמים באלה המתהלכים וכל (CD VII 4–5), and "all those who despise," המואסים וכל, in line 9, rather than the "camp group" of lines 6b–9a. Both groups are introduced with "all," וכל ... כל, and their subsequent fate, reward versus punishment, is outlined.⁵⁵ At the time of "the visitation"—the eschaton—one way will bring life, the other death.⁵⁶ The warning in VII 9 ff. counters the promise of reward in VII 4–5, although the warning has later been developed into a much longer section.

---

may have used the language of CD VII 4–5 to highlight the desirable qualities of all the members.

⁵²CD XX 3b–4a reads: "when his works become apparent, he shall be expelled from the congregation as one whose lot did not fall among those taught by God." In other words, the transgressor never truly belonged to the "men of perfect holiness" in the first place.

⁵³Highlighting the similarity with 1QS VIII 20ff., as well as the practice of expulsion as an example of a more rigorous rule of discipline for this group, Baumgarten claims that CD XX 2–8 refers to an elite, celibate group, which he identifies with the one in 1QS ("Qumran-Essene Restraints on Marriage,"13–24). However, in view of the expulsion ceremony described in 4Q266 11 5–21 and the preceding penal code (4Q266 10 ii 1–15), it is now known that strict rules were imposed on the community as a whole.

⁵⁴Davies, *Damascus Covenant*, 105ff. I have adopted his delineation.

⁵⁵Albert-Marie Denis emphasises the contrast between the two groups (*Les thèmes de connaissance dans le document de Damas* [Studia Hellenistica 15; Louvain: Universitaires de Louvain, 1967], 138).

⁵⁶A likely biblical background to CD VII 4b–10a is found in Leviticus 26, which outlines the basis for the covenantal agreement and compares two contrasting scenarios, the outcomes of obedience and of rejection of the covenant. Campbell suggests a connection between CD VII 9b and Lev 26:15, which both use the verb מאס ("reject") (*The Use of Scripture in the Damascus Document*, 147). Denis argues that Lev 26:43–6 forms the biblical backdrop to the passage (*Les thèmes de connaissance*, 138).

The reference to those who live in camps in CD VII 6b–9a does not form a part of this overall comparison between the just and the wicked, and does not serve as an antithesis to the first group. It is structurally set apart from the immediate context: first, instead of כל, the reference to those who live in camps begins with ואם ("and if"); second, no consequence of their behaviour in the form of reward or punishment is mentioned. Furthermore, the reference to life for a "thousand generations" does not refer, as Qimron claims, to the "continuity by God's promise" as opposed to "natural continuity" of those who marry and beget children.[57] Instead, CD VII 6, if taken literally, relates to the eschatological era and the fulfillment of the end-time promises by God to his remnant in the form of eternal life.[58] This eschatological perspective is common in the Admonition, in which the faithful are assured of God's blessings as reward. The community situates itself in the "time of evil," קץ הרשע (CD VI 10, 14; XV 7, 10; XII 23), when darkness still rules (CD IV 13), and Israel is blind (CD XVI 2–3).[59] The members of the covenant live at the verge of the new era when the wicked will be punished, but as part of the covenantal blessings, the loyal remnant, the community, will be rewarded with eternal life "for a thousand generations." It is difficult to see how this reward would only be bestowed upon an elite, celibate group, and not upon all members.

At first glance, the reference to those who live in camps (CD VII 6b–9a) looks out of place; the text would read better without it, since the reference to the camp group breaks the nice parallelism between the promise of the reward for the obedient and the warning about evils which will afflict the transgressors. The most reasonable conclusion is that the segment is an interpolation, as some scholars claim.[60] It was

---

[57] Qimron, "Celibacy in the Dead Sea Scrolls," 290–1. Baumgarten, similarly, points to the remarkable similarity with Pliny's description that the group of Essenes "has lasted—strange to say—for thousands of generations, though no one is born within it" ("Qumran-Essene Restraints on Marriage," 18–20).

[58] The life-giving reward for those who observe the rules of the community is based on Deut 7:9, where the expression אלף דור "thousand generations" is used with reference to the assurance that God will always, for all generations to come, keep his part of the covenant. In CD VII 6/XIX 1–2 it takes on the meaning of eternal life as a reward to the faithful ones. See Campbell, *The Use of Scripture in the Damascus Document*, 143; Dupont-Sommer, *The Essene Writings,* 132 n.5.

[59] On Belial's rule during the last period of history according to D and other Qumran texts, see Annette Steudel, "God and Belial," in *The Dead Scrolls: Fifty Years after their Discovery*, 332–6; "אחרית הימים in the Texts from Qumran," *RevQ* 16 (1993), 225–46.

[60] See Rubenstein, "Urban Halakhah and Camp Rules," 293; Johann Maier, *Die Texte vom Toten Meer* (Munich: Ernest Reinhardt, 1960), 2:52; Cothenet, *Les textes de Qumran*, 171; Jerome Murphy O'Connor, "A Literary Analysis of the Damascus Document VI,2–VIII,3," *RB* 78 (1971), 222; Campbell, *The Use of Scripture in the Damascus Document*, 137. Knibb views the passage as a possible secondary addition (*The Qumran Community*, 55).

likely inserted by a redactor, "for the sake of completeness," to make a statement concerning the importance of the whole family observing the laws of the covenant.⁶¹

CD VII 6b–7 quotes Jer 29:6, but with one modification; whereas Jer 29:6 explicitly includes both sons and daughers, בנים ובנות, CD VII 7 uses בנים in an inclusive sense: "And if they live in camps, according to the rule of the land, and take wives and beget children," ולקחו נשים והולידו בנים. Without the interpolation (CD VII 6b–9a), it is clear that the previous lines (4–6a) relate to the whole community—the just—as opposed to the wicked. As the text now reads, CD VII 4b–6a still addresses *all* who live according to the covenantal agreement, including those who are married and have children. Those who marry and live in camps are singled out, *from among the first group*, in order for the redactor to emphasise that the whole family, including women and children, should observe the laws and the community regulation.⁶² I take התהלכו ("they shall walk") as referring to the women and children.⁶³ They—women and children—should observe both the laws of the Torah (על פי התורה, "according to the Torah"), as well as the specific rules of the community (וכמשפט היסורים כסרך התורה, "and according to the precept established according to the rule of the Torah"), that is, the totality of the covenantal agreement. This is supported with a quote from Num 30:17, "as he said, 'Between a man and his wife, and between a father and his child,'" בין איש לאשתו ובין אב לבנו. CD VII 9a also includes sons by referring to לבנו, "his child," instead of "between a father and his daughter" (Num 30:17). Whereas Num 30:17 refers to the laws on oaths, CD VII uses the quote with reference to relationships between family members in a general way and makes the point that these should be governed by the laws and rules of the covenant.⁶⁴

---

⁶¹Knibb, The Qumran Community, 55.

⁶²The exact connotation of "the rule of the land," סרך הארץ, is not clear. Knibb understands the phrase, as "as men do" (*The Qumran Community,* 55). Elwolde suggests the emendation, כדרך הארץ, "in the customary way" ("Distinguishing the Linguistic and the Exegetical," 14). Although the suggestion is plausible, it is more likely that כסרך הארץ refers to a collection of laws, in accordance with the common use of סרך in D (see e.g., CD X 4; XII 19, 22; XIII 7; XIV 3, 12, see also, 4Q266 5 ii 14). Davis suggests that סרך הארץ is the label of the earliest law code in D ("History," 30–1).

⁶³In agreement with, among others, Knibb and Davies (Knibb, *The Qumran Community,* 55; Davies, *Damascus Covenant,* 142, 251).

⁶⁴See Knibb, *The Qumran Community,* 56. Campbell argues that the biblical text has been emended under influence of Mal 4:5, which reads "He will turn the hearts of parents to children and the hearts of children to their parents (והשיב לב־אבות על־בנים ולב־בנים על אבותם), so that I will not come and strike the land with a curse" (Campbell, *Use of Scripture in the Damascus Document,* 143). The similarities between Mal 4:5 and אב לבנו in CD VII 8–9 are not striking and any connection is impossible to verify.

The redactor stresses the importance of observing the law within the family by using the symbolically loaded imagery of camps, exile and restoration.[65] Just as the exiled population in Babylonia is exhorted by Jeremiah to marry, multiply, and cultivate the land, so the families in the camps in CD VII 6–7, who represent the exilic remnant, also have the duty to multiply and cultivate the land in preparation for the restoration.

5.4 Conclusion

The community behind D distinguished itself from the general society by its marital laws. According to discourse on the Nets of Belial (CD IV 12b–V 15a), the people outside of the community have been deceived by Belial to the extent that they are not even aware of their fornication. Two examples of fornication are given, both concerning illicit marriages: polygyny and marriage between a man and his niece. These marital combinations were generally accepted in the surrounding Jewish society and neither is prohibited in biblical law. In addition, the text criticises the contemporary population for not abstaining from sexual intercourse when a woman experiences vaginal bleeding. I suggested that an underlying polemic is directed against the practice of intermarriages with foreigners among the general population.

The prohibition of marriage between a man and his niece is based on an explicitly gender-inclusive reading of Lev 18:18. It is quite possible that reading biblical laws gender-inclusively was an accepted methodological principle in the community behind D, since D includes another example of a similar perspective from the early law code, namely, in the law on oaths of women. A prohibition of polygyny was likely a welcome reinterpretation of biblical law among the women in the community, as one can easily imagine that a household with several wives would often harbor tension and rivalry among the co-wives and their offspring. Certainly, biblical stories illustrate such hostility within families with several wives.[66] A tension between co-wives is also evident in the legal dispute between Babatha and the second wife after the death of their husband.[67] Furthermore, marriage contracts from Elephantine show that men

---

[65] The language of "camps" recalls the wilderness period (cf. Num 2:17; 32–34; 10:5–6, 25). The community behind D identified itself with the wilderness generation as well as with the exiled population in Babylonia and looked forward to the subsequent restoration. "Camps" should be seen as a place where the community prepared for the eschaton. For a discussion, see Jonathon Campbell, "Essene-Qumran Origins in the Exile: A Scriptural Basis?" *JJS* 46 (1995), 152–3; Shemaryahu Talmon, "The 'Desert Motif' in the Bible and in Qumran Literature," in *Biblical Motifs: Origins and Transformations* (ed. Alexander Altmann; Cambridge, Mass.: Harvard University Press, 1966), 31–63.

[66] E.g., see Gen 16:29–30.

[67] Lewis, *The Documents from the Bar Kokhba Period in the Cave of Letters*, 26.

sometimes had to promise not to take additional wives as part of the agreement.[68] This evidence suggests that a second wife was perceived to be undesirable for the first wife. The communal law prohibiting polygyny was hence beneficial for a wife as it gave her the security of being the sole wife of a man, not having to share possessions or marital relations with another wife.

The second passage in the Admonition that refers explicitly to women is found in CD VII 4b–9a, which highlights the duties of the families in the camps. Lines 6b–9a are likely an interpolation that is placed in a section that outlines the responsibility of members to live by the covenantal laws (CD IV 4 12b–VII 10a) and contrast the outcome of obedience versus disobedience to the laws. The passage immediately preceding the interpolation provides a summary of basic laws that members must observe (CD VI 14–VII 4a), which is followed by the promise of the reward for those who are "walking in these [the statutes] in holy perfection" (CD VII 4b–6a). The interpolation (lines 6b–9a) clarifies the preceding passage by emphasizing that *all* family members have the responsibility to observe and to live by these laws. The reference to the duties of those living in camps thus makes explicit that women and children, as part of the covenant people, must fulfill their part of the covenant agreement. The reference to all family members points to the inclusion of women and children within the covenant people. The group described as "those who walk in these [the statutes] in perfect holiness" (CD VII 4b–5a) may have included celibate persons, because the introduction of the interpolation (VII 6a) begins with "and if." Nevertheless, "those who walk in these in holy perfection" is used inclusively for all members, married or not.

---

[68]Bezalel Porten, "Five Fragmentary Aramaic Marriage Documents: New Collations and Restorations," *Abr-Nahrain* 27 (1989), 102–4; see also discussion by Collins, "Marriage, Divorce, and Family," 115–19.

6. COMMUNAL LAWS

6.1 Introduction

The following analysis treats those sections of the communal laws that pertain to women. The communal laws in D are distinct in that they prescribe regulations for a specific organized community, which I identify as Essene as I have explained above.[1] The laws that refer to women are those concerning the Examiner's supervision of marriage, divorce, and the education of children; laws regulating financial support for virgins; and from the penal code, laws concerning fornication with a wife and an offense to the Fathers and the Mothers.

Before examining the laws that explicitly concern women, I will begin by examining a section that describes the process of admission into the community (CD XV 5–15) and the subsequent list, which excludes certain people from entrance (CD XV 15 ff./4Q266 8 i 6–9). Although this section does not mention women, I will discuss whether this passage is, nevertheless, inclusive of women.

6.2 The Initiation Process and Excluded Categories: CD XV 5–XVI 2; 4Q266 8 I 1–10; 4Q270 6 II 5–10; 4Q271 4 II 1–4A

6.2.1 Introduction

Scholars have debated whether women could become full members in the sect behind the Scrolls. As I noted in Chapter 1, most scholars assume that women were marginal to the sect and unable to become full members. A key passage in this debate has been 1QSa I 9–11, which may require a wife to testify about her husband. While I will return to this passage below, I will first discuss CD XV 5–XVI 2/4Q266 8 i 1–10, which is an important text for examining the question about women's membership. CD XV 5–15 details the process of a formal initiation into the community whereby

---

[1] See above, p. 5.

children of members (XV 5) who reach maturity, as well as outsiders who are entering the community (XV 6b–7a), take the oath of the covenant. I will demonstrate below that the community marks a difference in degree of membership between full-fledged members and those who lack full membership status.[2] Furthermore, there are two main aspects that characterise full membership: taking the oath of the covenant at the initiation ritual and participating in a communal meeting. Below I will discuss whether women participated in these activities. In addition to examining the text in D, I will look at biblical precedents to taking the oath of the covenant.

The passage on initiation in CD XV 5–15 is followed by a list that excludes certain categories of people from entering "into the midst of the congregation" (CD XV 15a–17; 4Q266 8 i 6–9). Since only full members were allowed to enter, this section has a bearing on the issue of women's membership. My analysis will also treat the rules for initiation in 1QSa in some depth; these are particularly relevant because of the close relationship between 1QSa and the communal laws in D.[3] In addition, I will compare the list of excluded categories of people in D with similar lists in 1QSa and M. The purpose of this analysis is to answer the question whether or not full membership for women is a viable option in reconstructing the social reality of the community behind D.

The passage on the initiation process is part of a long section of rules that concerns oaths and vows (CD XV 1–XVI 20).[4] The text preceding CD XV 1 in MS A is lost, and no text immediately preceding this section is known from 4QD.[5] According to Hempel, CD XV 1–XVI 6a has been subject to heavy redaction. CD XV 1–5a is not associated with any literary stratum because of its fragmentary nature and "odd" content.[6] The reference to "the many" לרבים (line 8) has been added at a "Serekh Redaction," and CD XV 6b–7a is the product of a "Damascus Redactor" because of its polemical character.[7] In contrast to Hempel, I do not think that polemical passages *per se* can be dismissed as interpolations because of their similarity to the Admonition, and I consider lines 6b–7a as integral to the text.[8] Pointing to lists excluding certain

---

[2] It may be argued that "membership" is primarily a modern concept that should be used only to describe modern phenomena. But since there is a distinct admission process that marks the boundary between insiders and outsiders, "membership" is an appropriate term in this discussion.

[3] See above, p. 28.

[4] CD XVI 6b–20, which includes laws concerning binding oaths of women, belongs to Halakhah (see above p. 135).

[5] See DJD *XVIII*, 62–3.

[6] Hempel, *Laws*, 190.

[7] Ibid., 79–85.

[8] In agreement with most translators, I take CD XV 5–6a to refer to the formal enrolment of children of members (e.g., Baumgarten, Burrows, Martínez, Vermes, Rabin, Dupont-Sommer). Hempel, on the other hand, suggests, "And he who enters the covenant for all Israel..., together with their children who reach the age to pass over to the mustered...."; thus, she takes lines 5–6

categories of people in M, 1QSa, 4QMMT, and 4QFlor, Hempel argues that the list of similar exclusions in CD XV 15b–17a has an independent origin that has been incorporated here "by the author(s)" and applied to the context. The section on initiation is followed by exegetical comments on the oath of the covenant (CD XVI 2b–6a), which appear to be a later addition.[9] According to Hempel's scheme, of these redactional additions only the Serekh redaction has a provenance that clearly differs from the community of D. In addition, since the list of excluded categories is inserted by "the author(s)," it is contemporary with the bulk of communal laws. Therefore, the various literary segments on initiation and exclusion, with the exception of the possibly interpolated references to "the many," are relevant for my investigation of the extent of women's membership in the community behind D.

6.2.2 Key Aspects of the Initiation Rite in D

The section on children's entrance into full membership (CD XV 5ff.) is preceded by a short passage on rules related to the oath of the covenant. The exact meaning of CD XV 1–3 is debated. I follow the reading of this passage by Qimron, who proposes שבועת הבנים ("the oath of the children") at the end of line 1, rather than שבועת הבאים ("the oath of those who enter"), as the phrase is usually read. Qimron situates the passage within the context of the entrance rite. Accordingly, the first two lines of column XV prohibit anyone from using divine names or referring to "the Torah of Moses" (which contains the divine names) when taking an oath, with the *exception of* שבועת הבנים "the oath of the children" when they enter "by the curses of the covenant."[10] The use of curses in the initiation rite gives an indication of the solemn nature of the ceremony.

The introduction to the initiation rite (lines 5b–7a) in the passage on initiation reads:

5   והבא בברית לכל ישראל לחוק עולם את בניהם אשר יגיעו
6   לעבור על הפקודים בשבועת הברית יקימו עליהם וכן
7   המשפט בכל קץ הרשע לכל השב מדרכו הנשחתה

---

as a reference to new members and their children, which makes lines 6b–7 superfluous (*Laws*, 74, 77–9). However, הבא ברית ("he who enters the covenant") in CD XV 5 is the common term for present members (e.g., CD II 2) and the reference to "the oath of the children" שבועת הבנים in XV 1 (see below) shows that the oath under discussion is that of the children.

[9] CD XVI 2b–6a exhibits a distinct terminology and seems out of place. See Hempel, *Laws*, 86–90. Already Ginzberg considered lines 2–5 a later gloss (*An Unknown Jewish Sect*, 177).

[10] הבנים in CD XV 1 are thus identified as the הבנים in CD XV 5–6, who take the oath of the covenant when entering into the covenant. Qimron speculates that these curses may have been understood as a substitute for the divine names; alternatively, the oath of the covenant did include divine names. See Qimron, "Further Observations on The Laws of Oaths in the Damascus Document 15," 251–7; "לשבועת הבנים in the Damascus Covenant 15.1–2," *JQR* 81 (1990), 115–18.

5   And all who have entered the covenant for all of Israel as an eternal statute shall let their children,[11] who have reached (the age)
6   to cross over into those that are enrolled, take the oath of the covenant. Similar
7   is the precept during the entire time of evil for everyone who repents from his corrupt way.

Scholars are divided as to whether בניהם in CD XV 5 should be translated "their boys" or "their children." It will become clear further on in my investigation why I consider the gender-inclusive "their children" the correct translation.[12] The entrance into the community is described as "crossing over" לעבור into the group (CD XV 5–6a) of the enrolled, indicating that the mature children cross a distinct boundary within the community.[13] Lines 6b–7a clarifies that the rite also applies to outsiders who enter the community. The crossing over in this case, from outside the boundary of the group to the inside, is defined as a turning from a "corrupt way," מדרכו הנשחתה, in the present time of evil. The dualistic tone is sharp and aligned with the view of contemporary Israel in the Admonition.

CD XV 7b–11 explains that the Examiner examines the candidate (a mature child of a member or an outside candidate) before the candidate can take the oath. The object is to assess the character and intelligence of the candidate in order to decide whether the person should gain access to further information (lines 10a–11). 1QS VI 13–23 details a longer and more elaborate process, compared to D, for initiating new members.

Two main changes occur for the candidate who is accepted among the full members:[14] that person will receive additional knowledge (CD XV 10b–11) and be fully responsible for his (or her ?) deeds, as the candidate by oath promises to live according to the law of Moses.[15] The text emphasises that others are free from blame if

---

[11] The Hebrew text in these lines is difficult; it is unclear why הבא ברית is in the singular, while the suffix in את בניהם is in the plural.

[12] Translators offer both "boys" and "children." Baumgarten translates בניהם "their sons" ("The Damascus Document [CD])," 38) as does Rabin (*Zadokite Documents*, 72). Vermes (*The Complete Dead Sea Scrolls*, 136) and Wise, Abegg, and Cook (*Dead Sea Scrolls*, 65) translate the word "their children."

[13] עבר ("to cross over") appears frequently within the context of initiation and the renewal of the covenant ceremony in S. See 1QS I 16, 18, 20, 24 (יעבורו בברית; "they shall cross over into the covenant") and 1QS II 20, 21 (יעבורו; "they shall cross over").

[14] Nowhere does D elaborate on the age of the enrollment and taking the oath of the covenant. Possibly the age is assumed to be twenty, parallel to 1QSa I 8b–10a.

[15] The phrase לעבור על הפקודים ("to cross over into those that are enrolled") in CD XV 5–6 also appears in CD X 1–2. CD X 1–2 declares that this level of membership (לעבור על הפקודים) is required for testifying in court in a case that would bring the death penalty. Thus, full membership also means full responsibility within the community. 4Q269 8 ii 6/4Q271 2 13 uses the same expression in a prohibition against letting a young boy sprinkle water of purification at

The Communal Laws

the person transgresses from that moment on (CD XV 12–13a). If a person commits a significant error in legal observance, the Examiner is to teach that person for "one complete year" שנה תמימה (XV 13b–15a/4Q270 6 ii 7). The text continues (4Q266 8 i 6) with ולפי דעתה יקרב, "according to his knowledge, let him approach."[16] It is not specified to what קרב "approach" refers. In S, קרב ("approach") is used frequently with reference to the stages of admission for a candidate and the corresponding access to communal gatherings, which is likely the meaning here as well.[17] The verb also appears in a small fragment in D, 4Q266 5 i 13–14, where קרב ("to approach") is contrasted with רחק ("be far"), reminiscent of the admission process described in 1QS VI, which strengthens the suggested interpretation of קרב.[18] It is therefore likely that קרב ("to approach") in 4Q266 8 i 6 refers to new members' access to the communal assemblies. Thus, a new member who errs is barred from further access to those meetings that are restricted to full members; only after a full year of instruction by the Examiner may the candidate "approach" the communal meetings, provided that he or she possesses sufficient knowledge. A similar approach to transgressions is also found in the penal code, wherein a member who transgresses the communal rules is excluded from "the purity" for a specific length of time, depending on the crime.[19] "The purity" in the penal code refers to all objects and areas designated to be absolutely pure, including common meals and communal meetings.

---

the red cow purification rites, a view that is opposite to the Pharisaic one: וכול נער אשר לוא מלאו ימיו לעבור על הפקודים ("And any lad who is not of age to cross over into those that are enrolled shall not sprinkle") (*DJD XVIII*, 131). See Baumgarten, "The Red Cow Purification Rites in Qumran texts," 112–19. Finally, all members are mustered by their names at the meeting of all the camps, which may have taken place at the annual Renewal of the Covenant Ceremony. CD XIV 3–4 reads, "They shall all be enrolled by name (יפקדו כלם בשמותיהם) first the priests, second the Levites, third the Israelites, and fourth the proselytes." See Hempel, *The Damascus Texts*, 40–1.

[16]Instead of ולפי דעתה יקרב וכול היותו, CD XV 15 reads ולפי דעתה היותו, thus lacking a proper ending to the sentence. The omission of יקרב וכול was probably a mistake by the copyist.

[17]See 1QS VI 16, 19, 22; VIII 18; IX 15–16.

[18]4Q266 5 i 13–14 reads:

13   ]oo אִישׁ (ל) לפי רוחֹ[ו] יקר[בו
14   ]וֹח יֹחק{o}וּ לפי המבקר וֹ[כו]ל

13   ]each one according to [his] spirit [shall be brought n]ear
14   ]shall be removed by the word of the Examiner, and [al]l

[19]See 4Q266 10 i 14–15; 10 ii 1–15.

Readmission into full status depends upon a person's "knowledge" לפי דעתה (4Q266 8 i 6), in this case particularly referring to knowledge of the law.[20] The whole process is thus very similar to the probation period and readmission process described in 1QS VII 21, whereby a person may be promoted to full status after a two year probation, when he again will have access to the communal meetings depending on his knowledge.[21]

In sum, formal initiation and admission to communal meetings are two sides of the same coin. Through formal initiation, whereby a person becomes a full member, he (or she?) gains access to communal meetings. This privilege, however, will be withdrawn if the person sins, in which case he (or she ?) will temporarily be barred from meetings. Access to communal meetings is therefore not a permanent situation for full members, but depends on his (or her?) behaviour.

6.2.3 THE OATH OF THE COVENANT AND ITS BIBLICAL BACKGROUND

In order to pursue the question whether בניהם in CD XV 1 and 5 refers to young men only or if young women are included as well, it is important to look at biblical antecedents to the rite of taking the oath of the covenant. The initiation rite as described in D was part of an annual renewal of the covenant ceremony among the Essenes, which included both the candidates' taking the oath and a renewal ceremony whereby members renewed their commitment to the covenant by an oath. This ceremony was probably celebrated at the Feast of Weeks, Shavuot. The liturgy for the covenantal ceremony is described in detail in 1QS I 18–II 26,[22] but there are also traces of liturgical pieces related to the ceremony in several other documents from Qumran.[23] Differences between the texts may indicate that the outline of the ceremony

---

[20] The insight of a person is also important in the initial examination by the Examiner detailed in CD XIII 11–13: "let him [the Examiner] examine him [the candidate] with regard to his works and his intelligence (ושוכלו), his strength and might, and his wealth." The insight of a person is likely one aspect of the evaluation alluded to in 4Q266 5 i 13, which reads "according to his spirit."

[21] The difference between D and S concerning readmission is the gradual process in S and the length of time.

[22] Deuteronomy 27–31 has been particularly influential on the liturgy as described in 1QS I 18–II 26, especially in the framework of priestly recitations in the form of blessings and curses and the response of the people. But S also borrows elements from several biblical descriptions of a renewal of the covenant ritual. See Bilah Nitzan, *Qumran Prayer and Religious Poetry* (STDJ 12; Leiden: Brill, 1994) 129–30; Milik, *Ten Years*, 104. In agreement with scholars such as Murphy O'Connor, Pouilly and Delcor, Metso argues that the liturgical material in 1QS I 16–III 12 existed independently prior to its inclusion in S. She suggests that columns I–IV were not included in 4QS^d and 4QS^e (*Textual Development*, 113, 146–7).

[23] According to Daniel Falk, 5QRule (5Q13), the Berakhot (4Q286–290), and possibly the fragmentary texts 4QCommunal Ceremony (4Q275) and 5QCurses (5Q14) contain liturgical parts for the Festival (*Daily, Sabbath and Festival Prayers*, 217, 225, 236ff). Bilah Nitzan

changed during the course of the sect's history, or that different communities of Essenes may have celebrated the ceremony in different ways. From the evidence in S and D, it is apparent that the ceremony included three important elements: new members were initiated by oath, old members were mustered and affirmed their loyalty to the covenant, and disloyal members were expelled.

A description of a large gathering of people in 1QSa I 4–5 most likely alludes to the renewal of the covenant ceremony.[24] The text emphasizes the inclusion of women and children in the assembly: בבואום יקהילו את כול הבאים מטף עד נשים, "When they come they shall assemble all those who enter, from children to women" (1QSa I 4).[25]

The inclusiveness of the whole congregation in the covenant ceremony according to 1QSa is reminiscent of biblical precedents to the ceremony. Biblical narratives that describe a covenant ceremony commonly presume a large gathering of people, sometimes referring specifically to women and/or children, and sometimes not.[26] For example, the renewal of the covenant ceremony prescribed in Deut 31:9–13 highlights the presence of "women and children" in the assembly. Even when women are not mentioned, expressions such as "the people," or "the whole people," ought to be understood as indicating their presence. The overall inclusive character of the biblical

---

proposes basically the same documents (5Q13, 4QCurse [4Q280], 4Q286–290); see "4QBerhakhot[a–e] [4Q286–290]: A Covenantal Ceremony in the Light of Related Texts," *RevQ* 16 [1995], 488-9).

[24]Both Schiffman and Knibb link the introduction in 1QSa to a covenantal renewal ceremony. Whereas Shiffman points to similarities between this passage and Deuteronomy 29 (*The Eschatological Community of the Dead Sea Scrolls: A Study of the Rule of the Congregation* [SBLMS 38; Atlanta: Scholars Press, 1989], 11–13), Knibb points to Deut 31:11–12 (*The Qumran Community*, 146–7).

[25]For the full text, see below pp. 138–9.

[26]The Shechem ceremony in Deuteronomy 27–28 uses traditional androcentric language. At the same time, since all the people are addressed (Deut 27:1), one suspects that women were intended to be included as well. The suspicion is confirmed in subsequent curses and blessings that pertain to women: "the Lord will make you (ms) abound in prosperity, in the fruit of your (ms) womb (בטנך)" (28:11), and "cursed shall be the fruit of your (ms) womb (בטנך)" (28:18). In a secondary expansion of the curses in Deut 28:56–7, the fate of women is particularly explicit (see Judith Plaskow, *Standing Again at Sinai: Judaism From a Feminist Perspective*, [San Francisco: Harper, 1991], 25; Dorah O'Donnell Setel, "Exodus" in *Women's Bible Commentary*, 33). The description of the covenant ceremony in Josh 24:1–28 includes women by inference, in the statement "as for me *and my household, we* will *serve* the Lord" (24:15); thus "all the people" (24:2) includes the men and their households. The reform by Josiah is presented as a renewal of the covenant ceremony in 2 Kgs 23: 2–3; although women are not explicitly mentioned, children are mentioned (למקטן "from the smallest"), so one can assume that women are included as well among "all the people" who join the covenant. The Sinai tradition in Exodus 19, in contrast, stands out as unusual in its apparent exclusion of women from the covenant people. Their exclusion from "the people" is explicit in the commandment not to go near a woman for three days (Exod 19:15).

depictions of covenant-renewal ceremonies is even more impressive when one considers the general patriarchal perspective and male-oriented language throughout the Hebrew Bible.

The description of the initiation rite in CD XV entails several allusions to Deuteronomy 27–30, the 'Blessing and Curse' ceremony that Moses enacted before the people settled in the Land of Canaan (Deuteronomy 27–28), and the covenental renewal ceremony in chapters 29–30 at Moab.[27] A close parallel to the oath of initiation is found in the covenant ceremony depicted in Deut 29:10–12, where the people enter the covenant by taking an oath. The biblical text emphasises the inclusion of the whole people, including women, at the entrance into the covenant: "You stand assembled today, all of you... all the men of Israel, your children, your women... to enter into the covenant of the Lord your God, sworn by an oath... in order that he may establish you today as his people" (Deut 29:10–11). In addition, there are similarities between the initiation through an oath described in CD XV and the covenant ceremony described in Nehemiah 9–10. Nehemiah stresses the inclusive nature of the covenant ceremony whereby both men and women take an oath to observe the law of Moses; Neh 10:28–9 reads: "The rest of the people, the priests, the Levites... their wives, their sons, their daughters, all who have knowledge and understanding, join with their kin, their nobles, and enter into a curse and an oath to walk in God's law, which was given by Moses the servant of God, and to observe and do all the commandments..." Parallel to the entrance ritual in CD XV, both a curse and an oath are mentioned and only men and women who are knowledgeable should take the oath.

CD XV presents the covenant as a covenant of the whole people of Israel: "the covenant of *all of Israel*" (CD XV 5), and "the covenant Moses made with *Israel*" (CD XV 9). The references to Israel suggest that the inclusive nature of covenant rites as described in Deut 29:10–11, Deut 31:9–13 and Neh 10:28–9 has been preserved in the reenactment of the covenant ceremony, not only as it is described in 1QSa I 3–5, but also in the ceremony in the D community. The long biblical tradition of a public, inclusive assembly at covenant ceremonies, combined with the evidence of the presence of women and children at the covenant ceremony in 1QSa, make it plausible that, parallel to Neh 10:28–9, young women as well as young men formally entered the covenant by taking the oath of the covenant in the ceremony described in CD XV.

---

[27] CD XV 2 refers to "the curses of the covenant" (באלות הברית), parallel to Deut 29:21. CD XV 8–10 describes the oath of the covenant (cf. line 12) in terms reminiscent of Deut 30:2: "they shall muster him with the oath of the covenant which Moses made with Israel, the covenant to *re[turn t]o* the Torah of Moses with *all heart* and [with *all*] *soul*" (לש[וב א]ל תורת משה בכל לב [ובכל] נפש). In Deut 30:2, similarly, the people are to "*return* (ושבת) to the Lord your God... with *all* your *heart* and with *all* your *soul*" (בכל-לבבך ובכל-נפשך) [my italics].

6.2.4 MUSTERING AMONG THE ESSENES

The use of the verb פקד "to muster" (CD XV 6, 8) with reference to initiation may, on a cursory reading, suggest that only men are involved, because of the association of this verb with military service in the Hebrew Bible. Schiffman, for instance, comments that the mustering in the Pentateuch refers to males only.[28] However, whereas "mustering" in the Pentateuch commonly refers to enrollment into the army and occasionally mustering for tax purposes, there is no biblical antecedent for the type of "mustering" found in CD XV, which links enrollment to taking the oath of the covenant. CD XV 8 reads: "They shall *muster him with the oath of the covenant*" (emphasis mine).[29] The person taking the oath thereby takes on the responsibility of living according to the laws of the Torah, as well as the community's own interpretation of the Torah, "what is found" (הנמצא) (XV 10).[30] This is a very different obligation than conscription to the military or mustering to pay the temple tax. Consequently, one should not automatically assume that the mustering in the Pentateuch has the same implication or context in terms of gender.

1QSa uses the same term for adult members ("the mustered" הפקודים) as does D and can thus throw more light on the meaning of פקד in the context of membership.[31] Significantly, 1QSa clearly separates the conscription to the military service (alluded to in 1QSa I 12–13) from the formal entrance into full membership; the latter takes place at 20 years of age, while the former happens at the age of 25.[32] Thus, initiation into full membership should not be linked to mustering for military service, and so the use of פקד in CD XV should not be taken as evidence that the candidates for formal initiation were all male.

---

[28] Schiffman, *Sectarian Law*, 56–8

[29] In the census described in Num 1:2 ff., twenty years marks the age of adulthood when a man may serve in the military; see also Num 26:2. 2 Samuel 24 recounts David's census done for military purposes. Twenty is also the age for mustering into the military according to 11QT LVII 1–5, but 1QM VII 3 sets the age at twenty-five. For a census in relation to the duty to pay half a shekel in temple tax, see Exod 30:11–14; 38:26, which employ the verb פקד ("to muster"). Num 3:15 ff. and 4:2 refer to a Levitical census.

[30] This corresponds to "the hidden things" God has revealed to the community and which the larger Israel has failed to understand (CD III 12b–16a).

[31] Like D, 1QSa links "the mustering" into adulthood with knowledge and responsibility (1QSa I 8b–11). 1QSa adds that a person will enter (the exact term is missing) the adult group at the age of twenty and does not mention any formal examination.

[32] Schiffman notes that the age for military service and full membership in 1QSa is different, but still holds that mustering in 1QSa is connected to military service (*Sectarian Law*, 56).

6.2.5 1QSa

1QSa I 4–11 gives further evidence of the sectarian practice of formally enrolling children of members into full membership as well as of the participation of women in communal meetings. Since there are considerable similarities between the organizations behind D and 1QSa, as I have pointed out earlier, the description of the role of women in 1QSa has a bearing on the interpretation of D.[33] Parallel to D, 1QSa links formal enrollment (1QSa I 8b–11) to the annual renewal of the covenant ceremony (1QSa I 4–5). The passage refers specifically to women and children (I 4–5) in a manner reminiscent of the description of the renewal of covenant ceremony in Deut 31:9–13.[34]

1QSa I 4–11 is a very complex and difficult text, and the whole section needs to be taken into consideration for a proper evaluation of the gender of the participants. The Hebrew text is followed by a gender-inclusive translation (the reasons why this is the most appropriate approach are given below). 1QSa I 4–11 reads:

4 בבואום יקהילו את כול הבאים מטף עד נשים וקראו בא[וזניהם א]ת
5 [כ]וֹל חוקי הברית ולהבינם בכול משפֿ[טיה]מֿה פן ישגו במ[שוגגותיהמ]הֿ
6 וזה הֿסרך לכול צבאות העדה לכול האזרח בישראל ומן נעו[ר]יו
7 [יל]מֿדהו בספר ההגי וכפי יומיו ישכיליהו בחוקי[י] הברית ולֿ[פי שכלו]
8 [יי]סרו במשפטיהמה עשר שנים [י]בֿוא בטף ו[בן] עשרים שנֿ[ה יעבור על]
9 הפקודים לבוא בגורל בתוך משפֿ[ח]תֿו ליחד בעדֿ[ת] קודש ולוא יֿ[קרב]
10 אלֿ אשה לדעתה למשכבי זכר כי אם לפי מולואת לו עש[רי]ם שנה בדעתו [טוב]
11 ורע ובכן תקבל להעיד עליו משפטות התורא ולהתֿ[י]צֿב במשמע משפטים

4 When they come they shall assemble all those who enter, from children to women, and they shall read in [their] h[earing]
5 [al]l the statutes of the covenant, and instruct them in all [th]eir judg[ements] lest they stray in their errors.
6 And this is the rule for the hosts of the congregation, for all born in Israel. From the time of youth
7 they shall [ins]truct a person in the Book of Hagu, and according to age, they shall enlighten the youth in the precep[ts of] the covenant, and acc[ording to a person's understanding]

---

[33] See above, p. 28.

[34] See above, pp. 26–7. Schiffman points to a connection between the introduction in 1QSa I 1–5 and biblical models of a renewal of covenant ceremonies (*The Eschatological Community*, 13). Similarly, Knibb raises the possibility that lines 4–5 allude to the renewal of the covenant (*The Qumran Community*, 147).

8 [they shall] teach (him or her) their regulations. (For) ten years [the person] shall enter with the children.³⁵ And at twenty years of age, [he or she shall cross over into]
9 those enrolled, to enter the lot with his or her fam[il]y and join the holy Congre[gation]. But he shall not [approach]
10 a woman to know her by lying with her until he is fully twen[ty] years of age, at which time he knows [good]
11 and evil. And at that time she shall be received to bear witness of him (concerning) the judgments of the Law and to take her place at the hearing of the judgments.

Though scholars in general read 1QSa I 6–9 as referring to a male,³⁶ a close analysis reveals that a gender-inclusive reading is preferable. 1QSa I 4–5 declares that all those who enter, מטף עד נשים "from children to women," should be present at the assembly. Commenting on 1QSa I 4–5, Schuller states, "I propose that we continue reading with the same subject until the text alerts us to change (*i.e.*, in l. 9–10 ולא [קרב] אל אשה)."³⁷ Whether or not 1QSa I 4–5 should be taken as an interpretive key for determining the gender of the subject in the subsequent passage depends on the nature of the relationship between I 4–5 and I 6ff.³⁸ While I 1–3 introduces the end-

---

³⁵The reference to ten years has been interpreted in various ways; most translators connect the ten years with יבוא בטף ("[the person] shall enter with the children"). Ten years then refers to the time during which a person is counted as a child; see Schiffman, *The Eschatological Community*, 15–16. A problem with this view is that the next stage, between ten and twenty is not detailed. Nevertheless, since the stage of a נער ("a youth") is described in relation to education in lines 6–7, it may not have been necessary to describe this stage again.

³⁶See for example Schiffman's comments on 1QSa I 6–8: "Finally, and in accord with his demonstrated aptitudes and progress, *the young boy* would be taught the sectarian regulations..." (my italics), *The Eschatological Community*, 15.

³⁷Schuller, "Women in the Dead Sea Scrolls," in *Methods of Investigation of the Dead Sea Scrolls*, 123. Her gender inclusive reading has been criticised by Joan Taylor and Philip Davies ("On the Testimony of Women in 1QSa," 229–30). They point to the *vacat* in line 6, which they claim introduces a new section. It is true that line 6 starts a new section, namely rules for stages of life (childhood, youth, age of twenty, age of twenty-five, etc.). Nevertheless, this does not mean that the introduction in 1QSa I 1–5 is disconnected from what follows (see below). By comparison, there are several vacats at the beginning of a line in the description of the Renewal of the Covenant Ceremony in 1QS I 18–II 26 that introduce different segments of the ceremony (1QS I 21, II 11, 19).

³⁸In her source-critical study of 1QSa, Hempel argues that 1QSa I 6–II 11a comprises "traditional Essene legislation," while I 1–3 reflects a later "Zadokite recension," also apparent in 1QS V. She does not discuss to what stratum I 4–5 belongs ("The Earthly Essene Nucleus of 1QSa," 253–69). Nevertheless, a reading of the document that includes the initial description of the assembly for the renewal of the covenant in I 4–5 makes sense. There are allusions to the same ceremony in 1QSa I 8, "for ten years he or she shall come in with the children," and in line

time community who are faithful to the covenant, and I 4–5 relates to the renewal of the covenant ceremony, 1QSa I 6ff. describes the responsibilities of members according to their stages of life. According to Stegemann, the entire document is a rule book with regulations for various communal assemblies, and 1QSa I 1–5 relates rules for *every* assembly.[39] Thus, the description of the renewal of the covenant ceremony forms an introduction to the whole document (I 1–5), as well as providing a model for other communal meetings that follow. Stegemann suggests the following translation: "and this (= the following text) is the rule for every congregation (or: assembly) of Israel during the (present) last period (of history) if they assemble together."[40] Because the introduction stipulates that women attend, the presence of women is then expected in every assembly. It follows that the inclusion of both sexes is the norm for educational classes (1QSa I 6–8a), the entering into assemblies (with the parents) up to the age of ten (1QSa I 8b), as well as the formal entrance into the congregation at the age of twenty (1QSa I 8c–9) when a person makes the formal transition into full, adult membership. That I 9 refers to both men and women is confirmed in line 11, which explains that a wife is explicitly responsible for giving witness and will take her place in the meetings "for judgement" (1QSa I 11).[41]

There is further evidence in 1QSa that women participated in the communal assemblies. 1QSa I 25b–27a provides additional information about the responsibilities of the assembly and legislates specific purity rules. The text reads:

9, "to enter the lot in the midst of his or her family to join the holy congregation." In addition, the duties of members also constitute the basis for a type of ranking which would be important for the entrance at the renewal of the covenant ceremony. Finally, the main theme of the document is rules for communal meetings: while I 4–5 prescribes rules for the annual assembly (and provides a model for every meeting), 1QSa I 25ff provides rules for every type of assembly, and II 11–22 gives rules for the meeting at communal meals. Therefore there are not sufficient reasons to see 1QSa I 4–5 and I 6ff as separate units.

[39] Stegemann, "Some Remarks to 1QSa, to 1QSb, and to Qumran Messianism," 494.

[40] Ibid., 494. Although the passage is patterned on Deut 31:9–13, Stegemann does not hold that it refers specifically to the renewal of the covenant ceremony, but to every assembly. I suggest that the allusions to Deut 31:9–11 (lines 4–5) make it clear that the renewal of the covenant is specifically the topic in this passage at the same time as this assembly is presented as a model for "every Israelite congregation," כל עדת ישראל (line 1).

[41] There is no justification for some scholars' attempts to emend line 11 to refer to a male. In 1957, Joseph Baumgarten suggested two emendations to the text: תקבל should be יקבל and עליו should be על פי ("On the Testimony of Women," *JBL* 76 [1957], 266–69). Schiffman has promoted the proposed emendation in several of his publications. See *The Eschatological Community*, 18–19; *Sectarian Law*, 65; *Reclaiming*, 134–5. Davies and Taylor agree with Schuller that no emendation is necessary ("On the Testimony of Women in 1QSa," 226) and Baumgarten now also argues that no emendation is necessary (*DJD XVIII*, 165).

The Communal Laws

וא֯ם תעודה תהיה לכול הקהל למשפט או לעצת יֿחד או לתעודת מלחמֿה
וקדשום שלושת ימים להיות כול הבא עת[יד לע[צֿה

> And when there will be a convocation of the entire assembly for judgement or for the Council of the Community, or for a convocation of war, they shall sanctify them(selves) for three days, so that everyone who comes in shall be pre[pared for the Coun]cil.

According to the text, this meeting of the assembly takes place for various purposes, including "for judgement" למשפט. Since a woman is said to take her place in "the hearing of the judgements," במשמע המשפטים, in 1QSa I 11, the two passages concern the same kind of communal assembly. The expression כול הקהל, "the entire assembly" (1QSa I 25), recalls the gathering of the whole people in the biblical tradition, wherein קהל often includes both women and children.[42] The subsequent text qualifies the initial inclusiveness in 1QSa I 25 by the demand that the participants be knowledgeable, perfect in various ways (1QSa I 27–II 1), and free of blemishes (1QSa II 3–9). כול הקהל—"the entire assembly"—(I 25) then indicates that everyone in the community, including women, participates; the exception would be anyone—man or woman—who does not qualify due to impurity or imperfection, according to the specifics listed in the text.

Three days of purification precede the meeting of the assembly, which signifies its sacred status derived from the presence of the divine in the form of angels. The three days of sanctification recall the regulations for the Israelites at Mount Sinai (Exod 19:10–15) to prepare for the meeting with the Lord, including the directive by Moses "Do not go near a woman." Whereas the exhortation to prepare for meeting God in Exodus 19 applies specifically to men, the expression to "sanctify themselves" in 1QSa I 26 can apply equally to men and women. This period of purification for men and women would involve, among other things, abstention from sexual intercourse.[43]

In sum, an examination of the formal enrollment of grown-up children as recorded in 1QSa suggests that both young men and women are included. This has ramifications for the interpretation of D, as it enhances the likelihood that both male and female children of members are assumed to take the oath of the covenant according to CD XV 5. As I will demonstrate below, the omission of women from the list of excluded categories in D further strengthens this hypothesis.

---

[42] See e.g., Deut. 31:9–13; Neh 13:1; 2 Chr 20:5 (cf. 20:13); 30:25.

[43] This is one similarity between laws concerning entrance to the communal assembly and the temple, since 11QT XLV 11 requires that a man who has intercourse with his wife not enter the "city of the sanctuary" for three days.

6.2.6 LISTS OF EXCLUDED PERSONS

6.2.6.1 The List in D

4Q266 8 i 6b–9 excludes certain categories of people from entering "into the midst of the congregation" (lines 8–9). 4Q266 8 i 6b–9 reads (CD XV 15–17 underlined; 4Q270 6 ii 8–9 dotted underline)[44]:

וכול היותו אויל	6
[ומ]שׁוגע אל יבו[45] וכול פתי ושוגה וכה עינים לבלתי ראות	7
[ו]חגר או פסח או חרש או נער זעטוט א[ל יבו] איש	8
[מ]אֹלה אל תוך העדה כי מלאכֹ[י] הקוֹדֹ[ש בתוכם][46]	9

6   No demented
7   [f]ool shall enter (into the congregation). Neither shall any simple minded or errant person, nor one with dimmed eyes who cannot see,
8   [nor] a limping or lame or deaf person, nor a youth,[47] none
9   of these shall [come] into the congregation, for the ho[ly] angels [are in their midst.]

The list can be divided into the following categories: mentally challenged ("demented fool" אויל ומשוגע, "simple-minded" פתי), transgressors ("errant person," ושוגה), physically impaired (blind, limping, lame, deaf), and young persons ("youth," נער זעטוט). The emphasis is on mental and physical defects. The preoccupation with "unfit" persons, in the context of the entrance rite, shows that the ritual marks the crossing of a very distinct boundary only permitted to adult persons who are physically, morally, and mentally "fit." The list expands on the previous category of anyone who "proves to be a fool" when questioned by the examiner (CD XV 10b–11) and who consequently is excluded from initiation.[48]

The group of excluded categories in D is similar to other lists excluding "blemished" persons in 1QSa II 4–9 and 1QM VII 3–4. Since women are excluded according to the list in M, Schiffman claims that by analogy women would not be

---

[44]Double underline marks the overlap between CD XV and 4Q270 6.

[45]CD XV 15 lacks אל יבו; Baumgarten reconstructs 4Q270 6 ii 8 without אל יבו.

[46]4Q270 6 ii 10 adds after a short gap [מ]עֹטוֹ שני האד[ם, "the years of man have been diminish[ed"; cf. CD X 9, where the expression מעטיר ימו, "his days have been diminished," is part of an explanation as to why judges should not be older than 60 years. 4Q270 6 ii 10 likely was part of an explanation as to why some people became senile and physically impaired with old age and unfit to attend congregational meetings. See Baumgarten, *DJD XVIII*, 157.

[47]זעטוט carries the meaning "young man," "youth," or "student" as a variant of נער in rabbinic Hebrew; Jastrow, *Dictionary*, 407.

[48]A similar process is described in both 1QS (1QS V 20–23; VI 18) and CD XIII 11–13. Like the list in 4Q266 8 i 6–9, these passages reflect a concern about a person's intelligence and character.

allowed in the eschatological council of 1QSa either, nor in the council in D.[49] Is there any reason to assume that women would be excluded from communal assemblies according to D and 1QSa because they are excluded from the camp in M? In order to answer this question, it is necessary first to determine exactly from what the persons in the lists are excluded, and second, to examine which underlying principles guide the decision to exclude certain categories of people in all three lists.

6.2.6.2 Exclusion from What?

The summary statement in 4Q266 8 i 8b–9a specifies from what these people are excluded and for what reason: "none of these shall come [into] the midst of the congregation for holy angels [are in their midst]," א[ל יבו] איש [מ]אלה אל תוך העדה כי מלאכ[י] הקוד[ש בתוכם]. 1QSa uses similar expressions in 1QSa II 5 (בתוך העדה, "in the midst of congregation") and II 8 ([ב]תוך עדת א[נ]ושי השם, "in the midst of the congregation of the m[e]n of renown") to explain what the exclusion concerns. In addition, according to 1QSa, a simple-minded person is excluded from "the congregation of Israel" (עדת ישראל) (1QSa I 19–20), while blemished people can communicate their concerns indirectly to "the holy council" (עצת הקודש) (1QSa II 9). According to 1QSa II 4 a ritually defiled person is prohibited from entering "the assembly of God" (בקהל אלה).[50] Although there may be differences in the make-up of the communal bodies, these terms all connote communal meetings that have sacred status.

Some scholars assume that the lists of exclusion imply that these categories of people were excluded from the sect altogether; others have claimed that partial exclusion is implied.[51] There is clear evidence in D that persons with mental and

---

[49] Schiffman, *The Eschatological Community*, 51–2.

[50] Charlesworth proposes that the word is the Aramaic form for "God"; see "Rule of the Congregation (1QSa)," 115.

[51] Martínez and Trebolle Barrera argue that the bodily defects listed in 1QSa exclude a person from the community (*The People of the Dead Sea Scrolls*, 156). Michael Newton similarly argues that those who are excluded are banned from the community (*The Concept of Purity at Qumran and in the Letters of Paul* [Cambridge: Cambridge University Press, 1985], 50); cf. Howard Kee, "Membership in the Covenant People at Qumran and in the Teaching of Jesus," in *Jesus and the Dead Sea Scrolls* [ed. James Charlesworth; New York: Doubleday, 1992], 105). According to Schiffman, the physical defects in 1QSa exclude members from partaking in the assembly (*The Eschatological Community*, 38; "Purity and Perfection: Exclusion from the Council of the Community," in *Biblical Archaeology Today: Proceedings of the International Congress on Biblical Archaeology, Jerusalem 1984* [ed. J. Amitai; Jerusalem: Israel Exploration Society, The Israel Academy of Sciences and Humanities, in Cooperation with The American Schools of Oriental Research, 1985], 373–89). Similarly, Aaron Shemesh claims that "only unblemished people may enter into sacred assemblies and places" ("'The Holy Angels are in Their Council': The Exclusion of Deformed Persons from Holy Places in Qumranic and Rabbinic Literature," *DSD* 4 [1997], 180).

physical defects were living in the community.⁵² Furthermore, children—who are excluded according to the list in 4Q266 8 i 6–9—were obviously born into the community and very much belonged to the community and the covenant, as we have seen. Since children and people with physical and mental disabilites were part of the community, the list of exclusion in D consequently relates to exclusion from some aspect of communal life, not full exclusion. In comparison, 1QSa includes children (1QSa I 4–8), as well as physically and mentally challenged, persons in the community. Immediately following the list of excluded categories of people in 1QSa II 4–9 comes a rule that prescribes how these people can communicate any concerns to the holy council; hence, they are still part of the community.⁵³ It is thus evident that physically and mentally challenged people were part of the communities behind D and 1QSa, despite the fact that they were not allowed to enter into the communal meetings. In order to uncover the underlying principles for excluding members, a comparison between the lists in the three documents is necessary.

6.2.6.3 Principles for Exclusion: A Comparison

The following chart comparing the lists of excluded persons in D, 1QSa, and M clarifies their similarities and differences and facilitates the search for underlying guiding principles.

---

⁵²CD XIV 15 dictates that the community support a man who is "afflicted" (איש אשר י[ג]ונע), which refers to any kind of blemish. A rule on skin disease in CD XIII 6 assumes that a priest who is פתי ("simple-minded") still functions in the community.

⁵³1QSa II 9b–10: "And if [one of] these (who has a blemish) [has some]thing to say to the holy council, [they shall] question [him] in private, but the man [shall no]t enter into the midst of [the congregation] for he is afflicted" (ואל תוך [העדה לו]א יבוא כיא האיש מנוגע). According to 1QSa I 19–22, a person who is פיתי is prohibited from taking certain responsibilities in the community, but "he shall perform his service according to his ability."

Table 4: Excluded categories of people in D, 1QSa, and M

Defects	CD XV/4Q266 8 i 6–9	1QSa II 3–9	1QM VII 3–6
mental disability	demented fool, simple minded	—	—
moral inclination	errant person	—	—
physical defects	blind, limping, lame, deaf	afflicted in the flesh, crippled in legs or hands, lame, blind, deaf, dumb, stricken by visible blemish, tottering old man[54]	lame, blind, crippled, stricken by permanent blemish
age	youth	—	youth
sex	—	—	woman
purity	—	any human impurity	uncleanliness in flesh, not purified from discharge
excluded from	enter into the midst of congregation	take a stand in the midst of the congregation; stand firm in the midst of the congregation of the men of renown	enter the camp, go in battle
rationale	for the holy angels are in their midst	for holy angels are in their council	for the holy angels are together with their armies

There are a few striking differences and similarities. The rationale for excluding certain persons is the same in the three documents, which all refer to the presence of "holy angels." The similar wording shows literary dependence, though it is impossible to know the exact relationship.[55] While the three lists include physical defects, only D

---

[54] Age is not the primary issue here; instead any old man who cannot stand still is to be excluded, and the issue is therefore a physical one. See Shemesh, "Exclusion of Deformed Persons," 197; contra Schiffman, *The Eschatological Community*, 49.

[55] Compare 1QSa II 8–9, 4Q266 8 i 8b-9 and 1QM VII 6:

1QSa אל יב[ואו] אלה להתיצב [ב]תוך עדת א[נ]ושי השם כיא מלאכי קודש [בעד]תם

mentions the errant and the mentally disabled. Using the same expression, נער זעטוט ("youth"), both M and D include a youth in the lists, but only M refers specifically to women. While M and 1QSa refer specifically to impure people, D does not. In fact, the only category that is common to the three documents is the list of physical deformities, although the documents vary as to the deformities listed. The list of physical imperfections is thus the core of the lists and will be the starting point for my analysis.

It is generally accepted that the lists of physical defects are inspired by Lev 21:17–23, which gives a list of physical imperfections that disqualify a priest from serving in the sanctuary.[56] Lev 21:18–20 reads: "For no one who has a blemish (מום) shall draw near, one who is blind or lame, or one who has a mutilated face or a limb too long, or one who has a broken foot or a broken hand, or a hunchback, or a dwarf, or a man with a blemish in his eyes or an itching disease or scabs or crushed testicles."[57] The reason for the exclusion given in Lev 21:23 is that a person with a blemish should not profane (יחלל) the sanctuary.

Why did the sect apply some of the priestly list of physical imperfections to their own gatherings, whether in war or in the communal council? It has frequently been suggested that the Qumran community in some respects considered itself as a substitute for the temple and therefore applied the purity laws of the temple to its own community.[58] In the laws that exclude blemished people in D, 1QSa, and M, there is a

---

א[ל יבו]א איש [מ]אלה אל תוך העדה   כי מלאכ[י] הקוד[ש בתוכם] 4Q266
                                    כיא מלאכי קודש עם צבאותם   1QM

[56]There are restrictions listed in the Scrolls concerning entrance into the temple. 4QFlorilegium (4Q174) excludes an Ammonite, a Moabite, a mamzer, an alien, and a proselyte from entering the temple (4QFlor I 3–5). See Devorah Dimant, "*4QFlorilegium* and the Idea of the Community as Temple," in *Hellenica et Judaica: Hommage à Valentin Nikiprowetzky* (eds. André Caquot et al.; Leuven-Paris: Peeters, 1986), 165–89. The fragmentary text of 4QMMT B 39–41 contains a similar list (the Ammonite?, the Moabite, the mamzer, the eunuch). 11QT XLV 12–14 excludes the blind from entering the temple.

[57]With the exception of פסח (lame), different terms are used for the physical defects in 4Q266 8 i 6–9 compared to Lev 21:17–23, but three of the four categories mentioned in D are still part of the list in Leviticus 21 (blindness, limp, lameness). While both 1QSa and D include חרש ("deaf") in their lists, 1QSa also lists אלם ("dumb"). These categories are not mentioned in Leviticus 21. Possibly Exod 4:11 was influential in this regard, as Schiffman suggests ("Purity and Perfection," 378). For a detailed discussion of the variations of physical deformities and the philology of the terms in rabbinic texts, see Schiffman, *The Eschatological Community*, 37–52; "Purity and Perfection," 373–89.

[58]See, e.g., Schiffman, "The Impurity of the Dead in the Temple Scroll," in *Archaeology and History in the Dead Sea Scrolls*, 135–56; Bertil Gärtner argues that the Qumran community in a sense embodied the Temple (*The Temple and the Community in Qumran and the New Testament: A Comparative Study in the Temple Symbolism of the Qumran texts and the New Testament* [Cambridge: Cambridge University Press, 1965], 18). Newton writes, "The membership at Qumran, both lay and priestly, now represented the temple. It appears that in

similarity between the biblical legislation concerning the temple and the sectarian community laws, but one should be careful not to extend the parallels too far. Harrington notes that the sectarians applied more stringent rules to the temple than to their own community.[59] Although I agree with Harrington on this point, it appears certain that the rules concerning the *communal meetings* are influenced by the priestly purity rules of the temple. Not that the members at these meetings saw themselves as officiating priests in the temple, since D preserves the distinction between priests and laity in its legislation; instead the connecting link to the temple is to be found in the belief in the presence of angels.[60] As angels mark the presence of God in the temple, a divine presence through the holy angels is real also in the communal assembly. Like

---

particular they saw themselves, in their expiatory role, as constituting the two innermost and holy areas of the temple: the Holy Place and the Holy of Holies" (*The Concept of Purity*, 49). Qimron argues that the community at Qumran considered itself "a substitute for the Temple" ("Celibacy in the Dead Sea Scrolls," 291). For identification of the community as "the new Temple," see Martínez and Trebolle Barrera, *The People of the Dead Sea Scrolls,* 154–7. A similar notion is found in Colleen Conway, "Toward a Well-Formed Subject: the Function of Purity Language in the Serek Ha-Yahad," *JSP* 21 (2000), 103–5. Dimant claims that the community aspired to recreate "'the congregation of priests' officiating in the holy enclosure of the Tabernacle or the Temple-city" ("*4QFlorilegium* and the Idea of the Community as Temple," 165–89). John Kampen argues that "no spiritualisation" of the temple took place; instead, the community prepared itself for the eschatological temple ("The Significance of the Temple in the Manuscripts of the Damascus Document," in *The Dead Scrolls at Fifty*, 185–97).

[59]Harrington disputes the idea that the community saw itself as a substitute for the temple and applied the purity rules of the temple to that of the community. Instead the community was living according to the purity laws of the ordinary city in the Temple Scroll (*The Impurity Systems*, 51–7).

[60]A connection between the community and the temple is apparent in the theology of the Admonition. God has established "a sure house" (בית נאמן) in the community, a true priestly dynasty (CD III 19). This, however, does not necessarily comprise the whole community; the text emphasizes that one should support it, "hold fast" to it. In CD IV 3, the members (who should be understood to include women), are likened with "the Sons of Zadok." (For exegesis of this section, see Davies, *Damascus Covenant*, 90–5.) But in its legislation, D maintains a strict division between priests and lay members, and prescribes rules for the Temple in Jerusalem (not "a temple" in the community): a prohibition against entering the temple during flux and after childbirth in 4Q266 6 ii 3–4, 9; and restrictions on sending sacrifices to the Temple in CD XI 18–21. D maintains a strict view on priestly descent, disqualifying anyone from officiating in the Temple who emigrates from the land of Israel (4Q266 5 ii 8; see Baumgarten, "The Disqualification of Priests," 503–13). The members are divided into four groups at the mustering in CD XIV 3–6: "they shall all be mustered by their names; the priests first, the Levites second, the sons of Israel third, and the proselyte(s) fourth. And they shall be inscribed by their names, one after another, the priests first, the Levites second, the sons of Israel third, and the proselyte(s) fourth."

biblical laws protecting the holiness of the temple, sectarian laws prohibiting "blemished" persons from entering the communal assembly served to protect the sanctity of the assembly.

The blemishes of a priest are said to "profane" the sanctuary (Lev 21: 23). Most of these deformities in Lev 21:16–24 are related neither to the ability to carry out priestly duties nor to purity, but to aesthetics alone. Thus physical imperfection is opposed to holiness, as the person offering in the temple is "seen" by God. The Rabbis applied similar rules to pilgrims.[61] The texts from Qumran show that the sectarians also adopted the concept of holiness as related to bodily perfection and applied it to their communal meetings and the war camp. Accordingly, blemished persons were banned because of the real, close encounter with angels. The level of purity and physical perfection that was desired for the priests serving in the temple was thus extended to the communal meetings. This, however, does not rule out women's participation because the sectarian communal meetings were not restricted to priests, but were open to lay members. In comparison, Paul also believed that angels were present when members of the early church worshipped together; he instructed the congregation in Corinth that women should wear a head covering "because of the angels" (1 Cor 11:10).[62] That is, Christian communities provide an example where women and men did worship together in what they believed to be the presence of angels.

The demand for purity and perfection should be understood within the context of the sect's eschatological expectations. The presence of angels shows that the eschatological reality, for which the community prepared itself was, in a sense, already present in the community. By the exclusion of the impure and the imperfect, the communal meetings conspicuously foreshadowed the eschatological perfection of holiness and purity, as the members already enjoyed the company of the divine angels.[63]

Given that the list of blemishes in Lev 21:16–24 is applied to the communal assembly, why are other categories added in each list? The focus here is on broad categories, since details are not pertinent to the question of whether or not women took part in the assemblies. 4Q266 8 i 6–7 (and parallel copies) refers to the mentally challenged and the errant, which neither of the other texts do. Although mental

---

[61] Shemesh, "Exclusion of Deformed Persons," 179–206.

[62] Murphy O'Connor interprets 1 Cor 11:10 within the context of the lists of exclusion in 1QM VII 3–6, 1QSa II 3–9, 4Q266 8 i (based on to the translation provided by Milik in *Ten Years*, 114), and Lev 21:17–23, arguing that the uncovered head of a woman was like a bodily defect that would be deemed irreverent by the angels (*Paul and Qumran* [London: Geoffrey Chapman, 1968], 40–5).

[63] On the eschatological dimensions of the communal meetings, see W. Lyons and A. Reimer, "From Demonic Virus and Qumran Studies: Some Preventive Measures," *DSD* 5 (1998), 29.

deficiency is not part of the list in 1QSa, this text excludes the "simple minded" (איש פיתי) from full service in the congregation within the context of the official functions of the members in 1QSa I 19–22.[64] The exclusion of the mentally challenged has thus already been discussed in column one of 1QSa, and there is no need to repeat these rules when the exclusion of unfit persons is detailed in column two. In addition, in the introductory lines to the list of excluded categories, the text effectively excludes mentally challenged persons, as well as any errant person, since only those who are "discerning," "knowledgeable," "perfect of the way," and "men of valor" are allowed to attend the עצת היחד, "the council of the community" (1QSa I 27–8, II 2). Similarly, M limits participation in the holy war to those who are fit. 1QM VII 5 prescribes that the volunteers for war should be "perfect in spirit and body," ותמימי רוח ובשר, which clearly precludes mentally challenged persons and probably 'the errant' as well. Althogh D is the only text that explicitly excludes 'the errant,' the emphasis on perfection of the participants in the council in 1QSa and in the end time war in M reveals the same ideology. The reason someone who is mentally challenged should be banned from communal assemblies or war is obviously because such persons would simply not be capable of taking part in deliberations and judgments, and would not be fit to fight. An additional motive may be purity, as a mentally challenged person may not be entirely trustworthy in this regard. Finally, their exclusion reflects the general division of humans into perfect and imperfect.

Both 1QSa and 1QM ban a person suffering from any kind of impurity.[65] In addition, M specifically prescribes rules for a man who has a nocturnal emission. It is obvious that no impure person would be allowed to enter the assembly according to D either, as the presence of the holy angels clearly marks the space as sacred. However, the author apparently did not consider it necessary to mention the impure among those excluded, as their exclusion is self-evident. So far, D, 1QSa, and M, though differing on details, share a common ground by explicitly excluding the physically blemished and barring the mentally challenged, the impure, and possibly the errant (if not explicitly, then in principle, by emphasizing the perfection of the participants) from entering communal meetings and the war camp.

The last—and key—difference between the documents is the mention of a youth in D, the exclusion of boys and women in 1QM, the omission of both in 1QSa. Based on the exclusion of women from the war camp in 1QM, Schiffman concludes concerning 1QSa:

---

[64] According to 1QSa I 19b–22, a simple-minded person cannot "enter the lot to take his firm stand over the congregation of Israel" (אל יבוא בגורל להתיצב על עדת ישראל) nor participate in deciding legal cases or other matters of the congregation, nor battle. Instead, "he shall perform his service according to his ability."

[65] See 1QSa II 3–4; 1QM VII 5–6.

It is most likely that the very same regulation was in force regarding the eschatological council. Although women and children would be part of the sect, as is evident from 1QSa 1:6–11, their presence among the angels in the council of the community would not be allowed, as it was not in the military camp of the battle for the end of days.[66]

The rationale behind applying rules regarding women in M to other documents can be questioned. Although the lists are similar, M prescribes laws for an entirely different situation than do 1QSa and D, namely, the war camp. Accordingly, one should not *a priori* assume that the same rules apply to the war camp as to the congregational meetings described in D and 1QSa. Why are women and youths excluded from the war camp? Dupont-Sommer claims that "all access to the camp was forbidden to youth and women, doubtless because they were not specially sanctified for war and would defile the camp by their impure presence."[67] It is not clear why, in his estimation, women would be "impure," since women as well as men would be able to attain a ritually pure state. Nothing suggests that women in themselves were considered ritually impure in M, and indeed this would go against all purity laws in biblical and Qumran law that prescribe exact rules for purification of men and women after defilement.

The rules for the war camp in 1QM VII 3–6 are clearly inspired by the laws concerning the war camp in Deut 23:9–14, which, parallel to 1QM VII 3–7, includes rules for the exclusion of a person defiled by bodily discharge and rules for places to relieve oneself outside the camp. Deuteronomy 23 does not, however, mention blemished persons.[68] The ban of physically impaired and blemished persons was added in 1QM because Deut 23:14 emphasises the divine presence in the war camp: "because the Lord your God travels along with your camp... therefore your camp must be holy, so that he may not see anything indecent among you and turn away from you."[69] "Anything indecent" was interpreted as the blemishes that cause priests to be unfit from service (Lev 21:16–24), which consequently led to the inclusion of physical blemishes in the list in 1QM VII 3–6. In contrast to Deut 23:9–10, 1QM VII 3–6 also excludes women from the war camp together with youths. Though neither women nor youths are explicitly prohibited from entering the war camp in biblical rules, they are not mentioned as present either. Num 1:2–3 specifies that only men from twenty years of age and up should be conscripted for military service. Traditionally, soldiers have been men, not women or children. By excluding women and youths from the war camp, M makes explicit what is implicit in the biblical accounts. Women are excluded

---

[66]Schiffman, *The Eschatological Community*, 51; cf. "Purity and Perfection," 385
[67]Dupont-Sommer, *The Essene Writings*, 180 n.2.
[68]In her analysis of the purity of the Temple city, Japhet points out that the rules for the war camp in Deuteronomy are stricter than those for the Israelite camp in the wilderness ("The Prohibition of the Habitation of Women," 74).
[69]See Shemesh, "Exclusion of Deformed Persons," 194–5.

for practical purity reasons; not because women were impure, but as Yadin argues, because women constituted a threat to the purity of men by their very presence.[70] This corresponds to the traditional taboo against sex in connection with the holy war (for example, 2 Sam 11:11). The exclusion of boys from the war camp in M is related to the age requirements, which precede the list (1QM VII 1–3a), and may stem from a concern for the safety of children.

Just as the holiness of the holy council should be protected according to D and 1QSa, so the holiness of the war camp is to be maintained in the eschatological war. However, the situation of the war camp is entirely different from that of a communal assembly, and different kinds of impurity are considered threatening. In a war camp, the soldiers live for a longer period of time and sleep in tents. In such a situation, the presence of women, especially if they stayed overnight, would constitute a sexual temptation for the men. In a congregational meeting, sexual intercourse is not a possibility, and hence the presence of women is not a threat. Just as nocturnal emission is a concern in the rules for the war camp (1QM VII 4–5), but not, for obvious reasons, in a congregational meeting, so the presence of women is not a concern in the rules for the communal meetings as described in D and 1QSa. We can thus conclude that there is no reason to apply rules from M concerning the exclusion of women to the texts prescribing rules for the congregation in D and 1QSa.

Since women are not mentioned as a category of excluded people in D and 1QSa, this may in fact indicate that they are *not* excluded from entering the assembly.[71] It is admittedly an argument from silence, but since women commonly are mentioned beside children or youth, one would expect a reference to women—if indeed they were excluded—in 4Q266 8 i 8, which refers to a youth.[72] The omission of women is especially noticeable in comparison to 1QM VII 3b, which has the same expression for youths as 4Q266 8 i 8, נער זעטוט, and mentions women beside youths. Women are also mentioned beside youths by the same expression, נער זעטוט ואשה ("a young boy

---

[70]Yigael Yadin argues that boys were banned as a precaution against homosexual relations (*The Scroll of the War of the Sons of Light against the Sons of Darkness* [London: Oxford University Press, 1962], 71).

[71]Originally proposed by Schuller: "the point is that the authors of 1QSa did not exclude them [the women], again suggesting that women were considered as full members" ("Women in the Dead Sea Scrolls," in *Methods of Investigation of the Dead Sea Scrolls*, 124). More recently she has modified this proposal ("Women in the Dead Sea Scrolls," in *The Dead Sea Scrolls after Fifty Years*, 134).

[72]Compare references to women and children/youth in CD VII 7; 1QSa I 4; 11QT XXXIX 7–9. In addition, women are routinely grouped together with children and slaves in rabbinic literature, e.g., concerning not being accepted as witnesses in courts (*m. Seb.* 4:1) and being exempted from reciting the Shema (*m. Seb.* 3:3) and from "appearing before the Lord", i.e., doing pilgrimage to the temple (*m. Hag.* 1:1). On this topic, see Judith Baskin, "The Separation of Women in Rabbinic Judaism," in *Women, Religion, and Social Change*, eds. Yvonne Y. Haddad and Ellison B. Findley (Albany, NY: State University of New York Press, 1985), 7.

or a woman"), in 4QMiscellaneous Rules (4Q265) 3 3.[73] These examples show that the expression נער זעטוט ("youth") was frequently used together with ואשה ("and woman") when a rule applied to children *and* women. Consequently, the omission of a reference to a woman beside the youth in D is likely intentional, and indicates that women did enter into the congregational meetings.

6.2.7 Conclusion

The rite of initiation (CD XV 5–15) should be understood as a boundary-marking mechanism that was designed to separate the members of the community behind D from their fellow Jews. Thus through the rite of initiation, the insiders marked the boundary from outsiders as the children of the members took the oath of the covenant and progressed to the status of full members.[74] While the oath of the covenant marked the separation between insiders and outsiders, it also served to distinguish between full members in the community and those who had not yet attained this status.

The initiation ritual took place at the annual ceremony of the renewal of the covenant, a solemn ceremony that was inspired and patterned on covenantal rites in the Hebrew Bible. Such rites in the Hebrew Bible are conspicuous by their emphasis on the presence of the whole community. Above, I highlighted two passages from the Hebrew Bible—Deut 29:10–12 and Neh 10:28–9—that appear to have been particularly influential on the development of the covenantal rite as described in D and that explicitly include women in their discourses on the covenant rites. The presence of women and children at the renewal ceremony is apparent in 1QSa I 4–5. In light of the inclusive nature of the biblical renewal of the covenant ceremony, which is mirrored in the reference to the covenant being for *all Israel* in CD XV 5, it is likely that בניהם ("their children") in CD XV 1 and 5 refers to both male and female children and that both young men and women took the oath of the covenant. Furthermore, 1QSa gives clear evidence of the inclusion of women as full members among "those enrolled." Their status as full members is confirmed by the evidence of women's participation in the communal assembly in 1QSa, in which they testified about their husbands and listened to the deliberations.

---

[73]The text is restored: [אל] יואכל נער זעטוט ואשה [בזוב]ח הפסח, "[Let no] young boy nor a woman partake [of] the paschal [sacri]fice;" Baumgarten, "Miscellaneous Rules," in *DJD XXXV*, 63.

[74]In his sociological study on Jewish sects in Hasmonean times, Albert Baumgarten points out the difference between a sectarian view of membership and that of the mainstream Jewish population of the time, explaining that Jewish sects applied mechanisms of separation that other Jews normally applied to non-Jews "as a way of protesting against those Jews, and/or against Jewish society at large." The Essenes thereby built elaborate and efficient boundaries towards fellow Jews, in order to protect themselves from outsiders' "defiling" presence (*The Flourishing of Jewish Sects*, 9, 91).

Only full members were allowed to enter the communal meetings, and D, like 1QSa and M, details a list of people excluded from the communal deliberations. These documents rationalise the exclusion of some people by emphasising the presence of holy angels, which makes the communal meetings or a military camp sacred. Consequently, there are similarities between rules for entering the assembly, the war camp, and the temple, as the divine is present in all these sacred spaces. Nevertheless, one cannot assume that exactly the same rules apply to each sacred space. In particular, the situation of the war camp and that of the communal meeting is very different and therefore, to some extent, requires different rules. Accordingly, women are excluded from the war camp, but not necessarily from the communal meetings.

Highlighting the presence of angels, D and 1QSa ban certain people from the communal assembly in order to protect its purity and holiness. Impure people and less reliable people (those lacking full intellectual capacity) would pollute the sacred space, while those with physical imperfections would offend the divine by their appearance. In addition, no transgressors (morally corrupt) or children (lacking full membership status) were allowed entrance. None of these underlying reasons for exclusion are based on the sex of the persons involved. In other words, these principles do not apply to women's presence in the communal meeting more than to the presence of men. Women, as well as men, would be pure most of the time, but when they were impure they would be prohibited from attending. Neither would blemished women or men be allowed to participate in the meetings. The lists of excluded categories of people reveal the extent to which the sect was concerned about purity and holiness, in that it considered physical blemishes, mental disability, trangressions, and impurity threatening to the holiness of the congregation.

Although we usually think about membership in terms of the categories members/non-members—and certainly the Qumran documents often reflect these categories in dualistic terms such as 'the sons of light' versus 'the sons of darkness'—I have suggested that we need to recognize that there are degrees of membership. The matter of membership is more complex than simply insiders versus outsiders, because one can be a member in the sectarian communities behind D and 1QSa without attaining full membership status; so children and those who are physically and mentally disabled belong to the communities as members but not as full members.

In this section, I have considered membership first in relation to initiation into the congregation through taking the oath of the covenant and second, in relation to admittance into meetings that have a sacred status. Both these categories indicate full membership status. I have argued that there are reasons to think that women did participate in these activities and from that perspective they may be considered full members.

Does this mean that in the communities behind D and 1QSa women and men shared the same tasks? No, just as men had different functions within the community according to ability and ranking, so likely did women have different tasks amongst each other as well as in relation to men. But both men and women took part in the

6.3 MARRIAGE, DIVORCE, AND THE EDUCATION OF CHILDREN: 4Q266 9 III 1–10; CD XIII 15–19

6.3.1 INTRODUCTION

4Q266 9 iii 1–10/CD XIII 15–19 concerns the Examiner's responsibilities with regard to marriage, divorce (as I will argue below), and the education of children. This section sheds light on the subject of the role and status of women in the community behind D and, in addition, provides crucial information about the upbringing of children in the community. It forms a part of the rule for the Examiner in CD XIII 7b–20a, which begins with the introduction: "And this is the rule (סרך) for the Examiner of the camp."

4Q266 9 iii consists of several fragments that together make up a narrow column with about 20–25 letters per line.[75] While the end of CD XIII is damaged (CD XIII 16–22), 4Q266 9 iii supplements the CD text and improves the reading. Still, the combined text of 4Q266 9 iii 1–10/CD XIII 15–19 is incomplete.[76] There are a few textual differences between the two copies, which are shown below. I present the Cave 4 text, 4Q266 9 iii 1–10, because it is the most complete MS of this section. Where the wording of two copies differs substantially, I supply the text from CD in the column to the left.

6.3.2 THE TEXT: 4Q266 9 III 1–10; CD XIII 15B–19 UNDERLINED.

	1 [ואל י]עש [איש למקח ולממכר]
	2 [ד]בֿר כי אםׄ] הודיע למבקר[
	3 [א]שר במחנ[ה ועשה בעצה][78]
	4 [ולו] ישוגו וכן לכול לוקֿ[ח אשה]
ואל יעש איש דֿבׄרֿ[77] למקח ולממכר כי אם	
[עֿצֿהׄ וכן למגרש	5 הֿוֿאה בעצה[79] וֿכֿן יבן לֿ[מגרש] וֿהׄ[ ] ◦ ◦ ◦ [

---

[75] DJD XVIII, 70–1, Plate XI.

[76] There may be overlap also with lines 1–7 in the very narrow fragment 4Q269 10 ii as Stegemann proposes ("More Identified Fragments of 4QD^d [4Q269]," 497–501).

[77] Qimron restores דבר ("The text of CDC") instead of חבר, "association," as Rabin reads the word in CD XIII 15. Although Baumgarten and Schwartz follow Rabin's reading, they translate the word as if reading דבר ("The Damascus Document [CD]," 54). Commenting on 4Q266 9 iii 1-2, Baumgarten states that Qimron's reading is preferable in light of the word order in 4Q266, which differs from CD XIII 15 (DJD XVIII, 71).

[78] Rabin reads אמנה, (written) "agreement" (Neh 10:1); see Zadokite Documents, 67. But the traces of the first letter support a beth rather than an alef.

6 [וְהַ]ו̇אָה [ייַסֵּ]ר̇ את בניהם [ובנותם]
7 וֹטפם [ברו]ח̇ ע̇[נ]וָ̇ה ובא[הבת חסד]
8 אַל יטור לה̇[ם] בַּאף וע[ברה]
9 [ע]ל פשעיהם] וא[ת אשר איננו
10 [נקשר בש   מ[שפטיהם

1 [Let no man] do any[thing involving buying or selling]
2 unless [he informs the Examiner]
3 who is in the cam[p and acts with counsel]
4 so that they do not err. Likewise for anyone who tak[es a wife],
5 let it be with counsel, and likewise let him (the Examiner) guide [the man who divorces]
6 He (the Examiner) shall instruct their sons [and their daughters]
7 and their little children [in a spi]rit of hu[mi]lity and lov[ing-kindness.]
8 Let him (the Examiner) not keep rancour against th[em] with wrathful an[ger]
9 [be]cause of their failings, and against one who is not
10 [tied[80]bs   ]their [l]aws

6.3.3 Comments on the Text and Reconstruction

4Q266 9 iii 1–10 follows the text of CD XIII 15–19 closely for the most part, but there are a few notable differences. First, the word order differs slightly in 4Q266 9 iii 1–2 from that of CD XIII 15, but this does not affect the meaning. Second, the word יבן in 4Q266 9 iii 5 is missing in CD. It may have been omitted on purpose in CD, as the text reads better without it; יבן breaks the parallelism (indicated by underline) between וכן לכול לוקח אשה ("and likewise for anyone who takes a wife") in line 4 and וכן יבן למגרש ("and likewise let him guide one who divorces") in line 5. Third, the version in CD appears to have been longer. The approximate letter spaces in the gaps in CD XIII 17 and 19 indicate that CD would have contained additional words in the damaged portion of CD XIII 17–19 compared to the version in 4Q266 9 iii, but any reconstruction of the CD text remains uncertain.

---

[79] Qimron places the fragments that make up the right side of the column further apart, suggesting the longer reading והוׄ[שׂ]אה בעצה, "and she shall be married by counsel." While the switch in gender is not impossible, it would be surprising given the previous references to the man. Based on the reconstruction of 4Q266 9 iii 5, Qimron then proposes a new restoration of the parallel segment in CD, which has a gap longer than the text in 4Q266 9 iii. He suggests the reading והש[יא]ו א[תם ב]עצה "and they shall cause them to marry by counsel." It is unclear whether the tiny traces of the top of the letters support such a reading; see, Qimron, "לשיפור המהדורות של מגילות מדבר יהודה," 145.

[80] The meaning of "and against one who is not tied" is unclear. The stem קשר is rarely used in the Qumran Scrolls but occurs two more times in D (4Q267 5 ii 3/4Q266 5 i 10; CD XIII 10).

Baumgarten reconstructs [ובנותם?], "and their daughters" at the end of line 6. The *waw* in וטפם ("and their little children") allows for the reconstruction of a listing of three categories of young people; cf. ובכל־טפם נשיהם ובניהם ובנותיהם ("with all their little children, their wives, their sons, and their daughters") in 2 Chron 31:18. In the latter case, טף ("little children") is distinguished from "their sons" and "their daughters" which makes the proposed reconstruction ובנותם ("and their daughters") very plausible.

6.3.4 LITERARY STRATA

4Q266 9 iii 1–10/CD XIII 15–19 is part of "the rule for the Examiner of the camp," סרך המבקר למחנה (CD XIII 7–19), which in turn is a sub-section of a long rule for "the meeting of the camps" in CD XII 22–CD XIII 20.[81] Robert Davis assigns the section on the rule for the Examiner to the latest stratum, CDS4.[82] While the section forms part of the Community Organization, Hempel detects an underlying complex literary development.[83] Though different sources have been used, as Hempel demonstrates, the section still reads well as a coherent text, testifying to the redactional care with which these traditions were conjoined into a unit. Accordingly, the role prescribed for the Examiner is that of a teacher and a caring father both in the section

---

[81] Hempel points out that the partially preserved statement in CD XIII 20/4Q266 9 iii 11, "And this is the meeting of the camps for all the s[eed of]," fits well as a conclusion to the introduction in XII 22 (*Laws*, 126). A new heading appears to follow in CD XIII 22/4Q266 9 iii 14–15 as the text is restored; "these are the precepts for the Master (המשכיל)." See Baumgarten and Schwartz, "The Damascus Document (CD)," 54–5.

[82] Davis did not have access to the additional text in 4Q266 9 iii. For his discussion on CDS4, see "History," 88–9.

[83] The core of the rules for the Examiner is found in CD XIII 7 a,b, 12b–13, 15–16a, while CD XIII 9–10 and 14–15a are secondary additions. CD XIII 7c–8 stem from an independent tradition originally associated with the wise leader (משכיל) that has been merged with rules of the Examiner by the compiler of the laws. Hempel also detects evidence of a Serekh redaction in CD XIII 11–12a because of similarities to 1QS V 23a. These lines are the product of a Qumran redaction and are not from the community behind D (*Laws*, 117–26). Though I remain critical of the identification of the so-called Serekh redaction with Qumran, Hempel shows that there is a literary dependency between this stratum and S that points to a distinct layer. However, I remain undecided as to whether this layer is necessarily later than the rest of Community Organization, as much more study is needed on this issue. I will therefore not dismiss this stratum as irrelevant for illuminating the community behind D.

Hempel does not assign the last part of the Rule of the Examiner, including 4Q266 9 iii 3b–10, to any specific sub-stratum of the Community Organization. However, since these laws concern the power of the Examiner, there is no reason to doubt their integral part in this Rule. 4Q266 9 iii 3b–10 is closely connected by subject matter to the previous law in lines 1–3/CD XIII 15–16b, which Hempel considers part of the "core rule" (*Laws*, 117–18). The last part of the Rule for the Examiner (4Q266 9 iii 3b–10) should thus also be considered part of the original core.

CD XIII 7–10 in relation to the Many, and in CD XIII 17–19/4Q266 9 iii 6–10, concerning the children.[84] In addition, both segments use scriptural allusions.[85] While I recognise that there are underlying sources, I will read the passage as it stands since the whole text was compiled within the community behind D and is therefore relevant to the investigation into the D community.

6.3.5 A REFERENCE TO DIVORCE

There is a reference to divorce in line 5, [וכן יבן ל[מגרש ("and likewise let him guide [one who divorces]"), which is restored on the basis of למגרש וכן in CD XIII 17. In biblical Hebrew, גרש is used broadly for "driving out," while in the passive it refers specifically to a divorced woman, גרושה (e.g., Num 30:9; Lev 21:7, 14; Ezek 44:22). The standard term for divorce in biblical Hebrew is שלח (Deut 22:29; 24:1), whereas in rabbinic Hebrew גרש in the Piel is the common verb for "to give a letter of divorce." The question thus arises whether למגרש in D should be taken as a reference to someone who divorces, or to someone who is expelled.[86] Most translators read the word as a reference to someone who divorces.[87] In light of 4Q266 9 iii, it is now apparent that the immediate context concerns marriage; the reference to "one who takes a wife" in the preceding line (line 4) favours interpreting למגרש (line 5) as

---

[84] As the Examiner is portrayed as a father to the community—"his children"—in CD XIII 9–10, he again comes across as a loving father in 4Q266 9 iii 6–9/CD XIII 18–19, this time to the real children—the girls and boys—in the community. The exhortation to the Examiner to show loving kindness toward the children in 4Q266 9 iii 7 picks up on the pastoral role of the Examiner described in CD XIII 9–10: in CD XIII 9 he should "pity them (וירחם) as a father does his children" and CD XIII 18/4Q266 9 iii 7 instructs him to have a spirit of "humility and loving kindness." That the Examiner should be mercifully disposed is further emphasized by the negative command not to keep a grudge against them "because of their failings" (CD XIII 18/ 4Q266 9 iii 8).

[85] CD XIII 9–10 is cloaked in language from Ps 103:13; Ezek 34:12, 16; Isa 58:6; Hos 5:11; see Rabin, *Zadokite Documents*, 65–6. For the phrase באהבת חסד in CD XIII 18/ 4Q266 9 iii 7, see Mic 6:8. The phrase occurs no where else in D, but is a common expression in S: 1QS II 24; V 4, 25; VIII 2; X 26.

[86] Reading the word as a noun, Schechter suggested the translation "open space" as a plausible alternative to his translation, "to him who expels"; see *Fragments of a Zadokite Work*, 85 n.22.

[87] Rabin, Vermes, Martínez, Baumgarten, and Hempel take the word as a reference to someone divorcing (Rabin, *Zadokite Documents*, 66; Vermes, *The Complete Dead Sea Scrolls*, 142; Florentino García Martínez and Eibert J.C. Tigchelaar, *The Dead Sea Scrolls Study Edition*, 2 vols, [Cambridge: Eerdmans/Leiden: Brill, 1997–98], 1: 573; Baumgarten, "The Damascus Document [CD]," 55; Hempel, *Laws*, 115). According to Dupont Sommer, Fitzmyer, and Cook, the word refers to a banished person (Dupont Sommer, *The Essene Writings*, 158; Fitzmyer, "Divorce among First-Century Palestinian Jews," 103–10; Wise, Abegg, Cook, *Dead Sea Scrolls*, 71).

referring to divorce rather than expulsion. In addition, the verb used for expelling someone in the expulsion ceremony in D is שלח (4Q266 11 8, 14), not גרש.[88] Consequently, שלח would be the expected verb if our text referred to a banished member. Moreover, since the ordinances in 4Q266 9 iii 1–5/CD XIII 15–18 are restricting members from initiating an action on their own ("let no one do anything to buy or sell" and "similarly for one who takes a wife"), one expects the third stipulation, also introduced by "similarly," to involve some action taken by a member; that is, divorcing rather than "being banished." Finally, although some scholars have detected a prohibition of divorce in CD IV 20–1, the passage more likely condemns bigamy and not remarriage after divorce.[89] There is therefore sufficient reason for taking למגרש as a reference to one who divorces.

6.3.6 BUSINESS, MARRIAGE, AND DIVORCE: THE ROLE OF THE EXAMINER

The section begins with a rule requiring the Examiner to supervise any business transaction that a member of the community undertakes (4Q266 9 iii 1–4/CD XIII 15–16). The statute on business transactions is followed by the ordinances for the Examiner's supervision of marriage (lines 4–5) and divorce (lines 5–6). The three communal laws are linked together by repetition of the word וכן, "and similarly," which introduces both the topic of marriage and of divorce. These laws have been grouped together, since marriage and divorce—like business deals—involve transference of property, and all such transactions require the supervision of the Examiner.[90]

Two conditions are necessary before a person is allowed to make any business deal: (a) he or she should "inform" the Examiner and (b) that person must act with counsel (ועשה בעצ[ה]) (CD XIII 16). Subsequently, by the repetition of וכן, "and likewise," the text imposes the same conditions on one who marries or divorces. Concerning one who takes a wife, the text prescribes—parallel to business transactions—that "he (shall do it) with counsel" והואה בעצה (4Q266 9 iii 5). It is not entirely clear what kind of authority the Examiner assumes in the transactions—if it is merely providing counsel or giving permission. עצה encompasses various types of "counsel" in biblical Hebrew, including practical wisdom, political consultation, instruction, sagacity, design, etc.[91] In his study on עצה, Worrel points out that in

---

[88] In the penal code, the verbs for the act of expelling are unfortunately not preserved. But שלח is used in the penal code in S (1QS VII 16, 17, 25), and Baumgarten has reconstructed the penal code in 4Q270 with forms of שלח (4Q270 7 i 7, 14; *DJD XVIII*, 162–3).

[89] See above, section 5.2.2.

[90] Collins highlights the financial nature of both marriage and divorce contracts; see "Marriage, Divorce, and Family," 111–19. For an analysis of the economic aspects underlying this section, see Murphy, *Wealth in the Dead Sea Scrolls*, 82–3.

[91] The noun עצה ("counsel") is used as parallel to, for example, תבונה ("understanding") in Deut 32:28; Prov 5:5; 21:30; חכמה ("wisdom") in Jer 49:7; Prov 21:30; דבר ("word") in Judg

biblical Hebrew עצה, like the word דבר ("word"), carries more the meaning of an effective force than "the rather amorphous concept of advice."[92] In D as well, עצה carries several shades of meaning dependent on the context and sometimes assumes the force of a command.[93] עצה is used with reference to the Torah, לא בעצת תורה ("not by the counsel of the Torah"), in 4Q273 6 i.[94] Although the context is missing, "the counsel of the Torah" carries a meaning of absolute authority. The authority of a governing body, possibly from the wider Jewish society, is indisputable in CD XII 7–8 and expressed by the term עצה: "Let him not carry off any of their wealth so that they will not blaspheme, except by the counsel of the association of Israel, כי אם בעצת חבור ישראל."[95] Also, "the counsel" of the communal governing body in D carries absolute authority in the penalty code.[96] Worrel argues that the counsel provided in the communal body, both in CD and S, was connected to the idea of divine counsel, and was thereby "practically the equivalent of the counsel of God himself."[97] One example of this concept is found in CD XX 24–5, where the communal counsel is described as holy, implying that it was also absolute: "Each of them shall be judged according to his spirit according to the holy counsel (בעצת הקדש)."[98]

It is clear from the examples above that עצה often has the meaning of advice that carries the force of absolute authority. Of course, the effective force of the advice

---

20: 7; Isa 44:26. עצה ("counsel") is part of God's activities on behalf of his people and is often used together with "wondrous deeds" (see, e.g., Isa 25:1; 28:29; 29:15; Jer 32:19; Prov 1:30–1; Jer 49:20); see John Worrell, "עצה: 'Counsel' or 'Council' at Qumran?" VT 20 (1970), 65–7.

[92] Worrel, "עצה: 'Counsel,'" 67.

[93] עצה in plural is parallelled to בינה ("understanding") in CD V 17. 4Q266 5 ii 12 refers to "the counsel of the sons of Aaron," עצת בני אהרון. In this case, it is likely that the text prohibits seeking the counsel from priests defiled from staying abroad; DJD XVIII, 49–52.

[94] DJD XVIII, 198; cf. 1QS IX 9, 17.

[95] To which kind of association חבור ישראל ("association of Israel") refers remains enigmatic. Since the phrase is similar to the designation of the Jewish government, חבר היהודים ("association of the Judaeans"), on Hasmonean coins, it may refer to a governing body of Israel outside a sectarian community. See Rabin, Zadokite Documents, 61 n.8; see also Murphy, Wealth in the Dead Sea Scrolls, 84–6.

[96] עצה is used twice in the penal code in D: בעצת הר[ב]י[ם], "by permission of the Many" (4Q266 10 ii 7); "[He who in]sults his fellow without consultation (שלו בעצה) shall be [ex]cluded for one year and puni[sh]ed for s[ix months]" (4Q266 10 ii 2; cf. 1QS VII 10–11 concerning "permission," עצה, for leaving the session of the Many); see DJD XVIII 74–5. בעצה should likely be understood as "the counsel of the Many" in 4Q266 10 ii 2 though הרבים is not spelled out. בעצה in this case also pertains to permission.

[97] The authority of the counsel of a communal body, the Many, should be compared to the "council/counsel of the yahad," העצת היחד, in S (e.g., VIII 22). S also refers to "the counsel according to the Many," בעצה על פי הרבים (1QS VIII 19, 26).

[98] For the association of "counsel" with judgement, see Prov 1:29–31; 1QS VI 22–3; VIII 24–5.

depends on the authority of the one who delivers it. In D, the Examiner is accredited with extraordinary wisdom and with power over the individual members (CD XIII 7-10). Hence one should assume that the advice (עצה) of the Examiner was tantamount to an order and was not to be questioned. Though guidance certainly was also given, the Examiner had the authority to approve or disapprove any business deal or marriage.

While the first two clauses on business transactions and marriages use the word עצה ("counsel"), the last clause on divorce instead speaks of יבן in the *hiphil* ("teach," "give understanding," or "guide"). The consent of the Examiner is clearly required since the clause is connected to the previous one by the word וכן ("and likewise"). The text does not specify the content of the teaching or guidance that the Examiner provides and it is not clear what exactly יבן entails. In two other places in D, בין in the *hiphil* is used with the Examiner as the subject with reference to legal and theological matters.[99] Possibly the Examiner may investigate if divorce is halakhically and morally justified in a specific case. The involvement of the Examiner shows that although divorce might have occured, it was not taken lightly: a man was not free to divorce his wife at his own will.

The influence of the Examiner concerning divorce contradicts the traditional rights Jewish men held to divorce their wives at will (Deut 24:1–4; Sir 25:26).[100] The School of Hillel emphasized a man's absolute right to divorce for any cause, "even if she burned his dinner."[101] Such statements may give the false impression that divorce was unproblematic and spontaneous. Though divorce was routine, it always brought financial repercussions and was never a frivolous act.[102] A more stringent view is represented by Jesus, who prohibits divorce (except for adultery according to Matt. 5:32) and the House of Shammai which, similar to the Matthean Jesus, prohibits divorce for any reason except adultery. Such a strict position on divorce would provide stability for the woman, but also entail the risk of her living forever in a loveless, even abusive, relationship. Of course, she would run the same risk if the man alone had the right to initiate divorce, although in such a case she could hope for a bill of divorce, and try to influence her husband to give it to her. Nevertheless, in some segments of

---

[99] There is no parallel in D to the use of בין with ל followed by a personal indirect object (cf. 2 Chron 35:3; Dan 8:16; 11:33). Instead, elsewhere in D בין takes the direct object (see CD XIII 5–6, 8).

[100] Ben Sira 25:26 reads: "If she does not go as you direct, separate her from yourself."

[101] *M. Git.* 9–10. The debate between the houses of Hillel and Shammai focuses on reasonable cause for divorce, based on different interpretations of "something objectionable (ערות דבר) about her" in Deut 24:1. While the House of Hillel allowed divorce for any cause, the Shammaites restricted it to cases of adultery on the woman's part. For Jesus' prohibition of divorce, see Mt 5:32; 19:3–9; Mk 10:4–12; Lk 16:18; 1 Cor 7:10–11.

[102] There is no way to calculate the frequency of divorce, but it is treated as routine in literature and papyri; see Collins, "Marriage, Divorce, and Family," 149.

Jewish society, a woman was capable of divorcing her husband, in accordance with Roman customs.[103] This position, however, is not accepted or even discussed by the Rabbis, and it is uncertain how widespread the practice was.

The reason a member should not conduct business without the consent of the Examiner is explained by the phrase "so that they do not err" (ולו ישוגו) in line 4. שגה carries the meaning of sinning, especially inadvertently, and suggests that the main concern is to prevent any unintentional sin at the transactions.[104] Business transactions had to conform to all rules related to purity and tithing; one may therefore assume that the involvement of the Examiner was an extra safeguard against buying anything impure or anything that had not been properly tithed, given that purity and tithing are major issues in D.[105] In addition, in light of the prohibition against using the divine names or any substitute in oaths (CD XV 1–3) and the fact that oath formulas were

---

[103]There is evidence that women did initiate divorce in the Jewish society. Josephus provides examples of women divorcing their husbands, but also states that the practice was against the law (*Ant.* XV 259; XVIII 136; cf. Mk 10:11–12). Documents from Elephantine (fifth Century B.C.E.) give both marriage partners the right to initiate divorce; see Porten and Yardeni, *Contracts*, 33–3, 60–3, 78–83. An Aramaic Papyrus from Nahal Hever, *Papyrus Se'elim* 13 (134–5 C.E.), may be a Jewish bill of divorce written by a wife to her husband. This was the opinion of J. T. Milik, "Le travail d'edition des manuscripts du Desert de Juda," in *Volume du Congrès, Strasbourg 1956* (*VTSup*4; Leiden: Brill, 1956), 21. Bernadette Brooten highlights Milik's conclusions in her article "Konnten Frauen im alten Judentum die Scheidung betreiben? Überlegung zu Mk 10, 11–12 und 1 Kor 7, 10–11," *EvTh* 42 (1982), 65–80. In the publication of the papyrus by Ada Yardeni, in collaboration with Jonas Greenfield, Yardeni argues that the document is a receipt of a bill of divorce, not the actual bill of divorce itself; see *Nahal Se'elim Documents* (Jerusalem: Israel Exploration Society and Ben Gurion University in the Negev Press, 1995), 55–60 [Hebrew]. The papyrus is also published in Hanna Cotton and Ada Yardeni, *Aramaic, Hebrew, and Greek Texts from Naxal Hever and other Sites with an Appendix Containing Alleged Qumran Texts* (DJD XXVII; Oxford: Clarendon, 1997), 65–70.

Tal Ilan supports Milik's original conclusion ("Notes and Observations On a Newly Published Divorce Bill from the Judaean Desert," *HTR* 89 [1996], 195–202); so also Hannah Cotton and Elisha Qimron ("Xhev/Se ar 13 of 134 or 135 C.E.: A Wife's renunciation of Claims," *JJS* 49 [1998], 115). Ilan argues that women's right to initiate divorce was a common practice, but prohibited by the Pharisees, whose opinion became normative. See also Adiel Schremer, "Divorce in Papyrus Se'elim 13 Once Again: A Reply to Tal Ilan," *HTR* 91 (1998), 193–202, and the subsequent response by Tal Ilan, "The Provocative Approach Once Again: A Response to Adiel Schremer," *HTR* 91 (1998), 203–4. For a general discussion on a wife's right to divorce in Second Temple Judaism, see Gruber, "The Status of Women in Ancient Judaism," 162–3 ns. 44–5; Collins, "Marriage, Divorce, and Family," 119–21.

[104]Cf. CD XV 13–14: "Should he err (שגה) in any matter of the Torah revealed to the multitude of the camp, the Examiner shall ma[ke it known] to him and enjoin it upon him, and te[ac]h (him)..." See also Lev 4:13; Num 15:22.

[105]On purity, see e.g., restrictions concerning trading with gentiles CD XII 9–11; on agricultural laws, see 4Q266 6 iii–iv.

normal features of contracts and deeds, the supervision of the Examiner may have been needed to monitor the usage of oaths in the writings of contracts.[106] In sum, anyone in the community who considered doing business deals, or marrying or divorcing, needed the counsel of the Examiner to gain his advice as well as his approval or disapproval of the arrangement. These laws show the extraordinary authority the Examiner had over the lives of the members in the community behind D.

6.3.7 EDUCATION

The Examiner is presented as a teacher in D. In the description of the initiation process, the Examiner teaches recently initiated members who fail in some way (CD XV 14–15). The Rule for the Examiner (CD XIII 7–19) presents him as a teacher of wisdom who instructs the Many about God's doings in the world throughout history, relating to the Many the "wonder of his mighty deeds" (גבורות פלאו) and "the happenings of eternity" (נהיות עולם) (CD XIII 7–8). The Examiner is also responsible for some kind of instruction to the children within the community. The phrase "He shall instruct their sons [and daughters] and their children [in a spir]it of hu[mi]lity and lov[ing kindness]" in lines 4Q266 9 iii 6–7 echoes Micah 6:8: "He has told you, O mortal, what is good; and what does the Lord require of you but to do justice, and to love kindness (אהבת חסד), and to walk humbly with your God." In D, the Examiner is exhorted to give instructions in the spirit of kindness that Micah teaches. It should also be noted that the verse in Micah also encourages humility, as does the exhortation to the Examiner.[107] Given the context of humility and kindness, Baumgarten is no doubt correct in translating ייסר as "he shall instruct" rather than "discipline" or "rebuke."[108] In addition, the stem יסר is used in CD IV 8 and XX 31 with reference to the instruction of the members in the correct interpretation of the Torah.[109] Our text does not explain what the content of the instruction is. Since the Examiner in the same

---

[106] Murphy points out that oath formulas are common features in contracts and adds, "The fact that oaths are severely restricted in the Damascus Documents and the Rule... would raise the question whether covenanters could execute common deeds or conduct transactions in the outside world" (*Wealth in the Dead Sea Scrolls*, 369). Nevertheless, the stipulation CD XIII 15–16/4Q266 9 iii 1–2 suggests that members indeed could engage in business with outsiders, although under the supervision of the Examiner. Furthermore, since there are restrictions concerning business deals with gentiles, it should be taken for granted that trade with other Jews was allowed (CD XII 9–11).

[107] A different verbal stem is used in D, ענה ("be humble") compared to Mic 6:8, צנע ("be modest, humble").

[108] To discipline or to chasten are common meanings of יסר in the Hebrew Bible (e.g., Lev 26:18, 28; Hos 10:10; Jer 31:18) and occasionally the verb may allude to physical punishment (e.g., Deut 21:18; 22:18). Nevertheless, the verb can also mean "instruct" and "teach" (see, e.g., Isa 28:26; Hos 7:15; Prov 31:1).

[109] According to CD VII 5, to live by "his teaching" (i.e., God's) (יסורו) is part of the covenant relationship with God.

column is exhorted to instruct the Many in theology and scriptural interpretation (CD XIII 7–9), these subject matters would likely be part of the instruction to the children as well.

Scholars have suggested different identities for the characters in lines 6–9. By connecting lines 6–9 closely with למגרש ("one who divorces"), Tom Holmén holds that lines 6–9 concern a father and his children. According to this scenario, after a father has divorced their mother, the father should counsel the children. The identity of וה[ואה ("and he"; line 6) is accordingly the father.[110] However, since this piece of legislation appears in the Rule for the Examiner, it makes more sense that the Examiner is the implicit subject in these lines and not a divorcing father. Another problem is the identity of "their" sons, daughters, and children. Should "their" be taken in a communal sense, as a reference to the children of all members, or is the exhortation related specifically to the ordinance of divorce—and refers to the children of the divorced couple—as Holmén and Bilah Nitzan hold? The close examination of the context favours the identification of "their sons" with those of the entire community. If the "sons" were those of the divorcing father, one would expect a third person singular suffix, "his sons," since the divorced wife is not mentioned in the text. Moreover, the ordinances in 4Q266 9 iii 1–10/CD XIII 15–19 should be understood against the background of the Rule for the Examiner (CD XIII 7–19) as a whole. In this context, "their" in בניהם goes back to the references to the members in the third person plural, as used in CD XIII 7–10 ("the Many"; הרבים) as well as in CD XIII 16/ 4Q266 9 iii 4 (ולא ישוגו "so that they do not err"). Consequently, the reference to children in 4Q266 9 iii 6 should be understood as referring to the children of the community.

טף can denote nursing infants; it can collectively refer to young children; or it may refer to dependents in general, regardless of age.[111] טף in the Hebrew Bible is

---

[110]Holmén, "Divorce in CD 4:20–5:2 and 11QT 57:17–18," 403–4, see especially note 31. Bilah Nitzan takes a similar approach and interprets the passage as pertaining to the reproof of sons concerning someone divorcing their mother. The Examiner's role is hence to protect a father from being falsely accused by his sons. She translates lines 6–7 as follows: "And he [each man] will admonish their sons [and daughters] in a spirit of poverty and with compassion." See "The Laws of Reproof in 4QBerakhot (4Q286–290) in Light of their Parallels in the Damascus Covenant and Other Texts from Qumran," in *Legal Texts and Legal Issues*, 154–5.

[111]טף commonly denotes "children" in general, or those in a nomadic tribe who are not able to march to any great extent, i.e., the small children (*Hebrew Aramaic Lexicon*); see, e.g., Num 16:27; 2 Chr 20:13. M. O'Connor concludes that טף is sometimes used (in Numbers 31–32 in particular) as a general term for dependents ("Biblical Hebrew Lexicography: טף 'Children, Dependents' in Biblical and Qumran Hebrew," *JNSL* 25 [1999], 25–40). Deut 1:39 equates טפכם with "your children (בנכם) who do not yet know right from wrong"—thus young children in general. In Ezek 9:6, טף is distinguished from young men and women and connotes all young children (not only infants). In Num 31:18, הטף בנשים relates to young girls "who

sometimes distinguished from other children as denoting younger children, which is undoubtedly the case here. In this context, טף emphasises the inclusion of *all* children and shows that education should start at a fairly young age. We find a similar notion in Isa 28:9: "To whom shall he give instruction? To whom shall he explain a message? To those newly weaned from milk, just taken away from their mothers breasts."[112]

The reconstructed reference to daughters (ובנותם) is possible, but uncertain. Nevertheless, whether or not ובנותם ("their daughters") is the correct reconstruction, טפם ("their little children") combined with בניהם ("their sons" or "their children") makes clear that *all* children are the object of instruction. In other words, if there were no reference to daughters in the original text, בניהם should be translated gender inclusively as "children," and not "sons." By comparison, טף is used in a wide sense in 1QSa I 4–9 to include all children in the instruction in "the statutes of the covenant" and "their judgements." The phrase "from children to women," מטף עד נשים (1QSa I 4), makes it certain that girls are also included. The inclusion of all children, girls and boys, in the instruction in 1QSa I 4 thus strengthens the probability that girls are also to be instructed according to D (4Q266 9 iii 6–7).

There is additional information on the practice of educating children in 1QSa. The instruction "in their rules" and reading of the "statutes of the covenant" starts early—from childhood, מטף (1QSa I 4–5). In 1QSa I 6–8, it is clear that children receive a formal education as a stage in their lives as community members. 1QSa I 6–8 prescribes formal education of the young from "his (or her) youth" ([ומן נעו]ריו).[113] The word נעורים refers to early youth or childhood.[114] Thus, young boys and girls would get an extensive education, including in the Book of Hagu (1QSa I 7) and halakhah (the "statutes of the covenant" and "precepts"; 1QSa I 7–8).[115] The study of scripture suggests that teaching reading skills was part of the training. The prescription of education for children in 1QSa corresponds well with Josephus' claim that the Essenes were "versed from their early years (ἐμπαιδοτριβούμενοι) in holy books, various

---

have not known a man by sleeping with him," i.e., girls below marital age. One cannot detect an age-specific reference in the use of טף.

[112] For a discussion of this passage, see Gruber, "Breast-Feeding Practices in Biblical Israel and in Old Babylonian Mesopotamia," 80. He estimates that breast-feeding continued until the child was about three years of age.

[113] The term "youth," נעורים, does not refer to any specific gender.

[114] See Job 31:18; Schiffman argues that based on Tannaitic evidence, "we can conclude that early learning must have begun in the family setting, with actual schooling starting at six or seven" (*The Eschatological Community*, 15). It is questionable; however, if there is a direct link between Tannaitic evidence and 1QSa.

[115] It is not known what book is meant by the title *The Book of Hagu*. It may refer to the Torah or to a set of communal interpretations of the Torah; see Steven Fraade, "Hagu, Book of," *Encyclopedia of the Dead Sea Scrolls*, 1:327.

forms of purification, and sayings [lit. apophtegms] of the prophets" (*J. W* II 159).[116] The verb used for instructing the children in 4Q266 9 iii 6, יסר, is also used in 1QSa I 8.[117] In light of 1QSa I 4–8, it is evident that some kind of formal education for children is also implied by יסר in 4Q266 9 iii 6. Although 4Q266 9 iii does not specify the content of the instruction, this would likely include reading, as well as learning the correct interpretation of laws and the historical events, similar to the instruction mentioned previously in the document (CD IV 8; XX 31, XIII 8). Given the overall emphasis on studying and interpreting scripture in the sectarian literature of the Dead Sea Scrolls, it is not surprising that the Essene movement would consider the education of the young very important.

6.3.8 CONCLUSION

Our text highlights the authority of the Examiner over the personal lives of the community members, both men and women. The major decisions of individual members, such as marriage and divorce, were not personal issues any longer, but belonged to the communal realm. An emphasis on education in D is understandable in a community that focused on living correctly by the laws. The inclusion of girls in education should not be surprising, since it was obviously important for both sexes from a young age to understand the laws correctly, as well as to learn about the sectarian world view in order to fully endorse the community's way of life. Since the Examiner himself was responsible, the education and instruction of the children was given the utmost importance within the community. Correct instruction for the children was held to be the key to continuing perfection in the covenantal relationship for the community.

6.4 THE VIRGIN WITH NO REDEEMER: CD XIV 15–16; 4Q266 10 I 9

6.4.1 INTRODUCTION

CD XIV 12–17 stipulates rules for charitable contributions to the needy in the community and includes a list of the recipients. The rules are very precise: two days' salary each month should be given to the Examiner and the judges, who will provide help to the vulnerable and poor. The recipients include the sick, the poor, the elderly man, the physically handicapped, the Jewish captive in foreign land, the virgin who has no "redeemer," and the youth who has no one to help him financially.

---

[116] Dupont-Sommer proposes "sacred writings" rather than "by various purifications," emending the second word of διαφόροις ἁγνείαις, to ἁγίαις, "holy," and translating διαφόροις "writings"; *The Essene Writings*, 34.

[117] Four different verbs are used for instruction in the section: בין (1QSa I 5), למד (I 7), שכל (I 7), and יסר (I 8).

6.4.2 THE TEXT: CD XIV 12B–17A; PARALLEL: 4Q266 10 I 5–10 UNDERLINED

12 וֹזֶה סֶרֶךְ הָרַבִּים לְהָכִין כָל חפציהם שכר
13 שְׁנֵי יָמִים[118] לכל חדש למעיט ונתנו[119] על יד הַמְבַקֵּר והשופטים
14 מִמֶּנּוּ יתנו בעד[120] [פ]צָעָם וממנו [121]יַחֲזִיקוּ בְּיַד עֲנִי וְאֶבְיוֹן ולזקן אשר
15 [יכר]ע וְלֹאִישׁ אשר ינו[ג]ע ולאשר ישבה לגוי נכר ולבתולה אשר
16 אֵין לָהּ גֹ[וא]ל וְלֹנַעַ[ר]ֿ[122] א]שר אין לו דורש כל[123] עבודת הֶחָבֵר ולא
17 [יכרת בית החבר מיד]ֿם

12 And this is the rule for the Many to provide for all their needs: the wage of at least
13 two days per month is to be given to the Examiner and the judges.
14 From it they shall give for their [w]ounded, and from it they shall support the poor and the destitute, the old person who is
15 [bowed do]wn and the person who is affli[ct]ed, the one captured by a foreign people, the virgin who
16 has no re[deem]er, the you[th w]ho has no one to look after him,[124] (and) all the work of the association, so that
17 [the house of association[125] will] not [be cut off from among the]m.

---

[118]There appears not to be sufficient space in 4Q266 10 i 6 for inserting לכל חדש "per month." That the contribution should be made on a monthly basis may still be implicit in the 4Q266 text. See Baumgarten's translation of 4Q266 10 i 6: "[the earnings of at leas]t two [days (per month)] which will be given [to]..." (*DJD XVIII*, 72). Hempel, however, suggests that the shorter text is an earlier version referring to a one time charitable collection (*Laws*, 138).

[119]4Q266 10 i 6 reads וינתן (in the 3rd person singular).

[120]Following Qimron's reading; "The Text of CDC," 14. 4Q266 10 i 7 provides the two first letters of the word: פצ. Baumgarten's reconstruction [יתו]מים ("orphans"), which he translates, "their [s]ick" is certainly incorrect ("The Damascus Document [CD]," 56-7).

[121]4Q266 10 i 7 reads יֿ[חזקו בעד] הע[ני והאביון.

[122]The letters of לנע]ר in CD are hardly legible. According to Qimron, the traces in CD are best read as as לע[ו] ("The Text of CDC," 37). But in 4Q266 10 i 9 לנער is clear. Baumgarten thinks the traces in CD can be reconciled with לנער, that is, no variant reading is necessary. I agree with his reading. Rabin reconstructed ולע[למה א]שר אין לה דורש ("and for the virgin who has no one to seek her in marriage"), which would give a second category of women (*Zadokite Documents*, 70-1). This reading is not possible, because the next phrase in CD must be read as אין לו (not אין לה as Rabin read--but oddly 4Q266 has just לה). Also, if לעלמה were the correct restoration in CD, the top of the second *lamed* should appear.

[123]4Q266 10 i 9 reads ולכול.

[124]דורש is used in the general commandment to "care for the welfare of" a brother in CD VI 21–VII 1.

[125]בית החבר refers to the community at large, and the self-designation suggests that the community saw itself as a close-knit affiliation or fellowship of men and women. Murphy explains that the community presents itself as an alternative economic institution built on justice.

6.4.3 COMMUNAL SUPPORT

CD XIV 12–17 is part of "the rule for the assembly of all the camps," סרך מושב כל המחנות, in CD XIV 3–18a.[126] This section is immediately followed by the penal code (CD XIV 20–22/4Q266 10 i 14–15 preserves the beginning of the penal code). The text reflects a compassionate attitude towards the weak in the community. The concern for the vulnerable in society is well known from the Hebrew Bible, which frequently advocates assistance to the poor and needy.[127] A general commandment similar to the biblical commands, to support "the poor, destitute and proselyte," is found in the Admonition (CD VI 21). The stipulations in CD XIV 14–16 differ markedly from both the general biblical demands for charitable contributions and the instruction in CD VI 21, by being specific about the amount that should be given, and by determining the office-holder responsible for distributing the collections.[128] Thus, in the case of the community behind D, these precise stipulations sought to ensure that the vulnerable in the community would indeed get help.

The reference to the virgin with no redeemer is particularly interesting, since this passage reveals who, among the women in the community, were considered vulnerable and in need of assistance. In contrast to the Hebrew Bible, which commonly highlights the widow, together with the orphan and the alien,[129] as particularly in need of financial aid, it is striking that the widow is not mentioned in D.[130] In addition, the common term for "an orphan," יתום, is not used in the list in D, which instead refers to a youth without support, ולנע[ר א]שר אין לו דורש ("the you[th w]ho has no one to look after him"). Stegemann argues that the omission of widows and orphans indicates that they were cared for under family law, but he does not specify to which laws he

---

She interprets the reference to "the foundation walls of the assembly," יסדות אוש[י] הקהל (CD XIV 17–18/4Q266 10 i 11), in light of Ezek 22:29–31 where the prophet criticizes the people for not repairing the wall of the people; instead they are oppressing the poor and needy (*Wealth in the Dead Sea Scrolls*, 86).

[126] Hempel argues that the new heading in CD XIV 12, which reads "this is the Rule for the Many," וזה סרך הרבים, seems misplaced in the context of the Rule for the meeting of all the camps. It is therefore, she concludes, a secondary interpolation and the work of the Serekh redactor (*Laws*, 131–40). A second heading referring to the rule of the Many is odd, since CD XIV 17b concludes the rule with the words וזה פרוש מושב ה[מחנות], "this is the explanation of the assembly of the [camps]."

[127] See e.g., Lev 19:10–11; Deut 15:7–11; 24:17; 26:12; Ezek 22:29–30; Amos 2:6–7; Isa 1:23; 3:15.

[128] Murphy discusses the differences between CD XIV 12–16 and the biblical injunction to charity; see *Wealth in the Dead Sea Scrolls*, 83–7.

[129] E.g., Exod 22:22; Deut 14:29; 16:11, 14; Jer 49:11.

[130] Cf. CD VI 16–17, where "the sons of the pit" are accused of "preying on widows and murdering orphans," that is, attacking the most vulnerable groups in the society. The accusation is linked to stealing what rightfully belongs to the widows and orphans from the funds deposited in the temple; see Baumgarten and Schwartz, "The Damascus Document (CD)," 23 n.60.

refers.[131] That orphaned children were adequately taken care of in the community, as Stegemann holds, fits well with the picture of the close-knit community suggested by the communal laws in D. Nevertheless, the reference to the נער ("youth") lacking someone to care for him most certainly refers to a fatherless youth in need of assistance. Furthermore, the phrase "the virgin with no redeemer" refers to a woman who has no near kin to pay her dowry,[132] and thus she is likely orphaned too. Consequently, one may assume that while young orphans were protected in their childhood, they were in need of extra financial assistance when they reached adolescence.[133]

The text demonstrates the differing financial needs of poor young men and women; the young man lacks someone to support and protect him financially, while the young woman needs assistance in order to marry. The focus on marriage for women highlights the importance of women marrying. The ramifications for women who remained unmarried could be devastating, as they would not be able to fulfill the socially expected role of motherhood. Furthermore, if they were poor, unmarried women would lack the financial benefits that marriage provided and might end up as slaves or prostitutes.[134] The community behind D saw it as crucial to help such women by taking on the financial role that usually lay with the father, or "next of kin." By taking financial responsibility for young men and women, the community functioned as a surrogate family for them.

The omission of widows poses an interesting problem. Possibly, a poor widow would be included among the categories of the elderly or the poor. Still the omission, like that of the orphan, is likely intentional and indicates that widows, as a group, were not among the most vulnerable people. The rules for marriage in 4Q271 3 12, which is part of the older collection of laws that the community of D preserved and treasured, states that no-one should marry a woman who has had sexual experience, whether a young woman living in her father's house or a widow after she was widowed. A divorcee, on the other hand, is not mentioned. One may speculate, on the basis of this

---

[131] Stegemann, *The Library of Qumran*, 189.

[132] See Rabin, *Zadokite Documents*, 70; Murphy, *Wealth in the Dead Sea Scrolls*, 84; Stegemann argues that the phrase refers to brides whose families are unable to provide the dowry (*The Library of Qumran*, 189). Hempel translates the phrase: "the virgin who [has] no re[la]tives" (*Laws*, 132). גאל ("to redeem") is used in Ruth 4:1–10 concerning the right of a "next of kin" male to redeem the property of a relative. When Boaz redeems the property, he also acquires the widow, Ruth, as "next of kin" (cf. Lev 25:25).

[133] For the payment of dowry in marriage, see Michael Satlow, "Reconsidering the Rabbinic Ketubah Payment," in *The Jewish Family in Antiquity* (ed. Shaye Cohen; BJS 289; Atlanta. Ga.: Scholars Press, 1993), 133–51; Collins, "Marriage, Divorce, and Family," 113–15.

[134] Brian Capper describes the brutal consequences of poverty in the ancient world ("The New Covenant in Southern Palestine at the Arrest of Jesus," in *The Dead Sea Scrolls as Background to Postbiblical Judaism and Early Christianity* [ed. James Davila; STDJ 46; Leiden: Brill, 2003], 98–104).

rule, that the two categories of women, young women living at home and widows, would be the two most likely groups of women to marry. Divorcees, on the other hand, may not have been common in the community, as divorce was difficult for men to obtain, requiring as it did the permission of the Examiner (see above). If widows commonly remarried, they would not be vulnerable to abuse and exploitation, as were widows who remained unmarried.

6.5 THE PENAL CODE: CD XIV 20–23; 4Q266 10 I 14–15; II 1–15; 4Q269 11 I 4–8, II 1–2; 4Q270 7 I 1–15

6.5.1 INTRODUCTION

The communities behind the Dead Sea Scrolls had in place internal codes of penalties for the perpetrators of different offenses ranging from minor infringements of community laws to serious transgressions. Penal codes are known from D, S, and the fragmentary text of 4Q265. Two laws of the penal code in D concern women: namely, fornication with a wife, and murmuring against the Fathers and Mothers. These will be explored below, after a brief introduction to the penal codes.

6.5.2 THE PENAL CODES

The penal code in D appears immediately before the expulsion ceremony with which the document ends.[135] Before the publication of the 4QD text, only parts of three lines from the beginning of the penal code were known from CD XIV 20–3. A comparison between the penal codes in D, S, and 4Q265 reveals both similarities and differences between types of offenses and their subsequent punishments.[136] Several offenses appear in all three documents: for example, insulting another, dozing at assembly meetings, and laughing foolishly. A few parallel offenses appear only in S and 4Q265: lying, deceiving, and disobeying seniors (though 4Q270 includes offending Fathers and Mothers). Most of the offenses listed in D are parallel to those in S: for example, interrupting another member, sleeping during the assembly, walking out of the assembly, going naked before another, slandering. The offenses peculiar to D are: despising communal law (although this can be compared to apostasy after ten years in 1QS VII 22–4, which also leads to expulsion), offending the Fathers and the Mothers, and fornication with "his wife."

Both S and the D impose expulsion as the most severe penalty for offenses such as improper use of the divine name (1QS VI 27–VII 2) or despising the "law of the

---

[135] Stegemann, "Physical Reconstructions," 182–3.

[136] For a comparison between the penal codes see Baumgarten, "The Cave 4 Versions of the Qumran Penal Code," 268–76. See also Hempel, "The Penal Code Reconsidered," 337–48; Metso, "The Relationship between the Damascus Document and the Community Rule," 89–91.

Many" (4Q270 7 i 11).[137] There is no reference to expulsion in 4Q265, but then very little of the text is preserved. The common penalty in all documents is exclusion from הטהרה "the purity," or טהרת הרבים, "the purity of the many," which commentators usually interpret as pure food.[138] This punishment is often combined with another— נענש "be punished"— which involves food reduction (1QS VI 25).[139]

The many textual similarities and parallels in content in the three penal codes give clear evidence of a literary dependence among the documents. Their exact relationship, however, is hard to establish.[140] Hempel proposes a complex history of literary development, whereby parts of the penal code in D precede 1QS, while other parts follow it.[141] An important result of her analysis is that one cannot assume a straightforward development behind the penal legislation, such as a chronological order of the three penal codes. Instead, it seems that different communities at different stages modified common traditions of rules to suit their needs.

No offenses in 1QS or 4Q265 explicitly involve women. While the penal code in 4Q270 includes the two infringements that concern women, 4Q266 10 ii breaks off immediately before the section that in 4Q270 mentions women. Baumgarten points out that the 4Q266 version of the penal code must have been about two lines shorter than the one in 4Q270 and speculates that those laws that do not occur in 1QS may also

---

[137] Other offenses that carry expulsion as a penalty are: in 1QS, slandering the community (1QS VII 16), murmuring against the authority (VII 17), apostasy after 10 years (VII 24) and deliberate transgression of the law of Moses (VIII 22); in D: malice in capital matters (4Q266 10 ii 1), fornication with a wife (4Q270 7 i 12–13), and murmuring against the Fathers (4Q270 7 i 13–14).

[138] On טהרת הרבים, see Avemarie, "'Tohorat Ha-rabbim' and 'Mashqeh Ha-rabbim': Jacob Licht Reconsidered," 215–29.

[139] While נענש "be punished" in S and 4Q265 clearly refers to food reduction (in 4Q265 the food is reduced by a half, while in 1QS it is reduced by a quarter), D never specifies the meaning of the term. Baumgarten argues that the penalty in D involves something different, such as exclusion from deliberations, since food reduction would only work in a monastic community ("The Laws of the Damascus Document in Current Research," 54). I see no reason why communities that were made up of families could not also have had communal meals, and consequently food reduction as a penalty. Furthermore, there is no reason *per se* to believe that 4Q265, which has food reduction as a penalty, reflects an all male community, since there are laws elsewhere in the document that relate to women; for example, rules for eating the paschal lamb (4Q265 3) and concerning the purification period after childbirth (4Q265 7 11–17); see *DJD XXXV*, 63–4; 69–72.

[140] Baumgarten speculates that there was a movement away from the more rigorous penalties in 1QS and 4Q265 to the more lenient ones in D ("The Cave 4 Versions of the Qumran Penal Code," 274–5). Metso suggests that the two penal codes of S and D depend on a common source ("The Relationship between the Damascus Document and the Community Rule," 89–91).

[141] Hempel, "The Penal Code Reconsidered," 337–48.

The Communal Laws

have been left out in 4Q266.[142] However, the segment of three laws that are preserved only in 4Q270 is much too long to have been omitted in its entirety in 4Q266. Possibly, one of the three laws may have been lacking in the 4Q266 version, but it is impossible to know which one.

6.5.3 FORNICATION WITH A WIFE: 4Q270 7 I 12–13 (PARALLEL: 4Q267 9 VI 4–5 UNDERLINED)

6.5.3.1 Scholarly Points of Views

וֹאֲשֶׁר יִקְרֹ[ב] לזנות לאשתו אשר לא כמשפט ויצא ולֹא ישוב עוד

And he who approa[ches] to fornicate with his wife, contrary to the regulation, shall depart and not return again.

This law raises several questions which I will address below: How is it possible to fornicate within marriage? Why does this crime deserve expulsion? And how was the transgression monitored? Whereas the first question has drawn much attention, the other two have been subject to less scrutiny. Amongst the various interpretations of the nature of the transgression, Shemaryahu Talmon argues that the offense is specific to the Qumran compound where members would abstain from sexual relations for the period they were residing there.[143] According to John Kampen, the prohibition refers to violation of the purity laws of menstruation and childbirth.[144] Collins vaguely suggests that the offense concerns sex during menses or a period of abstention.[145] Angelo Tosato argues that the marriage union is illicit and that any sexual intercourse within that illegitimate union is considered זנות ("fornication").[146] Liliana Rosso Ubigli proposes that fornication here refers to sexual intercourse without the intention of procreation.[147] In a short study, Menachem Kister suggests the same interpretation, pointing to the use of זנות and זנה in rabbinic literature.[148] Baumgarten links the prohibition to "unnatural intercourse," which he does not clarify, adding that such an

---

[142] Baumgarten, *DJD XVIII*, 75.
[143] Shemaryahu Talmon, "The Community of the Renewed Covenant: Between Judaism and Christianity," in *The Community of the Renewed Covenant: The Notre Dame Symposium on the Dead Sea Scrolls* (eds. E. Ulrich and J. VanderKam; Notre Dame, Ind.: University of Notre Dame, 1994), 11.
[144] Kampen, "The Matthean Divorce Texts Reexamined," 157.
[145] Collins, "Family Life," 288.
[146] Angelo Tosato, "Su di una norma matrimoniale 4QD," *Biblica* 74 (1993), 401–10.
[147] Liliana Rosso Ubigli, "Il Documento Di Damsco e L'Etica Coniugale: A Proposito di un Nuovo Passo Qumranico," *Henoch* XIV (1992), 3–10.
[148] Menachem Kister, "Notes on Some Texts from Qumran," *JJS* (1993), 280–1. He refers to *m. Yebam.* 6:5; *y. Yebam.* 7c; and *b. Ketub.* 62b.

attitude is consistent with a ban against intercourse during pregnancy, which also is non-procreative.[149]

6.5.3.2 Interpreting לזנות

The suggestion of some scholars (e.g., Ubigli, Kister) that לזנות ("to fornicate") in 4Q270 7 i 13 refers to non-procreative sex is primarily based on the claim by Josephus that the Essenes only engaged in sex for purposes of procreation: "they [the Essenes] have no intercourse with them [their wives] during pregnancy, thus showing that their motive in marrying is not self-indulgence (ἡδονή), but the procreation of children" (*War* II 161). ἡδονή, "pleasure," or "pleasant lusts" here connotes physical pleasure. In its reproach against anyone who has sexual intercourse with a pregnant woman, the Catalogue of Transgressors (4Q270 2 ii 16) gives evidence of the same prohibition that Josephus ascribes to the Essenes.[150] These two sources certainly make very likely the suggestion that interprets the offense of fornication with a wife as non-procreative intercourse, a kind of intercourse which may have been understood as lustful.[151] A brief examination of the use of זנה and its Greek equivalent, πορνεύω, in D and in non-Qumranic literature, including rabbinic sources, strengthens this hypothesis.

The use of the verb זנה ("to fornicate") with reference to sexual intercourse within marriage conflicts with the basic meaning of the verb in Biblical Hebrew—to engage in sexual relations outside of or apart from marriage—that is, relations which are considered illicit.[152] The verb is used primarily with regard to the extramarital relations of women, since only women are obliged to restrict sexual relations to marriage.[153] But in Second Temple literature in general, the verb זנה ("to fornicate") is

---

[149] Baumgarten refers to a similar wording of כמ[ש]פט in 4Q271 3 15 in the context of examining the woman accused of not being a virgin before marriage. In this case he takes כמ[ש]פט as a reference to proper intercourse that would lead to a woman bleeding at her first intercourse; *DJD XVIII*, 165. Baumgarten has earlier argued that the law in 4Q270 7 i 12–13 most likely refers to some kind of violation of sexual abstinence ("The Cave 4 Versions of the Qumran Penal Code," 270).

[150] See above, pp. 109-11.

[151] My conclusion supports that of Kister and Ubigli. My analysis contributes to their discussions in that I highlight evidence in 1 Thessalonians and situate the law within the context of D as a whole. Furthermore, these studies do not evaluate competing interpretations, nor do they address issues concerning policing and women's testimony as I do below.

[152] *BDB* translates the verb "commit fornication," "to be a harlot" (p. 274). For a study of זנה ("to fornicate"), see Phyllis Bird, "'To Play the Harlot': An Inquiry into an Old Testament Metaphor," in *Gender and Difference in Ancient Israel* (ed. Peggy Day; Minneapolis: Fortress Press, 1989), 76. She notes that the activity of a prostitute is technically not illicit, since her sexuality is not the possession of any man (p. 77).

[153] There are a few exceptions where the verb זנה ("to fornicate") refers to sexual activity by men: "the people began to fornicate (לזנות) with the women of Moab" (Num 25:1); see also Hos 4:15.

commonly used for male sexual activity too. The Pseudepigrapha frequently links fornication with sexual desire and human failure to live by God's commands.[154]

זנה is used in a broad sense referring to sexual improprieties in general in the sectarian literature of the Dead Sea Scrolls. The verbal stem זנה occurs frequently in D where it is used either with reference to activities of outsiders or in warnings to community members. Furthermore, זנה is commonly associated with lust.[155] A prominent sin in the Admonition is to straying because of "eyes of fornication," עיני זנות (CD II 16–17). Since the eyes are an avenue to temptation, the "eyes of fornication" should be understood as lustful sexual desires that are in opposition to the will of God.[156] To follow one's own desire can lead to improper sexual relationships, such as those of the Watchers and the sons of Jacob, highlighted in the text (CD II 17–21; III 4–5).[157] The text contrasts the "eyes of fornication" with the eyes of the implied

---

[154] For example, in the Testament of the Twelve Patriarchs, promiscuity, or "spirit of promiscuity," τό πνεῦμα τῆς πορνείας, appears as a powerful force that snares and enslaves its victims, making men and women lose control and follow their sexual impulses and desires (T. Reu. 3.3; 5.3; 4:6-11; cf. 6:1ff.; for enslavement, see T. Jud. 15.2). For a detailed examination of the usage of πορνεία in Jewish literature from the Second Temple Period, see Lilliana Rosso Ubigli, "Alcuni Aspetti Della Conzione Della *Porneia* nel Tardo-Giudaismo," *Henoch* 1 (1979), 201–45.

[155] For example, according to CD VIII 5, the "princes of Judah" will be subject to God's wrath because "they have defiled themselves in ways of fornication" (ויתגוללו בדרכי זנות). And, in CD VII 1, members of the community are exhorted to "refrain from fornication (הזנות) according to the regulation."

[156] Cf. 1QS I 6. Num 15:39 clearly expresses the connection between eyes and desire, "you will remember all the commandments of the Lord and do them, and not follow the lust of (or 'fornicating after') your own heart and your own eyes" ולא־תתרו אחרי לבבכם ואחרי עיניכם אשר־אתם זנים אחריהם. Cf. Job 31:1; Prov 17:24; Eccl 4:8; Jub. 20:4–5; Matt 5:28–29a: "But I say to you that everyone who looks at a woman with lust has already committed adultery with her in his heart. If your right eye causes you to sin, tear it out and throw it away..." Davies' translation of the expression עיני זנות in CD II 16 as "lustful eyes" is very apropos (*Damascus Covenant*, 237). There is a close resemblance between עיני זנות and 2 Pet 2:14; the latter uses μοιχεύω ("commit adultery") rather than πορνεύω ("to fornicate"): ὀφθαλμοὺς ἔχοντες μεστοὺς μοιχαλίδος καὶ ἀκαταπαύστους ἁμαρτίας, "They have eyes full of adultery, insatiable for sin."

[157] The crimes of the Watchers are not further elaborated upon here, but their sin of having sex with earthly women is a common motif in the Pseudepigrapha. 1 Enoch 1–36 (The Book of the Watchers) greatly expands the biblical story about the Watchers into a book of its own (material from 1 Enoch is preserved in twelve scrolls from the Dead Sea Scrolls). The library from Qumran contained at least eight copies of The Book of Giants, which may have been part of the composition of Enoch and concerns the offspring of the union between the Watchers and human women (1QEnGiants[a,b] ar [1Q23-4]; 2QEnGiants ar [2Q26]; 4QEnGiants[a] ar [4Q203]; 4QEnGiants[b,c,d] ar [4Q530-3]; 6QpapEnGiants [6Q8]). See also Jub. 5:1–5; 7:21–25; 1QapGen II. Of the sins committed by "the sons of Jacob" (CD III 4–5), Judah's and Reuben's

audience of the Admonition; those who hear the Admonition will have their eyes opened so that they "may see and understand the works of God and choose that which he wants and despise that which he hates" (CD II 14–15). In addition, the midrash concerning the Nets of Belial (CD IV 12b–V 15a) refers to illicit marriages by the term זנות ("fornication"), namely bigamy (IV 20–21) and marriage between an uncle and a niece (V 7–11).[158] "Fornication" here refers to illegal sexual relations characteristic of the behaviour of the general population ruled by Belial.

There are two documents from the Second Temple Period, Tobit and 1 Thessalonians, that use πορνεία (the Greek equivalent to זנות) within the context of marriage, making them particularly relevant for the interpretation in D of the offense of fornication with a wife. In a prayer before consummating his marriage, Tobias says: "I am now taking this kinswoman of mine, not because of lust (οὐ διὰ πορνείαν) but with sincerity" (Tob 8:7).[159] In this case πορνεία describes sexual pleasures; one is not to marry for sexual gratification, but for sincere reasons.[160]

πορνεία is of great concern in the Pauline letters, which condemn all forms of non-marital sex as illicit.[161] Paul condemns improper sexual relations within marriage as πορνεία (here translated "lustful passion") in 1 Thess 4:3–6b:[162]

---

sexual transgressions are undoubtedly assumed: Judah slept with his daughter-in-law (Gen 38) and Reuben with his father's wife (Gen 35:22; 49:3–4). Their sins and punishments are elaborated upon in the Pseudepigrapha (see e.g., T. Reu. 1:6–10, T. Jud. 11–13; Jub. 33; 41; cf. Commentary on Genesis A [4Q252] V 3–7).

[158] The accusation concerning "lying with a woman who sees her bloody flux," דם זובה is not part of the net of "fornication," but of "defiling the sanctuary" (CD V 6–7).

[159] Four Aramaic copies of Tobit were found at Qumran and one Hebrew copy. Unfortunately, none of these copies preserves Tobit 8:7. For the Qumran fragments, see Jospeh Fitzmyer, "196–200: 4QpapTobit a ar, 4QTobit b–d ar, and 4QTobit e," in *DJD XIX*, 1–76.

[160] Wayne Meeks argues that, given the romance as a whole, the prayer is hardly intended to limit marriage to the production of children ("The Image of the Androgyne: Some Uses of a Symbol in Earliest Christianity," *HR* 13 [1973], 177 n.68).

[161] πορνεύω ("to fornicate, to commit sexual immorality") is rarely used in the Gospels, but the group of πορνεύω words occurs frequently in the Pauline letters and in the Book of Revelation. Although πορνεία is mostly used in a broad sense for sexual immorality, sometimes a specific sense can be derived; incest is called πορνεία in 1 Cor 5:1. On several occasions πορνεύω words are used alongside words related to μοιχεύω ("commit adultery"; e.g., Mk 7:21–2; 1 Cor 6:9; Heb 13:4). In these cases πορνεία refers to any illicit sex with the exception of adultery, i.e., pre-marital sex and possibly homosexual sex. In 1 Cor 7:2, marriage saves a man from πορνεία, which alludes to any form of pre-marital sex and perhaps sexual thoughts; Paul, the celibate, writes, "'It is well for a man not to touch a woman.' But because of cases of sexual immorality (διὰ δὲ τὰς πορνείας), each man should have his own wife and each woman her own husband." The group of πορνεύω words occurs frequently in lists of vices: Mk 7:21; 1 Cor 5:11; 6:9; 2 Cor 12:21; Gal 5:19; Col 3:5; 1 Tim 1:10; cf. Eph 5:3.

[162] While there is some debate about the authenticity of 2 Thessalonians, there is a wide consensus that 1 Thessalonians is an authentic Pauline letter. See e.g., Robert Jewett, *The*

The Communal Laws

4.3 τοῦτο γάρ ἐστιν θέλημα τοῦ θεοῦ, ὁ ἁγιασμὸς ὑμῶν, ἀπέχεσθαι ὑμᾶς ἀπὸ τῆς πορνείας, 4.4 εἰδέναι ἕκαστον ὑμῶν τὸ ἑαυτοῦ σκεῦος κτᾶσθαι ἐν ἁγιασμῷ καὶ τιμῇ, 4.5 μὴ ἐν πάθει ἐπιθυμίας καθάπερ καὶ τὰ ἔθνη τὰ μὴ εἰδότα τὸν θεόν, 4.6 τὸ μὴ ὑπερβαίνειν καὶ πλεονεκτεῖν ἐν τῷ πράγματι τὸν ἀδελφὸν αὐτοῦ

For this is the will of God, your sanctification: that you abstain from fornication (4) that each one of you know how to possess *your wife* in holiness and honour, (5) not in lustful passion, like the Gentiles who do not know God; (6) (and) in this matter (none of you) is to injure or exploit his brother. (my italics)

Σκεῦος in 1 Thess 4:4 is often understood as a reference to a man's body. In contrast, some scholars, such as Ernest Best, hold that σκεῦος refers to "wife" rather than "vessel." Best bases this interpretation on the parallel in 1 Pet 3:7 and the usage of כלי ("vessel") in a few instances in rabbinic Hebrew.[163] The usage of כלי ("vessel") for "wife" in 4QInstruction[b] (4Q416) 2 ii 21, כלי [ח]יקכה "the vessel/wife of your [bo]som" adds strong support for interpreting σκεῦος as "wife" in 1 Thess 4:4. As Strugnell has shown, κτάομαι ("acquire") within the context of marriage has sexual overtones, "to possess a woman sexually," or "to live with a woman."[164] The Christian attitude to marital sex is here contrasted with that of the Gentiles; whereas Christians who are pure and holy (1 Thess 3:13; 4:7) can engage in marital relations with holiness and sanctity, the sinful Gentiles, who do not know God, have sexual relations with lustful passion. As in Tobit, πορνεία is here used with regard to improper marital sexual relations, driven by desire and passion.

Early rabbinic legislation, which considers intercourse for non-procreative reasons in a few texts as illicit, should be briefly considered as well. The early Rabbis in general allow non-procreative sexual intercourse (such as during pregnancy) as well as the use of contraceptives in special cases, as long as men fulfill the positive

---

Thessalonian Correspondence: Pauline Rhetoric and Millenarian Piety (Philadelphia: Fortress Press, 1986), 1–30.

[163] See Ernest Best, *A Commentary on the First and Second Epistles to the Thessalonians* (New York: Harper and Row, 1972); cf. NRSV "that each one of you know how to control your own body in holiness and honor" (1 Thess 4:4). Another interpretation of 1 Thess 4:4 is that a man should get a wife to avoid fornication (similar to 1 Corinthians 7). For a discussion on different interpretations, see John Noonan, *Contraception: A History of Its Treatment by the Catholic Theologians and Canonists* (Cambridge, Mass.: Harvard University Press, 1965), 41.

[164] John Strugnell, "More on Wives and Marriage in the Dead Sea Scrolls: (4Q416 2 ii 21 [cf. 1 Thess. 4:4] and 4QMMT B)," *RevQ* 17 (1996), 537–47. The verb κτάομαι can also carry the meaning "win someone for oneself"; the meaning would then be that husbands should make their wives favourably inclined towards them for sexual intercourse (Best, *A Commentary*, 166).

commandment to procreate (Gen 1:28; 9:1, 7).¹⁶⁵ Nevertheless, a minority position considers marriage with a barren woman as promiscuous; words from the root זנה ("to fornicate") are used in some of these cases.¹⁶⁶ The case of a Levirate marriage deserves special attention because the sexual union is for the sole purpose of procreation. A levir is prohibited from having intercourse with his sterile levirate widow, since such a union would consitute בעילת זנות, according to the Mishnah.¹⁶⁷ Again, there is a connection between the root זנה ("to fornicate") and non-procreative sex. Although the Rabbis in general see sexual pleasure as a part of marital life, a stricter minority opinion surfaces, which views non-procreative sex between husband and wife as illicit.

In sum, there is evidence in certain Jewish and Christian writings from the Second Temple period, that is, in Tobit and 1 Thessalonians, of a view-point that considers sexual intercourse within marriage fornication when the driving force is pleasure. Moreover, there is evidence in rabbinic texts of a link between זנות ("fornication") and non-procreative sex. One may therefore conclude that the proposal "to fornicate" in the penal code refers to non-procreative (lustful) sex is likely the correct interpretation.

Moreover, serious objections can be raised against the alternative interpretations of 4Q270 7 i 12b–13a. There is no close connection between fornication and ritual impurity in D, which contradicts the suggestion by Kampen that the offense of fornicating with a wife concerns intercourse during a woman's period of impurity. In addition, all the offenses in the penal code in D concern specific sectarian regulations. Since none of the other offenses relate to biblical laws, one does not expect to find a biblical prohibition, such as that of sexual intercourse during menstruation, in the

---

¹⁶⁵ One contraceptive device was a sponge (*mok*) (*t. Nid.* 2:6); see Michael Satlow, *Tasting the Dish: The Rabbinic Rhetorics of Sexuality* (BJS 303; Atlanta: Scholars Press, 1995), 232–5.

¹⁶⁶ *M. Yebam.* 6:5: "A common priest must not marry a sterile woman (אילונית) unless he has already a wife and children. R. Judah says, 'Even though he already has a wife and children he must not marry a sterile woman for she is the harlot (זונה) mentioned in the Torah (Lev 21:7).' But the Sages say, 'A harlot (זונה) refers only to a proselyte, or to a freed bondwoman or to one who submitted to intercourse by nature of prostitution (בעילת זנות).'" A similar view of non-procreative sex as fornication appears in *y. Yebam.* 6:5, 7c; *b. Ketub.* 62b, in which the root זנה ("to fornicate") is used (see Kister, "Notes on Some New Texts from Qumran," 280–1). If the priest is sterile himself, there is no prohibition against marriage (*m. Yebam.* 8:6). One passage in the Tosefta prohibits any man (whether he has children or not) from marrying a sterile woman (*t. Yebam.* 8:4). This is contrary to other laws in Tosefta that permit a man to keep a sterile woman (e.g., *t. Ketub.* 1:3). On marriage with barren women, see Satlow, *Tasting the Dish*, 224–31.

¹⁶⁷ *M. Yebam.* 8:4–5; on this rule see Satlow, *Tasting the Dish*, 225.

penal code.¹⁶⁸ Therefore, it is more likely that the offense concerns a law unique to the community behind D.

The use of זנות ("fornication") with reference to illegal marriage unions in D (and 4QMMT) might be seen to support the suggestion by Tosato that it is the marriage union that is illicit in 4Q270 7 i 12b–13a. But the law is introduced by ואשר, "and he who," and is addressed to people in general rather than to a particular group whose marriages were considered illicit. Furthermore, since one may assume that the community behind D would reject those who were married illicitly (for example, a man and his niece, a man and his two wives), there would be no couples whose marriages were considered illicit within the community, and hence no need for a penalty. As to the suggestion by Talmon that the offense refers to a specific time of abstinence undertaken by members while residing at Qumran, this hypothesis is pure speculation and is part of an attempt to resolve the discrepancy between the claim that the Essenes were celibate and the many texts from Qumran that take marriage for granted.

6.5.3.3 Sexual Intercourse and Procreation: Opinions by Jewish Authors

The strict view that sexual relations in marriage are only for procreation is not unique to D. On the contrary, other literature from the Second Temple Period, such as the Testaments of the Twelve Patriarchs and 4 Maccabees, also displays a stringent attitude towards sexual intercourse within marriage.¹⁶⁹ Pseudo-Phocylides, a Jewish writer who harmonized Greek and Jewish thought, similarly advocated self-restraint within marriage.¹⁷⁰ These Jewish texts attest to the general influence of Hellenistic philosophy that often advocates moderation and self-control. Many Hellenistic writers

---

¹⁶⁸Cf. the penal code in 1QS VI 24–VII 27, where none of the rules are biblical. Transgression against דבר מתורת מושה, "one word of the Law of Moses," is dealt with in 1QS VIII 21b–23.

¹⁶⁹T. Iss. 2:3 praises Rachel for her strict attitude to sex within marriage: Εἶδε γάρ, ὅτι διὰ τέκνα ἤθελε συνεῖναι τῷ Ἰακώβ, καὶ οὐ διὰ φιληδονίαν, "For he [an angel] perceived that she wanted to lie with Jacob for the sake of children and not merely for sexual gratification." Cf. T. Jud. 10:2–3 where Er, Judah's first son, is killed by God because he did not want to impregnate Tamar. See also T. Iss. 3, which portrays the simple lifestyle of the son, who is hard working and has no desire for worldly pleasures, as an ideal way of life. His marriage at a late age is explained by his non-interest in sex: "I lived my life with singleness of vision. Accordingly, when I was thirty-five I took myself a wife because hard work consumed my energy, and pleasure with a woman (ἡδονὴν γυναικός) never came to my mind; rather sleep overtook me because of my labour" (3.5). For the English translation, see *The Old Testament Pseudepigrapha* (ed. James Charlesworth; New York: Doubleday, 1983), 1: 785–828.

¹⁷⁰See, e.g., Ps-Phoc 193–4: "Do not deliver yourself wholly unto unbridled sensuality towards your wife. For Eros is not a god, but a passion destructive to all." The author advocates a universal kind of practical ethics. Pieter van der Horst favours a date of composition between 30 B.C.E. and 40 C.E. and Alexandria as provenance; see van der Horst, "Pseudo-Phocylides: A New Translation and Introduction" in *The Old Testament Pseudepigrapha*, 2: 565–73.

promote a strict moral code which allows no deviance from the way of self-control and discipline, and includes a highly restricted view of sex within marriage. Both Josephus and Philo argue that marital sex should be for the sole purpose of procreation. The ideal that Josephus ascribes to the Essenes, of engaging in sexual intercourse for the reason of procreation alone, mirrors that of the author himself, as he states: "The law recognizes no sexual connexions except the natural union of man and wife, and that only for the procreation of children. The sexual union with males it abhors, and punishes anyone who engages in it with death."[171] It could—and has been—argued that Josephus imposes his own views on his description of the Essenes.[172] One may wonder, however, if it is not possible that Josephus' personal views and those of the Essenes may have coincided in their attitude towards sexuality. Josephus was a priest, devoted to the Torah, and clearly admired the Essenes, presenting them as ideal Jews to a Roman audience. It is very likely that they shared many ideals, including their view that intercourse must be for procreative purposes only.

Philo advocates moderation and restraint to a higher degree than does Josephus, and emphasises that the goal of marital relations is procreation.[173] Accordingly, he reproaches men who have sex with barren women, for they are "ploughing a hard and stony soil" and "they waste their seed of their own deliberate purpose."[174] He also condemns men who immoderately indulge in sex with their own wives for pleasure,[175] and explains that a Jewish man abstains from sex during the menstrual periods of his wife, not because of impurity, but in order not to waste his seed and energy.[176] In

---

[171] *Ag. Ap.* II, 199; cf. II 202.

[172] In his discussion of 4Q270 2 ii 15–16 from the Catalogue of Transgressors, Baumgarten argues that the underlying reason for abstention from sex during pregnancy is a concern for transmission of impurity from the woman through bleeding and not to avoid lust as Josephus claims ("A Fragment of Fetal Life and Pregnancy in 4Q270," 445–8; *DJD XVIII*, 146, in notes concerning line 16). I have previously argued against his interpretation (see pp. 109-11).

[173] *Joseph* 43: "We approach our virgin brides as pure as themselves, proposing as the end of our marriage not pleasure but the offspring of legitimate children." Although Philo can forgive those who continue being married to women who are found to be barren after marriage, he has only contempt for those who marry women they know are barren, comparing them with goats and declaring them "enemies of nature" (*Spec. Laws* 3:36).

[174] Although Philo condemns wasting of semen because it is non-procreative, this concept is not prevalent in Jewish thought at this time; see Satlow, *Tasting the Dish*, 246–64.

[175] *Spec. Laws* 3: 9: "Therefore, even that pleasure which is in accordance with nature is often open to blame, when anyone indulges in it immoderately and insatiably, as men who are unappeasably voracious in respect of eating, even if they take no kind of forbidden or unwholesome food; and as men who are madly devoted to association with women, and who commit themselves to an immoderate degree not with other men's wives, but with their own."

[176] *Spec. Laws* 3: 33–4. Roman medicine encouraged the husband to abstain from emission of semen some days before intercourse if he wanted to impregnate his wife, as this would increase the amount of semen; see Rouselle, *Porneia*, 18.

addition, Philo strongly abhors all forms of male homosexuality as being against nature and advocates the death penalty for such behaviour. In this case as well, the pursuit of lust and the resulting wasting of seed is part of the argument.[177] In his discussion on non-procreative sex, Philo does not condemn sex with pregnant women *per se*, but judging from Philo's principles this could be another example of "wasting the seed" and sex driven by pleasure rather than a desire for procreation. The underlying reason for the equating of non-procreative sexual intercourse within marriage with "fornication" in D may be found in a condemning attitude towards lustful sex. The Essenes in the D community may thereby, like Josephus and Philo, have been influenced by certain trends in the Hellenistic world that condemned sexual intercourse without intention to procreate and advocated sexual restraint.

6.5.3.4 *Enforcing the Law about Fornication*

Like the majority of laws in D, the stipulation about fornication in 4Q270 7 i 12–13 is androcentric and addresses a man: "he who approaches...," ואשר יקר[ב] לזנות לאשתו.[178] In this law, the exclusive focus on the man becomes even greater, as the penalty appears to apply only to the man. The discourse reflects a stern patriarchal attitude towards sexual activity: it is simply assumed that the man is the one initiating the sexual act that constitutes fornication and that the woman has no say in it. *He* is responsible, and thus *he* is penalized.

Gershon Brin has argued persuasively that the man alone is expelled from the sect. Accordingly, the man would be forced to divorce his wife.[179] He points out that if the wife were expelled with her husband, the community would be sanctioning the continuation of improper sexual acts. However, if both the man and the woman had been considered guilty, they likely would have been expelled together. From a sectarian point of view, members probably did not care about the continued improper behaviour of a couple if through their transgression they had already proved that they belonged with the outsiders. A more likely explanation for the punishment is that the man was punished because he alone was seen as responsible. Since the man alone was expelled, this law shows that the bond between the individual and the sect was more important than that within the biological family.

If the rule on fornication in 4Q270 7 i 12b–13a concerns sexual intercourse for a reason other than procreation, then the question of policing becomes an important one. It is apparent that one person in particular would be able to report sexual activities between a husband and wife, namely the wife herself. One may connect the law in 4Q270 7 i 12b–13a to the passage in 1QSa I 11 that gives the wife the responsibility to testify regarding her husband in matters of his obedience to the law: "And at that

---

[177] *Spec. Laws* 3: 39.

[178] Cf. CD XII 1, אל ישכב איש עם אשה בעיר המקדש, "let no man lie with a woman in the city of the sanctuary."

[179] Brin, "Divorce at Qumran," 242–3.

time she shall be received to bear witness of him (concerning) the judgments (משפטות התורא) of the Law and to take her place at the hearing of the judgments."[180] The following scenario can be envisioned. At meetings when the sectarian laws, המשפטים, were read to *all* members including women, wives occasionally were asked to testify about their husbands' behaviour. It was obviously crucial that women knew exactly what the laws entailed, since not only did they have to observe them themselves, but they were also obliged to keep track of their husbands' observance at home.[181] A wife would be the person best informed concerning a husband's observance of sexual laws, such as the prohibition against fornication and the ban on intercourse during the Sabbath from the Catalogue of Transgressors (4Q270 2 ii 15–16). The wife would know whether the man had ever engaged in sex when it was forbidden. A wife would also be the best person to testify on purity matters, many of which relate to sexual intimacy.[182] Since משפטים (1QSa I 11) refers to communal regulations in general, the law in 1QSa I 11 obligates a wife to give testimony, when needed, concerning her husband's observance of all aspects of the law.

6.5.3.5 Conclusion

Fornicating with one's wife results in the harshest penalty of all—expulsion with no readmittance. In light of the close link between זנות ("fornication") and Belial one can understand the severity of the crime. To engage in sex for reasons of lust and not procreation puts the perpetrator in the sphere of the outsiders, those who have fallen into the nets of Belial. Whoever engages in illicit sex demonstrates by his behaviour that he belongs among the outsiders ruled by Belial and not among the D community any longer. In 1 Thessalonians, fornication is associated with the practice of pagans as opposed to Christians; D presents a similar dichotomy whereby fornication belongs to the sphere of outsiders, that is, fellow Jews.

The teaching that one should refrain from sex unless it is performed for reasons of procreation was a familiar one in the Hellenistic world at the turn of the era. Philo and Josephus stress that sex within marriage is for procreation alone. A similar call for self-restraint and the control of all passions including sexual desires is found in a few works of the Apocrypha and Pseudepigrapha. Whereas these authors advocate moderation and self-control in marital relations in a general way, D is unique in

---

[180] On this passage, see my discussion pp. 140–2.

[181] The importance of women knowing the laws is emphasized in CD VII 7, והתהלכו על פי התורה וכמשפט היסורים כסרך התורה "then they [women and children] shall walk according to the Torah and the precept established according to the rule of the Torah"; see Davies, *Damascus Covenant*, 142; "Who Can Join the 'Damascus Covenant'?" *JJS* 46 (1995), 137; cf. 1QSa I 4–5. Davies and Taylor argue that the testimony of women in 1QSa I 11 concerns marital offenses only, not testimony in general ("On the Testimony of Women in 1QSa").

[182] Schuller (with input from George Brooke) mentions the possibility that the subject matter concerns a woman's menstruation cycle and purity, "Women in the Dead Sea Scrolls," in *Methods of Investigation*, 124.

legislating against non-procreative sexual intercourse and in enforcing a penalty for any transgressors.

At the same time, D does not mirror the strong emphasis on controlling desires and emotions found in Philo, the Testament of the Twelve Patriarchs, or the ethical teachings of many Hellenistic writers. D still reflects an underlying concern for the restriction of passions and desires, but in D this issue arises in relation to following the Law. To follow one's own will means to follow forbidden passions and desires rather than the will of God. This is expressed forcefully in the Admonition in the discourse on Israel's history (CD II 14–III 12a), which provides stern warnings against following "lustful eyes," leading to sexual sins.

Above, I sided with those scholars who claim that the offense of fornicating with one's wife in 4Q270 7 i 12–13 refers to sexual intercourse during pregnancy. It is impossible to know whether or not this offense also applied to other forms of non-procreative sexual intercourse, such as sexual relations with a barren or post-menopausal wife. There are no laws in D that give guidelines concerning when a woman would be considered infertile, as one might expect to find if indeed intercourse with a barren wife were prohibited.[183]

Whereas Josephus claims that the Essenes abstained from sex during pregnancy to demonstrate that intercourse had the sole function of procreation, I have earlier argued that a medical reason for abstaining from intercourse during pregnancy is given in the Catalogue of Transgressors (4Q270 2 ii 15–16). These two viewpoints appear contradictory at first. Nevertheless, there is no reason why there could not have been two different grounds for the regulation: sex during pregnancy was non-procreative and thus illegal and, in addition, intercourse during pregnancy could be harmful to the fetus. Hence the Essenes may have marshalled both ethical and medical reasons for advocating abstention from sex during pregnancy.

Furthermore, the Catalogue of Transgressors lists sexual relations during pregnancy and sexual relations between men in the same section (4Q270 2 ii 15–17). In light of Philo's perception of both non-procreative sex between husband and wife and homosexual sex as illicit, non-procreative sexual activity, it may be that a similar line of thought underlies the Catalogue of Transgressors. Accordingly, these crimes may have been considered similar in more than one respect; not only are both illicit sexual activity, but both types of sexual acts are done out of lust rather than for the reason of procreation.[184]

Based on 1QSa I 10–11, it appears that a wife was obliged to give testimony about her husband's observance of the laws. Her testimony may have concerned,

---

[183] By comparison, there are rabbinic laws stipulating when a wife is considered barren (namely, if she has not become pregnant after ten years of marriage; see e.g., *m. Yebam.* 6:6; *t. Yebam.* 8:4).

[184] Cf. *Ag. Ap.* 2: 199, in which Josephus contrasts procreative marital sex with non-procreative homosexual activity.

amongst other issues, his observance of sexual laws, such as abstention from sex during the Sabbath, during the pregnancy of a wife, and perhaps whether he ever intentionally tried to avoid pregnancy (e.g., anal intercourse, interrupted intercourse). A wife thereby took on the role of any member to report offenses committed by other members to the authority. The entire penal code, which mandates punishments for transgressions such as interrupting, insulting, showing oneself naked, and the serious offense of showing dissent, was based on an informant system, whereby members reported each other's wrongdoings to the communal authority. Such information was recorded, as evidenced by 4Q477.[185] There is no reason that the offense involving sexual intercourse would be any different in this regard, and a wife's testimony would have been necessary in order for the community to keep informed of her husband's obedience to the laws. The primary purpose would be to control the individual member's life, although one may also speculate that such information would be used in order to assess the man for any advancement within the internal hierarchy (see 1QSa I 19). The informant system that used wives to testify about husbands encouraged wives to put the loyalty to the community ahead of their loyalty to their husbands.

6.5.4 THE FATHERS AND MOTHERS IN THE PENAL CODE

6.5.4.1 The Text: 4Q270 7 i 13b–15a

vaca]t ואשר י̇לו[ן][186] על האבו̇ת	13
[וישלח] מן העדה ולא ישו̇ב [ואם] על האמות ונע̇נ̇ש עש̇ר[ת] ימים כי אין	14
לאמ̇[ו]ת רוקמה̇ בתוך	
[העדה] [vacat	15

---

[185] This picture is similar to Josephus' description in *War* II 141, where he claims that members at their initiation swear to expose liars and to conceal nothing from the members of the sect. Commenting on this passage, A. Baumgarten states, "An Essene was to be a permanent spy on activities of fellow members, and I suppose that the information provided by Essenes about each other was used by the leadership to control the lives of members." He also points to 4Qrebukes by the Overseer (4Q477) for evidence of how the members of the Qumran community were chastised for infringements of the communal laws (*The Flourishing of Jewish Sects*, 110–11).

[186] Although the verb, לון (murmur), is missing, the context suggests that the offense involves either offending or complaining about the Fathers and Mothers. The verb לון fits well since it requires על (cf. murmuring against the council of the congregation and against a fellow in 1QS VII 17). The other possibilities would be to reconstruct a verb for "offending" or "slandering," but none of the verbs used in this sense in the penal codes in D or 1QS take על (see, e.g., 4Q266 10 ii 2, 14-15, 1QS VII 4, 15).

13   [And whoever murm]urs against the Fathers
14 [shall be expelled] from the congregation and not return. [And if] (anyone) murmurs) against the Mothers he shall be penalized for te[n] days, for the M[o]thers do not have *rwqmh* in the midst of
15 [the congregation]

These few lines offer several interpretive problems: who are the Mothers and the Fathers, and what is *rwqmh*? I will offer tentative and limited answers to these questions, first concerning the titles the Fathers and the Mothers, and second concerning *rwqmh*.

6.5.4.2. The Fathers and the Mothers

6.5.4.2.1 Introduction

The identity of the groups, the Fathers and the Mothers, is not known. Knibb suggests that "the Fathers" is an honorific title applied to senior members of the community.[187] Baumgarten similarly considers Fathers and Mothers honorific titles, comparable to Brothers and Sisters, as mentioned in 4Q502 (see below).[188] Brian Capper, on the other hand, suggests that these groups are the elderly and vulnerable in the community who were in need of support.[189] No commentator, as far as I know, considers the האבות (the Fathers) and האמות (the Mothers) as referring to biological parents. Indeed, since the subject is in the singular ("and whoever..."), one would expect a singular reference to father and mother if biological parents were being discussed.[190] Thus it seems certain that the penalty code deals with two specific groups in the community: the Fathers and the Mothers. The question is whether the titles refer to all senior members, or to specific groups within the community. If the latter is correct, what status and function did these groups have?

6.5.4.2.2. The Titles Fathers and Mothers

The titles Father and Mothers are titles of respect. אבות in the Hebrew Bible is a common term for the Israelite ancestors, "the fathers" (e.g., Gen 48:15, 16; Exod 13:5; Deut 4:37; 10:22). אב in the singular may be used with regard to a teacher (2 Kgs 2:12), a prophet (2 Kgs 6:21), a priest (Judg 17:10; 18:10), an elderly person (1 Sam 24:12), a ruler or a chief (1 Chr 2:24, 42), and a "fatherly protector" (Isa 9:5; 22:20;

---

[187] Knibb, "Community Organization in the Damascus Document," *Encyclopedia of the Dead Sea Scrolls*, 1:138.

[188] Baumgarten, "The Cave 4 Versions of the Qumran Penal Code," 271.

[189] Capper, "The New Covenant in Southern Palestine," 103.

[190] Other cases of transgressions in the penal code in D are written in the third person singular, and the offended party is put in the singular, such as the case of one man stealing bread from another man (4Q270 7 i 11–12), and of one man fornicating with "his wife" (lines 12–13).

Gen 45:8; Ps 68:6). God is also called "Father" (Deut. 32:6; Isa 63:16; Jer 34:19). "Mother" is used honorifically once in the Hebrew Bible with respect to Deborah (Judg 5:7), who is called אם בישראל, "a Mother in Israel," in the sense of being a protector of the nation.

In the Dead Sea Scrolls, האבות, "the Fathers," is frequently used with reference to the Israelite ancestors. Although the sin of earlier generations occasionally is highlighted in the Qumran texts, אבות usually has an overwhelmingly positive sense. CD VIII 14–18 is particularly noteworthy, in that it identifies the members as the descendants of the recipients of the covenant, the Fathers, who, unlike העם ("the people"), have rightfully inherited the covenant.[191] אבות ("fathers") appears often in 1QSa and M as part of the title ראשי אבות העדה, "heads of the families [or clans] of the congregation," but this phrase appears unconnected to the title האבות ("the Fathers") in 4Q270 7 i.[192] There is, nevertheless, one reference to כול אבות העדה ("all the Fathers of the congregation") in 4QMyst[a] (4Q299) 76 3 that may be relevant.[193] The fragment is five lines long and only a few words remain, so that it provides little help for retrieving the context or the meaning of אבות העדה ("Fathers of the congregation"). The reference to אבות העדה ("Fathers of the congregation") allows for the possibility that the full title of "the Fathers" האבות in D is אבות העדה "the Fathers of the congregation" and, by inference, that the full title of אמות ("the Mothers") is אמות העדה ("the Mothers of the congregation").

4Q270 11 i 13–14 is the only instance in the non-biblical literature of the Dead Sea Scrolls where "the Mothers," אמות, occurs in the plural. In the wisdom text 4Q416, 4QInstruction[b], in which a man is admonished at length to honour and serve his parents, references to a mother and a father are in the singular. This wisdom passage forms part of the instruction in 4Q416 that reaffirms the social hierarchy of the day, namely, that of parents over children, and husbands over wives. Nevertheless, the authority of both parents is noteworthy, as is their common role as teachers of mystery: "they uncovered your ear to the mystery that is to come; honour them for the sake of your own honour..." (4Q416 2 iii 17b–18).[194]

---

[191]Cf. 4Q266 11 11–12: in the ritual of expulsion, the community is identified as descendants of "the fathers" who have received truthful regulations and holy precepts. See also 1QS II 9; 1QM XIII 7; XIV 8.

[192]See 1QSa I 16, 23–25, II 16; 1QM II 1, 3, 7; III 3–4. אבות in these cases carries the meaning of "clans" or "households" (cf. the use of ראשי אבות with reference to leaders of clans or households in the Israelite community in Exod 6:25; Num 31:26, Josh 14:1; 19:51). There are two references to אבות העדה in 1QM II 1 and 3, but also in these cases the full title ראשי אבות העדה may be assumed; see Yadin, *The Scroll of the War of the Sons of Light against the Sons of Darkness*, 263.

[193]Schiffman, "Mysteries," *DJD XX*, 86.

[194]See Daniel J. Harrington, *Wisdom Texts from Qumran* (New York: Routledge, 1996), 40–9. D. Harrington and J. Strugnell argue that גלה ("uncovered") in the third person singular should be corrected to the third person plural because of the context (*DJD XXXIV*, 122).

The Communal Laws 187

One document from the Dead Sea Scrolls, 4Q502, similarly to 4Q270 7 i 13–14, presents men and women in pairs. Unfortunately, the fragmentary nature of the text makes it notoriously difficult to interpret.[195] Although there is no reference to Fathers or Mothers in 4Q502, there are references to זקנים וזקנות ("elderly men and women" or "male and female Elders"; frag. 19 3), נערים ונע[רות] ("young men and women"; frag. 19 3), and בנים ובנ]נות ("sons and daughters" frag. 14 6).[196] אחים ("brothers"; frag. 9 11) and אחיות ("sisters"; frag. 96 1) are found but not together. White Crawford has recently argued that the terms זקנות and זקנים likely refer to male and female Elders, and I agree.[197] She highlights the phrase סוד זקנים, "council of Elders," in frag. 24 4, which certainly implies that the elders made up a council. Since female Elders are mentioned in the same document, one can assume that these also would take part in "the council of Elders."[198]

For further examples (other than in 4Q270 and Judges) of "mother" as a title, one has to look to sources later than the Dead Sea Scrolls. Pseudo-Philo's *Biblical Antiquities* (*LAB*) is particularly interesting because of its several references to "mother" as a title. Here, "mothers" is used for female ancestors.[199] As an important ancestor and heroine of the past, Tamar is called "our mother" (9.5). Another female protector, Deborah, who is also presented as a great teacher, is called "mother" in

---

[195]The original editor, M. Baillet, introduced the text as a marriage ritual ("Rituel de Mariage," in *Qumrân grotte 4: III [4Q482–4Q520]*; DJD VII; Oxford: Clarendon Press, 1982), 81–105. Based on a comparison with Philo's description of the Therapeutai, Joseph Baumgarten instead argues that the text describes a ritual by which elderly men and women renounced sexual intimacy ("4Q502, Marriage or Golden Age Ritual," *JJS* 34 [1983], 125–35). Michael Satlow proposes that 4Q502 is a New Year ritual ("4Q502 A New Year Festival?" *DSD* 5 [1998], 57–68). Johann Maier points to an allusion to Sukkot in the text (4Q502 99) ("Ritual of Marriage," *Encyclopedia of the Dead Sea Scrolls*, 2: 783).

[196]In addition, there is a reference to בת אמת "daughter of truth" (2 3), and possibly to "Adam and his wife," [אדם] ואשתו (1 3).

[197]White Crawford, "Mothers, Sisters, and Elders: Titles for Women in Second Temple Jewish and Early Christian Communities," 181–3.

[198]Satlow, "4Q502 A New Year Festival?" 65 n.33.

[199]Daniel J. Harrington dates the document to about 100 C.E. ("Pseudo-Philo: A New Translation and Introduction" in *The Old Testament Pseudepigrapha*, 2: 299). At the impending death of Jephthah's daughter it is said she will go away "and fall into the bosom of her mothers" (*LAB* 40.4). For a discussion of the mothers in Pseudo-Philo, see Cecilia Wassen, "The Story of Judah and Tamar in the Eyes of the Earliest Interpreters," *Literature and Theology* 8 (1994), 362–3; Betsy Halpern-Amaru, "Portraits of Women in Pseudo-Philo's *Biblical Antiquities*," in *'Women Like This': New Perspectives on Jewish Women in the Greco-Roman World* (ed. Amy-Jill Levine; Atlanta: Scholars Press, 1991), 83–106. In her study of Hannah's song, Joan Cook concludes that eschatological teaching is viewed as a function of motherhood in Biblical Antiquities ("Pseudo-Philo's Song of Hannah: Testament of a Mother in Israel," *JSP* 9 [1991], 103–14).

LAB, parallel to Judg 5:7. Calling the people "my sons" (33. 4), she commands them, "Obey me like your mother and heed my words" (33.1). In her case, the title "mother" emphasizes leadership and authority: "behold there has perished a mother from Israel and the holy one who exercised leadership in the house of Jacob" (33.6).[200] Greek and Latin inscriptions from Jewish diaspora communities add evidence that there was a tradition of using the epithet "mother" for a woman in a leadership position. Bernadette Brooten has collected and analysed references to μήτηρ συναγωγῆς, ("Mother of the synagogue"), corresponding to πατήρ συναγωγῆς ("Father of the synagogue"), and concluded that these were titles of the leaders in the synagogue.[201] Although these inscriptions stem from a later period than the Dead Sea Scrolls, they provide a close Greek parallel to the titles האבות and האמות ("Fathers" and "Mothers") in 4Q270 7 i 13–14, a parallel that is exact if the full titles in 4Q270 are Fathers and Mothers of the congregation.

In sum, the titles "Fathers" and "Mothers" carry positive connotations and are associated with leadership and authority. Although 4Q502 does not refer to Mothers and Fathers, the document provides evidence—parallel to 4Q270—of the existence of male and female leaders in the community, in this case, of male and female Elders.

6.5.4.2.3 The Offenses in 4Q270 7 i 13–14

To complain against the Fathers brought on the most severe punishment: expulsion with no return. The harsh punishment makes the transgression comparable to other offenses with the same outcome, such as slandering the Many (4Q270 7 i 6–7),[202] despising the law of the Many (line 11), or fornicating with a wife (lines 12–13). To offend another member did not lead to expulsion (4Q266 10 ii 2–3). לון is used twice in the penal code in S. Like complaining against the Fathers in 4Q270, murmuring against "the authority of the *yahad*" (והאיש ילון על יסוד היחד) leads automatically to expulsion (1QS VII 17–18). Neither case specifies the nature of the complaint. In contrast, complaining unjustly against a fellow member, רעה, warrants a punishment of six months according to S (1QS VII 17–18). Thus, the Fathers, like the *yahad* in S, were a group beyond reproach. The verb לון in the Hebrew Bible often carries the meaning of rebelling and involves disputing the authority of someone or some ones, which is likely the sense in the context of murmuring against the

---

[200] Cook, "Pseudo-Philo's Song of Hannah," 113.

[201] The six inscriptions Bernadette J. Brooten analyses range in date from the second to the sixth century C.E., with the exception of one which may stem from first century B.C.E. (*Women Leaders in the Synagogue: Inscriptional Evidence and Background Issues* [BJS 36; Chico, Calif.: Scholars Press, 1982], 57–64).

[202] The wording of the actual offense is lost. Baumgarten has restored the text based on 1QS VII 16–17.

Fathers.²⁰³ The offense can thus be compared to despising the judgment of another authoritative group, the Many, which, according to D (4Q270 7 i 11), also led to expulsion.²⁰⁴ The parallels in punishment indicate that the authority of the Fathers ranked as highly as that of the Many.

In contrast, complaining against the Mothers only carried with it ten days of penalty, the lightest penalty given for any crime in the penal code. The same length of penalty with no additional punishment in the form of exclusion (from the purity) is given in possibly two other cases in D: to anybody who gesticulates with his left hand while talking (as reconstructed in 4Q270 7 i 5/4Q266 10 ii 13–14) and to a person who leaves the assembly three times in one session (4Q266 10 ii 7–8).²⁰⁵ Thus, disputing the authority of the Mothers appears to be a minor infraction and on par with other minor offenses.

Although Josephus and Philo state that the Essenes showed the utmost respect for elderly members of their communities, it is also apparent that elderly members *lost* authority with age.²⁰⁶ D sets the upper age limit for serving as a judge as sixty, because of the risk of senility, and 1QSa excludes an "old man, איש זקן, who cannot maintain himself" from entering the Congregation.²⁰⁷ The title "Fathers" certainly indicates that the group consisted of senior members of the community. Nevertheless, the uniquely harsh sentence for murmuring against the Fathers suggests that the term refers to a distinct group within the community that held a special authoritative status in the community, not *all* senior members.

6.5.4.3 רוקמה

The discrepancy between the two punishments is explained in the text by the reference [כי אין לאמ[ו]ת רוקמה בתוך [העדה], "because the Mothers have no *rwqmh* in the midst of [the congregation]." *Rwqmh* is the only clue in the text about the rationale for the differentiation between the Fathers and Mothers.

The feminine noun רקמה refers to variegated material in biblical Hebrew, particularly embroidery or something of variegated colours.²⁰⁸ It is often used with reference to garments or fabrics, but any stones and metalwork can also be described

---

²⁰³ In the Hebrew Bible, לון is used in particular regarding Israel, which murmurs against Moses and God in the desert (e.g., Exod 15:24; 16:2; 17:3; Num 14:27)

²⁰⁴ Baumgarten also reconstructs the offense of slandering the Many in 4Q270 7 i 6–7 based on 1QS VII 16 (*DJD XVIII*, 162–3).

²⁰⁵ Cf. 1QS VII 15: "whoever stretches out his left hand in order to recline on it shall be punished (for) ten days."

²⁰⁶ Philo, *Hypoth.* 11:13; Josephus, *J.W.* II 146: "It is a point of honour with them to obey their elders."

²⁰⁷ CD X 6–10; 1QSa II 7.

²⁰⁸ *BDB*, 955b.

by the term רקמה.²⁰⁹ In rabbinic Hebrew רקמה carries the meaning of an embroidered garment.²¹⁰ Similarly, in the Dead Sea Scrolls *rwqmh* is used with reference to variegated material such as clothes and military items (see below), and it is therefore hard to understand the meaning of *rwqmh* in the discussion of Mothers and Fathers. Baumgarten suggests "authoritative status" but adds a question mark to indicate the uncertain meaning of the word. Cook translates the word "esteem" with no further explanation, and Vermes writes "*rwqmh* (distinction?)." That *rwqmh* carries the meaning of authority or esteem is derived solely from the context. A different approach is taken by Martínez, who proposes "for mothers there is no mingling (?) in the midst of [the congregation]."²¹¹

In an article devoted to the interpretation of רוקמה in 4Q270 7 i 14, John Elwolde offers a semantic analysis of the term רקמה and proposes that the term carried two meanings in Hebrew: one "embroidery" and a second, "essential being, authority, leadership, status."²¹² The second meaning is found in LXX Ps 138:15 (=MT 139:15), where the *hapax* רקמתי is translated as the noun ἡ ὑπόστασίς μου, "my substance." Elwolde argues that רקמתי in 11QPsᵃ XX 5–6 (corresponding Ps 139:15) was also understood as a noun carrying this meaning. Furthermore, LXX Ezek 17:3 renders הרקמה as τὸ ἥγημα, which Elwolde translates "leadership." Elwolde concludes that the scroll writers knew of both meanings and employed the term רקמה in 4Q270 7 i 14 to indicate that "mothers have no 'essential being,' 'authority,' or 'status' in the midst of the community, that is to say, they 'count for nothing' or 'have no (intrinsic) right to be' there."²¹³ There are three main obstacles to Elwolde's interpretation. First, רקמה, which is not an uncommon word in the Scrolls, usually means "embroidery." Second, if the mothers "count for nothing," why would murmuring against them be penalized? Third, the noun τὸ ἥγημα, in LXX Ezek 17:3 is a *hapax* and may carry the sense of "thought, purpose" rather than "leadership."²¹⁴

---

²⁰⁹Ezek 17:3: "A great eagle with great wings, and long pinions, rich in plumage in many colours" (אשר־לו רקמה); cf. multi-coloured stones in 1 Chr 29:2. *Riqmah* often refers to luxurious garments, traded by merchants and worn by royalty, e.g., Ezek 16:10 ואלבישך רקמה, "I clothed you with embroidered cloth" (cf. Ezek 16:13, 18; 26:16; 27:7, 24; Ps 45:14–15). רקמה can also function as an adjective in a construct chain; e.g., Ezek 16:18 ותקחי את בגדי רקמתך, "You took your embroidered garments." In a priestly context, מעשי רקם refers to the screens for the entrance to the tabernacle and its court (Exod 26:36; 27:16) and to the High Priest's sash (Exod 28:39; 39:29).

²¹⁰Jastrow, *Dictionary*, 1497.

²¹¹Martínez and Tigchelaar, *The Dead Sea Scrolls Study Edition*, 1:617.

²¹²John Elwolde, "*Rwqmh* in the Damascus Document and Ps 139:15," in *Diggers at the Well: Proceedings of a Third International Symposium on the Hebrew of the Dead Sea Scrolls and Ben Sira* (eds. T. Muraoka and J.F. Elwolde; STDJ 36; Leiden: Brill, 2000), 65–83.

²¹³Ibid., 73.

²¹⁴Liddell Scott, *A Greek-English Lexicon*, 763.

Before imposing an obscure meaning on the term, one should examine the use of *rwqmh* in the Dead Sea Scrolls to see if the term can be understood according to its common meaning of "variegated texture." If *rwqmh* is taken literally, then it might refer to some embroidered clothing—or piece of it— worn by the Fathers indicating a specific status within the community. Recently George Brooke has argued that the word רקמה should be taken literally and suggests that it refers to "a piece of embroidered cloth associated with priestly status."[215] His interpretation is based primarily on a comparison with Paul's use of ἐξουσία with reference to the authority manifested through wearing a veil in 1 Cor 11:10. My arguments (written before his publication) similarly point to a literal interpretation of the word as a reference to a piece of clothing, but I suggest a slightly different context.

Throughout history and across cultures, membership in a specific group or class has often been indicated by specific clothing. This is particularly evident in the Roman world of antiquity, where the costume of both men and women was imbued with symbolism. Forms, colours and decorations of the costume of men and woman signalled their precise status and function in society.[216] For women, the costume marked their marital status—girls, virgins of marital age, matrons, *matres familias*, widows, or even adulteresses. Josephus tells us that the Essenes always wore white, which would set them apart from the rest of the population.[217] Magness suggests that the Essenes only wore linen, a material difficult to dye, in contrast to the rest of the population, who wore mantles and tunics with coloured stripes.[218] She speculates that the Essene men may have worn clothing with designs made of a different weave rather than a different colour.[219] No clothing has been discovered from Qumran, but linen

---

[215] George Brooke, "Between Qumran and Corinth: Embroidered Allusions to Women's Authority," in *The Dead Sea Scrolls as Background to Postbiblical Judaism and Early Christianity*, 157–76

[216] See Shelley Stone, "The Toga: From National to Ceremonial Costume," in *The World of the Roman Costume*, (eds. Judith Lynn Sebesta and Larissa Bonfante; Madison, Wis.: University of Wisconsin Press, 1994), 13–45. Judith Sebesta explores the social and religious symbolism behind the costume of aristocratic Roman women, explaining that "in each stage of the Roman woman's life, costume served as a visual and tactile remainder of the virtue she should maintain and for which she should be respected" (p. 51); see "Symbolism in the Costume of the Roman Woman," in *The World of the Roman Costume*, 46–53.

[217] *J.W.* II 123. He also notes that the men wore linen loin-cloths when they bathed (II 129).

[218] Jodi Magness, "Women at Qumran?" in *What Athens has to do with Jerusalem: Essays on Classical, Jewish, and Early Christian Art and Archaeology in Honor of Gideon Foerster* (ed. Leonard Victor Rutgers; Interdisciplinary Studies in Ancient Culture and Religion 1; Peeters Publishers, 2002), 26–9.

[219] A child's garment with stripes formed of weave and not colour was discovered in the Cave of Letters; see Yigael Yadin, *The Finds from the Bar-Kokhba Period in the Cave of Letters* (Jerusalem: Israel Exploration Society, 1963), 211, 254, 257. Parts of an adult's tunic with similar weaved stripes was discovered in a cave in Wadi Murabbat (P. Benoit, Milik and de

textiles of scroll wrappers, covers, and packing pads for the scrolls jars were found in Cave 1. Sixteen of the linen cloths used as wrappers had a pattern consisting of "carefully woven or partly embroidered" blue threads, likely representing the ground plan of the temple.[220] The colour blue may have had a mystic value, and Magness suggests that the dye is the colour *tekhelet* (violet), a colour associated with the temple in the Hebrew Bible.[221] If the scroll wrappers were designed with a pattern to express a symbolic meaning, it is not impossible that the clothing of the Fathers also would have a pattern carrying a symbolic meaning.

Rwqmh in the Scrolls is commonly associated with the heavenly sphere. The word *rwqmh* occurs frequently in the *Sabbath Songs*, four times in 1QM, once in 4QBerakot[b], once in 4QPesher Isaiah[a], and once in 4QNarrative. In the War Scroll, רקמה is used in descriptions of shields, swords, and the girdle of the priests.[222] In 4QBerakhot[b], רקמה is used with reference to the luxurious garments of angels (4Q287 2 5), and in 4QPesher Isaiah[a] with reference to garments of the future messiah (4Q161 8–10 20).[223] The frequent use of *rwqmh* throughout the Sabbath Songs, where it is used in the descriptions of the heavenly sanctuary(ies) and the angelic priesthood, deserves special attention.[224] The mystical or numinous character of the Sabbath Songs has long been the subject of discussion.[225] Because of the lacunae in the text, as

---

Vaux, *DJD II*, 59, no 78); and a linen garment with such stripes in the Cave of Avior; see Magness, "Women at Qumran?" 28

[220] G. M. Crowfoot, "The Linen Textiles," in *Qumran Cave 1* (eds. Barthélemy and Milik; DJD I; Oxford: Clarendon Press, 1955), 24, Plate IV; Avigal Sheffer, "Textiles," *Encyclopedia of the Dead Sea Scrolls*, 2: 938–43; Yadin, *The Temple Scroll*, 1:198–200; Magness, "Women at Qumran?" 32–3.

[221] Crowfoot, "The Linen Textiles," 25; Magness, "Women at Qumran?" 32–3.

[222] See 1QM V 6, 9, 14. The girdle that is part of the priestly garments for battle is described as "embroidered with byssus, purple, and scarlet thread, and a brocaded pattern, work of a craftsman," וצורת רוקמה מעשה חושב (1QM VII 11). In addition, *rwqmh* is used in 4QNarrative (4Q462 1 5) but the immediate context is not clear; see Mark Smith, "462. 4QNarratives C," *DJD XIX*, 195–210.

[223] The pesher of the prophecy in Isa 10:33–4 and 11:1–5 narrates how God will provide the future royal Messiah with the law, the throne of glory, a holy crown, and "garment of variegated material," בגדי רוקמו[ת] (4Q161 8–10 20).

[224] The term occurs seven times in 4QShirShab and four times in 11QShirShab: Song 7, 4Q403 1 ii 1; Song 9, 4Q405 14–15 i 3, 6; Song 10, 4Q405 15 ii–16 4; Song 11, 4Q405 22 10–11; 4Q405 19ABCD 5 (see also parallel text in 11QShirShabb j–d–g–p); 4Q405 23 ii 7; Song 13, 11QShirShabb 8–7 5.

[225] There has long been a debate concerning the genre of the document. Without being able to go into this discussion in any depth, I agree with Carol Newsom when it comes to the *function* of the Sabbath Songs: "The language of the Sabbath Shirot, especially in its second half, does more than invite an analogy [between angelic and human priests]. It is extraordinarily vivid, sensuous language, both aurally and visually. What this does is to create and manipulate a virtual experience, the experience of being present in the heavenly temple and in the presence of

well as the elusive style of writing, it is sometimes difficult to know to what exactly *rwqmh* refers. However, the clothing of angels is described as variegated (*rwqmah*) as is the glory of God. The term is also often used in the descriptions of images on veils or brickwork of angelic beings, who take part in the praise of God.[226]

In light of the symbolism behind clothing in the ancient world, it is conceivable that the term *rwqmh* is used with reference to an embroidered garment that indicates the function of the Fathers in the community. Parallel to descriptions in which the term *rwqmh* appears–such as the special priestly clothing that indicates the status and function of the priests in battle (1QM VII 10) and the special clothing of the future Messiah that signals his royal status (4Q 4QpIsa^a 8–10 20)—*rwqmh* could very well refer to special clothing, or part of clothing with a special design, that would mark the particular status of the Fathers in the community. Such clothing—in whatever form— can be compared to *tzitzit*, the fringes attached to the four-cornered garment traditionally worn by Jewish men (Num 15:37–41), that according to the Talmud were imbued with symbolic meaning. These fringes included a cord dyed with the colour *tekhelet* (Num 15:38).[227] Similarly, *rwqmh* may well have been a special garment worn by some men that was associated with a symbolic meaning.

Given the frequent use of *rwqmh* in texts of mystical character, it is furthermore likely that the Fathers had a special function within spiritual practices in the community that aimed at creating a sense of communion with the heavenly sphere. If this interpretation is correct, then the text states that the Mothers did not—or should not—function in this capacity. Additional links between *rwqmh* and spiritual-mystical practices in Jewish literature outside the Dead Sea Scrolls corpus offer further substance to such a suggestion.

---

angelic priests who serve there" ("He has Established for Himself Priests," in *Archaeology and History in the Dead Sea Scrolls*, 115). Along the same vein, Joseph Baumgarten calls the literature "an early form of congregational mysticism" ("The Qumran Sabbath Shirot and Rabbinic Merkabah Traditions," *RevQ* 13 [1988], 201). The very real presence of angels in the community is expressed elsewhere in the sectarian literature (e.g., 1QSa II 8–9; 1QM VII 6; 1QH^a XI 21–3; XIV 13; XIX 11–12; 4QHod^a [4Q427] 7 i 6–13; 4Q266 8 i 9).

[226]Baumgarten notes that the idea of images in the temple being able to sing hymns is a strange concept, foreign to the Bible. In later Merkabah mysticism, however, the same notion appears. For example, in Hekhalot Rabbati, God is described as "He who is glorified with embroideries of song" (המהודר ברקמי שיר). Baumgarten concludes, "We now recognise that the root RQM was already used at Qumran for the embroideries of angelic figures which uttered songs of adorations" ("The Qumran Sabbath Shirot and Rabbinic Merkabah Traditions," 202–3). Cf. Gershom Scholem, *Jewish Gnosticism, Merkabah Mysticism, and Talmudic Tradition* (New York: The Jewish Theological Seminary of America, 1960), 26.

[227]The colour *tekhelet*, for example, was that of the "throne of glory" (*b. Menah.* 43b); for discussion on the practice of wearing "*tzitzit*" and the colour "*tekhelet*," see *Encyclopaedia Judaica* (New York: Macmillan, 1971).

6.5.4.4 rwqmh outside of the Dead Sea Scrolls

A possible clue to the usage of the term *rwqmh* in relation to the Fathers and Mothers may be found in the Testament of Job, a document with many similarities to Merkabah mysticism.[228] The three daughters of Job are given three "embroidered" cords, τὰς τρεῖς χορδὰς τὰς ποικίλας, an inheritance from Job (T. Job 46. 7). It is noteworthy that in LXX, ποικίλος is the common translation for רקמה.[229] ποικίλος, like רקמה, indicates complexity of various sorts, such as many coloured, embroidered, intricate, or in network of cords.[230] The cords derive from a three-stranded girdle that Job has received from God (T. Job 47.5). It was at that moment that God introduced the mysteries to Job, "things present and things to come" (47:9). The cords belong to the heavenly sphere: they are from heaven (46:8); they are vehicles for living in the heavens (47:3); and they link the carrier with the beings from above (47:11). They also function as a protection from evil (47:10) and disease (47:6).

According to the biblical text, the three daughters were given an inheritance along with their brothers (Job 42:15); nothing further is said about their inheritance. In contrast, in T. Job, the intricate cords provide the daughters with spiritual gifts, all related to communicating and understanding the heavenly sphere, and the daughters are able to praise God in the dialect of the angels. The daughters are told to wrap the cords around their breasts (T. Job 46.9).[231] The transformation of the first daughter,

---

[228] Pieter van der Horst points to an affinity between the Testament of Job and the 4QShirShab, and argues in favour of a Palestinian origin at the beginning of the Common Era for the former ("Images of Women in the Testament of Job," in *Studies on the Testament of Job* [eds. M. A. Knibb and P. W. van der Horst; SNTSMS 66; Cambridge: Cambridge University Press, 1989], 111). David Flusser groups together The Testament of Job, Joseph and Asenath, Apocalypse of Abraham, and The Sabbath Songs in his study on "Mystical Prayers" in "Psalms, Hymns and Prayers," in *Jewish Writings of the Second Temple Period*, 563–6. R.P. Spittler notices similarities between the Testament of Job and early Merkabah mysticism. He speculates that Test. Job may have been composed among the Egyptian Therapeutai, but he traces the interest in "angelic glossolalia" to a "Montanist apologist, probably of Jewish background" ("Testament of Job," in *The Old Testament Pseudepigrapha*, 1: 834). Howard C. Kee argues that Test. Job represents an earlier stage of Merkabah mysticism and is a Jewish composition from the early first century C.E.; see "Satan, Magic and Salvation in the Testament of Job," in *Society of Biblical Literature: 1974 Seminar Papers* (ed. G. MacRae; Cambridge, Mass.: Society of Biblical Literature, 1974), 1:53–76. John J. Collins argues that Test. Job is a first century Jewish Egyptian work ("Structure and Meaning in the Testament of Job," in *Society of Biblical Literature: 1974 Seminar Papers*, 1:35–52).

[229] E.g., 1 Chr 29:2; Judg 5:30; Ezek 16:10, 13, 18; 26:16; ἔργον ποικιλτοῦ in Exod 26:36; 28: 39 (=LXX 28:35); 38:18 (=LXX 37:16); 39:29 (=LXX 36:36).

[230] Robert Kraft, *The Testament of Job, According to the SV Text: Greek Text and English Translation* (ed. Robert A. Kraft; New York: SBL, Missoula, Mont.: Scholars Press, 1974), 79.

[231] Cf. 48.1; 49.1; 50.1. ζώνη, the common word for "girdle," is not used with reference to these cords. For a discussion of the various terms used for the girdle and the cords, see Van der

Hemera, is particularly noteworthy because of the close connection drawn between spiritual qualities and clothing in the passage (T. Job: 48.2–3):

> And she received another heart so that she no longer thought about earthly things. And she chanted verses in the angelic language and ascribed a hymn to God in accord with the hymnic style of the angels. And as she chanted the hymns, she permitted "the Spirit" to be inscribed on her garment.[232]

The theme of singing hymns in angelic dialect is strikingly similar to the content of the Sabbath Songs, with its focus on angelic praise. In light of the importance of the engraved images that are singing hymns in the Sabbath Songs, the mention of a garment that is engraved (χαράσσω) with the πνεῦμα, spirit, in T. Job 48 is particularly interesting.[233] It appears that the girdle is not only intricate, but also has inscriptions on it (whether in the form of text or figures). The carrier of an intricate (ποικίλος, the Greek word for *rwqmh*), engraved garment can sing in the dialect of angels and has the ability to participate in the angelic hymns. Thus in the Testament of Job, we have a further link between the term *rwqmh* and a spiritual-mystical tradition, pointing to communication between humans and angels.

Apart from T. Job there are other examples in Jewish and Christian literature of a connection between specific garments and the heavenly sphere. For example, in Ascension of Isaiah 9, righteous people are given new robes "of above" in the seventh heaven and become like the angels.[234] According to 2 Enoch 22:8–10, Enoch receives "clothes of Glory" in heaven and becomes like the angels. Levi, in a vision, is clothed with priestly garments and is anointed by "seven men in white clothing," probably angels. The text reads: "Arise, put on the vestments of the priesthood, the crown of righteousness, the oracle of understanding, the robe of truth, the breastplate of faith, the miter for the head, and the apron for prophetic power" (*T. Levi* 8:2). The story illuminates how both symbolic and real power is linked with priestly clothing. In the Jewish work Apocalypse of Zephaniah, Zephaniah puts on an angelic garment and is then able to join the angels in prayers, in their specific language (8.1–5).[235]

Horst, "Images of Women in the Testament of Job," 102; Spittler, "Testament of Job," in *The Old Testament Pseudepigrapha*, 1:864 n.46.

[232] Text and translation from Kraft, *The Testament of Job*.

[233] Spittler points to embroidered garments in the Merkabah tradition, and suggests that in Hemera's enscribed skirt we may see trace of early Merkabah traditions already present in the Sabbath Songs; see "Testament of Job," 866 n.48.

[234] Ascen Is. 9:2, 8–9, 18, 24–16; this part belongs to a Christian composition; see Knibb, "Martyrdom and Ascension of Isaiah," in *The Old Testament Pseudepigrapha*, 2:147.

[235] See O.S. Wintermute, "The Apocalypse of Zephaniah," in *The Old Testament Pseudepigrapha*, 1:514.

Pseudo-Philo recounts how the clothes from Moses convey specific power to the new carrier, Joshua. The garments of Moses, who was endowed with God's Spirit, evoke a change of mind in the recipient:

> And now you wait to no purpose, because Moses is dead. Take his garments of wisdom and clothe yourself, and with his belt of knowledge gird your loins, and you will be changed and become another man. ... And Joshua took the garments of wisdom and clothed himself and girded his loins with the belt of understanding. And when he clothed himself with it, his mind was afire and his spirit was moved... (*LAB* 20:2–3).[236]

In the later Merkabah mysticism, there was a technique to induce mystical, revelatory experiences by "putting on, or clothing" a garment or object into which God's name had been woven, לבוש את השם.[237] These examples all point to a firm tradition in Jewish and early Christian thought that connected special clothing with mystical power. Thus it is probable that the term *rwqmh* in the penal code in D refers to a piece of clothing (perhaps a cord) worn by the Fathers to indicate their authority as mystical mediators between the heavenly host and the earthly community.

6.5.4.5 Conclusion

The titles Mothers and Fathers suggest that the holders were viewed as fatherly and motherly protectors within the community where they held a high authority, with the authority of the Fathers surpassing that of the Mothers. The Fathers held a unique status in the Community behind D since anyone complaining against them would be expelled. The link between the Fathers and *rwqmh*, a term that occurs frequently in the Sabbath Songs, may be the key for understanding their unique position. Many Jewish documents from the Second Temple period are witness to a link between "powerful" clothing and communication with the heavenly sphere. Particularly noteworthy is the narrative in the Testament of Job about the wonderful, intricate strings that enable their carrier to sing in the dialects of angels. The many links between *rwqmh* and the mystical/spiritual context explored above suggest that the Fathers may have held a special function related to spiritual practices in the community that aimed at communicating with the heavenly beings. *rwqmh* may thus refer to a garment, or a part thereof, with specific design, embroidered or woven, that the Fathers used. Or it may be a symbolic term, referring to the spiritual power of the Fathers. In contrast, the

---

[236]Translation by Harrington, "Pseudo-Philo: A New Translation and Introduction." Van der Horst points to the the similarities between this story and that of Job's daughters, but does not think one tradition is dependant on the other; "Images of Women in the Testament of Job," 113.

[237]See Gershom Scholem, *Major Trends in Jewish Mysticism*, (3d ed. New York: Schocken Books, 1971), 77; see also Kee, "Satan, Magic and Salvation in the Testament of Job," 60.

Mothers lacked this role and had, therefore, less authority in the community. This does not preclude the possibility that the Mothers still held leadership positions in the community, but not in the same realm as those of the fathers. One possibility is that these women had special authority amongst the women in the community.

The vast discrepancy between the penalty for murmuring against the Fathers and that of murmuring against the Mothers highlights the different status of the two groups. The hierarchical difference is quite similar to that between a father and a mother in 4QInstruction^b, in which both parents are held in high esteem, but the status of a father greatly surpasses that of a mother. At the same time, it should be noted that the Fathers and the Mothers in D are mentioned together as a pair. In spite of the difference in penalties, the coupling of the two suggests that they were assumed to be closely related, and that both groups must have held some kind of authoritative position. In addition, the fact that the discrepancy between the penalties had to be explained ("because the Mothers do not have *rwqmh* within [the congregation]") suggests that it was unusual to differentiate drastically between the groups. This is the only time in any of the penal codes that a ruling is explained. Perhaps there was a need to justify the rulings to avoid controversy; perhaps the explanation was a response to an existing controversy.

6.6 Conclusion: Communal Laws

At the end of my analysis of communal laws that pertain to women, it is important to reflect upon the larger picture of the community that produced these laws. Several laws that I have presented above can best be understood as a product of a sectarian community. In what follows I will highlight some of the sectarian traits that are noticeable in the communal laws that relate to women in order to further our understanding of the community behind D and women's role within such an environment.

My discussion of the communal laws concerning women reveals that the families in the community behind D had come under extensive control of the leadership, particularly that of the Examiner. By overseeing the members' financial dealings, marriages, divorces, education of children, and financial help to the poor in the community, the Examiner exercised considerable influence over the personal lives of the members. The boundary between the communal and private spheres had been blurred by laws pertaining to family life, which gave the Examiner far-reaching power over the family and created an authoritarian environment.

There are many distinctively sectarian characteristics in the communal laws pertaining to the family in D. Although the members of the community behind D married and worked outside the community (CD XIV 12–13), their finances were supervised by the communal authority, as were matters of marriage and divorce. Furthermore, rebellious members were formally expelled, and any contact with them afterwards was forbidden (4Q266 11 14–16). These laws reflect a hierarchical organisation in which the communal authority strictly controlled the interaction between members and outsiders. The high level of control that the authority exerted over its members is particularly conspicuous in the penal code, which stipulated harsh punishments for what would seem to us today minor infringements of communal rules. A strong leadership in the community attempting to control the most private aspects of the members' lives is part of an overall strategy to retain members and distance outsiders. This kind of strict control that the communal authority exercised, apparent in both S and D, is typical of a sect, according to Bryan Wilson. He writes, "Sects have a totalitarian rather than segmental hold over their members: they dictate the member's ideological orientation to secular society; or they rigorously specify the necessary standards of moral rectitude; or they compel member's involvement in group activity"; and further, "Not only does the sect discipline or expel the member who entertains heretical opinions, or commits a moral misdemeanour, but it regards such defection as betrayal of the cause."[238]

Many sociologists emphasise *tension* with the socio-cultural environment as a central characteristic of sectarian ideologies, as well as their members' interactions with outsiders.[239] Combined with this notion, several sociological models add another factor: "the extent to which a religious group considers itself to be uniquely legitimate."[240] According to this two-dimensional model, a sect can be defined as a group that displays a strong tension vis-à-vis the general society and has a strong claim that it possesses the truth. Based on this model the community behind D is clearly a sect.[241] Many of the communal laws in D are part of an over-all strategy to set clear boundaries between insiders and the wider society, combined with an emphasis on strengthening the grid amongst the members. Such boundary-marking mechanisms are particularly expressed in laws concerning formal entrance rituals and expulsions. The community behind D shared with the S community the strict observance of the laws,

---

[238] Bryan Wilson, "An Analysis of Sect Development," *American Sociological Review* 24 (1959), 4.

[239] See, e.g., Rodney Stark and William Bainbridge, *A Theory of Religion* (Toronto Studies in Religion 2; New York: Peter Lang, 1987), 124–8; *The Future of Religion: Secularisation, Revival, and Cult Formation* (Berkely: University of California Press, 1985), 19–26 (see my description of this sociological model above, p. 13 n.50); Bryan Wilson, *The Social Dimensions of Sectarianism: Sects and New Religious Movements in Contemporary Society* (Oxford: Clarendon Press, 1990), 46–66.

[240] Jutta Jokiranta, "'Sectarianism' of the Qumran 'Sect': Sociological Notes," *RevQ* 20 (2001), 229; Ray Wallis, "The Cult and Its Transformation," in *Sectarianism: Analyses of Religious and Non-Religious Sects* (ed. R. Wallis; London: Peter Owen, 1975), 41–7. Meredith McGuire also highlights commitment to perfection as typical of a sect, *Religion: The Social Context* (3rd ed. Belmont: Wadsworth Publishing Company, 1992), 143–4.

[241] My presentation of sectarian traits of the D community is limited to the laws that I have analysed in my thesis. There are other sectarian characteristics in D that could be highlighted, but are outside of the scope of this study.

especially those regarding purity, and the erection of distinct boundaries between itself and non-members. The boundary between the community behind D and the external society is supported ideologically in the Admonition that outlines a dualistic worldview, placing the community within the Covenant of God, and Israel within the sphere of Belial's rule. Thus there are traits in the laws of D as well as in the ideology that reflect a tension vis-à-vis the general society, which is a feature characteristic of sects. In addition, the Admonition reveals an exclusive claim of possessing the truth, a claim typical of a sect. In spite of the lack of a theological discourse similar to that on the two spirits (1QS III 17–IV 1), there is a reference to ב]ני אור] "[so]ns of light" in the first line of the document (4Q266 1 a–b 1), which suggests a similar dichotomy in D between Light and Darkness. This dualistic outlook is evident throughout the Admonition, which sharply distinguishes between the Covenant and the sphere of Belial, whereby, as in S, redemption is possible only within the "in-group."[242] Consequently, withdrawal from society is necessary, and failure to do so is explicitly considered a sin.[243] Although the community behind D likely participated in the temple service, it also marked boundaries by viewing the temple and its priests as defiled, and by asserting that only those within the sect could validly use the temple service.[244] The difference in withdrawing from society between the communities behind S and D is only a matter of degree. While both communities have developed boundaries between themselves and the "threatening" outside world, S represents a more extreme form of isolationism.

This conclusion differs from some scholarly views that understand the community behind D as "living in the world" as opposed to the more secluded community behind S. In his study on sectarian traits in the Qumran texts, Philip Esler concludes that while S, which according to him originated at Qumran, was produced in a sect that is appropriately described as introverted, D—which reflects camps around Palestine—

---

[242] The entire Admonition reflects a dualistic world view by which two distinct ways of life are presented: to follow God's will or to stray from it. Those who observe God's law are a minority (the remnant); the rest of Israel is evil and ruled by Belial (CD IV 12–V 15; VII 4 ff.). The Admonition is not primarily interested in reforming outsiders, but wants to reinforce the commitment and loyalty of the insiders to the Covenantal community. John Martens highlights expressions of protest and tension vis-à-vis the general society in the Admonition; see "A Sectarian Analysis of the Damascus Document," in *Essays in Social Scientific Study of Judaism and Jewish Society* (eds. Simcha Fishbane and Jack Lightstone; Canada-Israel Conference on the Social Scientific Study of Judaism; Concordia University, 1990), 27–46.

[243] E.g., CD VIII 8 lists as a sin that each one "did not remove (נזרו) himself from the people" (cf. XIX 20b–21a) and CD VI 14–15 admonishes the readers or listeners "to separate (להבדל) (themselves) from the sons of the pit."

[244] For defilement of the temple, see CD IV 17–18; V 6–7. CD VI 11–14 indicates that only those who observe the Torah correctly will not "light his altar in vain"; see Philip Davies, "The Judaism(s) of the Damascus Document," in *The Damascus Documents: A Centennial of Discovery*, 34–5.

was written for people who should not be characterized as a sect, but as a reform movement.[245] Although Esler finds elements of isolationism in D, other evidence, such as attendance in the temple service and interaction with Gentiles, points to a reform movement. Furthermore, he claims that S contains stronger dualistic language than does D. My conclusion differs from his for several reasons. By taking the two main literary strata of the laws into consideration, the sectarian traits stand out clearly in the stratum of the communal laws, as opposed to the orientation of openness towards the society reflected in the early law code. Moreover, many of the rules in D that point to a sectarian environment occur in the 4QD fragments and are not taken into account by Esler, since his article was published prior to *DJD XVIII*.[246]

The status and role of women in this type of social environment is a difficult and complex issue. The sparse information about women in D provides a somewhat heterogeneous image. According to 4Q266 9 iii 6–7, it appears certain that young girls as well as young boys took part in the education provided by the community behind D. The education of the young people in the laws and interpretation of the Torah, as well as in the community's own history, was important in order to ensure a whole-hearted commitment to the New Covenant and also to ensure the young members' continued allegiance to the sect.

In the laws on charitable contributions, young men and women are among the recipients (CD XIV 15–16). The phraseology of these laws indicates that these youths were orphans. Since no young orphaned children are mentioned in the list, I agreed with Stegemann's suggestion that orphans were looked after from birth.[247] However, as youths, orphans were in need of added financial assistance. Here, the traditional roles of men and women come into play. While a young man needs financial assistance to get by, a young woman needs help in order to get married. Behind the law on charity, one recognizes an empathetic attitude towards the plight of unmarried women, who were unable to fulfill their role in society and by default became socially marginalised. Donations to support those otherwise unable to marry would have helped such women immensely. The request for charitable donations to the vulnerable in society is well-known in biblical texts. However, in contrast to the biblical tradition, donating money was made into law in D, and a system for contribution was put in place. Given the frequent biblical allusions to widows as a category of people among the most vulnerable in society, their omission in the list in D is curious. Perhaps their omission indicates that widows frequently remarried. In spite of laws that forbid

---

[245] Philip Esler, "Introverted Sectarianism at Qumran and in the Johannine Community," in *The First Christians' Social Worlds: Social-Scientific Approaches to New Testament Interpretation* (London: Routledge, 1994), 70–91. For a similar view see Anthony Saldarini, "Sectarianism," in *Encyclopedia of the Dead Sea Scrolls*, 2:855.

[246] See also Jokiranta ("'Sectarianism' of the Qumran 'Sect': Sociological Notes," 232–3), who points out that there are sectarian features in D.

[247] Stegemann, *The Library of Qumran*, 189.

"blemished" members of the community to enter certain communal meetings (4Q266 8 i 6–9), the laws on charity which includes disabled people (CD XIV 14–16) show that they were still very much part of the community. The laws also reveal a sympathetic view towards those stricken by physical disabilities, as well as the poor in the community.

Children and women clearly belonged in the community and the covenant. They were part of the in-group as opposed to the out-group. Nevertheless, children had a lesser status compared to full members. Like most ancient and modern societies, the community behind D had a rite of passage in place to mark adulthood, which in this case also meant attaining full membership. Though the text is not explicit on this point, there are hints that suggest that not only young men but also young women were enrolled in the community as full members when they reached a certain age (CD XV 5–15). Taking the oath of the covenant marked young men and women as members responsible and accountable for fulfilling the commandments. As full members they were also allowed entrance into communal meetings so holy that only ritually pure as well as physically and mentally fit adults could enter.

Few scholars consider the inclusion of women in these communal meetings a possibility, given the general assumption of the marginality of Essene women.[248] However, in the Essene milieu it would have been crucial that women knew every intricate detail of the laws they were obligated to observe; thus it makes sense that women at least attended meetings in which legal issues were discussed and judgements were made, as attested in 1QSa I 11. Furthermore since the women, like the men, had received some education in their childhood, they would have been capable of understanding deliberations and discussion around legal interpretations. It is not known whether women were allowed to participate actively in the communal deliberations, but there are hints in D that they at least attended, parallel to 1QSa.

It is within the area of marital laws that most information on women has been preserved. This is also an area that communal laws regulated strictly, and over which the Examiner had extensive authority. In accordance with the wider societal norms, virginity of the woman was a prerequisite for marriage. If any doubt about the virginity of a bride-to-be existed, midwives would examine her, as legislated in the early law code (4Q271 3 12–14a). The communal interpolation in lines 14b–15a gives the Examiner the right to select "trustworthy women." Accordingly, the power of the women experts was undermined by the Examiner in the communal laws. Likely his choice was quite limited, since only women with some experience of gynecology—that is, midwives—would be able to perform an examination. By having the right to approve or reject specific women as authorities in gynecological examinations, the male head of the community managed to gain some control, albeit very limited.[249] This

---

[248] See, e.g., Schiffman (*Reclaiming*, 135) and Stegemann (*The Library of Qumran*, 198).

[249] A similar development is noticeable in rabbinic tradition concerning the examination of women's bodies for the purpose of establishing the onset of menstruation and puberty. Here as

interpolation attests to the general tendency in communal laws to concentrate power in the hands of the Examiner even in the most intimate matters. This interpolation may be a sign of a suspicion as to the actual compliance of the female experts. Perhaps there was a suspicion of solidarity amongst women, and a fear that female physical examiners would side with the women suspected of having had pre-marital sexual relations and thus deceitfully exonerate them.

The responsibility of the Examiner to oversee members' business transactions (CD XIII 15–16) was part of his larger role as financial supervisor of the members' property. This is apparent elsewhere in the rule for the Examiner, which prescribes that he examine the possessions of aspiring new members (CD XIII 11–12) and also stipulates that no trade be allowed between the members, "the Sons of Dawn" (CD XIII 14).[250] From CD XIV 12–13, we know that the members of the community owned private property, but according to CD XIII 15–16 the power of the individual over his or her belongings was limited; any private purchase or sale was under the supervision of the Examiner, who could approve or reject the deal. This stipulation reveals the extent of the Examiner's power. It is likely that he scrutinized the halakhic aspects of financial transactions, but possibly also the commercial ones. It was important to ensure financial stability among the members, as the welfare of the whole community and, in particular, the less fortunate in the community, depended on the wealth of its members (CD XIV 12–16). The Examiner's supervision of marriage may have encompassed more than financial and halakhic considerations; he may also have considered aspects such as the sexual past of a woman and the genealogy of the husband, the latter being important in the Halakhah stratum of the document (4Q271 3 9–10).

The Examiner's supervision of divorce (4Q266 9 iii 5/CD XIII 17) merits some reflections. One may differ in opinion as to whether the sectarian way of divorce, which required the consent of the Examiner, was more advantageous for women or not compared to the general societal views on divorce. Traditionally, a husband had

---

well, Rabbis attempted to find ways to exercise control; one venue was by choosing the women who were to perform the examinations; see Charlotte Fonrobert, "Gynecological Exams in Rabbinic Literature: Women's Bodies between Female Autonomy and Male Control," *JAGNES* 4 (1993), 65–72.

[250] Since the rule is part of the legislation for the Examiner, one may surmise that it was one of his responsibilities to ensure that transactions of services and goods took place as free exchange with one another. Jospeh Baumgarten shows that the "Sons of Dawn," בני השחר, does not refer to outsiders, as has previously been assumed, but to fellow members; "The 'Sons of Dawn' in CDC 13, 14–15 and the Ban on Commerce Among the Essenes," *IEJ* 33 (1983), 81–5; see also Murphy, *Wealth in the Dead Sea Scrolls*, 58. Furthermore, the assistance of the Examiner to members experiencing troubles may also include those of financial nature (CD XIII 9–11); see Murphy, *Wealth in the Dead Sea Scrolls*, 40–4. The Examiner also received the monthly contributions (CD XIV 12–16); he recorded transgressions concerning financial relations with expelled members (4Q266 11 14–16).

unlimited rights to divorce his wife. But by the end of Second Temple period, his power in this regard was debated, as the school of Shammai and the Galilean teacher Jesus forbade divorce except in the case of adultery (according to Matthew). The sectarian rule in D, which requires the consent of the Examiner, comes somewhere in between the two main alternatives; a man could not divorce at will, but divorce was not prohibited *per se*. Perhaps such an arrangement was slightly more advantageous to women than the traditional practice that gave the husband the sole authority to initiate divorce. In a situation in which the ultimate decision lay in the hands of a third party—the Examiner—a woman would have more protection against a hasty, unwanted divorce than she would in the society outside the sect. At the same time, it appears that the woman was entirely excluded from the discussions between the husband and the Examiner, and had to accept the decision reached. The ordinances are put in explicitly gendered language: "let him (the Examiner) guide *the man who divorces*" (4Q266 9 iii 5/CD XIII 17). The text certainly does not imply that the woman took any part in the decision and she may have been bypassed completely in any discussions. Thus, in the case of sectarian divorce, authority was taken away from the husband and given to the Examiner, while the influence of the woman remained limited. Whether this situation was particularly beneficial for the woman can be debated.

The communal laws highlight the extensive authority of the Examiner over the personal lives of the community members, both men and women. In short, the major decisions of individual members, such as marriage and divorce, were not personal issues any longer, but belonged to the communal realm. The trend to exert communal authority over various aspects of members' lives is epitomized in the prescription to expel any man who "fornicates" with his wife (4Q270 7 i 13). I concluded that "fornication" here primarily refers to sexual relations during a wife's pregnancy; underlying the prohibition is a rejection of non-procreative sexual intercourse combined with a belief that intercourse during pregnancy may be harmful for the fetus. Like the majority of laws in D, the stipulation about fornication in 4Q270 7 i 12–13 is androcentric and addresses a man: "he who approa[ches] to fornicate with his wife," ואשר יק[ב] לזנות לאשתו. In this law, the exclusive focus on the man becomes even greater as the penalty appears to apply only to the man. The discourse reflects a stern patriarchal attitude towards sexual activity: it is simply assumed that the man is the one initiating the sexual act that constitutes fornication and that the woman has no say about it. *He* is responsible, and thus *he* is penalized.

I concluded above that the responsibility of policing the offence of fornication within the marriage may have rested particularly with the woman, since according to 1QSa I 11 she was obliged to testify about her husband's behaviour. It may seem rather surprising that women were allowed to testify and attend the judicial proceedings, a sentiment Schiffman expresses as part of his argument in favour of emending the 1QSa text: "It would be attractive for our argument to claim that women even testified in the sectarian legal system. However, then we would have a text allowing women to testify about one and only one thing: the conduct of their husbands.

Imagine what marriages this would have made!"[251] However, as part of a general informant system where members kept track of each other's trespasses, a wife's testimony against her husband makes perfect sense. A wife's testimony would have been necessary in order for the community to keep informed of her husband's obedience to the laws. This would require the wife to renounce her loyalty to her husband in favour of that to the community. Again, a sectarian stance is evident in that the interest of the community is put above that of the family. As Bryan Wilson explains, a sect typically demands total allegiance of its members: "a member is sectarian before he is anything else."[252] Similarly, Meredith McGuire emphasises that sects are characterized by a "total commitment" on the part of their members and explains that the internal power of the organization gives the movement strength against outside threats as well as against deviant and dissenting members.[253]

The right and responsibility to testify against her husband obviously gave a woman some influence in the intimate life of the marriage. Although the husband was assumed to be responsible for sexual advances, she could testify against him if he transgressed community rules on marital relations. For some women, the right to testify against a husband may very well have functioned as a safe-guard against sexual, as well as other, forms of abuse.

It is also in the penal code that the Mothers, a group of leading women, appear. Although not ranked as highly as the Fathers (4Q270 7 i 14), they held some authority in the community. Unfortunately, the text gives no hints as to the specific types of responsibilities which the Mothers held. Still, the title "Mothers" indicates that some women, likely among the senior members of the community, did have authoritative status in the community.

Judging from these communal laws, a typical woman in the community behind D would receive an education and, at adulthood, would formally enter the community by taking an oath, thereby obtaining full membership. Moreover, she would be able to attend communal meetings, presuming that she was ritually pure and unblemished. She would marry—with the permission of the Examiner—and have children. As a wife, she would ensure that no sexual intercourse took place during her menstrual periods nor during the nine months of pregnancy. She would be expected to report any transgression of laws that her husband might commit, including serious offences that would lead to his expulsion.

In many ways, the D community had become the extended family of its members, replacing the biological one. The new extended family provided benefits to its members in the form of education and financial support, if necessary. The ideological climate, as evidenced in the Admonition, gave the members an assurance that they

---

[251] See Schiffman, *Reclaiming*, 134–5.
[252] Bryan Wilson, *Religion in Sociological Perspective* (Oxford: Oxford University Press, 1982), 90–5.
[253] McGuire, *Religion: The Social Context*, 154.

belonged to the chosen ones, the Covenant, and that their observance of the laws was the correct path. At the same time, the freedom of the individual was limited in an organization that was strictly hierarchical. A member could be expelled if he or she did not subscribe to the strict rules of the community and submit himself or herself to the authority of the communal leadership.

My conclusions are complementary to Michael Satlow's proposition that the Essenes took an anti-family stance as part of their opposition to traditional social and power structures.[254] He concludes that the individual was subordinate to the group, and that the community was more important for the men than were their families. However, he characterizes the Essenes as egalitarian, pointing particularly to the uniform types of graves at Qumran. In my estimate, the community was far from egalitarian, but instead strongly hierarchical. Within this power structure, some aspects of the traditional authority of the husband as a *pater familias* were diminished in favour of the communal authority, leaving husband and wife relatively powerless. Although the wife and husband were relatively equal in their lack of power, both were at the same time subordinate to the authoritarian leadership.

---

[254]Michael Satlow, *Jewish Marriage in Antiquity* (Princeton: Princeton University Press, 2001), 21–4.

7. CONCLUSION

In this section I will highlight the main findings of my analysis and at the end propose directions for future research on women in the Dead Sea Scrolls. In this thesis I have attempted to read the legal section in D in terms of its two main literary strata, an early law code and a late communal collection of laws. The earliest stratum of laws is non-sectarian as opposed to the later sectarian stratum. The provenance of the earliest literary layer, the Halakhah section, is likely priestly circles in the first part of the second century B.C.E. It is possible that these circles correspond to "the root planting" (CD I 7–9) that was formed in the 170–160s B.C.E., about twenty years prior to the emergence of the Teacher of Righteousness. I concluded above that the formulators of the early law code should be seen as forerunners of the sectarian movement that emerged with the activities of the Teacher of Righteousness in the mid-second century B.C.E. There are laws from the early law code, including some concerning women, which by their highly stringent nature suggest that the early formulators had already begun to distinguish themselves from other priests by their strict interpretation of purity and Sabbath laws in particular. For example, laws prohibiting sexual intercourse in the City of the Sanctuary and the ban of sexual intercourse on the Sabbath cannot be considered 'mainstream.' A second observation is that the circles behind the Halakhah section were not celibate, but were deeply concerned about purity and marital regulations for women. Hence, celibacy, which was a trait of some Essenes—at least in the first century C.E., according to the Greek and Latin writers—may have been a late development in a movement that increasingly turned sectarian.

The earliest legal stratum reflects a halakhah grounded in biblical laws. Consequently, the early laws display a firm patriarchal stance, parallel to that of the Hebrew Bible. Following the biblical tradition in general, this law code sees female sexuality as a dangerous force, which threatens the societal norms and therefore must be closely guarded. Such a perspective is apparent above all in the demand for a physical examination of a prospective bride suspected of not being a virgin. Furthermore, an interpretation of the law of the *Sotah* accepts the biblical stipulation that a woman suspected of being an adulteress may be forced to undergo the demeaning ordeal of drinking "the water of bitterness." A similar double standard concerning the sexes is evident in the prescription that a father discloses any blemishes his daughter may have before marriage, without requiring the same disclosure of the prospective husband. Similar rules apply in the trade of goods as in the transfer of the bride from the father to the groom. The marital arrangements are described as a trade, and it is apparent that it is the woman who is being traded.

While exposing the patriarchal nature of the material, this study argues that there is also a tendency in the early law code to improve the position of women as compared to biblical law. This view is particularly evident in an uncompromising acceptance of women's oaths that, contrary to biblical law, allows for the annulment of an oath of a wife or a daughter only when it deviates from covenantal law. The tendency to better the position of women is also apparent in the interpretation of two biblical laws that sanction oppressive acts against women: the interpretation of the law of the *Sotah* and the law concerning the bride suspected of not being a virgin at the time of wedding. Unlike the description of the ordeal of the *Sotah* in Num 5: 11–31, 4Q270 4 1–11 appears to require witnesses to any suspicious behaviour of a wife before a husband can force her to undergo the ordeal. In addition, there is evidence that suggests that the woman is given a chance to defend herself at a preliminary hearing. These changes to the biblical law severely limit a husband's opportunities to force his wife to undergo the ordeal. In comparison to the biblical law on the slandered virgin in Deut 22:13–21, the law in 4Q271 3 12b–15 insists that a prospective bride with a bad reputation be examined *prior* to the wedding, rather than endorsing an inquiry afterwards. Thus, this legislation aims to avoid a situation described in Deuteronomy 22 in which a woman can face the death penalty after the wedding if the husband became suspicious about her prior virginal state; instead, she may face the risk of losing her honour.

The early law code demonstrates a great concern for purity laws and takes a stringent halakhic position in this regard. The correct observance of purity laws is equally as important for women as it is for men. According to this law code, men and women who are ritually impure from discharge (*zav, zavah*) transmit impurity in identical ways (4Q272 1 ii 3–18). Furthermore, the law code homogenizes impurity laws concerning sexual intercourse during a woman's period of menstruation and flux; whereby the same laws concerning impurity of the man apply in both cases (4Q266 6 ii 1–4). A law against "mingling" (CD XI 4–5) on the Sabbath suggests that for purity reasons the formulators of the law code banned sexual intercourse on the Sabbath. Purity reasons are also behind the law that prohibits sexual intercourse in the City of the Sanctuary (CD XII 1–2) and, in consequence, prohibits married couples from living there. Other Sabbath laws prohibit the wearing of perfume and spice bottles and the carrying of infants, which concern women in particular (CD XI 9–11) although these laws are phrased in the masculine.

The Catalogue of Transgressors (4Q270 2 i–ii), which likely stems from an independent source, rebukes those who transgress biblical laws as well as laws specific to the legislation of D. For example, the Catalogue rebukes any man who engages in homosexual relations and anyone who "approaches" his niece. The list also rebukes two female transgressors: a woman with a bad reputation who engages in sexual relations and an engaged woman sleeping with someone other than her fiancée. This list includes other transgressors of sexual laws, such as a person who has sexual intercourse with a pregnant woman and one who engages in sexual intercourse during the Sabbath. The many examples of sexual transgressors in the Catalogue testify to the general condemnation of sins of a sexual nature.

The Admonition and the Communal laws reflect a sectarian outlook. These parts likely developed during the second half of the second century B.C.E., given that the final composition of D is dated around 100 B.C.E. Little of the material in the Admonition concerns women per se, but women do appear in the context of accusations against the general population in the discourse on the Nets of Belial and in a reference to members living in the camps. In a radical reinterpretation of biblical law, the Admonition condemns bigamy as evil (CD IV 20–1) and revokes the traditional right of a householder to take several wives. This position is beneficial to women because women would not have to share their husbands, or their husbands' goods, with other women. Another marital union that is considered evil is that between an uncle and a niece (CD V 7–8). This sectarian law likely arose from a gender-inclusive interpretation of the prohibition against marriage between a man and his mother's sister in Lev 18:13.

The stratum of communal laws outlines regulations for a specific community and reflects a strict sectarian perspective, in which the communal authority exerts considerable control over the private members' lives. The main authoritative figure, the Examiner, has the power to approve or disapprove of divorce, marital unions, and members' business deals. Concerning marriage unions, the Examiner takes on the role that traditionally belongs to the parents. In contrast, in the early law code the father still has the sole responsibility (4Q271 3 7–10). The trend to subordinate the family unit to the group is also reflected in the penalty for fornicating with a wife (4Q270 7 i 13). I suggested that the woman's right to testify regarding her husband's behaviour should be understood within the general system of informants, or "spies," by which members report each other's offences to the communal authority. This shows that loyalty to the community is of paramount importance, superseding the loyalty to family members. The Examiner also has the right to select the women responsible for performing physical examinations on any woman suspected of being a non-virgin (4Q271 3 14b). Thus, while still exerting some authority, the female experts are subject to the authority of the Examiner. In short, the personal freedom of the members, both male and female, is limited in this sectarian environment. One consequence of this is that the traditional power differential between men and women in the family unit is diminished, whereby the traditional authority of the *pater familias* is weakened in favour of the communal leadership.

There is a communal responsibility to help the poor in the community, including any virgin who needs financial assistance with her dowry (CD XIV 15). These charity laws that require members to give the equivalent of two days' pay a month demonstrate a concern for the vulnerable in the community and show how the community, in some respects, has taken over the responsibilities that traditionally lay with the next of kin.

There is some, albeit limited, evidence in the communal legislation that suggests that men and women were considered equal in some respects. In the area of education, for example, both young girls and boys appear to be equally educated. In addition, this study argues that young women, as well as young men, took the oath of the covenant, whereby they became responsible and accountable for fulfilling the Commandments. As full members, women were allowed entrance into community meetings so holy that only full members who were ritually pure, unblemished, and mentally fit could enter. The appearance of a group of senior, authoritative women, known as "the Mothers" (4Q270 7 i 14), fits well with the view that women had full membership. Nevertheless, this group of senior women had considerably lower status than the Fathers. I proposed that the difference in status may be explained in terms of the possible spiritual role of the Fathers in the community. Given the hierarchical organization of the community behind D, it is possible that the tendency to affirm women's position in the communal laws is the result not so much of an enlightened attitude towards women, but of the diminishing of the "ordinary" male power in the family unit in the context of an authoritarian society.

Throughout D, there is a strict attitude towards improper sexual relations. Whereas the early law code singles out women in particular as likely sexual transgressors (women with bad reputation, widows who have had sexual relations post-widowhood), other literary layers of D express a condemning attitude towards men as well as women. Thus, in the Catalogue of Transgressors, both male and female transgressors of sexual laws are condemned. The Admonition displays a strong aversion to sexual immorality in general. In accusations against outsiders, men are particularly criticised for their sexual sins (CD IV 17; VIII 4–5). This stringent attitude towards sexual transgressions committed by men or women continues in the communal laws, in which a man "fornicating" with his wife is to be expelled. The harsh attitude towards non-marital sexual relations establishes the norm that restricts sexual relations to marriage, not only for women, in accordance with the long-standing tradition, but also for men. Hence, in the area of sexual morality, certain equality is noticeable.

Overall, D is written from an androcentric point of view, reflecting a patriarchal attitude towards women. Consequently, women are mentioned predominantly in instances where their behaviour affects men, such as in matters of impurity and marriage. At the same time, in spite of the androcentric perspective of the document, there are several regulations that improve women's legal position, compared to biblical law and communal laws, such as the prohibition against polygyny. This evidence provides a picture that does not easily fit either a fully positive or a negative evaluation when it comes to determining the status of women in the community behind D. Instead, as is often the case in the study of women in antiquity, the position of women turns out to be highly varied and heterogeneous. The material on women in D is yet another example of how complex the status of women was within the social structures of any given community in antiquity.

D provides much information on women in one Essene community among many, and the challenge is now to try to understand how this information relates to other documents from Qumran. As research continues to trace the complex relationship of all the various Qumran documents to one another, hopefully this effort will shed more light on the communities—and the position of women within these communities—behind the texts.

BIBLIOGRAPHY

1. EDITIONS AND TRANSLATIONS CITED OR QUOTED

BIBLES

Bruce M. Metzger and Roland E. Murphy eds. *The New Oxford Annotated Bible with the Apocryphal/Deuterocanonical Books: New Revised Standard Version.* New York: Oxford University Press, 1991.
Kittel, R., K. Elliger, W. Rudolph et al. eds. *Biblia Hebraica Stuttgartensia.* 5th ed. Stuttgart: Deutsche Bibelgesellschaft, 1997.
Aland, K., Matthew Black et al. eds. *The Greek New Testament.* 3rd ed. New York: American Bible Society, 1975.

THE DEAD SEA SCROLLS AND RELATED DOCUMENTS

Baumgarten, Joseph and Daniel Schwartz. "Damascus Document (CD)." In *Damascus Document, War Scroll, and Related Documents.* Vol. 2 of *The Dead Sea Scrolls: Hebrew, Aramaic, and Greek Texts with English Translations*, eds. James Charlesworth et al., 4–79. Tübingen: J. C. B. Mohr/Louisville, Ky.: Westminster John Knox Press, 1995.
Charlesworth, James and Loren Stuckenbruck. "Rule of the Congregation (1QSa)." In *Rule of the Community and Related Documents.* Vol. 1 of *The Dead Sea Scrolls: Hebrew, Aramaic, and Greek Texts with English Translations*, eds. James Charlesworth et al., 108–117. Tübingen: J. C. B. Mohr/Louisville, Ky.: Westminster John Knox Press, 1994.
Cothenet, É. "Le Document de Damas." In Vol. 2 of *Les Textes de Qumrân. Traduits et annotés*, ed. Jean Carmignac, 129–204. Paris: Letouzey et Ané, 1963.
Delcor, M. *Les hymnes de Qumrân.* Paris: Letouzey et Ané, 1962.
Dupont-Sommer, André. *The Essene Writings from Qumran.* Trans. G. Vermes. Gloucester, Mass.: Peter Smith, 1973.
Gaster, T. *The Dead Sea Scriptures in English Translation.* Garden City, N.Y.: Doubleday, 1956.
Holm-Nielsen, Svend. *Hodayot: Psalms from Qumran.* Acta Theologica Danica 2. Aarhus: Universitetsforlaget i Aarhus, 1960.
Lewis, Naphtali. *The Documents from the Bar Kokhba Period in the Cave of Letters.* Jerusalem: The Israel Exploration Society, 1989.
Licht, Jacob. *The Rule Scroll: A Scroll from the Wilderness of Judaea. 1QS, 1QSa, 1QSb, Text, Introduction, and Commentary.* Jerusalem: Bialik Institute, 1965 (Hebrew).
Lohse, Eduard. *Die Texte aus Qumran: Hebräisch und Deutsch. Mit masoretischer Punktation. Übersetzung, Einführung und Anmerkungen.* München: Kösel-Verlag, 1964.
Martínez, Florentino García and Eibert J. C. Tigchelaar. *The Dead Sea Scrolls Study Edition.* 2 vols. Cambridge: Eerdmans/Leiden: Brill, 1997–98.
Newsom, Carol. *Songs of the Sabbath Sacrifice: A Critial Edition.* HSS 27. Atlanta: Scholars Press, 1985.

Qimron, Elisha. "The Text of CDC." In *The Damascus Document Reconsidered*, ed. Magen Broshi, 9–49. Jerusalem: The Israel Exploration Society, 1992.

Rabin, Chaim. *The Zadokite Documents*. 2d ed. Oxford: Clarendon Press, 1958.

Schechter, Solomon. *Fragments of a Zadokite Work: Documents of Jewish Sectaries.* Cambridge: Cambridge University Press, 1910. Reprinted with "Prolegomenon" by J. A. Fitzmyer. New York: Ktav, 1970.

Schiffman, Lawrence. "Sectarian Rule (5Q13)" In *Rule of the Community and Related Documents* Vol. 1 of *The Dead Sea Scrolls: Hebrew, Aramaic, and Greek Texts with English Translations*, eds. James Charlesworth et al., 132–43. Tübingen: J. C. B. Mohr/ Louisville, Ky.: Westminster John Knox Press, 1994.

———. "Ordinances and Rules (4Q159=4QOrd^a, 4Q513=4QOrd^b)." In *Rule of the Community and Related Documents*. Vol. 1 of *The Dead Sea Scrolls: Hebrew Aramic, and Greek Texts with English Translations*, eds. James Charlesworth et al., 145–75. Tübingen: J. C. B. Mohr/Louisville, Ky.: Westminster John Knox Press, 1994.

Tov, Emmanuel, with the collaboration of S.J. Pfann. *The Dead Sea Scrolls on Microfiche: A Comprehensive Facsimile Edition of the Texts from the Judean Desert, with a Companion Volume.* Leiden: Brill, 1993.

Wacholder, Ben Zion and Martin G. Abegg. *A Preliminary Edition of the Unpublished Dead Sea Scrolls: The Hebrew and Aramaic Texts from Cave 4.* Fascicle 1. Washington: Biblical Archaeology Society, 1991.

Vermes, Geza. *The Complete Dead Sea Scrolls in English.* New York: Penguin Press, 1997.

Wise M., M. Abegg, and E. Cook. *The Dead Sea Scrolls: A New Translation.* San Francisco: HarperSanFrancisco: 1996.

Yadin, Yigael. *The Temple Scroll I–III*. Jerusalem: Israel Exploration Society, Archaeological Institute of the Hebrew University, Shrine of the Book, 1983.

———. *The Finds from the Bar-Kokhba Period in the Cave of Letters.* Jerusalem: Israel Exploration Society, 1963.

———. *The Scroll of the War of the Sons of Light against the Sons of Darkness.* London: Oxford University Press, 1962.

Yardeni, Ada in collaboration with Jonas Greenfield. *Nahal Se'elim Documents.* Jerusalem: Israel Exploration Society and Ben Gurion University in the Negev Press, 1995 (Hebrew).

Zeitlin, S. *The Zadokite Fragments: Facsimile of the Manuscripts in the Cairo Genizah.* Collection in the Possession of the University Library, Cambridge, England. JQRMS 1. Philadelphia: Dropsie College, 1952.

DISCOVERIES IN THE JUDAEAN DESERT

DJD I	Barthélemy D. and J. T. Milik. *Qumran Cave 1*. Oxford: Clarendon Press, 1955.
DJD II	Benoit, P., J. T. Milik et R. de Vaux. *Les grottes de Murabba'at.* Oxford: Clarendon Press, 1961.
DJDJ III	Baillet, M., J. T. Milik et R. de Vaux. *Les 'petites grottes' de Qumrân.* Oxford: Clarendon Press, 1962.
DJD V	Allegro, John M. *Qumran Cave 4*. Oxford: Clarendon Press, 1968.

DJD VII   Baillet, M. *Qumrân grotte 4. III (4Q482–4Q520)*. Oxford: Clarendon Press, 1982.
DJD X   Qimron E. and J. Strugnell. *Qumran Cave 4. V. Miqsat Ma'ase ha-Torah.* Oxford: Clarendon Press, 1994.
DJD XVIII   Baumgarten, J. M. *Qumran Cave 4. XIII. The Damascus Document (4Q266–273).* Oxford: Clarendon Press, 1996.
DJD XIX   Broshi, M., E. Eshel, J. Fitzmyer, E. Larson, C. Newsom, L. Schiffman, M. Smith, M. Stone, J. Strugnell and A. Yardeni, in consultation with J. C. VanderKam. *Qumran Cave 4. XIV. Parabiblical Texts. Part 2.* Oxford: Clarendon Press, 1995.
DJD XX   Elgvin T. and others, in consultation with J. A. Fitzmyer. *Qumran Cave 4. XV. Sapiential Texts. Part 1.* Oxford: Clarendon Press, 1997.
DJD XXII   Brooke, G. J., J. J. Collins, P. Flint, J. Greenfield, E. Larson, C. Newsom, É. Puech, L. H. Schiffman, M. Stone, and J. Trebolle Barrera, in consultation with J. Vanderkam, partially based on earlier transcriptions by J. T. Milik and J. Strugnell. *Qumran Cave 4. XVII: Parabiblical Texts. Part 3.* Oxford: Clarendon Press, 1996.
DJD XXVI   Alexander, P. and G. Vermes. *Qumran Cave 4. XIX: 4QSerekh Ha-Yahad.* Oxford: Clarendon Press, 1998.
DJD XXVII   Cotton H. M. and A. Yardeni. *Aramaic, Hebrew, and Greek Documentary Texts from Nahal Hever and Other Sites, with an Appendix Containing Alleged Qumran Texts.* Oxford: Clarendon Press, 1997.
DJD XXXI   Puech, Émile. *Qumrân Grotte 4. XXII. Textes Araméens Première Partie 4Q529–549.* Oxford: Clarendon Press, 2001.
DJD XXXIV   Strugnell, John, Daniel J. Harrington, Torlief Elgvin, in consultation with Joseph A. Fitzmyer. *Qumran Cave 4. XXIV: 4QInstruction (Musar leMevin): 4Q415 ff.* Oxford: Clarendon Press, 1999.
DJD XXXV   Baumgarten, Joseph M. et al. *Qumran Cave 4. XXV: Halakhic Texts.* Oxford: Clarendon Press, 1999.

RABBINIC LITERATURE

The Babylonian Talmud. Epstein I., ed. 6 vols. London: Soncino Press, 1961.
Mishnayoth. Blackman, Philip, ed. 6 vols. 3d ed. Gateshead, Eng.: Judaica Press, 1973.
The Tosefta. Neusner, Jacob, ed. 6 vols. New York: Ktav, 1977–86.

OTHER JEWISH LITERATURE

Charlesworth, James, ed. *The Old Testament Pseudepigrapha.* 2 vols. New York: Doubleday, 1983, 1985.
De Jonge, Marinus, ed. *Testamenta XII Patriarcharum: Edited according to Cambridge University Library MS. Ff. I.24 fol. 203a–262b with Short Notes by M. de Jonge.* PVTG 1. 2d ed. Leiden: Brill, 1970.
Josephus, *Works.* 10 vols. Ed. and trans. H. St. J. Thackeray (vols. 1–5), Ralph Marcus (vol. 5–8), Allen Wikgren (vol. 8), Louis H. Feldman (vols. 9–10). Loeb Classical Library.

London: Heinemann/New York: Putnam (vols. 1–4); Cambridge, Mass.: Harvard University Press (vols. 5–10), 1926–1965.
Kraft, Robert, ed. *The Testament of Job according to the SV Text: Greek Text and English Translation*. New York: SBL/Missoula, Mont.: Scholars Press, 1974.
Porten, Bezalel and Ada Yardeni, eds. *Contracts*. Vol. 2 of *Textbook of Aramic Documents from Ancient Egypt*. Jerusalem: Hebrew University/Winona Lake, Ind.: Eisenbrauns, 1986–93.
Yonge, C. D., ed. *The Works of Philo: Completed and Unabridged*: *New Updated Edition*. Peabody, Mass.: Hendrickson, 1993.

OTHER EARLY TEXTS

Fathers of the Church. 78 vols. Washington: Catholic University of America Press, 1947–2003.
Patrologia Graeca (PG). Ed. Jacques-Paul Migne. 161 vols. Paris: 1857–1866.
Patrologia Latina (PL). Ed. Jacques-Paul Migne. 221 vols. Paris: 1844–64.
Hippokrates. *Oevres complétes d'Hippocrate*. Ed. E. Littré. 10 vols. Paris: 1839–61. Reprinted in Amsterdam: 1962.
Soranus' Gynecology: Translated with an Introduction by Owsei Temkin. Baltimore: Johns Hopkins Press, 1956.

2. REFERENCE WORKS

The Anchor Bible Dictionary. Eds. David Noel Freedman, et al. 6 vols. New York: Doubleday, 1992.
Encyclopaedia Judaica. 16 vols. Jerusalem: Encyclopaedia Judaica/New York: Macmillan, 1971–2.
Encyclopedia of the Dead Sea Scrolls. Eds. Lawrence H. Schiffman and James C. VanderKam. 2 vols. New York: Oxford University Press, 1999.
A Greek-English Lexicon. Eds. Henry G. Liddell and Robert Scott. Revised by Henry Stuart Jones. Oxford: Clarendon Press, 1968.
Lexicon in Veteris Testamenti Libros. Eds. Ludwig Koehler and Walter Baumgartner. Leiden: Brill, 1953.
The New Brown-Driver-Briggs-Gesenius Hebrew and English Lexicon with an Appendix Containing the Biblical Aramaic. Eds. Francis Brown et al. Peabody, Mass.: Hendrickson Publishers, 1979.
ספר מלים: *Dictionary of the Targumim, Talmud Babli, Yerushalmi and Midrashic Literature*. Ed. Marcus Jastrow. New York: The Judaica Press, 1989.

3. GENERAL BIBLIOGRAPHY

Alexander, Philip. "Rules." In *Encyclopedia of the Dead Sea Scrolls*. 2:799–803.
Anderson, Gary. "Celibacy or Consummation in the Garden? Reflections on Early Jewish and Christian Interpretations of the Garden of Eden." *HTR* 82 (1989): 121–48.
Archer, Leonie J. *Her Price is Beyond Rubies: The Jewish Woman in Greco-Roman Palestine*. Sheffield: Sheffield Academic Press, 1990.

———. "The Role of Jewish Women in the Religion, Ritual and Cult of Graeco-Roman Palestine." In *Images of Women in Antiquity*, eds. Averil Cameron and Amélie Kuhrt, 273–87. Camberra: Croom Helm, 1983.
Avemarie, Friedrich. "'Tohorat Ha-Rabbim' and 'Maqsheh Ha-Rabbim': Jacob Licht Reconsidered." In *Legal Texts and Legal Issues: Proceedings of the Second Meeting of the International Organization for Qumran Studies, Cambridge, 1995: Published in Honour of Joseph M. Baumgarten*, eds. Moshe J. Bernstein, García Florentino Martínez, and John Kampen, 215–29. STDJ 23. Leiden: Brill, 1997.
Baer, Richard A. Jr. *Philo's Use of the Categories Male and Female*. Leiden: Brill, 1970.
Baltzer, Klaus. *The Covenant Formulary in Old Testament, Jewish, and Early Christian Writings*. Philadelphia: Fortress Press, 1971.
Bar-Adon, P. "Another Settlement of the Judean Desert Sect at 'En-Ghuweir on the Shores of the Dead Sea." *BASOR* 225 (1977): 1–25.
Baskin, Judith. "Rabbinic Judaism and the Creation of Woman." In *Judaism Since Gender*, eds. Miriam Peskowitz and Laura Levitt, 125–30. London: Routledge, 1997.
———. "The Separation of Women in Rabbinic Judaism." In *Women, Religion, and Social Change*, eds. Yvonne Y. Haddad and Ellison B. Findley, 3–18. Albany: State University of New York Press, 1985.
Baumgarten, Albert. *The Flourishing of Jewish Sects in the Maccabean Era: An Interpretation*. Kinderhook, N.Y.: Brill, 1997.
Baumgarten, Joseph M. "The Use of מי נדה for General Purification." In *The Dead Sea Scrolls Fifty Years after their Discovery: Proceedings of the Jerusalem Congress, July 20–25, 1997*, eds. Lawrence H. Schiffman, Emanuel Tov, and James C. VanderKam, 481–85. Jerusalem: Israel Exploration Society in cooperation with the Shrine of the Book, Israel Museum, 2000.
———. "Judicial procedures." In *Encyclopedia of the Dead Sea Scrolls*. 1:445–60.
———. "Damascus Document." In *Encyclopedia of the Dead Sea Scrolls*. 1:166–70.
———. "The Damascus Document Reconsidered." In *The Dead Sea Scrolls at Fifty: Proceedings of the 1997 Society of Biblical Literature Qumran Section Meetings*, vol. 2, eds. Robert Kugler and Eileen Schuller, 149–50. Early Judaism and Its Literature 15. Atlanta: Society of Biblical Literature, 1999.
———. "Scripture and Law in 4Q265." In *Biblical Perspectives: Early Use and Interpretation of the Bible in Light of the Dead Sea Scrolls. Proceedings of the First International Symposium of the Orion Center for the Study of the Dead Sea Scrolls and Associated Literature, 12–14 May 1996*, eds. Michael Stone and Esther Chazon, 25–33. STDJ 28. Leiden: Brill, 1998.
———. "The Red Cow Purification Rites in Qumran Texts." *JJS* 46 (1995): 112–19.
———. "A Fragment on Fetal Life and Pregnancy in 4Q270." In *Pomegranates and Golden Bells: Studies in Biblical, Jewish, and Near Easter Ritual, Law, and Literature in Honor of Jacob Milgrom*, eds. David P. Wright et al., 445–8. Winona Lake, Ind.: Eisenbrauns, 1995.
———. "The Laws about Fluxes in 4QTohora[a] (4Q274)." In *Time to Prepare the Way in the Wilderness: Papers on the Qumran Scrolls by Fellows of the Institute for Advanced Studies of the Hebrew University, Jerusalem, 1989–1990*, eds. Devorah Dimant and Lawrence H. Schiffman, 1–8. STDJ 16. Leiden: Brill, 1995.

—. "Zab Impurity in Qumran and Rabbinic Law." *JJS* 14 (1994): 273–7.

—. "Purification after Childbirth and the Sacred Garden in 4Q265 and Jubilees." In *New Qumran Texts and Studies: Proceedings of the First Meeting of the International Organization for Qumran Studies, Paris 1992*, eds. George Brooke and Florentino García Martínez, 3–10. STDJ 15. Leiden: Brill, 1994.

—. "The Purification Rituals in *DJD 7*." In *The Dead Sea Scrolls: Forty Years of Research*, eds. Devorah Dimant and Uriel Rappaport, 199–209. Leiden: Brill/Jerusalem: The Magness Press, 1992.

—. "The Cave 4 Versions of the Qumran Penal Code." *JJS* 43 (1992): 268–76.

—. "The Laws of the Damascus Document in Current Research." In *The Damascus Document Reconsidered*, ed. Magen Broshi, 51–62. Jerusalem: The Israel Exploration Society, 1992.

—. "The Disqualifications of Priests in 4Q Fragments of the 'Damascus Document,' a Specimen of Recovery of Pre-Rabbinic Halakha." In *The Madrid Qumran Congress: Proceedings of the International Congress on the Dead Sea Scrolls, Madrid 18–21 March 1991*, eds. Julio Trebolle Barrera and Luis Vegas Montaner, 2: 503–13. STDJ 11. Leiden: Brill, 1992.

—. "On the Nature of the Seductress in 4Q184." *RevQ* 57–58 (1991): 133–43.

—. "Qumran-Essene Restraints on Marriage." In *Archaeology and History in the Dead Sea Scrolls, The New York University Conference in Memory of Yigael Yadin*, ed. Lawrence H. Schiffman, 13–24. JSPSup 8. Sheffield: JSOT Press, 1990.

—. "The Qumran Sabbath Shirot and Rabbinic Merkabah Traditions." *RevQ* 13 (1988): 199–213.

—. "The 'Sons of Dawn' in CDC 13, 14–15 and the Ban on Commerce Among the Essenes." *IEJ* 33 (1983): 81–5.

—. "4Q502, Marriage or Golden Age Ritual?" *JJS* 34 (1983): 125–35.

—. "The Pharisaic-Sadducean Controversies about Purity." *JJS* 31 (1980): 157–70.

—. *Studies in Qumran Law*. Leiden: Brill, 1977.

—. "The Essene Avoidance of Oil and the Laws of Purity." *RevQ* 6 (1967): 183–92.

—. "On the Testimony of Women." *JBL* 76 (1957): 266–9.

Beall, Todd. *Josephus' Description of the Essenes Illustrated by the Dead Sea Scrolls*. Cambridge: Cambridge University Press, 1988.

Bengtsson, Håkan. *What's in a Name? A Study of Sobriquets in the Pesharim*. Uppsala: Uppsala University, 2000.

Bennett Elder, Linda. "The Woman Question and Female Ascetics Among Essenes." *BA* 57 (1994): 220–34.

Best, Ernest. *A Commentary on the First and Second Epistles to the Thessalonians*. New York: Harper and Row, 1972.

Biale, Rachel. *Women and Jewish Law: An Exploration of Women's Issues in Halakhic Sources*. New York: Schocken Books, 1984.

Bird, Phyllis. "'To Play The Harlot': An Inquiry Into An Old Testament Metaphor." In *Gender and Difference in Ancient Israel*, ed. Peggy Day, 75–94. Minneapolis: Fortress Press, 1989.

Black, Matthew. "The Tradition of Hasidean-Essene Asceticism: Its Origins and Influence." In *Aspects du Judéo-Christianisme: Collogue de Strasbourg 23–25 avril 1964*. Université des sciences humaines de Strasbourg. Centre de recherches d'histoire des religions, 19–33. Paris: Presses Universitaires de France, 1965.

———. *The Scrolls and Christian Origins: Studies in the Jewish Background of the New Testament*. BJS 48. Chico, Calif.: Scholars Press, 1961.

———. *The Essene Problem*. Friends of Dr. William's Library Fourteenth Lecture, 1960. Cambridge: W. Heiffer & Sons, 1961.

Bockmuehl, Marcus. "Redaction and Ideology in the *Rule of the Community*." *RevQ* 18 (1998): 541–57.

Borgen, Peder. "'At the Age of Twenty' in 1QSa." *RevQ* 10 (1961–62): 267–77.

Bradley, Keith. "The Social Role of the Nurse in the Roman World." In *Discovering the Roman Family: Studies in Roman Social History*, 13–36. New York/Oxford: Oxford University Press, 1991.

———. "Wet-Nursing at Rome: A Study in Social Relations." In *The Family in Ancient Rome: New Perspectives*, ed. Beryl Rawson, 201–29. Ithaca, N.Y.: Cornell University Press, 1986.

Brenner, Athalya. "An Afterword: The Decalogue–Am I an Addressee?" In *A Feminist Companion to Exodus–Deuteronomy*. Vol. 6 of *The Feminist Companion to the Bible*, ed. A. Brenner, 255–8. Sheffield: Sheffield Academic Press, 1994.

Brewer, David Instone. "Deuteronomy 24:1–4 and the Origin of the Jewish Divorce Certificate." *JJS* 49 (1998): 230–43.

———. "Nomological Exegesis in Qumran 'Divorce' Texts." *RevQ* 18 (1998): 561–79.

Brin, Gershon. *The Concept of Time in the Bible and the Dead Sea Scrolls*. STDJ 39. Leiden: Brill, 2001.

———. "Divorce at Qumran." In *Legal Texts and Legal Issues: Proceedings of the Second Meeting of the International Organization for Qumran Studies, Cambridge, 1995: Published in Honour of Joseph M. Baumgarten*, eds. Moshe J. Bernstein, Florentino García Martínez, and John Kampen, 231–44. STDJ 23. Leiden: Brill, 1997.

———. "לשתי הוראות בעניני נישואין מקומראן" ("Two Instructions on Marital Matters from Qumran"). *Bet Miqra* 142 (year 40) Nisan 5755 (1995) (Hebrew): 224–31.

Brooke, George. "Between Qumran and Corinth: Embroidered Allusions to Women's Authority." In *The Dead Sea Scrolls as Background to Postbiblical Judaism and Early Christianity*, ed. James Davila, 157–76. STDJ 46. Leiden: Brill, 2003.

Brooten, Bernadette J. "Early Christian Women and Their Cultural Context: Issues of Method in Historical Reconstruction." In *Feminist Perspectives on Biblical Scholarship*, ed. Adela Yarbro Collins, 65–91. Chico, Calif.: Scholars Press, 1985.

———. "Konnten Frauen im alten Judentum die Scheidung betreiben? Überlegung zu Mk 10, 11–12 und 1 Kor 7, 10–11." *EvTh* 42 (1982): 65–80.

———. *Women Leaders in the Ancient Synagogue*. BJS 36. Chico, Calif.: Scholars Press, 1982.

Broshi, Magen. "Was Qumran, Indeed, a Monastery? The Consensus and Its Challengers: An Archaeologist's View." In *Caves of Enlightenment: Proceedings of the American Schools of Oriental Research Dead Sea Scrolls Jubilee Symposium (1947–1997)*, ed. James H. Charlesworth, 19–37. North Richland Hills, Tex.: Bibal Press, 1998.

———. "Anti-Qumranic Polemics in the Talmud." In *The Madrid Qumran Congress: Proceedings of the International Congress on the Dead Sea Scrolls, Madrid 18–21*

March 1991, eds. Julio Trebolle Barrera and Luis Vegas Montaner, 2:589–600. Leiden: Brill, 1992.

Broshi M. and Hanan Eshel. "The Greek King is Antiochus IV (4QHistorical Text=4Q248)." *JJS* 48 (1997): 120–9.

Buchanan, George W. "The Role of Purity in the Structure of the Essene Sect." *RevQ* 4 (1963–64): 397–406.

Büchler, Adolph. "Purity and Family Impurity in Jerusalem before 70 C.E." In *Studies in Jewish History*, 64–98. London: Oxford University Press, 1956.

Budd, Philip. *Leviticus*. The New Century Bible Commentary. Grand Rapids, Mich.: Eerdmans, 1996.

Callaway, Philip. "Qumran Origins: From the Doresh to the Moreh." *RevQ* 14 (1990): 637–50.

———. *The History of the Qumran Community: An Investigation*. JSPSup 3. Sheffield: Sheffield Academic Press, 1988.

Campbell, Jonathan. *The Use of Scripture in the Damascus Document 1–8, 19–20*. New York: Walter de Gruyter, 1995.

———. "Essene-Qumran Origins in the Exile: A Scriptural Basis?" *JJS* 46 (1995): 143–56.

Cansdale, Lena. "Women Members of the *Yahad* according to the Qumran Scrolls." *Eleventh World Congress of Jewish Studies*, 215–22. Jerusalem: World Union of Jewish Studies, 1994.

Cantarella, Eva. *Pandora's Daughters: The Role and Status of Women in Greek and Roman Society*. Baltimore: The Johns Hopkins University Press, 1987.

Capper, Brian. "The New Covenant in Southern Palestine at the Arrest of Jesus." In *The Dead Sea Scrolls as Background to Postbiblical Judaism and Early Christianity*, ed. James Davila, 90–116. STDJ 46. Leiden: Brill, 2003.

Caqout, André. "Grandeur et pureté du sacerdoce: Remarques sur le Testament de Qahat (4Q542)." In *Solving Riddles and Untying Knots: Biblical, Epigraphic, and Semetic Studies in Honor of Jonas C. Greenfield*, eds. Ziony Zevit, Seymour Gitin, and Michael Sokoloff, 39–44. Winona Lake, Ind.: Eisenbrauns, 1995.

Chance, John. "The Anthropology of Honor and Shame: Culture, Values, and Practice." *Semeia* 68 (1994): 139–49.

Clark, Gillian. "Roman Women." In *Women in Antiquity*, eds. Ian McAuslan and Peter Walcot, 36–55. New York: Oxford University Press, 1996.

———. *Women in Late Antiquity: Pagan and Christian Life-Styles*. Oxford: Clarendon Press: 1993.

Cohen, Shaye. "Hellenism in Unexpected Places." In *Hellenism in the Land of Israel*, eds. John Collins and Gregory Sterling, 217–23. Notre Dame, Ind.: University of Notre Dame Press, 2001.

———. "Menstruants and the Sacred in Judaism and Christianity." In *Women's History and Ancient History*, ed. Sarah Pomeroy, 273–99. Chapel Hill, N.C.: University of North Carolina Press, 1991.

Collins, John. J. "Family Life." In *Encyclopedia of the Dead Sea Scrolls*. 1:287–90.

———. "Marriage, Divorce, and Family in Second Temple Judaism." In *Families in Ancient Israel*, eds. Leo Perdue, Joseph Blenkinsopp, and Carol Meyers, 104–62. Louisville, Ky.: Westminster John Knox Press, 1997.

———. *The Sceptre and the Star: The Messiahs of the Dead Sea Scrolls and Other Ancient Literature*. New York: Doubleday, 1995.
———. "Was the Dead Sea Sect an Apocalyptic Movement?" In *Archaeology and History in the Dead Sea Scrolls: The New York University Conference in Memory of Yigael Yadin*, ed. Lawrence H. Schiffman, 25–51. JSPSup 8. Sheffield: JSOT Press, 1990.
———. "The Origin of the Qumran Community: A Review of the Evidence." In *To Touch the Text: Biblical and Related Studies in Honor of Joseph A. Fitzmyer, S.J.*, eds. Maurya P. Horgan and Paul J. Kobelski, 159–78. New York: Crossroad, 1989.
———. *Between Athens and Jerusalem*. New York: Crossroad, 1983.
———. "Structure and Meaning in the Testament of Job." In *Society of Biblical Literature: 1974 Seminar Papers*, ed. G. MacRae, 1:35–52. Cambridge, Mass.: Society of Biblical Literature, 1974.
Conway, Colleen. "Toward a Well-Formed Subject: The Function of Purity Language in the Serek Ha-Yahad." *JSP* 21 (2000): 103–20.
Cook, Joan. "Pseudo-Philo's Song of Hannah: Testament of a Mother in Israel." *JSP* 9 (1991): 103–14.
Coppens, J. "Le célibat esséniens." In *Qumrân: Sa piété, sa théologie et son milieu*, eds. Mathias Delcor et al., 295–303. Bibliotheca Ephemeridum Theologicarum Lovaniensium 46. Paris: Duculot, Gembloux, 1978.
Cotton, Hannah and Elisha Qimron. "Xhev/Se ar 13 of 134 or 135 C.E.: A Wife's Renunciation of Claims." *JJS* 49 (1998): 108–18.
Crawford, Sidnie White. "Mothers, Sisters, and Elders: Titles for Women in Second Temple Jewish and Early Christian Communities." In *The Dead Sea Scrolls as Background to Postbiblical Judaism and Early Christianity*, ed. James Davila, 177–91. STDJ 46. Leiden: Brill, 2003.
———. "The Meaning of the Phrase עיר הקדש in the Temple Scroll." *DSD* 8 (2001): 242–53.
———. "A Comparison of the 'A' and 'B' Manuscripts of the Damascus Document." *RevQ* 12 (1987): 537–53.
Cross, Frank Moore. *The Ancient Library of Qumran*. 3d ed. Minneapolis: Fortress Press, 1995.
———. "Introduction." In *Scrolls from Cave I: The Great Isaiah Scroll, The Order of the Community, The Pesher to Habakkuk*, eds. F. M. Cross, John Trevor et al. Jerusalem: Albright Institute of Archaeological Research and the Shrine of the Book, 1974.
Cross, Frank Moore and Esther Eshel. "Ostraca from Khirbet Qumran." *IEJ* 47 (1997): 17–28.
Davies, Philip. "The Judaism(s) of the Damascus Document." In *The Damascus Document: A Centennial of Discovery. Proceedings of the Third International Symposium of the Orion Center for the Study of the Dead Sea Scrolls and Associated Literature, 4–8 February, 1998*, eds. Joseph M. Baumgarten, Esther G. Chazon, and Avital Pinnick, 27–43. STDJ 35. Leiden: Brill, 2000.
———. "Reflections on DJD XVIII." In *The Dead Sea Scrolls at Fifty: Proceedings of the 1997 Society of Biblical Literature Qumran Section Meetings*, vol. 2, eds. Robert Kugler and Eileen Schuller, 151–65. Early Judaism and Its Literature 15. Atlanta: Society of Biblical Literature, 1999.
———. "Was There Really a Qumran Community?" *CurBS* 3 (1995): 9–35.
———. "Who Can Join the 'Damascus Covenant'?" *JJS* 46 (1995): 134–42.
———. "Damascus Rule." In the *Anchor Bible Dictionary*. 2:8–10.

———. "Redaction and Sectarianism in the Qumran Scrolls." In *Scriptures and Scrolls: Studies in Honour of A. S. Van der Woude on the Occasion of His 65th Birthday*, eds. F. García Martínez, A. Hilhorst and C. J. Labuschagne, 152–63. VTSup 49. Leiden: Brill, 1992.

———. "Communities at Qumran and the Case of the Missing 'Teacher.'" *RevQ* 15 (1991): 275–86.

———. "The Birthplace of the Essenes: Where is 'Damascus?'" *RevQ* 14 (1990): 503–19.

———. "Halakhah at Qumran." In *A Tribute to Geza Vermes: Essays on Jewish and Christian Literature and History*, eds. Philip Davies and Richard White, 37–50. JSOTSS 100. Sheffield: JSOT Press, 1990.

———. "The Teacher of Righteousness and the 'End of Days.'" *RevQ* 13 (1988): 313–17.

———. "How Not to Do Archaeology: The Story of Qumran." *BA* (1988): 203–7.

———. *Behind the Essenes: History and Ideology in the Dead Sea Scrolls*. BJS 94. Atlanta: Scholars Press, 1987.

———. "The Temple Scroll and the Damascus Document." In *Temple Scrolls Studies: Papers Presented at the International Symposium on the Temple Scroll, Manchester, December 1987*, ed. George Brooke, 201–10. JSPSup 7. Sheffield: JSOT Press, 1987.

———. *Damascus Covenant: An Interpretation of the "Damascus Document."* JSOTSup 25. Sheffield: JSOT Press, 1983.

———. *Qumran*. Guildford, Surrey: Lutterworth Press, 1982.

———. "The Ideology of the Temple in the Damascus Document." *JJS* 33 (1982): 287–301.

Davies, P. and Joan Taylor. "The So-Called 'Therapeutae' of De Vita Contemplativa: Identity and Character." *HTR* 91 (1998): 3–24.

———. "On the Testimony of Women in 1QSa." *DSD* 3 (1996): 223–35

Davis, Robert. "The History of the Composition of the 'Damascus Document.'" Ph.D. dissertation. Harvard University, 1992.

Dean-Jones, Lesley. *Women's Bodies in Classical Greek Science*. Oxford: Clarendon Press, 1994.

Demand, Nancy. *Birth, Death and Motherhood in Classical Greece*. Baltimore: The Johns Hopkins University Press, 1994.

Denis, Albert-Marie. *Les thèmes de connaissance dans le document de Damas*. Studia Hellenistica 15. Louvain: Universitaires de Louvain, 1967.

De Vaux, R. *Archaeology and the Dead Sea Scrolls: The Schweich Lectures of the British Academy 1959*. London: Oxford University Press, 1973.

Dimant, Devorah. "The Qumran Manuscripts: Contents and Significance." In *Time to Prepare the Way in the Wilderness: Papers on the Qumran Scrolls by Fellows of the Institute for Advanced Studies of the Hebrew University, Jerusalem, 1989–1990*, eds. Devorah Dimant and Lawrence H. Schiffman, 23–58. STDJ 16. Leiden: Brill, 1995.

———. "4QFlorilegium and the Idea of the Community as Temple." In *Hellenica et Judaica: Hommage à Valentin Nikiprowetzky*, eds. André Caquot et al., 165–89. Leuven-Paris: Peeters, 1986.

———. "Qumran Sectarian Literature." In *Jewish Writings of the Second Temple Period*, ed. Michael E. Stone, 483–550. Compendia Rerum Iudaicarum ad Novum Testamentum, Section 2. The Literature of the Jewish People in the Period of the Second Temple and the Talmud 2. Assen, The Netherlands: Van Gorcum/Philadephia: Fortress Press, 1984.

Doering, Lutz. "Purity Regulations Concerning the Sabbath in the Dead Sea Scrolls and Related Literature." In *The Dead Sea Scrolls Fifty Years after their Discovery: Proceedings of the Jerusalem Congress, July 20–25, 1997*, eds. Lawrence H. Schiffman, Emanuel Tov, and James C. VanderKam, 600–2. Jerusalem: Israel Exploration Society in cooperation with the Shrine of the Book, Israel Museum, 2000.

Dover, K. J. "Classical Greek Attitudes to Sexual Behaviour." In *Women in the Ancient World: The Arethusa Papers*, eds. John Peradotto and J. P. Sullivan, 143–57. Albany: State University of New York Press, 1984.

Driver, Godfrey R. *The Judean Scrolls: The Problem and a Solution*. Oxford: B. Blackwell, 1965.

———. "Two Problems in the Old Testament Examined in the Light of Archaeology." *Syria* 33 (1956): 73–7.

Dupont-Sommer, André. "La problème des influences étrangères sur la secte juive de Qoumrân." *Revue d'histoire et de philosophie religieuses* 35 (1955): 75–92.

Eisenman, Robert. *James, the Brother of Jesus: The Key to Unlocking the Secrets of Early Christianity and the Dead Sea Scrolls*. New York: Viking, 1996.

———. *The Dead Sea Scrolls and the First Christians*. Rockport, Mass.: Element Books, 1996.

Eisenman, Robert and Michael Wise. *The Dead Sea Scrolls Uncovered*. Rockport, Mass.: Element Books, 1992.

Elder, Linda Bennet. "The Woman Question and Female Ascetics among Essenes." *BA* 57 (1994): 220–34.

Elwolde, John. "Distinguishing the Linguistic and the Exegetical: The Biblical Book of Numbers in the Damascus Document." *DSD* 7 (2000): 1–25.

———. "*Rwqmh* in the Damascus Document and Ps 139:15." In *Diggers at the Well: Proceedings of a Third International Symposium on the Hebrew of the Dead Sea Scrolls and Ben Sira*, eds. T. Muraoka and J. F. Elwolde, 65–83. STDJ 36. Leiden: Brill, 2000.

Epstein, Louis. *Marriage Laws in the Bible and the Talmud*. Cambridge, Mass.: Harvard University Press, 1942.

Esler, Philip. "Introverted Sectarianism at Qumran and in the Johannine Community." In *The First Christians' Social Worlds: Social-Scientific Approaches to New Testament Interpretation*, 70–91. London: Routledge, 1994

Falk, Daniel. *Daily, Sabbath and Festival Prayers in the Dead Sea Scroll*. STDJ 27. Leiden: Brill, 1998.

Falk, Ze'ev W. *Introduction to Jewish Law of the Second Commonwealth*, vol.1. Leiden: Brill, 1972.

Fishbane, Michael. "Accusations of Adultery: A Study of Law and Scribal Practice in Numbers 5:11–31." *HUCA* 45 (1974): 25–45

Fitzmyer, Joseph. "Marriage and Divorce." In *Encyclopedia of the Dead Sea Scrolls*. 1:511–14.

———. "The Gathering in of the Teacher of Righteousness." In *The Dead Sea Scrolls and Christian Origins*, 261–5. Studies in the Dead Sea Scrolls and Related Literature. Grand Rapids, Mich./Cambridge, UK: Eerdmans, 2000. Originally published as "The Gathering In of the Community's Teacher." *Maarav* 8 (1992): 223–38.

———. "Divorce among First-Century Palestinian Jews." *ErIsr* 14 (1978): 106–10.

———. "The Matthean Divorce Texts and Some New Palestinian Evidence." *TS* 37 (1976): 197–226.
Flusser, David. "Psalms, Hymns and Prayers." In *Jewish Writings of the Second Temple Period*, ed. Michael E. Stone, 551–77. Compendia Rerum Iudaicarum ad Novum Testamentum, Section 2. The Literature of the Jewish People in the Period of the Second Temple and the Talmud 2. Assen, The Netherlands: Van Gorcum/Philadelphia: Fortress Press, 1984.
Fonrobert, Charlotte. "Gynecological Exams in Rabbinic Literature: Women's Bodies Between Female Autonomy and Male Control." *JAGNES* 4 (1993): 65–72.
Fraade, Steven. "Hagu, Book of." In *Encyclopedia of the Dead Sea Scrolls*. 1:327.
———. "Ascetical Aspects of Ancient Judaism." In *Jewish Spirituality*, ed. Arthur Green, 1: 253–88. World Spirituality 13. New York: Crossroad, 1986.
Frymer-Kensky, Tikva. "Deuteronomy." In *The Women's Bible Commentary*, eds. Carol Newsom and Sharon Ringe, 52–62. London: SPCK, 1992.
———. "The Strange Case of the Suspected *Sotah* (Numbers V 11–31)." *VT* 34 (1984): 11–26.
Fuller, Russell. "Text-Critical Problems in Malachi 2:10–16." *JBL* 110 (1991): 47–57.
Gärtner, Bertil. *The Temple and the Community in Qumran and the New Testament: A Comparative Study in the Temple Symbolism of the Qumran Texts and the New Testament*. Cambridge: Cambridge University Press, 1965.
Gilmore, David. "Anthropology of the Mediterranean." *Annual Review of Anthropology* 11 (1982): 175–205
Ginzberg, Louis. *An Unknown Jewish Sect*. New York: Ktav, 1976. Revised and updated version of *Eine unbekannte jüdische Sekte*, 1922 ed.
Golb, Norman. *Who Wrote the Dead Sea Scrolls: The Search for the Secret of Qumran*. New York: Scribner, 1995.
———. "The Dead Sea Scrolls: A New Perspective." *The American Scholar* 58 (1989): 177–207.
———. "The Problem of Origin and Identification of the Dead Sea Scrolls." *Proceedings of the American Philosophical Society* 124 (1980): 1–24.
Greenfield, Jonas. "The Words of Levi Son of Jacob in Damascus Document IV, 15–19." *RevQ* 13 (1988): 319–22.
Gropp, Douglas. "Slavery." In *Encyclopedia of the Dead Sea Scrolls*. 2:884–6.
Grossman, Maxine. *Reading for History in the Damascus Document: A Methodological Study*. STDJ 45. Leiden: Brill, 2002.
Gruber, Mayer, I. "Women in the Religious System of Qumran." In *Judaism in Late Antiquity. Part Five, The Judaism of Qumran: A Systematic Reading of the Dead Sea Scrolls*, eds. Alan Avery-Peck and Jacob Neusner, 1:173–196. Leiden: Brill, 2001.
———. "Breast-Feeding Practices in Biblical Israel and in Old Babylonian Mesopotamia." In *The Motherhood of God and Other Studies,* eds. Jacob Neusner et al., 69–107. South Florida Studies in the History of Judaism 57. Atlanta: Scholars Press, 1992.
———. "Women in the Cult according to the Priestly Code." In *Judaic Perspectives on Ancient Israel*, eds. J. Neusner et al., 35–48. Philadelphia: Fortress Press, 1987.
Guillaumont, Antoine. "A propos du célibat des Esséniens." In *Hommages à André Dupont-Sommer*, 395–404. Paris: Librarie Adrien Maisonneuve, 1971.

Hachlili, R. "Burial Practices at Qumran." *RevQ* 16 (1993): 253.
Halpern-Amaru, Betsy. *The Empowerment of Women in the Book of Jubilees*. SJSJ 60. Leiden: Brill, 1999.
———. "Portraits of Women in Pseudo-Philo's *Biblical Antiquities.*" In *'Women Like This' New Perspectives on Jewish Women in the Greco-Roman World*, ed. Amy-Jill Levine, 83–106. Atlanta: Scholars Press, 1991.
Hansson, Ann Ellis. "The Medical Writer's Woman." In *Before Sexuality: The Construction of the Erotic Experience in the Ancient Greek*, eds. David Halperin et al., 309–37. Princeton N.J.: Princeton University Press, 1990.
Hanson, K. C. "The Herodians and Mediterranean Kinship, Part I: Genealogy and Descent." *BTB* 19 (1989): 75–84.
———. "The Herodians and Mediterranean Kinship, Part II: Marriage and Divorce." *BTB* 19 (1989): 142–51.
Hanson, K.C and Douglas Oakman. *Palestine in the Time of Jesus: Social Structure and Social Conflicts*. Minneapolis: Fortress Press, 1998.
Harrington, Daniel J. *Wisdom Texts from Qumran*. New York: Routledge, 1996.
Harrington, Hannah K. *The Impurity Systems of Qumran and the Rabbis: Biblical Foundation*. SBL Dissertation Series 143. Atlanta: Scholars Press, 1993.
Hauptman, Judith. *Rereading the Rabbis: A Woman's Voice*. Boulder, Colo.: WestviewPress, 1998.
Hempel, Charlotte. *The Damascus Texts*. Companion to the Qumran Scrolls 1. Sheffield: Sheffield Academic Press, 2000.
———. "The Laws of the Damascus Document and 4QMMT." In *The Damascus Document: A Centennial of Discovery. Proceedings of the Third International Symposium of the Orion Center for the Study of the Dead Sea Scrolls and Associated Literature, 4–8 February, 1998*, eds. Joseph M. Baumgarten, Esther G. Chazon, and Avital Pinnick, 69–84. STDJ 35. Leiden: Brill, 2000.
———. "4QOrd^a (4Q159) and the Laws of the Damascus Document." In *The Dead Sea Scrolls: Fifty Years after Their Discovery: Proceedings of the Jerusalem Congress, July 20–25, 1997*, eds. Lawrence H. Schiffman, Emanuel Tov, and James C. VanderKam, 372–6. Jerusalem: Israel Exploration Society in cooperation with the Shrine of the Book, Israel Museum, 2000.
———. *The Laws of the Damascus Document: Sources, Tradition, and Redaction*. STDJ 29. Leiden: Brill, 1998.
———. "The Penal Code Reconsidered." In *Legal Texts and Legal Issues: Proceedings of the Second Meeting of the International Organization for Qumran Studies, Cambridge, 1995: Published in Honour of Joseph M. Baumgarten*, eds. Moshe J. Bernstein, Florentino García Martínez, and John Kampen, 337–48. STDJ 23. Leiden: Brill, 1997.
———. "The Earthly Nucleus of 1QSa." *DSD* 3 (1996): 253–69.
Hengel, M., J. H. Charlesworth, and D. Mendels. "The Polemical Character of 'On Kingship' in the Temple Scroll: An Attempt at Dating 11QTemple." *JJS* 37 (1986): 28–38.
Himmelfarb, Martha. "Impurity and Sin in 4QD, 1QS, and 4Q512." *DSD* 8 (2001): 9–37.
———. "Sexual Relations and Purity in the Temple Scroll." *DSD* 6 (1999): 11–36.
Holmén, Tom. "Divorce in CD 4:20–5:2 and 11QT 57:17–18 Some Remarks on the Pertinence of the Question." *RevQ* 18 (1998): 397–408.

Hübner, H. "Zolibat in Qumran." *NTS* 16 (1970–71): 153–67.
Ilan, Tal. "The Provocative Approach Once Again: A Response to Adiel Schremer." *HTR* 91 (1998): 203–4.
———. *Mine and Yours are Hers: Retrieving Women's History from Rabbinic Literature*. Leiden: Brill, 1997.
———. "Notes and Observations On a Newly Published Divorce Bill from the Judaean Desert." *HTR* 89 (1996): 195–202.
———. *Jewish Women in Greco-Roman Palestine*. Peabody, Mass.: Hendrickson Publishers, 1995.
Isaksson, Abel. *Marriage and Ministry in the New Temple: A Study with Special Reference* to *Mt. 19.12–13 and 1 Cor. 11.3–6* . Uppsala Universitet Nytestamentliga Seminar Acta 24. Lund: C. W. K. Gleerup, 1965.
Iwry, Samuel. "Was There a Migration to Damascus? The Problem of שבי ישראל." *ErIsr* 9 (1969): 80–8.
Jackson, Bernard S. "Damascus Document IX, 16–23 and Parallels." *RevQ* 9 (1977–8): 445–50.
———. *Essays in Jewish and Comparative Legal History*. Leiden: Brill, 1975.
Japhet, Sarah. "The Prohibition of the Habitation of Women: The Temple Scroll's Attitude Toward Sexual Impurity and Its Biblical Precedents." *JANES* 22 (1993): 69–87.
Jewett, Robert. *The Thessalonian Correspondence: Pauline Rhetoric and Millenarian Piety*. Philadelphia: Fortress Press, 1986.
Jokiranta, Jutta. "'Sectarianism' of the Qumran 'Sect': Sociological Notes." *RevQ* 20 (2001): 223–39.
Kampen, John. "The Significance of the Temple in the Manuscripts of the Damascus Document." In *The Dead Scrolls at Fifty: Proceedings of the 1997 Society of Biblical Literature Qumran Section Meetings,* vol. 2, eds. Robert Kugler and Eileen Schuller, 185–97. Early Judaism and Its Literature 15. Atlanta: Society of Biblical Literature, 1999.
———. "The Matthean Divorce Texts Reexamined." In *New Qumran Texts and Studies: Proceedings of the First International Organization for Qumran Studies, Paris 1992*, eds. George Brooke and Florentino García Martínez, 149–67. STDJ 15. Leiden: Brill, 1994.
———. "A Fresh Look at Masculine Plural Suffix in CD IV, 21." *RevQ* 16 (1993): 91–7.
Karlsen Seim, Turid. *The Double Message: Patterns of Gender in Luke and Acts*. Nashville: Abingdon Press, 1994.
Kee, Howard. "Membership in the Covenant People at Qumran and in the Teaching of Jesus." In *Jesus and the Dead Sea Scrolls*, ed. James Charlesworth, 104–22. New York: Doubleday, 1992.
———. "Satan, Magic and Salvation in the Testament of Job." In *Society of Biblical Literature: 1974 Seminar Papers*, 53–76.
King, Helen. *Hippocrates' Woman: Reading the Female Body in Ancient Greece*. New York: Routledge, 1998.
———. "Producing Woman: Hippocratic Gynaecology." In *Women in Ancient Societies*, eds. Leonie Archer, S. Fischler, and M. Wyhe, 102–14. New York: Routledge, 1994.
Kister, Menahem. "Notes on Some New Texts from Qumran." *JJS* 44 (1993): 280–90.

Knibb, Michael A. "Community Organization in the Damascus Document." In *Encyclopedia of the Dead Sea Scrolls*. 1:136–8.

———. "The Place of the Damascus Document." In *Methods of Investigation of the Dead Sea Scrolls and the Khirbet Qumran Site: Present Realities and Future Prospects*, eds. M. Wise et al., 149–60. Annals of the New York Academy of Sciences 722. New York: New York Academy of Sciences, 1994.

———. "The Interpretation of *Damascus Document* VII, 9b–VIII, 2a and XIX 5b–14." *RevQ* 15 (1991): 243–51.

———. *The Qumran Community*. Cambridge: Cambridge University Press, 1987.

———. "Exile in the Damascus Document." *JSOT* 25 (1983): 99–117.

Kosmala, Hans. "The Three Nets of Belial." *ASTI* 4 (1965): 91–113.

Kraemer, Ross S. *Her Share of the Blessings*. New York/Oxford: Oxford University Press, 1992.

———. "Jewish Women in the Diaspora World of Late Antiquity." In *Jewish Women in Historical Perspective,* ed. Judith R. Baskin, 43–65. Detroit: Wayne State University Press, 1991.

———. "Monastic Jewish Women in Greco-Roman Egypt: Philo Judaeus on the Therapeutrides." *Signs* 14 (1989): 342–70.

Kugler, Robert. "Rewriting Rubrics: Sacrifice and the Religion of Qumran." In *Religion in the Dead Sea Scrolls*, eds. John J. Collins and Robert A. Kugler, 90–112. Grand Rapids, Mich.: Eerdmans, 2000.

Laato, Antii. "The Chronology of the Damascus Document of Qumran." *RevQ* 15 (1992): 605–7.

Laperrousaz, Ernest-Marie. "Brevès remarques archaeologiques concernant la chronologie des occupations esséniens de Qoumrân." *RevQ* 12 (1986): 199–212.

———. *Qoumrân, l'établissement essénien des bords de la Mer Morte: Histoire et archéologie du site*. Paris: A & J Picard, 1976.

Levine, Baruch A. "The Temple Scroll: Aspects of its Historical Provenance and Literary Character." *BASOR* 232 (1987): 5–23.

Licht, Jacob. "Some Terms and Concepts of Ritual Purity in The Qumran Writings." In *Studies in the Bible Presented to Professor M. H. Segal*, eds. J. M. Grintz and J. Liver, 300–9. Publications of the Israel Society for Biblical Research 17. Jerusalem: Kiryat Sepher, 1964.

Lieberman, Saul. "The Discipline in the So-Called Dead Sea Manual of Discipline." *JBL* 71 (1951): 199–206.

Liver, J. "The Half-Shekel Offering in Biblical and Post-Biblical Literature." *HTR* (1963): 173–98.

Lyons, W.J. and A.M. Reimer. "The Demonic Virus and Qumran Studies: Some Preventative Measures." *DSD* 5 (1998): 16–32.

Magness, Jodi *The Archaeology of Qumran and the Dead Sea Scrolls*. Grand Rapids, Mich.: Eerdmans, 2002.

———. "Women at Qumran?" In *What Athens Has to Do with Jerusalem: Essays on Classical, Jewish, and Early Christian Art and Archaeology in Honor of Gideon Foerster*, ed. Leonard Victor Rutgers, 26–9. Interdisciplinary Studies in Ancient Culture and Religion 1. Leuven: Peeters Publishers, 2002.

———. "The Chronology of the Settlement of Qumran in the Herodian Period." *DSD* 2 (1995): 58–65.
Maier, Johann. "Ritual of Marriage." In *Encyclopedia of the Dead Sea Scrolls*. 2:783.
———. *Die Texte vom Toten Meer*. Munich: Ernest Reinhardt, 1960.
Maier, Johann and Kurt Schubert. *Die Qumran-Essener: Texte der Schriftrollen und Lebensbild der Gemeinde*. München: E. Reinhardt, 1973.
Marcus, Ralph. "Philo, Josephus and the Dead Sea Yahad." *JBL* 71 (1952): 207–9.
Martens, John. "A Sectarian Analysis of the Damascus Document." In *Essays in the Social Scientific Study of Judaism and Jewish Society*, eds. Simcha Fishbane and Jack Lightstone, 27–46. Canada-Israel Conference on the Social Scientific Study of Judaism. Montreal: Concordia University, 1990.
Martínez, Florentino García. "The Temple Scroll and the New Jerusalem." In *The Dead Sea Scrolls After Fifty Years: A Comprehensive Assessment*, eds. Peter W. Flint and James VanderKam, 2: 431–60. Leiden: Brill, 1998.
———. "New Perspectives on the Study of the Dead Sea Scrolls." In *Perspectives in the Study of the Old Testament and Early Judaism: A Symposium in Honour of Adam S van der Woude on the Occasion of his 70th Birthday*, eds. Florentino García Martínez and Ed Noort, 230–48. VTSup 73. Leiden: Brill, 1998.
———. "Damascus Document: A Bibliography of Studies 1970–89." In *The Damascus Document Reconsidered*, ed. Magen Broshi, 63–83. Jerusalem: The Israel Exploration Society, 1992.
Martínez, Florentino García and Julio Trebolle Barrera. *The People of the Dead Sea Scrolls*. Trans. Wilfred Watson. Leiden: Brill, 1995.
Martínez, Florentino García and A.S. van der Woude. "A 'Groningen' Hypothesis of Qumran Origins and Early History." *RevQ* 14 (1990): 521–41
Martin, Dale. "Slavery and the Ancient Jewish Family." In *The Jewish Family in Antiquity*, ed. Shaye Cohen, 113–29. BJS 289. Atlanta: Scholars Press, 1993.
Marx, A. "Les racines du célibate essénien." *RevQ* 7 (1970): 323–42.
Mason, Steve. *Flavius Josephus on the Pharisees*. Leiden: Brill, 1991.
———. "Josephus and the Pharisees Reconsidered: A Critique of Smith/Neusner." *SR* 17 (1988): 455–69.
Matthews, Victor and Don Benjamin. "Social Sciences and Biblical Studies." *Semeia* 68 (1994): 7–21.
McGuire, Meredith. *Religion: The Social Context*. 3d ed. Belmont: Wadsworth Publishing Company, 1992.
McKane, W. "Poison, Trial by Ordeal and the Cup of Wrath." *VT* 30 (1980): 475–92.
Meeks, Wayne. "The Image of the Androgyne: Some Uses of a Symbol in Earliest Christianity." *HR* 13 (1973): 165–208.
Mendelsohn, S. *The Criminal Jurisprudence of the Ancient Hebrews*. 2nd ed. New York: Hermon Press, 1968.
Metso, Sarianna. "The Relationship between the Damascus Document and the Community Rule." In *The Damascus Document: A Centennial of Discovery. Proceedings of the Third International Symposium of the Orion Center for the Study of the Dead Sea Scrolls and Associated Literature, 4–8 February, 1998*, eds. Joseph M. Baumgarten, Esther G. Chazon, and Avital Pinnick, 85–93. STDJ 35. Leiden: Brill, 2000.

———. "In Search of the Sitz im Leben of the Community Rule." In *Provo International Conference on the Dead Sea Scrolls*, eds. Donald Parry and Eugene Ulrich, 306–15. STDJ 30. Leiden: Brill, 1999.

———. "Constitutional Rules at Qumran." In *The Dead Sea Scrolls after Fifty Years: A Comprehensive Assessment*, eds. Peter W. Flint and James VanderKam, 1:186–210. Leiden: Brill, 1998.

———. *Textual Development of the Qumran Community Rule*. STDJ 21. Leiden: Brill, 1997.

Milgrom, Jacob. "4QTohora[a]: An Unpublished Qumran Text on Purities." In *Time to Prepare the Way in the Wilderness: Papers on the Qumran Scrolls by Fellows of the Institute for Advanced Studies of the Hebrew University, Jerusalem, 1989–1990*, eds. Devorah Dimant and Lawrence H. Schiffman, 59–68. STDJ 16. Leiden: Brill, 1995.

———. "The City of the Temple: A Response to Lawrence H. Schiffman." *JQR* 85 (1994): 125–8.

———. *Leviticus 1–16: A New Translation with Introduction and Commentary*. Vol. 3 of The Anchor Bible. New York: Doubleday, 1991.

———. *JPS Torah Commentary: Numbers*. Philadelphia: Jewish Publication Society, 1990.

———. "The Scriptural Foundations and Deviations in the Laws of Purity of the Temple Scroll." In *Archaeology and History in the Dead Sea Scrolls: The New York University Conference in Memory of Yigal Yadin*, ed. Lawrence H. Schiffman, 83–99. JSPSup 8. Sheffield: JSOT Press, 1990.

———. "The Case of the Suspected Adulteress, Numbers 5:11–31: Redaction and Meaning." In *Women in the Hebrew Bible: A Reader*, ed. Alice Bach, 475–82. New York: Routledge, 1999. First published in *Creation of Sacred Literature: Composition and Redaction of the Biblical Text*, ed. Richard Elliot Freedman, 69–75. Berkeley: University of California Press, 1981.

———. "Further Studies in the Temple Scroll." *JQR* 71 (1980): 89–106.

———. "The Temple Scroll." *BA* 41 (1978): 105–20.

———. "Studies in the Temple Scroll." *JBL* 97 (1978): 501–23.

———. "The Bethrothed Slave-Girl, Lev 19:20–22." *ZAW* 89 (1977): 43–50.

Milik, Jósef.T. "Milkî-sedeq and Milkî-resa dans les anciens écrits juifs et chrétiens." *JJS* 23 (1972): 95–144.

———. *Ten Years of Discovery in the Judean Wilderness*. London: SCM Press, 1959.

———. "Le travail d'édition des manuscrits du Desert de Juda." In *Volume du Congrès, Strasbourg 1956*, 16–26. VTSup 4. Leiden: Brill, 1956.

Moehring, Horst R. "Josephus on the Marriage Customs of the Essenes." In *Early Christian Origins: Studies in Honour of Harold R. Willoughby*, ed. Allen Wikgren, 120–7. Chicago: Quadrangle Books, 1961.

Murphy, Catherine. *Wealth in the Dead Sea Scrolls and in the Qumran Community*. STDJ 40. Leiden: Brill, 2002.

Murphy-O'Connor, Jerome. "The Judean Desert." In *Early Judaism and its Modern Interpreters*, eds. Robert Kraft and George Nickelsburg, 119–56. Vol. 2 of *The Bible and Its Modern Interpreters*, ed. Douglas A. Knight. Philadelphia: Fortress Press, 1986.

———. "The Essenes and Their History." *RB* 81 (1974): 215–44.

———. "The Original Text of CD 7:9–8:2=19:5–14." *HTR* 64 (1971): 379–86.

———. "A Literary Analysis of the Damascus Document VI,2–VIII, 3." *RB* 78 (1971): 210–32.
———. "An Essene Missionary Document? CD II, 14–VI, 1." *RB* 77 (1970): 201–29.
———. *Paul and Qumran*. London: Geoffrey Chapman, 1968.
Neusner, Jacob. *A History of the Mishnaic Law of Purities. Part Twenty-Two: The Mishnaic System of Uncleanness*, ed. J. Neusner. SJLA 6. Leiden: Brill, 1977.
———. "By the Testimony of Two Witnesses in the Damascus Document IX, 17–22 and in Pharisaic-Rabbinic Law." *RevQ* 8 (1972–5): 197–217.
———. *The Idea of Purity in Ancient Judaism*. Leiden: Brill, 1973.
Newsom, Carol A. "He Has Established for Himself Priests." In *Archaeology and History in the Dead Sea Scrolls: The New York University Conference in Memory of Yigal Yadin*, ed. Lawrence H. Schiffman, 101–20. JSPSup 8. Sheffield: JSOT Press, 1990.
———. "'Sectually Explicit' Literature from Qumran." In *The Hebrew Bible and Its Interpreters*, eds. William Propp, Baruch Halpern, and David Noel Freedman, 167–87. Winona Lake, Ind.: Eisenbrauns, 1990.
Newton, Michael. *The Concept of Purity at Qumran and in the Letters of Paul*. Cambridge: Cambridge University Press, 1985.
Nitzan, Bilah. "The Laws of Reproof in 4QBerakhot (4Q286–290) in Light of their Parallels in the Damascus Covenant and Other Texts from Qumran." In *Legal Texts and Legal Issues: Proceedings of the Second Meeting of the International Organization for Qumran Studies, Cambridge, 1995: Published in Honour of Joseph M. Baumgarten*, eds. Moshe J. Bernstein, Florentino García Martínez, and John Kampen, 149–65. STDJ 23. Leiden: Brill, 1997.
———. "4QBerhakhot $^{a-e}$ (4Q286–290): A Covenantal Ceremony in the Light of Related Texts." *RevQ* 16 (1995): 487–506.
———. *Qumran Prayer and Religious Poetry*. STDJ 12. Leiden: Brill, 1994.
Nodet, E. "La loi à Qumran et Schiffman." *RB* 102 (1995): 38–71.
Noonan, John. *Contraception: A History of Its Treatment by the Catholic Theologians and Canonists*. Cambridge, Mass.: Harvard University Press, 1965.
O'Donnell Setel, Dorah. "Exodus." In *The Women's Bible Commentary*, eds. Carol A. Newsom and Sharon H. Ringe, 26–35. Louisville, Ky.: Westminster/John Knox Press, 1992.
O'Connor, M. "Biblical Hebrew Lexicography: טף 'Children, Dependents' in Biblical and Qumran Hebrew." *JNSL* 25 (1999): 25–40.
Paterson Corrington, Gail. "The Milk of Salvation: Redemption by the Mother in Later Antiquity and Early Christianity." *HTR* 82 (1989): 393–420.
Plaskow, Judith. *Standing Again at Sinai: Judaism from a Feminist Perspective*. San Francisco: Harper, 1991.
Phillips, Anthony. *Ancient Israel's Criminal Law: A New Approach to the Decalogue*. New York: Schocken Books, 1970.
Pomeroy, Sarah B. *Goddesses, Whores, Wives, and Slaves: Women in Classical Antiquity*. New York: Schocken Books, 1975.
Porten, Bezalel. "Five Fragmentary Aramaic Marriage Documents: New Collations and Restorations." *Abr-Nahrain* 27 (1989): 80–105.

Pressler, Carolyn. "Wives and Daugthers, Bond and Free: Views of Women in the Slave Laws of Exodus 21:2–11." In *Gender and Law in the Hebrew Bible and the Ancient Near East*, eds. Victor Matthews, Bernard Levinson, and Tikva Frymer-Kensy, 147–72. JSOTSup 262. Sheffield: Sheffield Academic Press, 1998.

———. "Sexual Violence and Deuteronomic Law." *A Feminist Companion to Exodus-Deuteronomy*, ed. Athalya Brenner, 102–12. Feminist Companion to the Bible 6. Sheffield: Sheffield Academic Press, 1994.

Qimron, Elisha. "לשיפור המהדורות של מגילות מדבר יהודה," ("Improvements to the Editions of the Dead Sea Scrolls"). *ErIsr* 26 (1999): 142–6 (Hebrew).

———. "Further Observations on the Laws of Oaths in the Damascus Document 15." *JQR* 85 (1994): 251–7.

———. "Celibacy in the Dead Sea Scrolls and the Two Kinds of Sectarians." In *The Madrid Qumran Congress: Proceedings of the International Congress on the Dead Sea Scrolls, Madrid 18–21 March 1991*, eds. Julio Trebolle Barrera and Luis Vegas Montaner, 1:286–94. STDJ 11. Leiden: Brill, 1992.

———. "לשבועת הבנים in the Damascus Covenant 15.1–2." *JQR* 81 (1990): 115–18.

———. "The Holiness of the Holy Land in the Light of a New Document from Qumran." In *The Holy Land in History and Thought*, ed. Moshe Sharon, 9–13. Leiden: Brill, 1988.

———. "The Halacha of Damascus Covenant. An Interpretation of 'Al Yitarev'." In *Proceedings of the Ninth World Congress of Jewish Studies, Jerusalem, Aug 1985*, Vol.1. Jerusalem: World Union of Jewish Studies, 1986: 9–15 (Hebrew).

———. "Davies' the Damascus Covenant," *JQR* 77 (1986): 84–7.

———. *The Hebrew of the Dead Sea Scrolls.* HSS 29. Atlanta: Scholars Press, 1986.

Rabinovitch, N. L. "Damascus Document IX, 17–22 and Rabbinic Parallels." *RevQ* 9 (1977–8): 113–16.

Rajak, Tessa. "Women Benefactors and Community Practices." In *The Jews Among Pagans and Christians in the Roman Empire*, eds. J. Lieu, J. North, and T. Rajak, 22–7. London/New York: Routledge, 1992.

Rawson, Beryl. "The Roman Family." In *The Family in Ancient Roman: New Perspective*, ed. B. Rawson, 1–57. Ithaca, N.Y.: Cornell University Press, 1986.

Riaud, Jean. "Les Thérapeutes d'Alexandria dans la tradition et dans la recherche critique jusqu'aux découvertes de Qumrân." In *Aufstieg und Niedergang der römischen Welt: Geschichte und Kultur Roms im Spiegel der neureren Forschung* 2/20/2, 1189–1295. Berlin: De Gruyter, 1987.

Richardson, Neil. "Some Notes on 1QSa." *JBL* 76 (1957): 108–22.

Rouselle, Aline. *Porneia: On Desire and the Body in Antiquity*. Trans. Felicia Pheasant. Oxford: Basil Blackwell, 1988.

Rubenstein, Arie. "Urban Halakhah and Camp Rules in the Cairo Fragments of the Damescene Covenant." *Sefared* 12 (1952): 283–96.

Safrai, Shmuel. "Jerusalem in the Halacha of the Second Temple Period." In *The Centrality of Jerusalem: Historical Perspectives*, eds. Marcel Poorthuis and Chana Safrai, 94–113. Kampen, Netherlands: Kok Pharos Publishing House, 1996.

———. "Teaching of Pietists in Mishnaic Literature." *JJS* 16 (1965): 15–33.

Sakenfeld, Katherine Doob. "Numbers." In *The Women's Bible Commentary*, eds. Carol A. Newsom and Sharon H. Ringe, 45–51. Louisville, Ky.: Westminster/John Knox Press, 1992.
Saladarini, Anthony. "Sectarianism." In *Encyclopedia of the Dead Sea Scrolls*. 2:855.
Sanders, E. P. *Judaism: Practice & Belief 63 B.C.E.–63 C.E.* London: SCM Press/Philadelphia: Trinity Press International, 1992.
———. *Jewish Law from Jesus to the Mishnah: Five Studies.* London: SCM Press/ Philadelphia: Trinity Press International, 1990.
Satlow, Michael. *Jewish Marriage in Antiquity*. Princeton: Princeton University Press, 2001.
———. "4Q502 A New Year Festival?" *DSD* 5 (1998): 57–68.
———. *Tasting the Dish: The Rabbinic Rhetorics of Sexuality*. BJS 303. Atlanta: Scholars Press, 1995.
———. "Reconsidering the Rabbinic Ketubah Payment." In *The Jewish Family in Antiquity*, ed. Shaye Cohen, 133–51. BJS 289. Atlanta: Scholars Press, 1993.
Schiffman, Lawrence. "The Relationship of the Zadokite Fragments to the Temple Scroll." In *The Damascus Document: A Centennial of Discovery. Proceedings of the Third International Symposium of the Orion Center for the Study of the Dead Sea Scrolls and Associated Literature, 4–8 February, 1998*, eds. Joseph M. Baumgarten, Esther G. Chazon, and Avital Pinnick, 133–44. STDJ 35. Leiden: Brill, 2000.
———. "Sabbath." In *Encyclopedia of the Dead Sea Scrolls*. 2: 805–7.
———. "*Ir Ha-Miqdash* and Its Meaning in the Temple Scroll and Other Qumran Texts." In *Sanctity of Time and Space in Tradition and Modernity,* eds. A. Houtman, A. Poorthuis, and J. Schwartz, 95–109. Leiden: Brill, 1998.
———. "The Place of 4QMMT in the Corpus of Qumran Manuscripts." In *Reading 4QMMT: New Perspectives on Qumran Law and History*, eds. John Kampen and Moshe Bernstein, 81–98. SBLSymS 2. Atlanta: Scholars Press, 1996.
———. "The Theology of the Temple Scroll." *JQR* 85 (1994): 118–21.
———. "The Temple Scroll and the Nature of Its Law: The Status of the Question." In *The Community of the Renewed Covenant: The Notre Dame Symposium on the Dead Sea Scrolls*, eds. E. Ulrich and J. VanderKam, 37–55. Notre Dame, Ind.: University of Notre Dame, 1994.
———. *Reclaiming the Dead Sea Scrolls*. Philadelphia: The Jewish Publication Society, 1994.
———. "Pharisaic and Sadducean Halakhah in Light of the Dead Sea Scrolls." *DSD* 3 (1994): 285–99.
———. "New Halakhic Texts from Qumran." *HS* 34 (1993): 21–31.
———. "Laws Pertaining to Women in the Temple Scroll." In *The Dead Sea Scrolls: Forty Years of Research*, eds. Devorah Dimant and Uriel Rappaport, 210–28. Leiden: Brill/Jerusalem: Magness Press, 1992.
———. "The Law of Vows and Oaths (Num. 30: 3–16) in the Zadokite Fragments and the Temple Scroll." *RevQ* 15 (1991): 199–214.
———. "The New Halakhic Letter (4QMMT) and the Origins of the Dead Sea Sect." *BA* 53 (1990): 64–73.
———. "The Impurity of the Dead in the Temple Scroll." In *Archaeology and History in the Dead Sea Scrolls: The New York University Conference in Memory of Yigal Yadin*, ed. Lawrence H. Schiffman, 135–56. JSPSup 8. Sheffield: JSOT Press, 1990.

———. *The Eschatological Community of the Dead Sea Scrolls: A Study of the Rule of the Congregation.* SBLMS 38. Atlanta: Scholars Press, 1989.

———. "*Miqsat Ma'aseh Ha-Torah* and the Temple Scroll." *RevQ* 14 (1989–90): 435–57.

———. "Architecture and Law: The Temple and its Courtyards in the Temple Scroll." In *From Ancient Israel to Modern Judaism: Intellect in Quest of Understanding, Essays in Honor of Marvin Fox*, eds. J. Neusner, Ernest Frerichs, and Nahum Sarna, 1: 267–84. BJS 159. Atlanta: Scholars Press, 1989.

———. "The Temple Scroll and the Systems of Jewish Law of the Second Temple Period." In *Temple Scroll Studies: Papers Presented at the International Symposium on the Temple Scroll, Manchester, December 1987*, ed. George J. Brooke, 239–55. JSPSup 7. Sheffield: JSOT Press, 1987.

———. "Exclusion from the Sanctuary and the City of the Sanctuary in the Temple Scroll." *HAR* 9 (1985): 301–20.

———. "Purity and Perfection: Exclusion from the Council of the Community." In *Biblical Archaeology Today: Proceedings of the International Congress on Biblical Archaeology, Jerusalem 1984*, ed. J. Amitai, 373–89. Jerusalem: Israel Exploration Society, The Israel Academy of Sciences and Humanities, in cooperation with the American Schools of Oriental Research, 1985.

———. "Legislation Concerning Relations with Non-Jews in the Zadokite Fragments and in Tannaitic Literature." *RevQ* 11 (1983): 379–89.

———. *Sectarian Law in the Dead Sea Scrolls: Courts, Testimony and the Penal Code.* BJS 38. Chico, Calif.: Scholars Press, 1983.

———. *The Halakah at Qumran*, ed. Jacob Neusner. SJLA 16. Leiden: Brill, 1975.

Scholem, Gershom. *Major Trends in Jewish Mysticism.* 3rd ed. New York: Schocken Books, 1971.

———. *Jewish Gnosticism, Merkabah Mysticism, and Talmudic Tradition.* New York: The Jewish Theological Seminary of America, 1960.

Schremer, Adiel. "Qumran Polemic on Marital Law: CD 4:20–5:11 and Its Social Background." In *The Damascus Document: A Centennial of Discovery. Proceedings of the Third International Symposium of the Orion Center for the Study of the Dead Sea Scrolls and Associated Literature, 4–8 February, 1998*, eds. Joseph M. Baumgarten, Esther G. Chazon, and Avital Pinnick, 147–60. STDJ 35. Leiden: Brill, 2000.

———. "Divorce in Papyrus Se'elim 13 Once Again: A Reply to Tal Ilan." *HTR* 91 (1998): 193–202.

Schuller, Eileen. "Women in the Dead Sea Scrolls." In *The Dead Sea Scrolls after Fifty Years: A Comprehensive Assessment*, eds. Peter W. Flint and James VanderKam, 2:117–44. Leiden: Brill, 1998.

———. "Evidence for Women in the Community of the Dead Sea Scrolls." In *Voluntary Associations in the Graeco-Roman World*, eds. John S. Kloppenborg and Stephen G. Wilson, 252–65. New York: Routledge, 1996.

———. "Women in the Dead Sea Scrolls." In *Methods of Investigation of the Dead Sea Scrolls and the Khirbet Qumran Site: Present Realities and Future Prospects*, eds. Michael Wise et al., 115–31. Annals of the New York Academy of Sciences 722. New York: New York Academy of Sciences, 1994.

Schuller, Eileen and Cecilia Wassen. "Women: Daily Life." In *Encyclopedia of the Dead Sea Scrolls*, 2: 981–4.
Schürer, Emil. *The History of the Jewish People in the Age of Jesus Christ (175 B.C.–A.D. 135)*. 3 vols. Trans. T. A. Burkill, edited and revised by Geza Vermes and Fergus Millar. Edinburgh: Clark, 1979.
Sebesta, Judith. "Symbolism in the Costume of the Roman Woman." In *The World of the Roman Costume*, eds. Judith Lynn Sebesta and Larissa Bonfante, 46–53. Madison, Wis.: University of Wisconsin Press, 1994.
Sheffer, Avigail. "Textiles." In *Encyclopedia of the Dead Sea Scrolls*. 2: 938–43.
Shemesh, Aaron. "4Q271.3: A Key to Sectarian Matrimonial Law." *JJS* 49 (1998): 244–63.
———. "'The Holy Angels are in Their Council': The Exclusion of Deformed Persons from Holy Places in Qumranic and Rabbinic Literature." *DSD* 4 (1997): 179–206.
Sievers, Joseph. "The Role of Women in the Hasmonean Dynasty." In *Josephus, the Bible, and History*, eds. Louis H. Feldman and Gohei Hata, 132–46. Detroit: Wayne State University Press, 1989.
Sheridan, Susan Guise. "Scholars, Soldiers, Craftsmen, Elites? Analysis of French Collection of Human Remains from Qumran." *DSD* 9 (2002): 199–248.
Simon, Marcel. *Jewish Sects at the Time of Jesus*. Trans. James H. Farley. Philadelphia: Fortress Press, 1967.
Sissa, Guilia. "Maidenhood Without Maidenhead: The Female Body in Ancient Greece." In *Before Sexuality: The Construction of the Erotic Experience in the Ancient Greek*, eds. David Halperin et al., 339–64. Princeton N.J.: Princeton University Press, 1990.
Sly, Dorothy. *Philo's Perception of Women*. Atlanta: Scholars Press, 1990.
Smith, Morton. "The Description of the Essenes in Josephus and in the Philosophumena." *HUCA* 29 (1958): 273–313.
Solomon, Avi. "The Prohibition Against Tevul Yom and Defeilement of the Daily Whole Offering in the Jerusalem Temple in CD 11:21–12:1: A New Understanding." *DSD* 4 (1997): 1–20.
Stagg, Evelyn and Frank. *Woman in the World of Jesus*. Philadelphia: Westminster Press, 1978.
Stark, Rodney and William Bainbridge. *A Theory of Religion*. Toronto Studies in Religion 2. New York: Peter Lang, 1987.
———. *The Future of Religion: Secularisation, Revival, and Cult Formation*. Berkely: University of California Press, 1985.
Stegemann, Hartmut. "Towards Physical Reconstructions of the Qumran Damascus Document Scrolls." In *The Damascus Document: A Centennial of Discovery. Proceedings of the Third International Symposium of the Orion Center for the Study of the Dead Sea Scrolls and Associated Literature, 4–8 February, 1998*, eds. Joseph M. Baumgarten, Esther G. Chazon, and Avital Pinnick, 177–200. STDJ 35. Leiden: Brill, 2000.
———. The *Library of Qumran: On the Essenes, Qumran, John the Baptist, and Jesus*. Grand Rapids, Mich./Cambridge, U.K: Eerdmans, 1998. Originally published as *Die Essener, Qumran, Johannes der Täufer und Jesus* (1993).
———. "More Identified Fragments of 4QD^d (4Q269)." *RevQ* 18 (1998): 497–509.
———. "Some Remarks to 1QSa, to 1QSb, and to Qumran Messianism." *RevQ* 17 (1996): 479–505.

———. "The Qumran Essenes—Local Members of the Main Jewish Union in Late Second Temple Times." In *The Madrid Qumran Congress: Proceedings of the International Congress on the Dead Sea Scrolls, Madrid 18–21 March 1991*, eds. Julio Trebolle Barrera and Luis Vegas Montaner, 2:83–166. STDJ 11. Leiden: Brill, 1992.

Steudel, Annette. "God and Belial." In *The Dead Scrolls: Fifty Years after Their Discovery 1947–1997: Proceedings of the Jerusalem Congress, July 20–25, 1997,* eds. Lawrence H. Schiffman, Emanuel Tov, and James C. VanderKam, 332–40. Jerusalem: Israel Exploration Society in cooperation with the Shrine of the Book, Israel Museum, 2000.

———. "The Houses of Prostration: CD XI, 21–XII. 1.–Duplicates of the Temple (1)." *RevQ* 16 (1993): 49–67.

———. " אחרית הימים in the Texts from Qumran." *RevQ* 16 (1993): 225–46.

Stone, Shelley. "The Toga: From National to Ceremonial Costume." In *The World of the Roman Costume*, eds. Judith Lynn Sebesta and Larissa Bonfante, 13–45. Madison: University of Wisconsin Press, 1994.

Strugnell, John. "More on Wives and Marriage in the Dead Sea Scrolls (4Q416 2 ii 21 [cf. 1 Thess. 4:4] and 4QMMT B)." *RevQ* 17 (1996): 537–47.

———. "The Qumran Scrolls: A Report on Work in Progress." In *Jewish Civilization in the Hellenistic Roman Period*, ed. S. Talmon, 94–106. Philadelphia: Sheffield Academic Press, 1991.

———. "Notes en Marge du Volume V des 'Discoveries in the Judean Desert of Jordan'." *RevQ* 26 (1970): 163–276.

———. "Flavius Josephus and the Essenes: Antiquities XVIII.18–22." *JBL* 77 (1958): 106–15.

Stulman, Louis. "Enchroachment in Deuteronomy: An Analysis of the Social World of the D Code." *JBL* 109 (1990): 613–32.

Sukenik, Eleazar L. *Otzar Ha-Megilloth Ha-Genuzoth*. Jerusalem: Baliak, 1954 (Hebrew).

Talmon, Shemaryahu. "The Community of the Renewed Covenant: Between Judaism and Christianity." In *The Community of the Renewed Covenant: The Notre Dame Symposium on the Dead Sea Scrolls*, eds. E. Ulrich and J. VanderKam, 3–24. Notre Dame, Ind.: University of Notre Dame, 1994.

———. "The Emergence of Institutionalized Prayer in Israel in the Light of the Qumran Literature." In *Qumrân: Sa piété, sa théologie et son milieu*, ed. M. Delcor, 265–84. Paris: Gembloux/Leuven: University Press, 1978.

———. "The 'Desert Motif' in the Bible and in Qumran Literature." In *Biblical Motifs: Origins and Transformations*, ed. Alexander Altmann, 31–63. Cambridge, Mass.: Harvard University Press, 1966.

Taylor, Joan. "The Cemeteries of Khirbet Qumran and Women's Presence at the Site." *DSD* 6 (1999): 285–323.

Tigchelaar, Eibert. "More Identifications of Scraps and Overlaps." *RevQ* 19 (1999): 61–8.

Tigay, Jeffrey. "Examination of the Accused Bride in 4Q159: Forensic Medicine at Qumran." *JANES* 22 (1993): 129–34.

Trebilco, Paul R. *Jewish Communities in Asia Minor*. Cambridge: Cambridge University Press, 1991.

Todd, Emmanuel. *The Explanation of Ideology: Family Structures and Social Systems*. Oxford: Blackwell, 1985.

Tosato, Angelo. "Su di una Norma Matrimoniale 4QD." *Biblica* 74 (1993): 401–10.
Ubigli, Liliana Rosso. "Il Documento Di Damsco e L'Etica Coniugale: A Proposito di un Nuovo Passo Qumranico." *Henoch* 14 (1992): 3–10.
———. "Alcuni Aspetti Della Conzione Della *Porneia* nel Tardo-Giudaismo." *Henoch* 1 (1979): 201–45.
VanderKam, James. *The Dead Sea Scrolls Today*. Grand Rapids, Mich.: Eerdmans, 1994.
VanderKam, James and Peter Flint. *The Meaning of the Dead Sea Scrolls: Their Significance for Understanding the Bible, Judaism, Jesus, and Christianity*. San Francisco: HarperSanFrancisco, 2002.
Van der Horst, Pieter. "Images of Women in the Testament of Job." In *Studies on the Testament of Job*, eds. M. A. Knibb and P. W. van der Horst, 93–116. SNTSMS 66. Cambridge: Cambridge University Press, 1989.
Vermes, Geza. *Post-Biblical Jewish Studies*. Leiden: Brill, 1975.
———. "Sectarian Matrimonial Halakhah in the Damascus Rule." *JJS* 25 (1974): 197–202.
Vermes, Geza and Martin Goodman. *The Essenes According to the Classical Sources*. Sheffield: JSOT Press, 1989.
Wachholder, Ben Zion. "The Preamble to the Damascus Document: A Composite Edition of 4Q266–4Q268." *HUCA* 69 (1998): 31–47.
Wacker, Marie-Therese. "Methods of Feminist Exegesis." In *Feminist Interpretation: The Bible in Women's Perspective*, eds. Luise Schottroff, Silva Schroerer, and Marie-Therese Wacker, 63–82. Minneapolis: Fortress Press, 1998.
Wallis, Ray. "The Cult and Its Transformation." In *Sectarianism: Analyses of Religious and Non-Religious Sects*, ed. R. Wallis, 35–47. London: Peter Owen, 1975.
Wassen, Cecilia. "The Story of Judah and Tamar in the Eyes of the Earliest Interpreters." *Literature and Theology* 8 (1994): 354–66.
Wegner, Judith R. *Chattel or Person? The Status of Women in the Mishnah*. New York: Oxford University Press, 1992.
———. "The Image and Status of Women in Classical Rabbinical Judaism." In *Jewish Women in Historical Perspective*, ed. Judith R. Baskin, 68–93. Detroit: Wayne State University Press, 1991.
Weinfeld, Moshe. *The Organizational Patterns and the Penal Code of the Qumran Sect: A Comparison with Guilds and Religious Associations*. NTAO 2. Göttingen: Vandenhoeck & Ruprecht, 1986.
Westbrook, Raymond. "The Female Slave." In *Gender and Law in the Hebrew Bible and the Ancient Near East*, eds. Victor Matthews, Bernard Levinson, and Tikva Frymer-Kensky, 214–38. JSOTSup 262. Sheffield: Sheffield Academic Press, 1998.
Wilson, Bryan. *The Social Dimensions of Sectarianism: Sects and New Religious Movements in Contemporary Society*. Oxford: Clarendon Press, 1990.
———. *Religion in Sociological Perspective*. Oxford: Oxford University Press, 1982.
———. "An Analysis of Sect Development." *American Sociological Review* 24 (1959): 3–15.
Winter, Paul. "Sadokite Fragments IV 20, 21 and the Exegesis of Genesis 1:27 in Late Judaism." *ZAW* 68 (1956): 71–84.
Wise, Michael O. "4QFlorilegium and the Temple of Adam." *RevQ* 15 (1991): 103–32.
———. *A Critical Study of the Temple Scroll from Qumran Cave 11*. SAOC 49. Chicago, Ill.: The Oriental Institute of the University of Chicago, 1990.

Worrell, John. "עצה: 'Counsel' or 'Council' at Qumran?" *VT* 20 (1970): 65–74.
Yadin, Yigael. "L'attitude essénienne envers la polygamy et le divorce." *RB* 79 (1972): 98–9.

Index of Biblical Texts

Hebrew Bible

Genesis
1:27 116
1:28 178
7:9 116
9:1 178
9:7 178
16:29–30 128
19:8 73
24:14 79
24:15 79
24:48 79
34:1–31 84
35:16–19 58
35:22 176
38 .... 82, 176
45:8 186
46:26 63
48:15 185
48:16 185
49:3–4 176

Exodus
1:5 63
4:11 148
6:25 186
13:5 185
15:24 189
16:2 189
16:29 96
17:3 189
19 .... 137, 143
19:1 27
19:10–15 143
19:15 .... 98, 137
20:7 107
20:8 93
20:10 70
20:16 8

21:7–11 71
21:9 .... 61, 69
21:10 .... 61, 68
21:26–27 71
22:22 169
23:1–2 88
26:36 .... 190, 194
27:16 190
28:39 .... 190, 194
30:11–14 139
31:12–17 93
38:18 194
38:26 139
39:29 .... 190, 194

Leviticus
4:13 163
5 70
5:7 70
5:10 70
7:20 56
11 40
12 .... 47, 54
12–15 .... 46, 104
12:1–5 .... 53, 55
12:2 53
12:2–5 55
12:2–8 .... 55, 56
12:4 .... 3, 54, 55, 58
12:6 57
12:6–7 57
12:17 46
13–14 47
15 .... 48, 49, 52, 53, 58
15:1–15 47
15:2 48
15:2–15 48
15:4–12 49
15:7 .... 48, 50, 53
15:11 .... 48, 50

Leviticus (*continued*)
- 15:13–15 48
- 15:16–18 .... 47, 49
- 15:18 .... 49, 98, 101
- 15:19 .... 49, 50, 53, 119
- 15:19–22 50
- 15:19–24 47
- 15:20–23 50
- 15:22 53
- 15:24 .... 52, 119
- 15:25 .... 50, 53, 58, 119
- 15:25–30 47
- 15:29 54
- 15:31 .... 55, 56
- 18:6–18 120
- 18:13 .... 121, 209
- 18:18 .... 116, 128
- 18:22 109
- 19:10–11 169
- 19:19 76
- 19:20 68
- 19:20–22 .... 59, 68, 71
- 19:22 70
- 20:10 62
- 20:13 109
- 20:18 46
- 21 .... 80, 148
- 21:7 .... 73, 77, 159, 178
- 21:7–8a 80
- 21:13 73
- 21:13–14a 80
- 21:14 .... 77, 159
- 21:16–24 .... 150, 152
- 21:17 73
- 21:17–23 .... 74, 148
- 21:18–20 148
- 21:23 .... 148, 150
- 22:3 56
- 22:28 110
- 25 73
- 25:14 .... 73, 74
- 25:25 170
- 26 125
- 26:15 125
- 26:18 164
- 26:28 164
- 26:43–46 125

Numbers
- 1:2ff 139
- 1:2–3 152
- 2:17 128
- 2:32–34 128
- 3:15 139
- 4:2 139
- 5 63
- 5:2 53
- 5:11–21 67
- 5:11–31 .... 59, 61, 106, 208
- 5:13 .... 61, 66
- 5:14 64
- 5:15 .... 64, 67
- 5:17 64
- 5:18 .... 64, 67
- 5:20 67
- 5:21 .... 62, 63
- 5:21–23 64
- 5:22 .... 62, 66
- 5:24 .... 62, 64
- 5:27 .... 62, 63
- 5:27–28 .... 62, 66
- 5:28 63
- 7:11–18 54
- 7:20–21 56
- 9:9–14 54
- 10:5–6 128
- 10:25 128
- 11:12 96
- 14:27 189
- 15;22 163
- 15:37–41 193
- 15:38 193
- 15:39 175
- 16:27 165
- 19 50
- 22:23 56
- 25:1 174
- 26:2 139
- 30 .... 92, 93, 117
- 30:1–16 91

Index of Biblical Texts

30:2	91
30:3	91
30:3–16	92, 93, 106
30:6	92
30:6–15	91
30:7–16	92
30:8	92
30:9	92, 159
30:11	91
30:13	91, 92
30:14	92
30:17	123, 127
31–32	165
31:17	73
31:18	73, 165
31:26	186
31:35	73
35:30	62

Deuteronomy

1:39	165
1:41	114
4:27	185
7:9	122
10:22	185
13:2–19	82
14:29	169
15:7–11	169
16:11	169
16:14	169
17:6	65
17:17	116
19:15	62, 65, 88
19:15–20	88
21:1–9	62
21:1–14	69
21:18	164
21:22	55
22	73, 77, 208
22:5	73
22:6–7	110
22:9	77
22:9–11	76
22:10–11	73
22:13–19	73
22:13–21	81, 82, 84, 106, 108, 117, 208
22:13–29	82, 108
22:18	164
22:19	81
22:20–21	82
22:20–24	62
22:21	82, 108
22:22	77
22:23	107
22:23–24	77, 85
22:23–27	68
22:28–29	117
22:29	159
23	152
23:9–10	152
23:9–14	152
23:14	152
23:22–24	93
23:23	91, 92
22:23–27	108
23:24	121
24:1	73, 159, 162
24:1–4	117, 162
24:17	169
26:12	169
27	73
27–28	137, 138
27–30	138
27–31	136
27:1	137
27:15–26	107, 108
27:18	73
27:20–22	108
28:11	137
28:18	137
28:30	108
28:56–67	137
29–30	138
29:10–11	138
29:10–12	138, 154
29:21	138
30:2	138
31:9–11	142
31:9–13	137, 138, 139, 142, 143

Deuteronomy (*continued*)
31:11–12 137
32:6 186
32:28 160

Joshua
14:1 186
19:51 186
24:1–28 137
24:2 137
24:15 137

Judges
5:7 .... 186, 188
5:30 194
7:30 63
17:10 185
18:10 185
20:7 160

Ruth
3:3 73
4:1–10 170

1 Samuel
24:12 185

2 Samuel
11:11 153
24 139

2 Kings
2:12 185
6:21 185
23:2–3 137

1 Chronicles
2:24 185
2:42 185
23:13 77
29:2 .... 190, 194

2 Chronicles
20:5 143
20:13 .... 143, 165
30:25 143
31:18 158
35:3 162

Nehemiah
9–10 138
10:28–29 ....138, 154
31:1 143

Job
31:1 175
31:18 166
42:15 194

Psalms
45:14–15 190
68:6 186
68:30 68
103:13 159
138:15 (LXX) 190
139:15 190

Proverbs
1:29–31 161
1:30–31 161
5:5 160
17:24 175
21:30 160
31:1 164

Ecclesiastes
4:8 175

Isaiah
1:23 169
3:15 169
9:5 185
10:33–34 192
11:1–5 192
22:20 186
24:17 113
25:1 161
28:9 166
28:26 164
28:29 161

Index of Biblical Texts

29:15 161
44:26 161
58:6 159
63:16 186

Jeremiah
3:8 82
29:6 127
31:18 164
32:19 161
34:19 186
49:7 160
49:11 169
49:20 161

Ezekiel
9:6 165
16:8 73
16:10 .... 190, 194
16:13 .... 190, 194
16:18 .... 190, 194
17:3 (LXX) 190
22:29–31 169
26:16 .... 190, 194
27:7 190
27:24 190
34:12 159
34:16 159
44:22 .... 80, 159

Daniel
8:16 162
11:33 162

Hosea
4:15 174
5:11 159
7:15 164
10:10 164

Amos
2:6–7 169

Micah
6:8 .... 159, 164

Malachi
2:14 73
2:16 117
4:5 127

New Testament

Matthew
5:28–29a 175
5:32 162
12:11 93
19:3–9 162
19:4 116

Mark
7:21 176
7:21–22 176
10:4–12 162
10:10–12 116
10:11–12 163

Luke
11:27 57
14:5 93
16:18 162

1 Corinthians
5:1 176
5:11 176
6:9 176
7:2 176
7:10–11 162
11:10 .... 150, 191
11:11 150

2 Corinthians
12:21 176

Galatians
5:19 176

Ephesians
5:3 176

Colossians
3:5 176

1 Thessalonians 174, 176, 178, 182
3:13 177
4:3–6b 176
4:4 177
4:7 177

2 Thessalonians 176

1 Timothy
1:10 176

Hebrews
13:4 176

1 Peter
3:7 177
2 Peter
2:14 175

Revelation 176

Index of Dead Sea Scrolls

1. The Damascus Document

Cairo Damascus Document (CD)

I–VI 11	26
I–VIII	21
I 1	25, 26, 34
I 1–II 1	33
I 1–VII 9	33
I 2	22
I 3–11	24
I 5–7	24
I 7	22
I 7–9	40, 207
I 9–11	24
I 11	24
I 13–18a	33
II 2	25, 34, 133
II 5–III 16	22
II 11	22
II 14	25, 34
II 14–15	176
II 14–III 12a	183
II 15–16	124
II 16	175
II 16–17	175
II 17–21	175
III 4–5	175
III 12b–16a	139
III 19	149
IV 3	149
IV 8	164, 167
IV 9	110
IV 12–V 15	22, 113–114, 128, 176, 199
IV 12–VI 2	22
IV 12–VII 10a	125, 129
IV 13	126
IV 16–VI 1	33
IV 17	210
IV 17–18	114, 120
IV 19–21	20
IV 19–V 15	114
IV 19c–20a	33
IV 20–21	114–118, 160, 176, 209
IV 21	116
V 6–7	114, 118–120, 199
V 7–8	209
V 7–11	79, 109, 120–122, 176
V 9–11	29, 121
V 12	76
V 13–15	20
V 17	161
V 18–VI 2	20
VI 5	25
VI 10	22, 126
VI 11–14	199
VI 11–VII 4	26
VI 14	22, 126
VI 14–15	199
VI 14–VII 4a	129
VI 16–17	169
VI 17–18	199
VI 19	25
VI 21	169
VI 21–VII 1	168
VII 1	175
VII 4ff	199
VII 4–5	123–125
VII 4b–6a	123–124, 127, 129
VII 4–8	123
VII 4b–9a	129
VII 4b–10a	122–123, 125–128
VII 5ff	26
VII 6	126
VII 6–7	127
VII 6–9	6, 33, 113, 126–128
VII 6–15	122
VII 7	30, 182
VII 8–9	127
VII 9	33, 125, 127
VII 9b–VIII 2a	20

CD (*continued*)

VII 10–VIII 2a	33
VII 14–VIII 2a	20
VII 15	25
VII 19	25
VIII 2b–18	33
VIII 4–5	210
VIII 5	175
VIII 8	199
VIII 12c–13	27
VIII 14–18	186
VIII 21	25
IX–XVI	21, 26, 36
IX 1–10b	38
IX 2	23
IX 6	55
IX 7–9	19
IX 10b–14	38
IX 11	30
IX 14	39
IX 16b–X 3	65
IX 21	69
IX 21–23	87
IX 23	69
IX 23–X 3	88
X 1–2	87, 134
X 4	23, 127
X 4–10	28
X 6–10	189
X 9	144
X 10	23
X 10b–13	38
X 14	23, 93
X 14–XI 18b	38, 46, 94
X 17–19	95
X 19	93
X 22	76, 95
X 23	30
XI 1	95
XI 3–4	94
XI 4	39
XI 4–5	94–95, 208
XI 7–8	95, 96
XI 7–9	39
XI 9–10	94
XI 9b–11	13, 95–97, 208
XI 9–21	43
XI 10–11	39
XI 11	94, 96
XI 12	70, 97
XI 12b–XII 2a	40
XI 13–14	93
XI 14–15	35, 39, 94
XI 17	39
XI 17–21	39
XI 18a	98
XI 18b	41
XI 18–21	38, 40, 149
XI 18b–XII 1a	98
XI 18b–XII 20	97
XI 21b–22a	102
XI 21b–XII 1a	41
XI 21b–XII 2a	38
XI 21b–XII 6a	41
XII 1	39, 181
XII 1–2	40, 41, 43, 45, 97–99, 101, 102, 103, 104, 208
XII 1–12	8
XII 2–4	35
XII 2b–6a	38, 41
XII 5–6	70
XII 6b–11a	38, 39, 71, 98
XII 7–8	161
XII 8–11	30
XII 9–10	39
XII 9–11	163, 164
XII 10	30
XII 10–11	43, 69, 70, 97
XII 11b	40
XII 11b–15a	40
XII 11b–18	38, 40, 98
XII 11b–20a	40, 41
XII 12	29
XII 13–14	40
XII 14–18	40
XII 15–16	40
XII 15–17	40
XII 19	23, 30, 127
XII 19–20a	41, 98
XII 22	23, 127, 158

XII 22–XIII 7	28
XII 22–XIII 20	158
XII 23	28, 30, 126
XII 23b–XIII 1a	98
XIII	124
XIII 2–7	28
XIII 5–6	35, 162
XIII 6	146
XIII 7	23, 158
XIII 7–8	158, 164
XIII 7–9	165
XIII 7–10	162, 165
XIII 7–19	28, 158, 165
XIII 7b–20a	156
XIII 8	162, 167
XIII 9–10	158, 159
XIII 9–11	202
XIII 10	157
XIII 11–12	158, 202
XIII 11–13	136, 144
XIII 12b–13	158
XIII 14	202
XIII 14–15	158
XIII 15–16	30, 158, 160, 164, 202
XIII 15–18	160
XIII 15–19	156–159, 165
XIII 15–XIV 2	116
XIII 16	165
XIII 16–22	156
XIII 17	115, 116, 117, 202, 203
XIII 17–19	159
XIII 18–19	159
XIII 20	28, 158
XIII 20–21	28
XIV 1–2	124–125
XIV 3	28, 127
XIV 3–4	135
XIV 3–6	26, 149
XIV 3–10	37
XIV 3–18a	169
XIV 6–8	35
XIV 11–12	35
XIV 12	127, 169
XIV 12–13	30, 197, 202
XIV 12–16	169, 202
XIV 12–17	167–171
XIV 14–16	169, 201
XIV 15	146, 210
XIV 15–16	43, 167, 200
XIV 17b	169
XIV 17–18	169
XIV 20–22	169, 171
XV	138, 144, 147
XV 1	132, 133, 136, 154
XV 1–2	13
XV 1–3	133, 163
XV 1–5a	38, 132
XV 1–XVI 6a	132
XV 1–XVI 18	91
XV 1–XVI 20	132
XV 2	138
XV 5	132, 133, 134, 136, 138, 143, 154
XV 5–6	132, 133, 134,
XV 5–10	12
XV 5–15	131–132, 154, 201
XV 5–XVI 2	43, 131
XV 5–XVI 6	26
XV 6b–7a	132
XV 6	139
XV 7	126
XV 7–11	134
XV 8	139
XV 8–11	138
XV 9	138
XV 10	110, 126, 139
XV 10b–11	134, 144
XV 12–13	135
XV 13–14	163
XV 13–15	135
XV 14–15	164
XV 15	131, 144, 156
XV 15–17	132, 133, 144
XVI 2–3	126
XVI 2–6	133
XVI 6–9	92
XVI 6–12	39, 90–93, 106, 121
XVI 6–15	38
XVI 6–20	132
XVI 7	122

CD (continued)

XVI 9	91
XVI 10–12	42, 92
XVI 13ff.	39
XVI 13–17	90
XIX–XX	21
XIX 1–2	122, 126
XIX 3	122
XIX 4	122
XIX 5–6	122
XIX 5b–14	20
XIX 7–32a	33
XIX 20b–21a	199
XIX 33–34	25
XIX 33b–XX 22b	24, 33
XIX 33–XX 34	33, 124
XIX 35b–XX 1a	23
XX 1	24, 33
XX 1–8	124–125
XX 3–4	125
XX 8–9	34
XX 12	25
XX 13b–15a	23
XX 14	24, 33
XX 22	99
XX 24–25	161
XX 27b–34	33
XX 28	24
XX 28b–30	27
XX 31	34, 35, 164, 167
XX 32	24
XX 32–33	33
XX 33–34	21, 33

4QD Cave 4 Damascus Document

4Q266	21–23
1 1	26
1 a–b	21
1 a–b 1	26, 34, 199
1 a–b 5	25, 34
1 c–f	21
2 i 1–5	21
2 i 1–6	124
2 i 4	124
3 iii	20
4	33
4 7–8	21
5 i 1–2	65
5 i 10	157
5 i 12	99
5 i 13	136
5 i 13–14	135
5 i 17	34
5 ii 1–16	39, 40
5 ii 3	55
5 ii 4–14	78
5 ii 5–8	39
5 ii 12	161
5 ii 14	127
6 i	38
6 i a–e	46
6 i 4	85
6 i 10	85
6 i 13	101
6 i 14	46, 103, 104
6 i 14–16	42, 45, 47, 58
6 i 14–6 ii 3	46
6 i–iii	39, 40
6 ii	46, 47, 101
6 ii 1–2	52, 103
6 ii 1–4	51, 208
6 ii 1–13	42, 45–46, 51–58
6 ii 2	119
6 ii 2–3	52, 53, 58, 104
6 ii 2–13	103
6 ii 3	54
6 ii 3–4	52, 53, 54, 149
6 ii 3–13	47
6 ii 3b	53
6 ii 4	54, 102
6 ii 5–9	57
6 ii 5–13	51, 55
6 ii 6	119
6 ii 9	149
6 ii 10	55, 56
6 ii 10–11	55, 58
6 ii 11	57
6 ii 13	103, 104
6 iii–iv	39, 163
6 iii 1–3	46

6 iii 2–5	40
8 i	150
8 i 1–10	131
8 i 6	135, 136
8 i 6–7	150
8 i 6b–9	131, 132, 144–147, 148, 201
8 i 8	153
8 i 8b–9a	145, 147
8 i 9	28, 193
8 iii 6–9	28
9 iii	167
9 iii 1–2	156, 164
9 iii 1–4	160
9 iii 1–5	160
9 iii 1–10	43, 156–159, 165
9 iii 1–19	116
9 iii 3b–10	158
9 iii 4	165
9 iii 5	115, 117, 160, 202, 203
9 iii 6	165, 167
9 iii 6–7	164, 166, 200
9 iii 6–10	159
9 iii 7	159
9 iii 11	158
9 iii 15	26
10 i 5–10	168
10 i 6	168
10 i 7	168
10 i 9	167, 168
10 i 11	169
10 i 14–15	135, 169, 171
10 ii	35, 172
10 ii 1	55, 172
10 ii 1–15	125, 135, 171
10 ii 2	161, 184
10 ii 2–3	188
10 ii 7	161
10 ii 13–14	189
10 ii 14–15	184
11	21
11 5–21	34, 125
11 7	34
11 8	160
11 8–21	27
11 9b–13	34
11 11–12	186
11 14	160
11 14–16	197, 202
11 17	27
11 18	110
11 21	34
12	63, 65
12 1–9	59–60
12 2	64
12 4–9	68
12 6	68
13	59, 60
13 4	59
13 5	59

4Q267

5 ii 3	157
5 ii 5	99
6	39
7 12–14	71, 72
9 v 1–2	124
9 vi 4–5	173

4Q268

4Q269

7	39, 40
8 i 3–ii	39
8 ii 5	110
8 ii 6	134
9 1–8	71, 72
9 9	72
10 ii	156
11 i 4–8	171
11 ii 1–2	171

4Q270	171
2 i	33, 34
2 i 16–17	108
2 i 16–19	43, 107–109
2 i 18–19	95
2 i 19–21	107
2 i–ii	33, 34, 107, 208
2 ii 13–14	109
2 ii 15	110

4Q270 (continued)

Reference	Pages
2 ii 15–16	180, 182, 183
2 ii 15–17	109–111, 183
2 ii 15–19	20, 43
2 ii 16	111, 112, 174
2 ii 17	112
2 ii 18	112
2 ii 19	26, 34
2 ii 19–21	27
2 ii 20	34, 112
2 ii 21	34
3 i	46
3 ii 18	39
4	39, 59, 63, 65, 106
4 1	63
4 1–10	103
4 1–11	208
4 1–21	42, 59–61
4 2	65, 67
4 2–4	64
4 3	65–66
4 4	66
4 5–8	64
4 7	67
4 9	67
4 12–21	68–71
4 13–17	97, 104
5	60
5 10	72
5 14–21	71, 72
5 19	80
5 21	85
6	144
6 ii 5–10	131
6 ii 7	135
6 ii 8–9	144
6 ii 10	144
6 ii 19–21	90
6 v	35
6 v 15–16	95
6 v 16	95
6 v 16–17	70
7 i	35, 186
7 i 1–15	171
7 i 5	189
7 i 6–7	188, 189
7 i 7	160
7 i 11	172, 189
7 i 11–12	185
7 i 12–13	172, 173, 174, 178, 179, 181, 183, 203
7 i 12–15	43
7 i 13	174, 203, 209
7 i 13–14	172, 187, 188
7 i 13b–15a	184–185
7 i 14	160, 190, 204, 210
10 1–2	72
11 i 13–14	186

4Q271

Reference	Pages
4Q271	79
2 1–6	39
2 12	110
2 13	134
3	60, 73, 75, 80, 87, 89
3 1–2	74
3 1–4a	72
3 1–14a, 15	39
3 1–15	105
3 3–4	74
3 4b–9a	74–76, 105
3 4b–15	71–73
3 4–5	74
3 6–7	74
3 7–8	72
3 7–10	209
3 7b–14a, 15b	42
3 9	16, 75, 103
3 9b–10a	76–80, 202
3 10–12	80, 85, 103, 115
3 10–15	80–85
3 12	108, 170
3 12–13	108
3 12b–14	85, 201
3 12b–15	105, 106, 208
3 13	81, 89, 108
3 14	82, 85, 88, 209
3 14–15	43, 73, 81, 88
3 15	174
4 ii 1–4a	131
4 ii 7–12	90

5 i 1–2	94
5 i 5–7	95
5 i 9	35
5 i 17–18	97, 98

4Q272

1 i–ii	39, 40
1 ii	46, 49, 58
1 ii 3	46, 103, 104
1 ii 3–4a	48
1 ii 3–18	42, 45–46, 47–51, 58, 208
1 ii 6	48
1 ii 7	48, 49
1 ii 7b–9a	49
1 ii 8	119
1 ii 8–10	50
1 ii 11–17	50
1 ii 12	110
1 ii 13, 15–16	50
1 ii 15–18	46

4Q273	21
4 ii	40
5	72, 89
5 4–5	89
6 i	161

5Q12	19

6Q15	19
5	107, 109

2. OTHER TEXTS

Cave 1

1QH Hodayot	76
XIV 13	193
XV 21–2	96
XI 21–23	193
XIX 11–12	193

1QM (=1Q33) War Scroll	6, 27, 155, 192
II 1,3,7	186
III 3–4	186

V 6, 9, 14	192
VII 1–3a	153
VII 1–7	6, 12
VII 3	139, 153
VII 3–4	144
VII 3–6	147, 150, 152
VII 4–5	74, 153
VII 5	151
VII 5–6	151
VII 6	147, 193
VII 10	193
VII 11	192
XIII 7	186
XIV 8	186

1QpHab Pesher Habakkuk	25, 27
VIII 8	25
IX 9–10	25
XI 4–5	25

1QS Rule of the Community	5, 27, 31, 132, 138, 172
I–IV	136
I 1–III 12	30
I 4–5	137
I 6	175
I 9–11	131
I 16	134
I 16–III 12	136
I 18	134
I 18–II 26	136
I 20	134
I 24	134
I 24b–25	27
II 9	186
II 20	134
II 21	134
II 24	159
III 17–IV 1	199
V–XI	30
V 4	159
V 13	69
V 20–23	144
V 23a	158
V 24	159

1QS (continued)
VI 135
VI 16 135
VI 16–21 69
VI 18 144
VI 19 135
VI 22 135
VI 24–VII 27 179
VI 25 .... 69, 172
VI 27–VII 2 171
VII 3 69
VII 4 184
VII 10–11 161
VII 15 184
VII 16 .... 160, 172, 188, 189
VII 17 .... 160, 172, 184, 188
VII 17–18 188
VII 21 136
VII 22–24 171
VII 24 172
VII 25 160
VIII 2 159
VIII 5 76
VIII 18 135
VIII 20ff 125
VIII 21–23 179
VIII 22 172
VIII 24–25 69
IX 15–16 135
XI 11 76
X 26 159

1QSa (=1Q28a) Rule of the
Congregation 5, 15, 27, 28, 30
  41, 133, 137, 139, 143,
  145, 148, 152, 155, 166
I 1–5 .... 141, 142
I 1–3 141
I 2 28
I 4 .... 153, 166
I 4–5 .... 140, 141, 154, 166
I 4–8 .... 145, 167
I 4–9 166
I 4–11 140–142
I 5 167

I 6–8 166
I 6–9 141
I 6–II 11a 28, 141
I 7 .... 28, 166, 167, 189
I 7–8 166
I 7–17 28
I 8 .... 141, 167
I 8–II 26 141
I 8b–10a 134
I 8b–11 .... 139, 140
I 9–10 141
I 10–11 183
I 11 .... 88, 143, 181, 182, 201, 203
I 12–13 139
I 14 28
I 14–15 182
I 15–18 28
I 16 186
I 17–19 28
I 18–II26 136
I 19 184
I 19–20 145
I 19–22 .... 146, 151
I 21 141
I 23–25 186
I 25 143
I 25ff 142
I 25b–27a 142–143
I 26 12
I 27–28 151
I 27–II 1 143
I 29–II 1 28
II 2 151
II 3–4 151
II 3–9 .... 143, 147, 150
II 4 145
II 4–9 .... 144, 145
II 5 145
II 5b–9a 74
II 8–9 .... 28, 145, 147, 193
II 9b–10 146
II 11 141
II 11–22 142
II 15 28

II 16 186
II 19 141

1QSb (=1Q28b) Blessings 27

1QapGen Genesis Apocryphon
II 175

1Q23–24 1QEnGiants[a,b] ar 175

Cave 2
2Q26 2QEnGiants ar 175

Cave 4
4QS[b,d,e] (4Q256, 4Q258, 4Q259)
Community Rule 31, 136

4Q159 4QOrdinances[a] 6, 15, 28,
29, 36, 71, 83,
2–4 .... 73, 82, 83, 84, 85, 89
6–10 73
8–10 82

4Q161 4QPesher Isaiah[a] 192
8–10 20 .... 192, 193

4Q174 4QFlorilegium 133
I 3–5 148

4Q197 4QTobit[b] ar
4 ii 17 79

4Q203 4QEnGiants[a] ar 175

4Q213a 4QAramaic Levi[b]
3–4 84

4Q221 4QJubilees[f]
7 6 55

4Q248 4QHistorical Text A
7 99

4Q251 4QHalakha A 6, 29

1–2, 3–7 93
1 4–5 96
1 7 94
8 1–2 71
12 2–3 109
17 2 121

4Q264b 4QHalakha B
I–II 93

4Q265 4QMiscellaneous Rules 6, 28,
29, 171, 172
3 .... 12, 172
3 3 .... 54, 154
6 93
6 4 96
7 1–5 93
7 55
7 11–17 172
7 14–15 55

4Q274 4QTohorot A 6, 28, 29, 119
1 i 5 94
1 i 6 29
1 i 7–8 53
1 i 8 60
1 i 8b–9a 49
2 i 54
2 i 6 29

4Q275 4QCommunal Ceremony 136

4Q276 4QTohorot B[a] 28

4Q277 4QTohorot B[b]
1 ii 13 54

4Q280 4QCurses 137

4Q278 4QTohorot C 6, 28

4Q286–290 4QBerakhot[a–e] 136,
137, 192
4Q287 2 5 192

4Q298 4QWords of the Sage to the Sons of Dawn
1–2 i 26
3–4 ii 26

4Q299 4QMysteries^a
76 3 186

4Q340 4QList of Netinim 78

4Q392–399 4QMMT A–F 6, 15, 27, 29, 36, 79, 133, 179
4Q394 3–7 i 16–19 54
4QMMT B 29–33 100
B 36–38 110
B 39–41 148
B 39–49 120
B 48 94
B 48–49 120
B 59–62 100
B 75–82 77
4QMMT C 120
4QMMT D 120

4Q400–407 Songs of the Sabbath Sacrifice (4QShirShabb[a–h]) 194
4Q403 1 ii 1 192
4Q405 14–15 i 3,6 192
4Q405 15 ii–16 4 192
4Q405 22 10–11 192
4Q405 19ABCD 5 192
4Q405 23 ii 7 192

4Q415 4QInstruction[a] 75
2 ii 7 73
11 6–7 .... 74, 75

4Q416 4QInstruction[b] 6, 93, 197
2 i–ii 71
2 ii 17 71
2 ii 21 177
2 iii 17–18 186
2 iv 7b–10 93

4Q418a 4QInstruction[e]
167 6 75

4Q427 4QHodayot[a]
7 i 6–13 193

4Q462 4QNarrative 192
1 5 192

4Q477 4QRebukes by the Overseer 27, 184
4Q502 4QRitual of Marriage 6, 185, 188
1 3 187
2 3 187
9 11 187
14 6 187
19 3 187
24 4 187
96 1 187

4Q512 4QRitual of Purification
10–11 5 57
iv 1–5 94

4Q513 4QOrdinances[b] 6
2 ii 120
10 ii 3 120

4Q514 4QOrdinances[c] 6

4Q530–533 4QEnGiants[b,c,d] ar 175

4Q542 4QTestament of Qahat
1 i 5–6 78

5Q13 5QRule 27, 136, 137

5Q14 5QCurses 136

Cave 6
6Q8 6QpapEnGiants 175

Cave 11

11QT Temple Scroll	4, 6, 15, 27, 29, 36, 46, 93, 99, 104, 115
XXXIX 7–9	153
XLV 4–7	94
XLV 7–8	49, 101
XLV 7–12	8
XLV 9–10	54
XLV 11	143
XLV 11–12	29, 40, 49, 98–102
XLV 12–14	148
XLV 15–16	49
XLV 16–17	100
XLVI 9–10	100
XLVI 13–16a	100
XLVI 15–16	100
XLVI 15–17	29, 99
XLVI 16b–18	100
XLVI 17–18	100
XLVI 18	101
XLVII 3b–5a	101
XLVII 9	99
XLVII 12–13	99
XLVIII 14–17	99, 100
XLIX 12	40
XLIX 20–21	54
L 2	94
L 12	54
L 15–16	54
LI 3	54
LI 5	54
LII 5–7	110
LIII 11–14a	93
LIII 14b–LIV 7	93
LIV 4–5	117
LVII 1–5	139
LVII 17b–19a	115, 117
LXIII 10–15	69
LXIII 14	69
LXV 7–15	82
LXV 7–LXVI 4	117
LXV 12	99
LXVI 8–11	117
LXVI 15–17	121
LXVI 16–17	109

11Q5 11QPsalms[a]
XX 5–6 190

11Q17 Songs of the Sabbath Sacrifice (11QShirShabb)
8–7 5 192

INDEX OF ANCIENT AUTHORS

1. APOCRYPHA AND PSEUDEPIGRAPHA

Apocalypse of Zephaniah 195
Ascension of Isaiah 195
Ben Sira 84, 162
1 Enoch 3, 4, 175
2 Enoch 195
Jubilees 3, 4, 27, 55, 79, 84,
                          93, 95, 114, 175, 176
Judith 79
4 Maccabees 179
Psalms of Solomon 114, 118
Pseudo-Philo 187–188, 196
Pseudo Phocylides 179
Sirach 162
Testament of Twelve Patriarchs 175,
                                             179, 183
Testament of Issachar 179
Testament of Job 194, 195, 196
Testament of Judah 175, 176, 179
Testament of Levi 84, 114, 195
Testament of Reuben 175, 176
Tobit 77, 79, 81, 176, 177, 178

2. JOSEPHUS AND PHILO

Josephus 2, 3, 5, 9, 87, 88, 91,
         105, 112, 118, 123, 163, 166, 174,
         180, 181, 182, 183, 184, 189, 191

Philo 2, 3, 8, 9, 66, 70, 78, 97,
                   105, 180, 181, 182, 183, 189

3. RABBINIC LITERATURE

BABYLONIAN TALMUD
Shabbat 97
Yebamot 66, 77, 81, 86, 111
Ketubbot 86, 173, 178
Nedarim 91
Sotah 66
Niddah 111

MISHNAH
Shevi'it 153
Shabbat 96, 97
Hagigah 91, 153
Yebamot 80, 86, 87, 173, 178, 183
Ketubbot 57, 73, 75, 76,
                                   83, 84, 86, 87, 118
Nedarim 91, 92
Sotah 64, 66, 67, 87
Gittin 73, 117, 162
Qiddushin 75, 76, 78, 117
Sanhedrin 84, 87
Arakhin 84
Keritot 118
Zabim 49

PALESTINIAN TALMUD
Yebamot 173
Ketubbot 86
Nedarim 91

SIFRA
Mezora 53
Emor 80

SIFRE NUMBERS 66

TOSEFTA
Shabbat 57, 96
Yebamot 178, 183
Ketubbot 75, 178
Sotah 64
Baba Batra 75
Menahot 193
Niddah 178

257

www.ingramcontent.com/pod-product-compliance
Lightning Source LLC
Chambersburg PA
CBHW020645300426
44112CB00007B/242